VASARI'S WORDS

The *Lives of the Artists* as a History of Ideas in the Italian Renaissance

In this book, Douglas Biow analyzes Vasari's *Lives of the Artists*—often considered the first great work of art history in the modern era—from a new perspective. He focuses on keywords and shows how they address a variety of compelling, culturally determined ideas circulating in late Renaissance Italy. The keywords chosen for this study investigate five seemingly divergent, yet still interconnected, ideas. What does it mean to have a "profession," *professione*, and possess "genius," *ingegno*, in the visual arts? How is "speed,"*prestezza*, valued among visual artists of the period and how is "time," *tempo*, conceptualized in Vasari's narrative and descriptions of visual art? Finally, how is the "night," *notte*, conceived and visually represented as a distinct span of time in the *Lives*? Written in an engaging manner for specialists and non-specialists alike, *Vasari's Words* places the *Lives*—a truly foundational and innovative book of Western culture—within the context of the modern discipline of intellectual history.

Douglas Biow is the Superior Oil Company-Linward Shivers Centennial Professor in Medieval and Renaissance Studies and Director of the Center for European Studies at the University of Texas at Austin. He is the author of five prior books, including most recently *The Culture of Cleanliness in Renaissance Italy* (2006), *In Your Face: Professional Improprieties and the Art of Being Conspicuous* (2010), and *On the Importance of Being an Individual: Men, Their Professions, and Their Beards* (2015). He has been the recipient of a number of scholarly awards, including NEH, Delmas, and Guggenheim fellowships.

VASARI'S WORDS

The Lives of the Artists *as a History of Ideas in the Italian Renaissance*

DOUGLAS BIOW
University of Texas, Austin

CAMBRIDGE
UNIVERSITY PRESS

CAMBRIDGE
UNIVERSITY PRESS

University Printing House, Cambridge CB2 8BS, United Kingdom

One Liberty Plaza, 20th Floor, New York, NY 10006, USA

477 Williamstown Road, Port Melbourne, VIC 3207, Australia

314–321, 3rd Floor, Plot 3, Splendor Forum, Jasola District Centre, New Delhi – 110025, India

79 Anson Road, #06-04/06, Singapore 079906

Cambridge University Press is part of the University of Cambridge.

It furthers the University's mission by disseminating knowledge in the pursuit of education, learning, and research at the highest international levels of excellence.

www.cambridge.org
Information on this title: www.cambridge.org/9781108472050
DOI: 10.1017/9781108641227

First published 2018
Reprinted 2019

Printed in the United Kingdom by Print on Demand, World Wide

A catalogue record for this publication is available from the British Library.

Library of Congress Cataloging-in-Publication Data
Names: Biow, Douglas, author.
Title: Vasari's words : the 'Lives of the artists' as a history of ideas in the Italian Renaissance / Douglas Biow, University of Texas, Austin.
Description: New York: Cambridge University Press, 2019. |
Includes bibliographical references and index.
Identifiers: LCCN 2018029873 | ISBN 9781108472050 (hardback)
Subjects: LCSH: Vasari, Giorgio, 1511–1574. Vite de' piu eccellenti pittori, scultori et architettori. | Renaissance–Italy.
Classification: LCC N7483.V37B56 2019 | DDC 709.2–dc23
LC record available at https://lccn.loc.gov/2018029873

ISBN 978-1-108-47205-0 Hardback

For my mother,

Margot H. Feely

(in light of her love for printed books and the visual arts,

as a once-upon-a-time copyeditor, production editor, and book editor,

first at the Spiral Press and then the Metropolitan Museum of Art)

with gratitude and love for all that she has done

for me

Without a doubt those who are the inventors of anything notable receive the greatest attention from the pens of writers of histories [*Senza dubbio coloro che sono inventori d'alcuna cosa notabile hanno grandissima parte nelle penne di chi scrive l'istorie*].

—Giorgio Vasari, "The Life of Duccio, Painter of Siena," the *Lives* (1568)

CONTENTS

ILLUSTRATIONS

PREFACE

This book was drafted initially with some urgency. Not because there was a deadline for it. And not because I was coming up for tenure or promotion and needed a book in print to show for myself. It was drafted originally with some urgency because it came into being while I faced the possibility of death. Not my death, to be sure, but my mother's. And nothing so sharpens the mind, I've discovered, as facing the real possibility that someone who has been there for you your entire life might actually be dying. So while I stayed in the hospital for days on end and commuted by airplane between Austin and NYC for roughly a month and a half, I did what I suppose a research scholar does instinctively as a coping mechanism, especially while suspended in that sort of Magic Mountain-like limbo world of the modern American hospital and the modern American jetliner, where a sense of time eerily disappears and one hour, one day, one week starts to blend almost imperceptibly into another. I disassociated, writing away on the plane, stuffed into a cramped chair with my laptop propped open before me, or tapping away on the keyboard in the hospital, sometimes through the long insomniac nights. Needless to say, while it didn't help my mother that I busily read and wrote (she eventually survived her illness thanks to the miracles of modern medicine), it did help me. Beyond keeping me creatively engaged through that troubling, frantic period, it allowed me to feel that I was honoring, perhaps even memorializing in some measure, two of the things she cared about in her own professional life and still cares about deeply: printed books and visual art. In any event, that was the genesis of this book, which is dedicated exclusively to Giorgio Vasari's landmark *Le Vite de' più eccellenti pittori, scultori, e architettori* (*The Lives of the Most Excellent Painters, Sculptors, and Architects*, 1550/68)—a pioneering book that has determined the course of modern thinking about the visual arts and still remains, in the words of the art historian Alina Payne, an "indestructible palimpsest." Indeed, as Payne puts it in terms suited to this entire study, "we still rely on [Vasari's] information, we are still guided by his judgments, and we still tacitly perpetuate his prejudices. More important—and this applies to the field at large, not only to Renaissance scholarship—we also depend on his model of historical interpretation of the arts, on his choice of how to reconcile or appear to reconcile the domains of reality and writing."[1]

It should hardly be surprising, then, that over time, as I turned from the initial spark of inspiration to the persistence of scholarly dedication, I gradually became aware that Vasari's *Lives* is not just a book full of stories about visual artists, some reasonably entertaining, some not. Nor is it just a book full of biased judgments that (not without some heated controversy) have set the direction of most art historical narratives of the Italian Renaissance since its first appearance in print in precisely the middle of the sixteenth century. Nor is it just a book full of facts from time to time mined by scholars as a quarry of information and misinformation about the visual art of the period. Vasari's *Lives*, I came to realize, is also a book about ideas—or at least what we might call "cultural values" or "cultural concerns" or "culturally shared forms of solving difficult artistic problems through the actual material making of visual art." In Vasari's hands those ideas are developed so that they thematically permeate the *Lives* from beginning to end. And this fascinated me. Never before had I come across a book in the vernacular that could lay claim to being the origin of so many different ideas that had long captured my imagination regarding the Italian Renaissance in general and the visual arts in particular. These ideas, which have found their way into various books and articles I have authored over my career, concern such things as the connections between professionalism and humanism; the links between art, genius, and institutionalized training; the relationship between allegory and realism, teleology and timelessness, exemplarity and inimitability, practice and theory, the visual and the verbal; the complex ties binding productivity, speed, facility, industriousness, and labor in a period of conspicuous consumption; the way men belonging to or aspiring to be part of the cultural elite felt compelled to behave in a manner that allowed them to stand out without appearing too indecorously conspicuous in the context of court culture; and the dialectical interplay between the individual and the community.

The more I worked on this book, however, the more I became aware that Vasari helped originate ideas about the visual arts I had never seriously considered before, such as what it means to represent the night visually during a period that had also become increasingly invested economically, socially, and culturally in conquering—or in the words of one scholar, "colonizing"—the pervasive darkness of the night as a distinct span of time. Put differently, I came to discover that Vasari may not have been a profoundly original thinker—he was certainly not a philosopher like Marsilio Ficino and Pietro Pomponazzi, and he was by no means a deep-thinking humanist like Lorenzo Valla and Angelo Poliziano—but he was nevertheless a great synthesizer, developer, and disseminator of fascinating ideas that were circulating in the period. Additionally, the more I read the *Lives*, the more I became convinced that Vasari came upon those ideas not just through his interactions with members of the cultural elite but also through the fundamental process of having been a practitioner himself, a thoughtful and accomplished, if not pathbreaking, maker of visual art. Moreover, Vasari gave voice to those ideas for the first time in a single, comprehensive, massive book dedicated specifically to tracing the development of the visual arts over roughly three hundred years. And so he can be said to stand historically at the origin of certain strands of thought and concerns and values and artistic problem-solving that helped define the Italian Renaissance in the visual arts. In this respect, Vasari was not just an important biographer and mythographer, crafting (with the help of others) a host of lasting verbal portraits of artists whose lives he both recounts and invents. Indeed, in the second edition of his book he even included the novelty of reproducing visual portraits of those artists when he could locate reasonable likenesses of them. He was also someone who laced his entire book with ideas, so many of which necessarily derived from his long involvement with the practice of making visual art himself and above all from his deep investment in *disegno* ("design"), conceived as both a mechanical *and* an intellectual art. What is more, all those ideas that are laced throughout Vasari's book—ideas such as the generative concept of *disegno* itself—were associated with a host of artists discussed within the *Lives*, even though predictably enough they find their fullest formulation ultimately in the now legendary figures whom he was most bent on mythologizing, namely Leonardo, Michelangelo, and Raphael. So it is with this book. While it cuts through the *Lives* from beginning to end and covers a host of artists, both familiar and unfamiliar, canonical and not, it necessarily devotes many more pages to those whom Vasari considered to be the most transformative and exceptional. Those were the visual artists around whom a number of key ideas inevitably coalesced.

In presenting Vasari's *Lives* as a history of compelling ideas that grow out of his reflections on the changing nature of the visual arts and the professional identities of their creators in the period, I have sought to write this book in an economical, anti-pedantic, anti-polemical, and sometimes even breezy, down-to-earth manner, largely in an effort to try to reach the broadest possible audience, including someone just like my mother, who was trained at Vassar College in art history long ago and worked for years as a book editor at the Metropolitan Museum of Art. For while Vasari may be a household name for scholars working on the Renaissance, and especially those in the field of art history, his *Lives* itself is rarely read, much less in its entirety.[2] And the scholarship dedicated to the *Lives*, a good deal of which has been synthesized in this book, does not always help broaden his appeal to those who are not highly specialized scholars devoted to such academic pursuits as tracking down Vasari's sources and making selective use of his text as a fund of information for artists about whom we sometimes have absolutely no other data. Those dedicated and often eloquent scholars have also dutifully examined Vasari's elaborate network of social relations and artistic connections; they have detected how much of the *Lives* may or may not have been actually written by him; and they have painstakingly documented who his collaborators were in the making of both editions of the book as well as identified the ways in which they contributed to it. Along with that, they have explored the dynamic and complex connections between the visual and the verbal; investigated his thoughts about periodization, historical development, style, biographical writing, and exemplarity; and, among other worthy endeavors, offered intricate and sometimes brilliant close readings of his prose.

In making the claim that Vasari's *Lives* should indeed be better read as a book of ideas, I am not suggesting that it is a particularly riveting book to read, either in English or, for that matter, in its original sixteenth-century Italian. I am not one of those scholars who finds Vasari to be a superb writer or storyteller, although I have spent much of the past few years reading and rereading the *Lives*, a few times from beginning to end, in an effort to detect overarching patterns of meaning as the book unfolds as a series of biographies modeled in part on works of classical antiquity, from Plutarch's *Parallel Lives* (ca. 100 CE), to Suetonius' *The Twelve Caesars* (121 CE) or *Lives of Illustrious Men, Grammarians, and Rhetoricians*, to Diogenes Laertius' *Lives and Opinions of Eminent Philosophers* (third century CE). Perhaps to the puzzlement of some, then, this book, whose title openly declares that it is about "Vasari's words," does not explore in any detail Vasari's narrative style. Vasari was certainly not a bad writer. And thanks no doubt in part to the rudimentary training he received early in his life in the classicizing educational and cultural program of the *studia humanitatis*—a program of studies devoted primarily to poetry, grammar, rhetoric, moral philosophy, and history—Vasari was unquestionably a far better writer than most of those concerned with the visual arts when it came to articulating his thoughts in a period when a number of artists were taking on the role of author, such as Lorenzo Ghiberti in the fifteenth century or the immodest and belligerent Benvenuto Cellini in the sixteenth. But Vasari was definitely not, to my mind, a great or rhetorically gifted writer. There are excellent books and articles devoted to focusing on Vasari's style, and there are also excellent books and articles dedicated to arguing that Vasari was something of a formalist whose *Lives* is a tightly constructed narrative on a par with some of the greatest works of imaginative literature written in any language. This book is not one of them. By "Vasari's words" I mean not Vasari's prose style. Rather, in keeping with Raymond Williams's critical strategy for dissecting the "vocabulary of a culture and society,"[3] I mean instead Vasari's "keywords," or at least the handful of keywords I have selected for discussion, each of which serves to capture various cultural concerns and values and distinctly visual problems that I have labeled as "ideas"—ideas that grow out of his (as well as necessarily my) reflections on the professional identity of artists in his period. Nor, I should say in passing, is this book meant to be exhaustive in its treatment of its subject. The keywords I have chosen to focus on serve to open up a new way of coming to terms with an influential, canonical book and, just as important, a new way of understanding late Renaissance culture, with the hope that some of the insights arrived at through my approach to the *Lives* will also perhaps be of interest to art historians, even as the book undoubtedly covers terrain that will inevitably be familiar to some, particularly those devoted to studying Vasari. Consider it, then, a book that anatomizes the *Lives* in an effort to show how Vasari's interconnected practices of making visual art and writing about it shaped—and was shaped by—certain key ideas of the Italian Renaissance. It is also, I should add, a book that presumes some basic knowledge on the part of the reader about the Italian Renaissance generally and Italian Renaissance art specifically.[4]

Finally, a very brief word about Vasari's life and career. The son of a potter, Vasari was born on July 30, 1511 in Arezzo, an important provincial town not far from Florence. The painter Luca Signorelli, Vasari's cousin, recognized the young Vasari's talent early on and recommended him to the stained-glass maker Guillaume de Marçillat, who took him on as a pupil in Arezzo. In 1524, Cardinal Silvio Passerini, impressed with the thirteen-year-old Vasari's abilities and intellect, took him under his protection and brought him to Florence. There Vasari acquired a rudimentary humanistic education—alongside Ippolito and Alessandro de' Medici—under the tutelage of Pierio Valeriano, the author, among other works, of the dialogue *De litteratorum infelicitate* (*On the Ill Fortune of Learned Men*) and an early book on hieroglyphs. In Florence Vasari also became a lifelong devotee and eventually mythologizer of Michelangelo. And in the same city he enjoyed being part of the circle of mannerist painters associated with Andrea del Sarto, Baccio Bandinelli, and Francesco Salviati. Because of his deep investment in Florence, Vasari would also later come to be associated closely with the city, both its artistic heritage and its cultural influence. He became a favored artist in the court of Cosimo I, eventually appointed to oversee the construction of such vast, imperial projects as the extensive pictorial decoration of much of Palazzo Vecchio and the building of the bureaucratically handsome architecture of the Uffizi, a monumental work of institutional architecture *par excellence*. Yet Vasari, it is important to stress, traveled far and wide throughout much of central and northern Italy, spending much time in Rome, where he also assiduously studied antiquities. He received numerous commissions, from Pisa to Pistoia, Naples to Venice, Bologna to Cortona, Camaldoli to Rome, some of them quite staggering in size and conception. And wherever he went in his far-reaching travels, he collected information and drawings, gradually building up a wide network of friends, correspondents, patrons, informants, humanists, literati, and colleagues who shared his cultural, intellectual, and aesthetic interests.

His paintings typically were well received in his own time, even if posterity has not been kind to them. Today art historians tend to view him as a largely derivative, though technically polished, thoughtful artist who had a predilection for incorporating learned allegories into his works of art and who contributed to the development of what has been called the relief-style mode of painting of the mannerist period that arose after the death of Raphael.[5] His monumentalizing visual art produced later in his life is also closely associated today with the formation of the Florentine/Tuscan grand-ducal, bureaucratic state and Duke Cosimo I's potent and transformative role in the formation of a sort of disciplinary state control over the arts. Vasari typically worked on a grand scale in both painting and architecture and was a relentless advocate, like Michelangelo, for the importance of *disegno* as the basis for making great art in the modern style, as opposed to, say, *colorito*, which privileged—as it was exemplified often in Venetian oil painting of the period—the deliberate blurring of contours and the gradual building up of form through the expressive, expansive, and studied application of paint. Finally, Vasari knew how to manage, as a sort of impresario, a large body of assistants as he completed one massive project after another. The best of his artwork displays a learned command of the visual language of Michelangelo and Raphael and classical antiquity. Exemplary in this regard are not his truly massive projects, impressive and sophisticated though they can be as complex visual programs. Rather, he now is more appreciated for the sometimes elegant, stylish, and at times clever frescoes he designed for his own house in Arezzo, a house Vasari purchased in 1540 and whose interior design he began in 1542 and had mostly finished in 1548, about the time he earnestly began writing the first edition of the *Lives*. In his fashionably furnished house, Vasari surrounded himself with decorations that he felt conferred on him honor, fame, glory, and status, including a room full of portraits of Michelangelo and a variety of other distinguished visual artists whom he considered to be the greatest of his day and in whose midst he obviously felt he belonged. He died in Arezzo on June 27, 1574, roughly two months after Cosimo I, the patron to whom he dedicated both editions of the *Lives*, and whose Florence he helped transform visually into a monumental, bureaucratic state. Shortly afterwards he was buried in the church of Santa Maria della Pieve in Arezzo where, because of a major restoration in later years, not even a plaque remains today to identify his tomb.

ACKNOWLEDGMENTS

This book, like my others, could not have been written without the assistance of a number of people. First, my thanks to my hyper-efficient staff, Sally Dickson and Nhi Nguyen, for taking care of the Center for European Studies and covering for me during my prolonged absences in NYC and then, later, twice in Cornwall, CT. I am also indebted once again to Wayne Rebhorn for reading through the manuscript at various stages and assisting me greatly with the extensive and sometimes belabored revisions, as well as helping me to see, as he is so remarkably capable of seeing, the forest for the trees. I am also indebted to Mirka Benes, Julia Guernsey, Ann Johns, Eva Struhal, and Louis Waldman, five superb art historians who talked to me at length about a range of issues that have to do with visual art generally, read through the entire book in its various iterations, and generously assisted me with a number of key revisions. I am also greatly indebted to Daniela Bini for periodically checking and correcting, along with Wayne Rebhorn, the translations, and Cathy Brandewie, a clear, perceptive, and elegant writer, for copyediting parts of my manuscript and making helpful editorial suggestions. My thanks as well to Gerd Blum, Carl Blyth, Rita Comanducci, Clemente Fedele, Alison Frazier, Susan Gayland, Tracie Matysik, Walter Melion, Tom Pangle, Guy Raffa, Michael Schmidt, Jeff Smith, Nancy Struever, Tom Willette, and Paul Woodruff for taking the time to talk or write to me about a variety of issues as they arose while I worked on the project, although I recognize that my strategies for addressing certain issues, my decision to concentrate on certain areas of scholarship at the expense of others, and my overall conclusions will not always meet their satisfaction.

As always I am grateful to Wendy Nesmith and her ILL staff for tracking down various books for me and even purchasing some for the library collection. I am also grateful to Merry Burlingham for kindly heeding my request and purchasing some rather obscure books for the permanent library collection as I worked on this project. The nucleus of Chapter 1 was delivered as a talk at the annual Renaissance Society of America Conference in March 2015 and then in a far more developed format at the conference "Translators and Printers in Renaissance Europe: Framing Identity and Agency" at the University of London in September 2016 organized by Andrea Rizzi. Chapter 3 was presented at a seminar devoted to European Art at the Newberry Library in April 2016. Some early formulations of Chapter 5 were presented in a truly inchoate format at my home university at different events organized by Brian Levack and Seth Garland for the Institute for Historical Studies, whose theme that year happened to be devoted to the topic of darkness and night; a much more fully developed version of Chapter 5 benefited greatly from being workshopped at a seminar for the Centre for Renaissance and Early Modern Studies at the University of York organized by Helen Smith in March 2017. My thanks to all those who attended those events and provided me with helpful feedback. Finally, I owe so very much to Beatrice Rehl for her sustained encouragement and interest in this project as it evolved, thanks in no small measure to her (often witty but always gracious) input, as well as Mark Rosen of The University of Texas at Dallas and the other extremely helpful (in this case anonymous) reader for the press.

Cambridge University Press gratefully acknowledges the support of the Office of the President at The University of Texas at Austin, which provided funds toward the publication of this book.

This book is dedicated to my mother, who studied art history at Vassar College in the 1950s, who has had such a positive and guiding influence on my life, who has taught me how to survive and appreciate literature and art, and who has always been there for me through thick and thin.

NOTES ON TRANSLATION

Vasari's Words focuses on keywords as an organizing principle and investigative strategy for capturing ideas through a historically contextualized "close reading," rather than a laboratory-modeled, computer-generated, analytics-driven mode of "distant reading," to borrow Franco Moretti's phrase. Yet oddly enough it includes little Italian in its central portions. This is the case because it seemed to me cumbersome and distracting to provide the complete Italian in the actual body of the book for the English translations of the *Lives* contained within it, especially for Anglo-American readers who are not exactly fluent in sixteenth-century Italian prose yet are still curious about Vasari, the *Lives*, and the Italian Renaissance. Moreover, one of my aims in writing *Vasari's Words* was to reach a variety of readers, including those who may not understand Italian at all or, for that matter, have any particular interest whatsoever in Vasari, the *Lives*, or even the Italian Renaissance but are nevertheless interested in reflecting, as I have sought to do, on how to investigate a foundational book of a period and by extension its culture through a singular, thematic focus on keywords. In that context, including all the Italian for the translated passages in the body of my book seemed to me unwise for those readers as well. That said, I have highlighted a host of words, phrases, and sentences in Italian, bracketing as well as italicizing them, to underscore the importance of the frequency of those keywords in the *Lives*, to emphasize their sometimes pervasive but often subtle linguistic power, and/or to call attention to the cluster of associations they give rise to within Vasari's culture.

Additionally, I have left a few Italian words in the original language when I found them to be untranslatable. Consequently, *disegno*—a complex term that for Vasari encompasses everything from "drawing" to "design" to "forethought" to "invention" to "intention" to "plan" to the material realization of a highly developed "Idea" or set of ideas, and that is *not* in fact a crucial keyword studied in this book since it has been so thoroughly examined elsewhere in the context of Vasari's *Lives*—largely remains italicized as *disegno* throughout, as does the term *sprezzatura*, yet another word for which I can find no apt English equivalent ("nonchalance" or "insouciance" or just "being cool" simply won't do). The same holds true for the word *grazia*, whose English cognate, "grace," only captures one aspect of the meaning of the complex Italian Renaissance term. Indeed, in sixteenth-century Italian, the word *grazia*—a loaded term in Baldassar Castiglione's lexicon of keywords, for instance—can mean everything from theological "grace," the sort of grace that is bestowed upon one from on high; to the suave "grace" of, say, a skilled charmer with words; to the "grace" of someone mysteriously born with a natural ability to do something ever-so-brilliantly without the slightest training whatsoever; to the "grace" one warmly receives as a favor—a sort of "gratuity" as an expression of thanks— from someone of rank and authority; to the "grace" one feels as a form of gratitude for protection, recognition, and reward. *Grazia*, to use one of Dante Alighieri's terms, is a "polysemous" word, which a number of scholars have already explored in depth and are still investigating.

Finally, unless otherwise indicated, all citations from the *Lives* are taken from Giorgio Vasari, *Le vite de' più eccellenti pittori, scultori, e architettori nelle redazioni del 1550 e 1568*, ed. Rosanna Bettarini and Paola Barocchi, 6 vols. (Florence: Sansoni, 1966–87). All translations, modified for accuracy, are from Giorgio Vasari, *Lives of the Painters, Sculptors and Architects*, trans. Gaston Du C. De Vere, intro. David Ekserdjian (New York, NY: Knopf, 1996). I have also consulted the rich commentary contained in the volumes of Giorgio Vasari, *Le vite de' più eccellenti pittori, scultori, e architettiori*, 9 vols., ed. Paola della Pergola, Luigi Grassi, and Giovanni Previtali, revisions by Aldo Rossi, notes and bibliography by Giovanni Previtali and Paola Ceschi (Novara: Istituto Geografico De Agostini, 1967). References throughout, placed in parenthesis, are first to the English and then Italian versions of the text; abbreviations are as follows: G = Giuntina edition, T = Torrentiniana edition. For the sake of space, I have not registered where there are variations, as there often are as we move from the 1550 Torrentiniana to the 1568 Giuntina edition, but readers can readily compare them in the online Barocchi-Bettarini edition of Vasari 1966–87, http://vasari.sns.it/consultazione/Vasari/indice.html, where the two editions are conveniently set one above the other (the Giuntina above the Torrentiniana).

INTRODUCTION

Meanwhile, the Lord Duke Cosimo desiring that the Book of the Lives, already brought almost to completion with the greatest diligence that I had found possible, and with the assistance of some of my friends [*già condotto quasi al fine con quella maggior diligenza che a me era stato possibile e con l'aiuto d'alcuni miei amici*], should be given to the printers, I gave it to Lorenzo Torrentino, printer to the Duke, and so the printing was begun [*e così fu cominciato a stamparsi*].[1]

—Giorgio Vasari, "Description of the Works of Giorgio Vasari," the *Lives* (1568)

At one point in his discussion of Raphael Sanzio's life, Giorgio Vasari (fig. 1) turns to identify the various philosophers peopling the *School of Athens* (fig. 2),[2] doing so in a manner we can only presume viewers in his own time would have done. In the center of the painting, Vasari points out, is the brooding, white-bearded Plato holding a copy of the *Timaeus* as he gestures upwards toward the transcendent, abstract realm of Ideas; striding beside him is the meditative, frowning, dark-bearded Aristotle with his *Ethics* in his hand as he gestures instead downward, toward the sublunary physical world and, presumably, the imminent realm not of metaphysics but of virtuous behavior and praiseworthy action; below them both is the cynic Diogenes, stretched out half-naked across the steps, indiscreetly lounging about with his tell-tale cup by his side; and diagonally across is the white-robed astrologer Zoroaster bearing a star-studded globe of the cosmos. Note as well, Vasari observes, that Raphael (1483–1520) has cleverly incorporated into the painting, in typical Renaissance fashion, the likenesses of several contemporaries: Federigo II, the Duke of Mantua; the architect Donato Bramante; and, tellingly, his own self-portrait. The painting thus functions at one level as a sort of guessing game. It has been ingeniously designed for those inquisitive readers who, pausing to take a break in a lull of scholarly concentration, lift their heads up

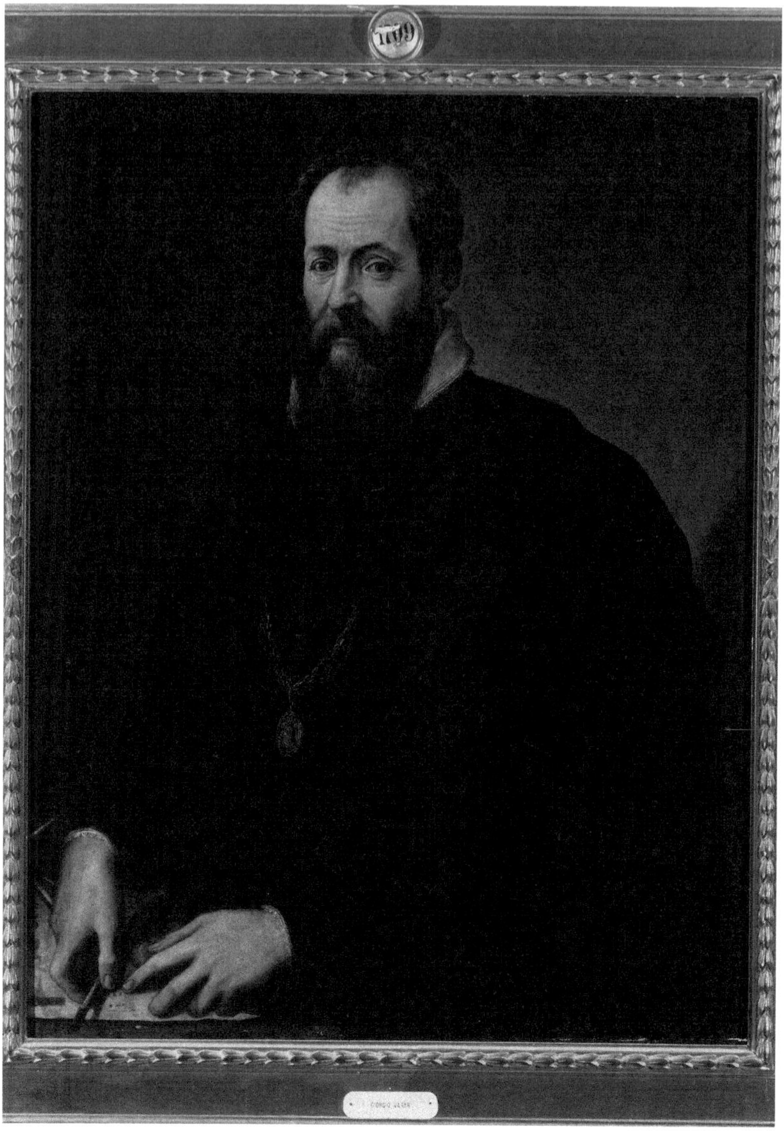

1. Followers of Giorgio Vasari (1511–1574), *Portrait* (ca. 1550–66/8). Galleria degli Uffizi, Florence, Italy. Photo credit: Scala/Art Resource, NY.

from their books in Julius II's personal library and take a moment to wonder who those different, pensive figures depicted on the wall really were in classical antiquity, even as a number of them do not carry antique scrolls but anachronistically and therefore puzzlingly hold bound volumes (not unlike the ones stacked up on low shelves in the Stanza della Segnatura itself).[3]

But whatever those learned readers may or may not have thought, for Vasari the *School of Athens* was designed to dramatize how the visual artist who actually painted the fresco, and whose self-portrait conspicuously appears in it, should be thought of as a maker of ideas, a sort of philosopher himself through the very process of painting, in which he deployed various strategies for rendering those ideas, and the world itself, visible to the eye.[4] Or to put the matter differently, for the artist Vasari authoring the *Lives*, the painting of frescoes based on the mastery of *disegno*, as Raphael so evidently did, should be viewed as no less an expression of ideas than writing them down in books. The *School of Athens* should therefore be viewed not as the simple illustration of an idea but as a material object that, like a seminal book of philosophy, generates ideas on its own. It is a visionary work to ponder,[5] like the precious bound books in Julius II's private library, precisely because it is the inventive product of a contemplative visual artist with ideas of his own and a deep grounding in *disegno* conceived not just as a mechanical but also, more importantly, as an intellectual art—an art that requires extensive planning, forethought, and complex problem-solving. Or, as Vasari at one point summarily puts it early in the *Lives*, "*disegno*"—rooted as it is in the deft manual ability to draw and craft sharp, accurate outlines—"is none other than a visible expression and declaration of a concept that is there

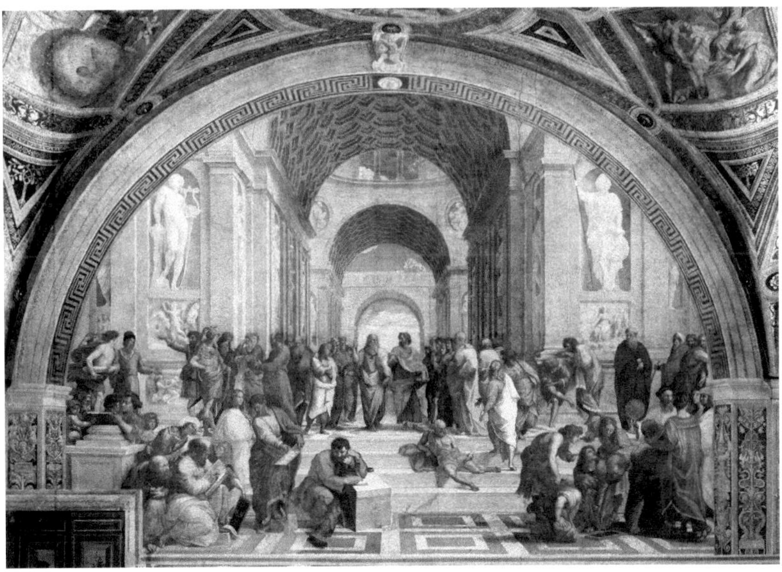

2. Raphael (Raffaello Sanzio, 1483–1520), *The School of Athens* (ca. 1510–12). Stanza della Segnatura, Vatican Palace, Rome, Italy. Photo credit: Scala/Art Resource, NY.

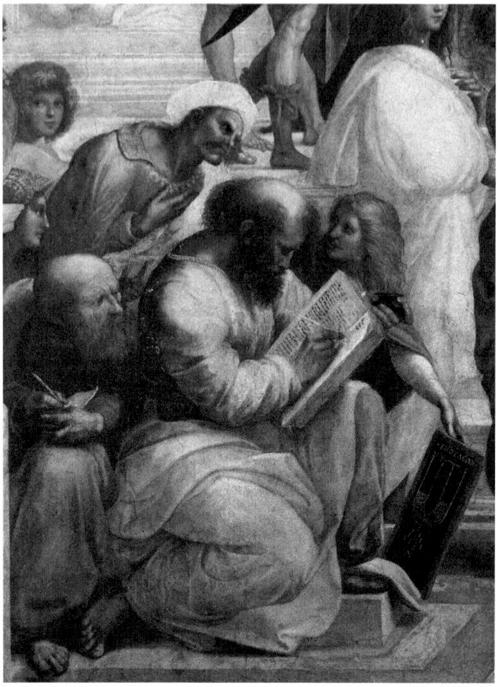

3. Raphael (Raffaello Sanzio, 1483–1520), *The School of Athens* (ca. 1510–12). Detail of Pythagoras grouping and tablet. Stanza della Segnatura, Vatican Palace, Rome, Italy. Photo credit: Scala/Art Resource, NY.

in one's mind [*una apparente espressione e dichiarazione del concetto che si ha nell'animo*] and of that which others have imagined and fashioned as an idea in their minds [*e di quello che altri si è nella mente imaginato e fabricato nell'idea*]" (G1.111). The emphasis here is placed, and shall be in the context of this study, on the last crucial word: *idea*.

For all intents and purposes, then, Vasari seems to be a perfectly reliable guide as he identifies one ancient man of ideas after another and invites us to do the same, had we ever been admitted into Julius II's private library in the sixteenth century and had the privilege of seeing the fresco firsthand, perhaps in the process of consulting some of those rare bound books, which included many precious ones dedicated to pagan philosophy. But then Vasari suddenly botches the job. He has been recalling the group of figures positioned at the bottom left of the fresco, just where the stairs begin to move up toward the basilica-like structure (fig. 3), which is perhaps even intended to allude to what the new St. Peter's under construction might

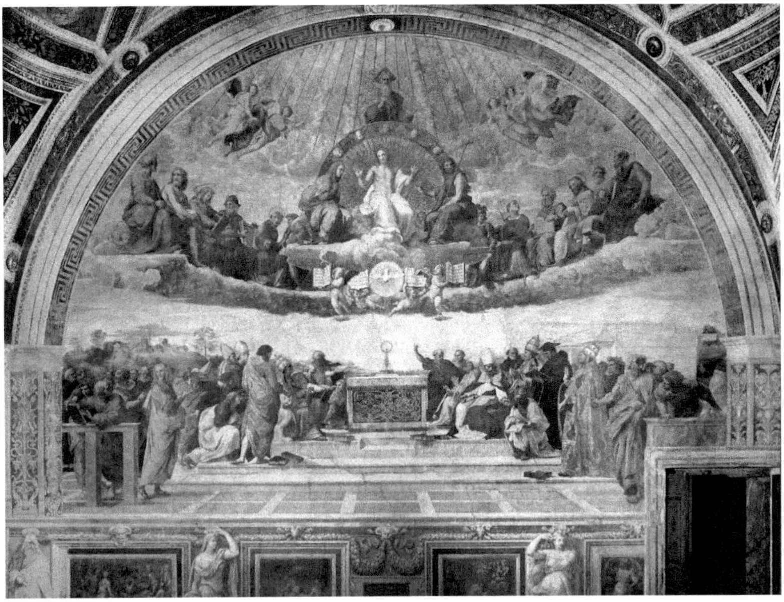

4. Raphael (Raffaello Sanzio, 1483–1520), *La Disputa, Theology* (ca. 1510–12). Stanza della Segnatura, Vatican Palace, Rome, Italy. Photo credit: Erich Lessing/Art Resource, NY.

look like when finished, and he then makes the following rather bizarre observation:

> Behind St. Matthew [*sic*], who is copying the characters from the tablet wherein are the figures (which is held before him by an angel [*sic*]), and writing them down in a book, he painted an old man who, having placed a piece of paper on his knee, is copying all that St. Matthew writes down; and while intent on his work in that uncomfortable position, he seems to twist his head and his jaws in time with the motion of the pen. (1.718, G4.167)

Vasari has here egregiously blundered. Or so it would seem. The crouched man writing in the book is not St. Matthew but Pythagoras, as any undergraduate student with ready access to Wikipedia can immediately tell you. And there is not an angel to be seen in the entire fresco. If you want angels, look to the facing wall, to the *Disputation of the Holy Sacrament* (fig. 4). There are six of them there, divided into two groups of three on either side of Christ in heaven, not to mention all those winged, floating putti incorporated into both the billowy clouds forming a cushioned bench for the saints and the gilded representation of the abstract realm of the blessed.

How, then, could this have possibly happened? How could a trained and learned practitioner, who was able to reconstitute a host of images in his book by relying so often on the power of his prodigious memory alone, get things so right in one moment and so wrong in another? This particular question may seem all the more pressing in the case of this specific secular image of the *School of Athens*, which over time has become so iconic that it encapsulates in our own era the genius of Raphael as a contemplative, visionary painter and the High Renaissance generally as a period when so many texts of pagan philosophy were being dutifully recovered, printed, and studied.[6] For Raphael's *School of Athens*, so full of pagans suavely staged here and there, is self-evidently *not*, I think it is safe to say, about evangelists—at least not on the surface. And yet Vasari's confusion makes some sense within the larger historical/typological context that makes up the integrated series of frescoes forming the entire Stanza della Segnatura, leaving aside the fact that, as Giovanni Pietro Bellori observed long ago,[7] an intermediary source almost certainly muddled Vasari's recollection. In describing Raphael's *School of Athens*, Vasari was no doubt "looking," as Marcia B. Hall has likewise observed, "at the 1523 print by Agostino Veneziano (ca. 1490–ca. 1540), in which Matthew was substituted for Pythagoras."[8] And yet, whatever the cause of Vasari's blunder, whether he had simply failed to recall the painting correctly in his mind's eye or far more probably was working from an inexact source as the basis for his slightly flawed description, the *School of Athens* is clearly about illumination. In literary terms, it is about the sort of natural light associated with the pagans in the *Divina Commedia* (*Divine Comedy*, 1321), whose author, Dante Alighieri, also happens to be the one poet who makes an appearance in *both* the *Parnassus* and the *Disputation* of the Stanza della Segnatura: he is at once a muse-inspired writer of fantastical, imaginative literature *and* a *poeta theologus* (poet theologian) of divinely inspired, Christian verbal art. Accordingly, just as Dante's Virgil in the *Divine Comedy* effectively sees through a glass darkly as he advances, Moses-like, toward the promised land of revelation but can never witness it as soon as Beatrice (typologically configured as Christ) descends into the redeemed garden of Eden, so too Raphael's enlightened yet still confused pagans advance—as Plato and Aristotle do—toward the truth of Christian theology and the mystery of the sacrament on the opposite wall, fueled by their own longing for revelation in their pursuit of wisdom. Guided by their pagan ideas, they can arguably see this truth through a glass darkly but they cannot really comprehend what they see. Nor can they fully bear witness to it as they stride through the basilica-like structure, moving against the current of the dynamic orthogonals while debating complex ideas, just as peripatetic philosophers were wont to do in antiquity.

In this context, it is entirely fitting that Vasari mistakes Pythagoras for St. Matthew receiving the word of God as it is dictated to him, even if the direct cause for Vasari's blunder was that he was probably working from Veneziano's print as the contaminating source. For pagan illumination in this painting is meant to be seen as revelatory in its own right. It is a worldly, intellective light that instinctively yearns for, and thereby advances in its own right toward, the higher, sublime, revealed light and truth of the Gospels pictured on the facing wall and bound in the four opened volumes held aloft by the cheerful winged putti on either side of the Holy Ghost figured conventionally as a dove. Vasari's apparent blunder, albeit occasioned by relying on Veneziano's print, thus calls attention not to what is recognizably *in* the painting or *on* the surface of it, but what iconographically underpins it: the larger truth that pagan illumination and Christian enlightenment can and should be reconciled, with the former prefiguring the latter. Literally Vasari is wrong, but allegorically he is absolutely right. Pythagoras is a pagan prefiguration of Christian harmony, the very harmony that the entire fresco cycle serves to give concrete material shape to in pictorial form and that is worked out philosophically in the harmonic structures on the tablet as a visual configuration of musical and mathematical ideas.[9] As such, the act of painting in the library should be viewed as an expression on Raphael's part of the active, physical making and shaping of ideas visually.[10]

The core argument of *Vasari's Words* is that the *Lives of the Artists* should also be read, like the illuminating, visionary *School of Athens*, as itself an illuminating, visionary work that gives expression to ideas through the creative process of making tangible things—or, as I have preferred to call it in my subtitle, a history of ideas. Moreover, as a series of integrated biographies that collectively account for various developments within a well-defined period and serve to teach through examples, the *Lives* can be construed as a history in the highly rhetoricized and classicized conception of the term *historia/istoria* (history/story) in the Italian Renaissance.[11] And authoring a history was something that Vasari, inspired by the writings of various Renaissance humanists, considered one of the worthiest things anyone could do. History, after all, was largely understood in the Renaissance to be, rhetorically speaking, about teaching through examples. And Vasari aimed to teach, among other things, ideas through the hundreds of examples that make up the collective biographies of his *Lives* and, in the process, aggressively advance as a practitioner-writer a certain program of both making and looking at visual art. Directly related to this argument is the crucial notion underpinning this book that the ideas of the *Lives* can be profitably captured by focusing on keywords as a form of "semantic cultural analysis" and "semantic critical analysis" of the sort described by the anthropological linguist Anna Wierzbicka, developed almost half a century ago in a memorable manner by the Marxist critic Raymond Williams, and recently practiced in cultural and intellectual history by Martin Jay and in literary and cultural studies by the comparatist Roland Greene.[12] In this respect the *Lives* is not just a history of ideas written *in* the Italian Renaissance, as the subtitle of this book announces, but also very much a history of ideas *about* the Italian Renaissance.

My secondary argument is that by examining those ideas through keywords, synthetically understood—in the encapsulating words of Wierzbicka—"as focal points around which entire cultural domains are organized,"[13] we can appreciate all the better how the *Lives* itself has a formal design, somewhat along the lines of how Vasari, at least in part, conceptualizes the Renaissance notion of *disegno* in the visual arts. Much as a good painting for Vasari is thought out in terms of its overall *disegno*, with hidden geometric forms typically underpinning the composition within a rationally and mathematically organized space, so too Vasari's *Lives* is thought out in terms of its overall *disegno*,[14] with a variety of compelling and complementary ideas providing an underlying thematic structure from beginning to end. To phrase the matter somewhat differently, the ideas permeating the book are not only interesting in and of themselves. In Renaissance rhetorical terms, which are also the terms that underpin Vasari's conception of *disegno*, he makes the ideas permeating the book work at the service of invention (*inventio*: the discovery of arguments) and disposition (*dispositio*: the arrangement of arguments), thereby providing a general, skeletal structure that gives shape to much of the *Lives* itself. A good work of visual art is grounded for Vasari in ideas that have been developed through the mechanical *and* intellectual process of *disegno*, of drawing as a way of generating and working out ideas, as a cognitive act fueled by the power of memory working at the service of an overall, unifying argument; so, too, I contend, does the *Lives* through the process of writing itself. Simply put, the book has a design to it, and the ideas both inform and arise out of that design. However, as for the book's overall linguistic style (in Renaissance rhetorical terms its *elocutio*), that is a different matter altogether, in no small measure because Vasari's words were not always in fact his own, as the art historians Charles Hope, Thomas Frangenberg, and Marco Ruffini have persuasively argued.[15] Less than half of the book in both the 1550 Torrentiniana and 1568 Giuntina editions may even, it appears, have been written by Vasari (figs. 5 and 6). And that makes issues related to matters of style all the more complex and intriguing when thinking about Vasari's words in the *Lives*—or rather, in many instances we might say "Vasari's"

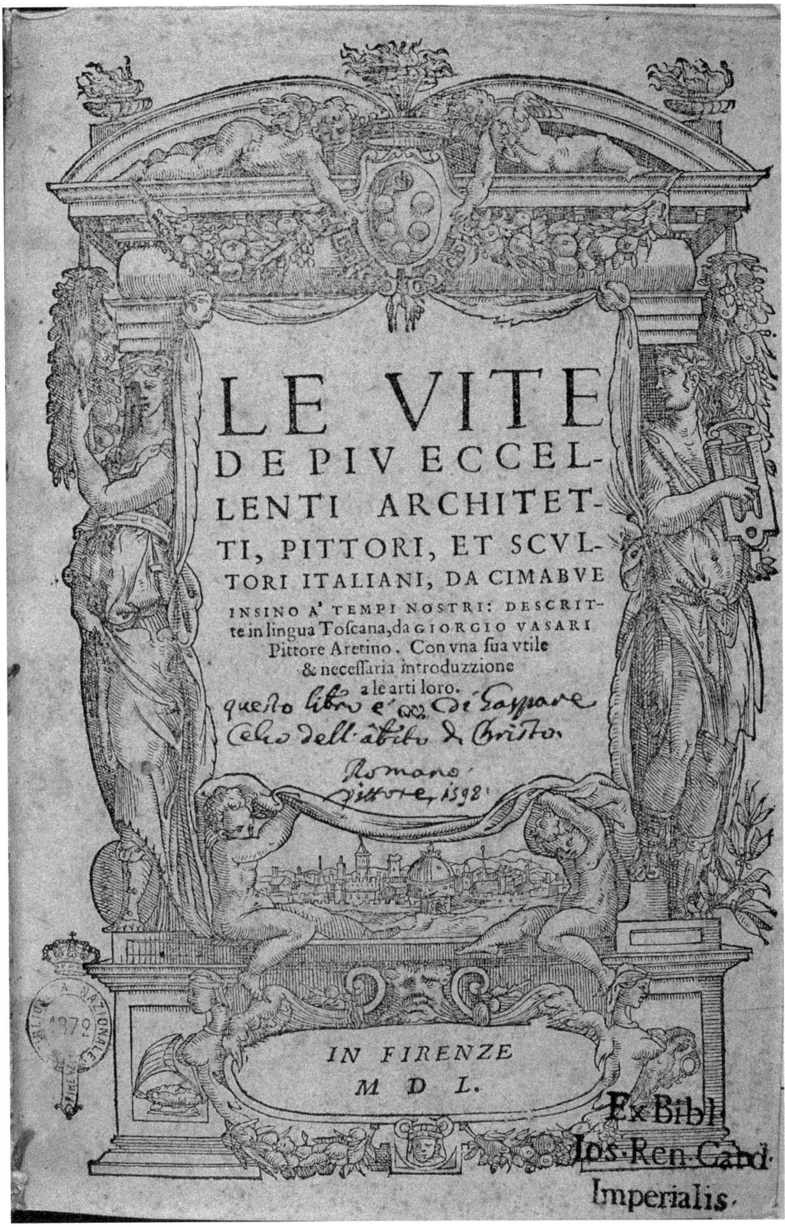
LE VITE
DE PIV ECCEL-
LENTI ARCHITET-
TI, PITTORI, ET SCVL-
TORI ITALIANI, DA CIMABVE
INSINO A' TEMPI NOSTRI: DESCRIT-
te in lingua Toſcana, da GIORGIO VASARI
Pittore Aretino. Con vna ſua vtile
& neceſſaria introduzzione
a le arti loro.
questo libro e' di Gasparre
Celio dell'abito di Christo
Romano
pittore 1598

IN FIRENZE
M D L.

Ex Bibl.
Ios. Ren. Card.
Imperialis.

5. Giorgio Vasari (1511–1574), *Le vite dei piu eccellenti architetti, pittori, et scultori italiani, da Cimabue insino a' tempi nostri: descritte in lingua toscana, da Giorgio Vasari ...; Con una sua utile & necessaria introduzzione a le arti loro*. Florence: Appresso Lorenzo Torrentino, 1550. Title page. Biblioteca Nazionale, Florence, Italy. Photo: Sergio Anelli. Photo credit: Mondadori Portfolio/Art Resource, NY.

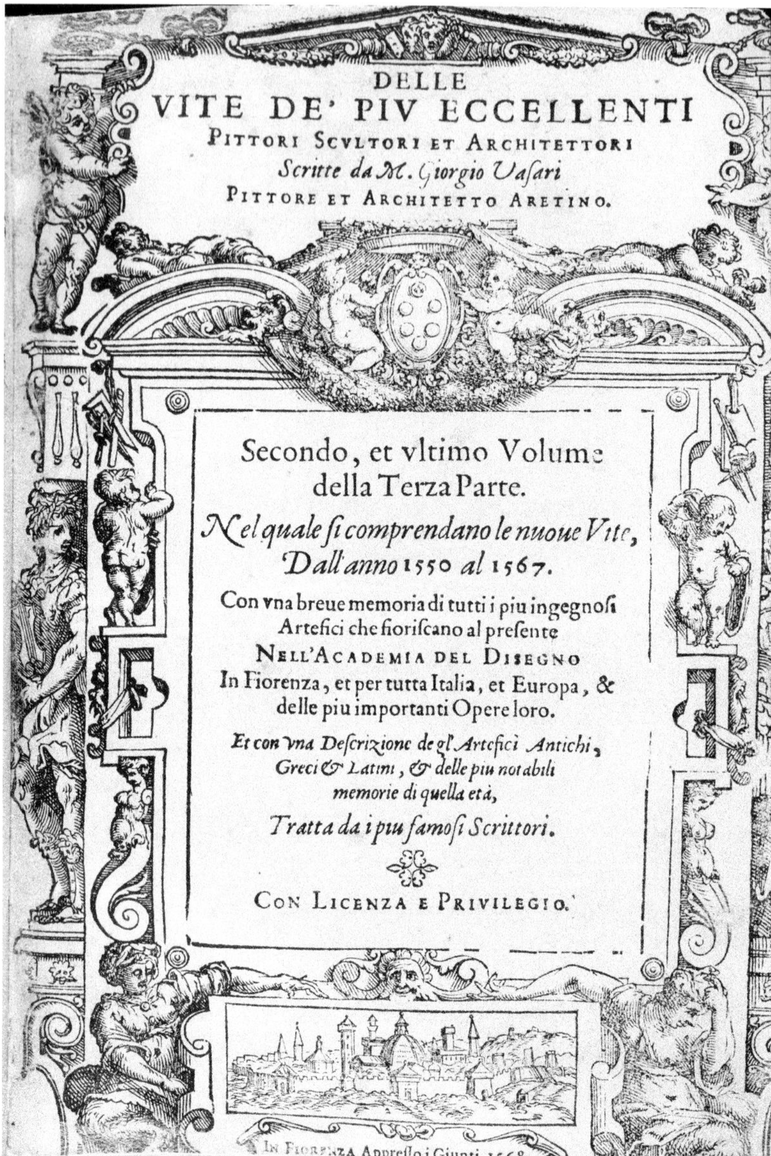
DELLE
VITE DE' PIV ECCELLENTI
PITTORI SCVLTORI ET ARCHITETTORI
Scritte da M. Giorgio Vasari
PITTORE ET ARCHITETTO ARETINO.

Secondo, et vltimo Volume
della Terza Parte.
Nel quale si comprendano le nuoue Vite,
Dall'anno 1550 al 1567.
Con vna breue memoria di tutti i piu ingegnosi
Artefici che fioriscano al presente
NELL'ACADEMIA DEL DISEGNO
In Fiorenza, et per tutta Italia, et Europa, &
delle piu importanti Opere loro.
Et con vna Descrizione de gl'Artefici Antichi,
Greci & Latini, & delle piu notabili
memorie di quella età,
Tratta da i piu famosi Scrittori.

CON LICENZA E PRIVILEGIO.

IN FIORENZA Appresso i Giunti. 1568.

6. Giorgio Vasari (1511–1574), *Le vite de' piu eccellenti pittori, scultori, e architettori, di nuouo dal medesimo riviste et ampliate con i ritratti loro et con l'aggiunta delle vite de' vivi, & de' morti dall'anno 1550 insino al 1567*. Florence: Appresso i Giunti, 1568. Biblioteca B. 2898 1–2. Title page. Casa Buonarroti, Florence, Italy. Photo credit: Scala/Art Resource, NY.

words, if the use of such ungainly quotation marks were not so terrible an eyesore. In any event, from a purely literary point of view, I can think of no major work of the Italian Renaissance, written either in poetry or prose, the vernacular or Latin, that has been deemed (albeit not without some fierce debate) the product of such extensively shared authorship.

Vasari's Words thus focuses on how five interconnected ideas arise, evolve, and are resolved in the *Lives*. Each idea is captured through a keyword, with each keyword in its turn directing our attention to new cultural values identified by Vasari as important to understanding, appreciating, and/or ensuring the future of this new and vibrant age labeled by him a *rinascita* (rebirth).[16] Chapter 1, "*Professione*/Profession," lays the conceptual groundwork for the book by investigating, as do the four subsequent chapters, matters of professional concern. Accordingly, it examines the way that Vasari not only rethinks artistic labor as a profession but also the very idea of what it means to have a profession in the visual arts in his culture. In the process Vasari creates a new individual and collective identity for visual artists of his *rinascita* while at the same time ascribing a new, elevated cultural value to their work as professionals—or, as Vasari prefers to dub them in a few instances, as *professori*: that is to say, as men who can profess, and thus publicly proclaim, exceptional mastery over a determinate area of expertise. Chapter 2, "*Ingegno*/Genius," then considers what is economically, socially, culturally, and individually needed to achieve true excellence in this newly conceived *professione* of the visual arts. In view of that, Chapter 2 examines the importance Vasari attributes in the *Lives* to the value of recognizing genius, cultivating genius, acknowledging the limits of genius, tracing the lineage of genius, differentiating various qualities of genius, and, most importantly, shaping genius in the *professione* of the visual arts through a combination of longstanding and entirely new, institutionalized programs of education and collaboration. Hence, for Vasari, one must not merely have *ingegno* to become a truly great painter, sculptor, or architect. One must diligently and properly cultivate *ingegno* through dedicated, disciplined *fatica* (labor) and socially accepted forms of professional training. And therein lies the importance Vasari attributes, at least partly in the second edition of his *Lives*, to the cultural value of the new pedagogical program of educating visual artists in their *professione*—an education that was a chief function of the newly instituted, state-sponsored, Florentine Accademia del Disegno (Academy of Design). Chapter 3, "*Prestezza*/Speed," then examines how the very idea of speed is culturally valued in the *Lives*. Speed, we come to learn, is a new feature that distinguishes some exceptional artists of remarkable *ingegno* as possessing a professional advantage within an increasingly competitive art market driven by consumers with lots of cash or credit at their disposal and a voracious appetite for commissioning and purchasing both small- and large-scale works of visual art. Moreover, the third chapter demonstrates how, remarkably enough, no author writing before Vasari had ever linked the historical development of the visual arts in any given period to the ever-increasing speed with which excellent paintings, sculptures, or buildings were being masterfully produced. In this way speed becomes for Vasari a new and highly valued feature of his *rinascita* as he traces how visual artists develop technically and conceptually over roughly three hundred years as professionals.

The first three chapters of this book can thus be said to offer a triumphalist reading of the *Lives*, with visual artists in Vasari's book being recognized as having an elevated *professione* and a new, distinguished program of education dedicated to training and nurturing their *ingegno* within it, as well as a new ability to produce works with staggering and ever-increasing *prestezza* as laborers, thereby progressively enhancing the value of their *professione* over time. By contrast, the fourth chapter examines how Vasari was painfully aware that all historical periods eventually stagnate, wane, and come to an end, and thus he labors to ensure that his lavishly praised *rinascita* will continue to endure and be remembered for both its small and grand achievements. Chapter 4, "*Tempo*/Time," the penultimate chapter of this book, consequently investigates the importance Vasari attributes to the cultural value of using time productively in this newly conceived *professione* of the visual arts. By the same token, Vasari reveals throughout the *Lives* how he is plagued by the fear that much of his celebrated *rinascita* will not survive through time, since so many of its praiseworthy artifacts were being destroyed even in the very period in which he was writing. But as a professional painter who has taken up for the time being the role of the professional author, he is nevertheless defiantly bent on doing everything he can as he writes the *Lives* to sustain the art he admires and preserve it over time. Chapter 5, "*Notte*/Night," the last and longest chapter of this book, then returns to the overriding triumphalist reading of the *Lives* and explores how issues of temporality play themselves out in terms of visual, as opposed to verbal, representation. The final chapter does so by investigating the way that a certain span of time dominated by darkness—the period most commonly associated with sleep both then and in our own time—was not just economically, socially, and culturally conquered during the period in which Vasari lived but, we learn in the *Lives*, visually as well. In this regard, Vasari viewed as a major professional achievement in the Italian Renaissance the ability to take the universally shared temporal experience of the night and represent it naturalistically in visual form, so that the idea of the night, with all its manifold and complex associations, is convincingly materialized through the process of painting as a thick, all-encompassing, and at times impenetrable, enveloping darkness. And here, significantly enough, it is not Michelangelo (1475–1564) who teaches us how to represent the night as a distinct span of time but, instead, the other great, exemplary artist in the second edition of the *Lives*: Raphael, the intellectual, "philosophical," visionary, and princely painter with whom this Introduction began.

This book is therefore devoted not to analyzing visual art closely in the process of reflecting on the *Lives*. Rather, it is devoted to revealing how Vasari, as a practitioner turned author, serves as a useful and informative guide as he helps us to think about the broader process of cultural and historical formation that was taking place in the context of the creation of a newly conceived *professione* of the visual arts. To be sure, Vasari's comments on the particular details of paintings may repeatedly fall short of what we as art historians would do today. And occasionally Vasari botches the job along the way, as he did in mistaking Pythagoras for St. Matthew in the *School of Athens*. But Vasari nevertheless repeatedly brings to light certain key issues that we may occasionally ignore as we yearn to unpack a work of visual art with great subtlety and sophistication. In the case of the *Deliverance of St. Peter*, for instance, which I discuss in the final chapter of this book, Vasari seizes upon the concept of the "night" in a way that no one before him had done in writing about visual art. He thus brings to our attention the very idea that here, for the first time, night has been represented materially in an altogether novel manner in the difficult, complex medium of fresco on the grand scale. In this instance, Vasari recognized that something significant was going on in Raphael's tour-de-force painting when it comes to representing the night. Night as a distinct span of time, he gives us to understand, had evidently become an important matter of concern both for him and others within the specific, local culture of mid-sixteenth-century Italy. And to his credit, Vasari found that in this case it was the exceptional Raphael who had overcome the difficulty of representing the darkness of night in a visually breathtaking and innovative manner. For some scholars, then, Vasari may be just the starting point in the process of analyzing works of art and artists of the past and in seeking to pursue a more nuanced understanding of, say, how the darkness of night might function meaningfully and symbolically in a particular painting, such as Raphael's *Deliverance of St. Peter* or his transformative, highly dramatic, "visionary," and perhaps "tragic" *Transfiguration*.[17] By contrast, Vasari constitutes in this book both the beginning *and* endpoint of my inquiry. Accordingly, I have tried to give Vasari his due and understand him, as best I can, on his own terms, beginning with a highly focused reading in the first chapter of how he treats the very term *professione* in the *Lives* and then, in the following four chapters, exploring how a variety of ideas unfold organically from it.

In this light, I have borne in mind as I wrote this book the following trenchant observation delivered by Michael Baxandall at the very outset of his *Patterns of Intention: On the Historical Explanation of Pictures*. "We do not explain pictures," he wrote polemically, "we explain remarks about pictures—or rather, we explain pictures only in so far as we have considered them under some verbal description or specification."[18] For Baxandall, the language of talking about visual art is in the end all that we have when it comes to making sense of it. This crucial point, so central to an understanding of the *Lives* as an innovative book containing literally hundreds of *ekphrases*,[19] is rendered especially evident when we turn to reflect on the critical language that Vasari uses to make sense of visual art and the lives of the excellent producers of it. Similarly, as Quentin Skinner and others have consistently maintained in the context of integrating the insights of linguistics into the discipline of intellectual history, the words chosen by writers in specific moments in time served to construct meaning as "speech acts"—which is to say as intentional, linguistic performances—that aimed to have an impact within an historically determined culture. Consequently, when Vasari, for instance, deploys the word *professione* over and over again to describe visual artists, he is not just designating what they do, one by one, as individual painters, sculptors, architects, and the like in the period he labels a *rinascita*. He is also publicly declaring, I argue in Chapter 1, that those same visual artists collectively belong to a diverse yet unified fellowship of extremely accomplished laborers who now and for evermore have a *professione* of the sort that Vasari is self-consciously fashioning for them through the act of writing the *Lives* itself. And Vasari, drawing on the achievements of men such as the fifteenth-century humanist Leon Battista Alberti (1404–1472), verbally constructed this new *professione* for these likeminded visual artists in a period when professionalism itself had become increasingly a matter of great cultural concern.

The *Lives*, it is thus the burden of this book to show, should not be read as just a humanist-inspired, Plinian-modeled, and Plutarchan-cum-Suetonian structured history of art—indeed as the first great, sustained work of art history in the modern era, as well as a work of art history that even to this day remains a contested yet still perennial, "revolutionary," reference point as a master narrative of the period.[20] Nor should the *Lives* be read as just a history of the lives of certain memorable visual artists and their sometimes dazzling accomplishments and/or weird personalities, all recounted with some literary dexterity on Vasari's part as he draws on narrative models available to him in the vernacular, such as those by Dante Alighieri, Giovanni Boccaccio, and Franco Sacchetti, and takes on the role of a storyteller and mythographer.[21] The *Lives* should also be read as a history that seriously engages ideas. More precisely, I argue in this book that the *Lives* should be read as a history of ideas that arises in no small measure out of Vasari's varied, complex, and interrelated reflections on the changing nature of professional identity within the visual arts of his time. Consequently, if as scholars in the humanities we are at all interested not just in knowing something about the putative lives of "excellent" visual artists of the period but also in knowing something about the ideas that underpinned and sustained what they did as professionals and why they did it, then the *Lives* certainly merits being read by not just art historians, a number of whom—from Robert Williams, Svetlana Alpers, Patricia Rubin, and Alessandro Nova to Philippe Sohm, David Summers, Roland Le Mollé, Marco Ruffini, and Paola Barocchi—have already explored some of the nuances of Vasari's critical vocabulary. Vasari's book should also be read by literary, intellectual, and cultural historians, who have often disregarded the *Lives* as an important document for understanding the historically determined horizons of expectations that defined the period of the Italian Renaissance and some of the complex ideas that animated it. Moreover, recognizing that a number of those culturally determined ideas pervade the book from beginning to end should in its turn also encourage us to realize that Vasari's massive, sprawling *Lives* should be read from beginning to end.[22] Only by doing so is it possible to appreciate fully how the *Lives*, like an accomplished work of visual art for Vasari, is itself formally constructed as a book with a comprehensive *disegno*, in the sense that it is a book governed from beginning to end by a constellation of well-conceived, complementary, and compelling ideas: ideas that unfold with an internal logic; ideas that obviously mattered to Vasari personally and professionally; and ideas that underpinned how his culture understood the extraordinarily impressive output of visual art in the period that we commonly call—in no small measure thanks to Vasari's input and indeed "Vasari's" words—the Italian Renaissance.

Finally, a brief word about whether *this* book, which examines Vasari's *Lives* as history of ideas, should itself be construed as a history of ideas in the context of the modern discipline of intellectual history, a discipline that has witnessed major shifts over the past several decades, ever since it was first informally established at Johns Hopkins University under the guidance of A. O. Lovejoy and George Boas. To be sure, in many ways this book is not a history of ideas when it comes to thinking about the way the discipline of intellectual history has customarily defined it, and this is especially true when it comes to thinking about the Italian Renaissance. When concentrating on that particular period, the conventional scholarly move—at least over the past few decades—has been to consider the history of ideas in the context of the history of philosophy, or the history of rhetoric, or the history of science, or the history of medicine, or the history of political thought, or the history of religion, or the history of antiquarianism, or the history of education, along with, more recently, the history of scholarship, collecting, readership, editing, patronage, publishing, museum-building, reception, emotions, and sexuality—or some such combination. But I see no reason why the ideas investigated in this book—whether we in fact define them as cultural concerns, cultural values, cultural mythologies, or cultural modes of problem-solving embodied in the process of actually making visual art—should not in their own right be viewed as legitimate areas of scholarly inquiry within the discipline of intellectual history, even if some of them, such as *professione*, *prestezza*, and *notte*, do not typically fit into the sets of interests conventionally associated with a history of ideas dedicated to Renaissance Italy. For the history of ideas has been a capacious and interdisciplinary area of study from its inception, as the intellectual historian Anthony Grafton most recently elucidated in an article dedicated to marking the moment when he became one of the principal editors of the foundational *Journal of the History of Ideas*.[23] And it is in this spirit that this book can be construed as a contribution to the history of ideas within a "revitalized" discipline that, as Darrin M. McMahon envisions it, "ought at the very least to be eclectic, reveling in the interdisciplinary ideal that first defined it."[24] In any event, that is the spirit with which this book was written, as it draws on art, literary, intellectual, and cultural history to argue that Vasari's *Lives* should indeed be read as a history of ideas.

So how, then, should this book be understood in the context of the modern, evolving discipline of intellectual history as a history of ideas? It is certainly by no means the sort of book that seeks to argue that Vasari's ideas are peculiarly interesting in the manner of those explored, for instance, in Carlo Ginzburg's landmark *The Cheese and the Worms*, with Vasari serving as an idiosyncratic character processing various cultural concerns of his era in his own unique way and from a distinctly peripheral space.[25] Far from idiosyncratic, Vasari was—and certainly aimed to be—a quintessential "insider," even if he originally came from the provincial town of Arezzo.[26] He thus comes across, both in his book and in his life, as the very opposite of the atypical outsider, of some bizarre, Menocchio like creature applying pressure from the margins to standard modes of thinking or behaving, thereby conflating and upsetting the normativized distinctions between the high and the low yet offering in the process new and challenging insights into different habits of thought, some theologically heretical, some not. Vasari's ideas, in sum, are those of someone who sought to work and live within the traditional but still evolving spaces of elite, centralized power and who did everything he could throughout his career to adhere to, and inform others about the value of adhering to, largely accepted modes of thought and behavior. Nor, for that matter, does this book maintain that Vasari addresses and explores ideas in his *Lives* that transcend context, although this is not to say that Vasari's concerns as they are expressed in the *Lives* may not feel at times strikingly familiar to many of us living and working in the West today, such as his almost obsessive, neoliberalist-like concern with efficiency, speed, and productivity, much less his concern for the importance of fashioning a unifying professional identity for all those collectively working in the visual arts in Italy, as well as his deep desire to institutionalize an enduring model and curriculum for training professionals within a state-sponsored academy embedded in a repressive, authoritarian state—a state that brilliantly regulated certain social and cultural behaviors at court, in the city, and in the realm. Rather, this is a book that argues in a largely unpolemical fashion for a return to something we might simply call good, old-fashioned thinking about big ideas by investigating where they made their first appearance here historically in the visual arts; how they grew out of a variety of concerns circulating in a specific culture among the highly verbal, educated elite; and how they articulated comprehensively in a single volume the importance of thinking seriously about visual art—not just verbal art—as a powerful, creative form for generating ideas themselves. Or to frame the issue in a manner that fits in with Vasari's overall historical project, this book reminds us once again that the works of visual artists, and not just the writings of humanists, philosophers, theologians, poets, and statesmen, say, should be viewed as core components of the creation, development, articulation, circulation, and dissemination of compelling ideas in the Italian Renaissance.

I begin, then, with the beginning, or rather with how Vasari in 1568 describes near the end of the *Lives* how the very idea of the book itself originally came into being through a collaborative process. The year is 1546, the place Rome. Several distinguished humanists and poets coming originally from various regions of southern, central, and northern Italy have gathered together at the magnificent Palazzo Farnese. These men have come there to dine and presumably do what men of their education, profession, and station always love doing whenever they can find a chance to meet as an informal group in the evening: converse, banter, tell jokes, perform agreeably for one another, and just generally share ideas in a pleasant setting modeled on the symposia of classical antiquity. Paolo Giovio (1483–1552), a humanist from Como with a vested interest in collecting antiquities and enriching his private museum of portraits at his stylish lakeside villa back home, is present at the gathering. So too are Annibale Caro (1507–1565, born in Civitanova Marche), Porrino Gandolfo (d. 1552, born in Modena), Francesco Maria Molza (1489–1544, also born in Modena), Claudio Tolomei (1492–1556, born in Ascanio), and Romolo Quirino Amaseo (1489–1552, born in Udine).[27] Present as well at the illustrious gathering is Vasari, the only Tuscan-born among the lot, who, albeit not a humanist or poet, presumably enjoys the company of these sorts of highly literate gentlemen and their convivial, entertaining discussions. For these men who belong to the cultural elite can talk a lot, they can talk well, and they can talk about a variety of ideas.[28] And one of the ideas they eventually talk about that evening is how they would like to possess a comprehensive history of the visual arts of their time, beginning with Cimabue (ca. 1240–ca. 1302) and ending with the present. However, the book they have in mind—or rather the book that Giovio in particular has in mind to complement his museum at home, since he is indeed the great promoter of this particular humanist-inspired project that evening—is no ordinary book devoted exclusively to the visual arts. It must contain the sort of relevant, detailed information about visual artists and their works, both past and present, that only a truly well-connected practitioner could reliably know. Needless to say, that sort of innovative book of history, which has no extant classical precedent, is something that Pliny the Elder, the Roman encyclopedist who memorably traced the development of the visual arts in classical antiquity, did not construct when he wrote his monumental *Naturalis historia* (*Natural History*, 77–9 CE).[29] It is also certainly not the sort of innovative book that any one of the esteemed authors gathered together at the Palazzo Farnese could have ever even begun to think about writing on his own. After all, each of them, unlike the exceptional humanist Leon Battista Alberti, who lived and wrote roughly a century before Giovio, Caro, Gandolfo, Molza, Tolomei, and Amaseo, lacked any experience whatsoever in the actual practice of making visual art. Nor, as non-practitioners with absolutely no training in *disegno*, would any of those humanists and poets present at the gathering have ever presumably been in a position to talk with supreme authority about the ways in which the actual making of visual art not only required mechanical skill but also functioned as a cognitive act, as a way of solving distinctly visual problems and generating distinctly visual ideas.[30]

But fortunately there was Vasari. At which point we can only imagine what went through the minds of those learned gentlemen as the host, Cardinal Alessandro Farnese (1520–1589), seated presumably in full public view on a dais as he ate,[31] gently urged Vasari to take on the task of at least assembling the essential, preliminary material for it, if not actually writing the book—something that Vasari, as it turns out, had already been actively and prudently doing for some time. Vasari, they must have been thinking, while admittedly not a trained or rhetorically gifted writer, is a professional painter who seems to possess essential information about virtually every visual artist worth knowing, both past and present. What is more, he collects and sometimes beautifully frames samples of their drawings in a special, voluminous book of his own making and design—a fascinating, unique collection of images, distinct in conception and purpose from a master's functional pattern book devised for workshop training, use, and production. Along with that, Vasari is prompt and reliable and industrious and, yes, extremely quick, a man of exceptional artistic facility. So he never wastes time and will perform the job efficiently, perhaps without breaking a sweat in the process. As it so happens, that is precisely what Vasari did in 1546 as he finished a large fresco cycle for Cardinal Farnese at breakneck speed, albeit not in the same room in which they presently dine and converse. He is certainly literate, having received some rudimentary training in the *studia humanitatis* in his youth, and is reasonably articulate. Word has it—or, more precisely, Vasari himself would have it (G5.512)—that he even memorized much of the *Aeneid* at one point, before leaving Arezzo to be educated in Florence with the Medici children. He obviously gets on with humanists, he comports himself well with others in the elevated social world of the cultural elite, and he understands, as only an accomplished practitioner intimately can, how truly excellent painters, sculptors, and architects work out and generate ideas visually through the mechanical and intellectual art of *disegno*. He will therefore make a good potential collaborator on just such a worthy literary project if any one of those humanists present at the gathering in Rome finally chooses to write the proposed book with the assistance of Vasari and in the process inevitably seeks to surpass the canonical Plinian model that has survived from antiquity. And lastly, Vasari has an obvious talent, a "genius," in the classical sense of the word, for taking on massive projects, managing people to complete them on schedule, and performing somewhat hyperproductively for others with the aim of dutifully pleasing, if not downright stupefying at times, everyone concerned. That settles it. Vasari is the right man for the job. Or at least he is the right man for getting the job started by collecting all the necessary preparatory material for it.

That, more or less, is how Vasari in 1568 would have us understand the way in which the idea of the *Lives* initially came to light twenty-two years earlier in 1546 and how, with Giovio's urging and the warm encouragement of others, he eventually became the sole recognized author of it on the printed title page of both editions (figs. 5 and 6), although I have admittedly added an entire paragraph of local narrative color to my own fanciful rendition of what went on in the minds of those gentlemen attending the evening dinner party in Rome. Yet whether or not this elite dinner gathering actually occurred as Vasari imaginatively describes it at the very end of his book, or as I have liberally summarized it toward the very beginning of mine, matters little—and indeed there are sound reasons to suspect that the foundational event as described by Vasari did not in fact take place either then or even, perhaps, ever, not least because one of the named interlocutors allegedly present at it, Molza, was by then already long dead.[32] What matters in the end is that Vasari evidently *wants* us to understand that the idea of the *Lives* as a verbal and cultural artifact was initially born out of a conversation with a group of elite humanists and poets. That is the book's presumed genesis. And that is crucial. For as the art historian David Cast has recently emphasized, and as Vasari himself often enough gives us to understand in various ways in both editions of the *Lives*, conversation was an ever-present, highly cultivated, and even elaborately theorized feature of sixteenth-century Italian culture. And not just humanist culture. On the one hand there were the high-minded, fashionable conversations of the cultural elite, such as those described by Baldassar Castiglione (1478–1529) in his landmark *Cortegiano* (*The Courtier*, 1528) and Stefano Guazzo (1530–1593) in his influential *La civil conversazione* (*Civil Conversation*, 1574), in addition to all those amiable conversations described by any number of writers composing elegant, classicizing dialogues in Latin and the vernacular, along with the sometimes ponderous, sometimes jocular, sometimes heady conversations that presumably took place in such newly occupied social spaces as museums, loggias, sculpture gardens, academies, and even, curiously enough, catacombs. On the other hand there were the everyday, informal conversations that took place in such interactive, free-flowing social spaces as bookshops, apothecary shops, barbershops, markets, baths, taverns, courtyards, brothels, piazzas, street corners, artists' *botteghe* (workshops), or just the steps before a city cathedral, such as the fanciful, heterogeneous conversations dramatized by Anton Francesco Doni (1513–1574) in his *I marmi* (*The Marble Steps*, 1552–3), or Pietro Aretino (1492–1556) in his scandalously pornographic *Ragionamenti* (*Discourses*, 1534–6), or, for that matter, by any number of early sixteenth-century authors of ludic plays inspired by the revival of classical comedy, particularly the Roman comedies of Terence and Plautus.[33]

This is important given the stated focus of this book, because one of the privileged topics of conversation during the period in which Vasari wrote the *Lives* was in fact centered on words. More precisely it was centered, among other matters, on (1) which words we should use on a daily basis in order to be marked with distinction as a person of good taste and respectable social standing; (2) which regions, courts, or cities of Italy offer the best examples of word choice in current speech and writing patterns; (3) which works of canonical literature we should take as our enduring models of good diction in the context of speaking and writing well; (4) whether we should in fact turn to literature itself as the basis for deciding which words to use in speaking and writing well; (5) whether we should ground the vernacular in the best of all possible customs of past and current language usage rather than in canonical literature; (6) whether we should adhere to a single linguistic model or a number of such models for codifying the vernacular; and (7) whether a full-blown grammar of a living, mutable language can in fact ever be written in a world that was not unified politically, socially, economically, and culturally.[34] This intense focus on appropriate word choice as a topic of keen interest among the cultural elite in Italy had a long history, with roots going all the way back to the fourteenth century and Dante's recently recovered *De vulgari eloquentia* (*On Eloquence in the Vernacular*, ca. 1303–5). But the topic came to life in earnest in sixteenth-century Italy, particularly after the publication in 1524 of Gian Giorgio Trissino's *Epistola de le lettere nuovamente aggiunte a la lingua italiana* (*Epistle Concerning the Letters Recently Added to the Italian Language*) and then, soon on its heels, Pietro Bembo's landmark *Prose della volgar lingua* (*Prose Writings on the Vernacular*) in 1525. And the topic continued to occupy and challenge the minds of mid-sixteenth-century Italian writers dedicated to giving concrete and lasting shape to a language still very much in a formative state and, for a host of thinkers, in need of being codified and classicized.

Among the many writers concentrating on this particular issue were three Florentines: Carlo Lenzoni (1501–1551), Pierfrancesco Giambullari (1495–1555), and Giovan Battista Gelli (1498–1563).[35] All three men, possessing distinctly different backgrounds, were contemporaries of Vasari, close friends, and members of the newly formed Accademia Fiorentina (Florentine Academy), an institution that Cosimo I (1519–1574) appropriated in 1540 for his own dynastic purposes. The Accademia Fiorentina had briefly survived as the Accademia degli Umidi (Academy of the Wet Ones) before Cosimo I took it over and calculatingly enlarged its membership with men favorable to his overall cultural politics. All three men shared largely similar views about the so-called *questione della lingua* (debate over the language) and freely supported Cosimo I's ideological program of instrumentalizing the Accademia Fiorentina to assert the linguistic dominance of Florence over Tuscany, as well as its influence ideally over other territories far and wide, thereby hopefully making Florentine some time in the not too distant future the purified and regulated universal language for those engaged throughout Italy in such politically sensitive activities as state governance and diplomacy. Finally, all three men wrote about the *questione della lingua* from the early 1540s to the mid-1550s. Often enough they included each other as dramatis personae in their writings, and some of those writings were indeed formally fashioned in a conversational mode as dialogues. In sum, Lenzoni, Giambullari, and Gelli collectively addressed a variety of linguistic matters of keen interest to members of the Accademia Fiorentina precisely during the period in which Vasari took up the onerous task of writing the *Lives*, beyond just assembling the essential, preparatory materials for its initial drafting.[36]

Now, my aim in calling attention to the *questione della lingua* in the context of thinking about how the *Lives* putatively emerged out of a conversation initiated in Rome in 1546 is not to rehearse the sixteenth century's largely academic, sometimes heavily politicized, and often decidedly parochial, urbane, elitist, and ideologically charged debate over the very language used in the local culture in which Vasari, as a practicing painter, composed the *Lives* and self-consciously took on the role of an author. Rather, my aim here is a more modest one. It is to suggest that there is good reason to question what sort of impact the thoughts and treatises of Lenzoni, Giambullari, and Gelli might have had on the *Lives* in terms of actual word usage. For as the art historian Marco Ruffini has cogently argued, there is indeed strong evidence that these three Florentine writers, along with a few others in Florence addressing similar sorts of linguistic concerns—such as Vincenzo Borghini (1515–1580) and Cosimo Bartoli (1503–1572), for instance[37]—shared with Vasari a large ideological and aesthetic investment, specifically in the context of thinking about the overarching *questione della lingua*, in a "programmatic reaction against a cultural tradition dominated by literary authors and masterpieces."[38] More precisely, as Ruffini has demonstrated, there is good reason to believe that men such as Giambullari, who helped revise Vasari's 1550 manuscript, "along with other editors" invested in this particular art historical project, "saw the *Lives* as a vehicle for and embodiment of their views about language."[39] So what about the words themselves? If Vasari was indebted to the thoughts of these and other Florentine authors on matters related to the *questione della lingua*, did he—under their sometimes persistent editorial influence and scrutiny—also actually write in a manner that would satisfy the expectations of Lenzoni, Giambullari, Gelli, and others in terms of what constituted good and pure Florentine when we descend to the granular level of examining the words used in composing the *Lives* and consider such matters as orthography, sentence structure, grammar, and diction? Did Vasari, that is to say, consistently, conscientiously, and rigorously adhere to "the rules to render prose beautiful and rhythmic [*le regole da far bella et numerosa la prosa*]"[40] as they are set forth, for instance, by Lenzoni at the end of his posthumously printed *In difesa della lingua fiorentina, et di Dante* (*In Defense of the Florentine Language and of Dante*, 1556), precisely as his book's subtitle announces?[41]

And the answer to those questions is largely no, as Vasari himself seems to acknowledge in various places in the *Lives*.[42] From beginning to end Vasari's *Lives* is hardly written in a consistently pure, polished Florentine, as Giambullari imagines in his lengthy grammar book composed for Cosimo I's son, *De la lingua che si parla e scrive in Firenze* (*On the Language That Is Spoken and Written in Florence*, 1551).[43] Rather, the *Lives* is effectively written in a sort of mixed salad greens of Italian vernaculars, albeit primarily in a rich and varied and indeed sometimes even elegant "Tuscan language [*lingua Toscana*]" (fig. 5), as the opening title page of the 1550 edition advertises. There are many reasons why that is the case, not least the fact that Vasari was born and educated in Arezzo, so writing in pure Florentine, as Gelli and Lenzoni surely would have insisted, could not have come naturally to him.[44] Vasari was Tuscan, not Florentine. And for Gelli, as well as for his various companions of the Accademia Fiorentina dedicated to thinking about such linguistic matters, that made all the difference in the world. As Gelli synthetically puts it in his *Ragionamento sopra la difficultà di mettere in regole la nostra lingua* (*Discourse Concerning the Difficulty of Furnishing Rules for Our Language*, 1551), "all or the major part of foreigners," which is to say all those people who are not strictly from Florence, "confess and tacitly agree that the language they look for and hold as good is only Florentine." And with this statement Gelli specifically means the more refined, elevated vernacular spoken by "the noble and true Florentine citizens," the very elite Florentines whom Gelli—as a shoemaker and hosier by trade—aspired to be accepted by as a longstanding and dedicated member of the Accademia Fiorentina.[45] Furthermore, the editors of the *Lives*—particularly Borghini and Caro—deliberately wanted Vasari to adopt the unaffected, informal, and sometimes technical mode of speech appropriate to a practicing visual artist taking on the role of an author. So Vasari consciously eschewed, as he puts it, "the long and ornate periods, choice words, and other ornaments of learned speech and writing [*gl'ornati e lunghi periodi, la scelta delle voci e gli altri ornamenti del parlare e scrivere dottamente*]" (2.1067, G6.412–13; see also especially 1.25, G1.29).[46] In this respect, for Vasari to attempt to write in a pure, measured, and polished Florentine throughout the *Lives*, from the very beginning to the very end, only would have served to undermine what was deemed to be the book's proper rhetorical register. Stylistically, it would have deprived the *Lives* of sounding like the work of a Tuscan artisan writing in his own natural, unaffected mode of speech about men of typically low to modest social station by making his book appear inappropriately and ostentatiously the elevated linguistic product of Florentine literati writing biographies of illustrious members of the cultural elite. And that was a stratum of society to which visual artists as a generalized group did not belong, even as Vasari calculatingly strove to lift them up in stature through the very writing of the *Lives* itself.[47]

But one additional and extremely important reason that the *Lives* was not written in Florentine, or at least not consistently written in a pure, polished, and measured Florentine throughout, has to do with the fact that what distinguishes Vasari's book from, say, the learned academic treatises and dialogues of Giambullari, Lenzoni, and Gelli—much less the stylistically varied books composed in the vernacular by a variety of the other sixteenth-century Italian writers so far mentioned in this Introduction—is that Vasari did not in truth author the *Lives* all by himself. Not, according to some, by a long shot. Instead, the *Lives*, as a number of scholars have argued,[48] was the product of a collaborative literary effort, much as the idea for the book itself, as Vasari imaginatively tells the story at the very end of the Giuntina edition of the *Lives*, was born out of a collaborative conversation in a gathering composed of humanists and poets coming from distinctly different regions of Italy, all of whom surely must have spoken a slightly different form of the vernacular.[49] Hence, even though a number of men invested in disseminating the Florentine language far and wide had a hand in directly editing, revising, and contributing at times lengthy passages or whole sections to Vasari's book, the *Lives* ultimately reads here and there as a hybrid text, a work of stylistic bricolage, precisely because various people from so many different regions of Italy actually contributed to it in substantive ways.[50] Put differently, the *Lives* as a discourse is distinctly dialogic in its plurilingual style, to borrow and adapt Mikhail Bakhtin's famous critical terms. But it is strikingly monologic in its commitment to certain key ideas that Vasari steadfastly mulls over again and again with a relentless persistence as the titular author ostensibly governing it all.[51] And five of those ideas are indeed the focus of this book dedicated to Vasari's—or, as it were, "Vasari's"—words.

Before turning to those ideas and examining how they build upon one another to construct a largely triumphant narrative about economic, social, cultural, and aesthetic success in the visual arts of Vasari's *rinascita*, I close by briefly conjuring up a thoroughly imaginary yet still plausible event that I will situate not in the past of mid-sixteenth-century Italy but some time in the near present. The place in question is not a sumptuous, richly decorated, and candlelit palace in Rome full of amiable humanists and poets at a convivial gathering in the evening as they talk about a unique book of art history they would like to see written in the near future. Instead, the place is a sparsely furnished, probably threadbare, fluorescent-lit seminar room in a modern research university somewhere in America with a handful of humanities graduate students sitting around a rather large table with various initials crudely scratched into its thinly veneered and poorly varnished surface. All the students attending the first day of the late afternoon class have a copy of Vasari's *Lives* in hand and periodically look at it, as if seeing it for the first time, with a sense of grim foreboding, wondering if this is indeed the right class for them. The book they have purchased, which they have been told is essential reading for an understanding of the Renaissance in general and thus constitutes the exclusive focus of the class, is an inexpensive edition in the original Italian with small type and thin margins, and it runs, dauntingly, even without a single word of substantive commentary, to just under 1,400 pages. The immense book, whose edition is indeed ominously called "I Mammut" (The Mammoths), is thick and heavy—not easy to hold in one's lap or prop up when lying in bed but certainly useful for keeping a door jammed open.[52] And then there's the syllabus. It contains a list of secondary readings that seems to go on forever. No doubt, somewhere in the well-stocked library there are also thick, weighty volumes devoted to all those proceedings that ritually get organized and eventually find their way into print to celebrate the anniversaries that commemorate important moments in a canonical author's life: his birth, his death, the dates marking the printings of his major books. One student, whose primary focus is on modern Italy and computational criticism, wonders why everyone in the now rather amorphous, interdisciplinary field of Italian Studies is still constrained to take a distribution of classes across historical periods and, like a character out of Italo Calvino's *Se una notte di inverno un viaggiatore* (*If on a Winter's Night a Traveler*), fantasizes briefly about being able to feed at least the secondary literature into a computer that somehow magically scans, mines, and condenses the essential information into a few synthetic, digitally processed paragraphs, thereby relieving the uninterested reader of the task of actually having to cope with mounds of scholarship. But no matter. For the moment the secondary literature can be set aside. It is time to see what this book, hyped as the first book of art history in the modern era, is all about. It is time to attend to Vasari's words.

I

PROFESSIONE/PROFESSION

I am remembering at the end of my discourse [*nella fine del ragionamento*] that it is necessary, for whoever yearns to be praised, with regard to the beauty and value of their works, to follow in the footsteps of the best and the most worthy, because whoever wishes to follow rightly the model of history can make the labors of the dead seem less beautiful by means of his [own] honorable labors. So, my fellow artists/artisans [*artefici miei*], may I offer you as much assistance [*vi faccia di giovamento*] as the works and deeds of those whom I go about imitating in our profession [*che io vado imitando nella nostra professione*].

—Giorgio Vasari, "Conclusion to the Work, to the Artists/Artisans and Readers [*Artefici et a' Lettori*]," the *Lives* (1550)[1]

For some time now scholars in Europe and the United States have been thinking seriously about the notion of professional identity in Renaissance Italy. Thanks to them we currently have at our disposal a large number of studies devoted to examining the social networks and daily lives of people who actually practiced professions, just as we presently have at our command a variety of studies dedicated to articulating how different people from different walks of life and places wrote about professions in various occasions and contexts, not just during the Italian Renaissance but also in other periods both directly before and after it throughout Europe.[2] For their part, literary scholars have also occasionally demonstrated a keen interest in exploring the complex and sometimes nuanced ways in which professions and professional identity impinged on the artistic production of Renaissance writers of instructional treatises and imaginative literature.[3] In my view—and some scholars, such as the intellectual and cultural historian George McClure, seem to be in substantial agreement with this overall assessment—the widespread Renaissance interest in professions and professional identity intensified greatly in sixteenth-century Italy.[4] This was the century, after all, in which both practitioners and non-practitioners alike wrote an unprecedented number of treatises—far more than any prior century—directly addressing what was required in order to succeed in everything from being an ambassador, courtier, prince, cardinal, soldier, and secretary to that of a sculptor, architect, painter, metallurgist, engineer, cook, goldsmith, surgeon, medic, and steward. It was also notably the century that experienced a profound shift in a "rhetoric of profession," as McClure has demonstrated, with rhetoric here understood not just as the formal art of persuasion but as a discourse that is bounded with traceable *topoi* (commonplaces) and that is historically and culturally determined. This shift in a rhetoric of professions involved, among other things: a marked attention to professional self-definition; a truly broad-based cultural exploration, leveling, and secularization of professions; an increased attention to the value of vocational choice and work as a source of happiness and self-worth; a popularizing of these issues through the commercial press and in the vulgar tongue; an astonishing proliferation of the topic of professions in a variety of less learned cultural forms, from encyclopedic compendia to chronicles, to jokes, to civic rituals, to carnival songs, to parlor games; and an extraordinary increase in—as well as cultural acceptance of and resistance toward—different professions as indeed professions. This widespread investment in professions culminated toward the end of the sixteenth century in Tomaso Garzoni's cornucopian *La piazza universale di tutte le professioni del mondo* (*The Universal Piazza of All the Professions in the World*, 1585/7), a massive, quirky, and encyclopedic book—in many ways indebted to Leonardo Fioravanti's equally massive, quirky, and encyclopedic *Dello specchio di scientia universale* (*Concerning a Mirror of Universal Knowledge*, 1564)—that covered virtually every profession under the sun, from that of the Petrarchan-modeled, humanist scholar ensconced in his study to, at the opposite end of the social spectrum, that of the lowly street cleaner.

In many ways Vasari is an ideal person to examine in the context of thinking about issues related to "professionalism." This is a distinctly modern term employed anachronistically throughout this book to designate not the organizing, controlling, and credentialing of exclusionary labor in the full-blown capitalist economies of the large, complex, bureaucratic nation states of the West in the nineteenth, twentieth, and twenty-first centuries. Rather, the term "professionalism" is here used to characterize, for the lack of a better word, the formative but still quite pervasive investment in the concept of professional identity in the brokerage, patronage, guild-controlled, gift-giving, and proto-capitalist market economies of the small but increasingly bureaucratic courts, republics, princedoms, and duchies of late Renaissance Italy. Periodically cast as a forerunner of the modern discipline of art history,

Vasari was a practicing painter and architect who wrote extensively about visual artists, primarily painters, sculptors, and architects, but also goldsmiths, engravers, printmakers, manuscript illuminators, medalists, gem carvers, stained-glass makers, woodcarvers, embroiderers, and what we would probably just loosely call today "interior decorators" or "designers." More to the point, throughout his monumental *Lives*, Vasari was obsessed with the very notion of professions, using the word *professione* and its variants over and over again to characterize the work of visual artists in both the Torrentiniana edition of 1550 and the Giuntina edition of 1568. In the process of doing so, he articulated a new conception of institutionalized artistic labor grounded in the activities of Michelangelo and the Accademia del Disegno. He did this, moreover, precisely in a period when "guild memberships, business experience and workshop practices," as Rita Comanducci succinctly puts it, "no longer retained the crucial role they had enjoyed until the recent past." Indeed, with the advent of the principality and the diminished role of the guilds in the governance of Florence, the workshop master, who previously enjoyed the possibility of being able to hold a political office, serve as a highly respected member of the Florentine Republic, and thereby acquire social visibility and social advantages, "was losing prestige and respectability vis-à-vis the court noble."[5] At the same time, in the course of evoking through *ekphrasis* a host of works of visual art from the time of Cimabue to his present,[6] Vasari also created a strikingly new role for himself as someone who could speak chorally for a profession and, up to a point, position himself as a professional author collaborating with, and being guided by, a variety of accomplished writers situated among the cultural elite, including, but not limited to, those already mentioned in the Introduction to this book.

Let us begin, then, with the word *professione*. For the most part Vasari uses it as a virtual synonym for "art," with the term "art" understood—like the concept of *techne* from the time of the ancient Greeks—as a highly specialized, determinate, rational, communicable, reliable, teachable, and often rule-bound form of skillfully applied and socially valued knowledge.[7] To be sure, in the strictest sense of the term, a "profession" signifies *the area of expertise* practiced by someone with significant training in it, while an "art," at least as the concept unfolded historically, typically signifies *the form of knowledge* that the practitioner puts into practice in the course of expertly working in the profession. So the two terms can indeed be set side by side without being seen as entirely redundant in meaning, as when, for instance, Vasari refers to Michelangelo as having surpassed everyone else in ability "in every art [*ciascheduna arte*] and every profession [*ogni professione*]" (2.642, G6.3). Phrased differently, in theory we can say that an art as a form of knowledge put into practice (the know-how of rhetoric, say, which allows one to be a rhetorician) underpins a profession as an area of expertise (actually being a rhetorician who applies that knowledge of rhetoric with admirable skill). But a profession (being a rhetorician) does not underpin an art (rhetoric). And yet, in reality the two terms are used often enough interchangeably in the *Lives*, as well as in Italian Renaissance culture, where *artes* can also refer to guilds, such as the twenty-one major and minor *arti/artes* of Florence, and where one of the definitions synthetically applied to the term *professione* in the *Vocabolario degli Accademici della Crusca* (*Lexicon of the Academicians of the Crusca*, 1612) is, in fact, *ars*.[8] Simply put, then, Vasari can treat the two terms *arte* and *professione* in fundamentally the same way, as equivalents, for the obvious reason that they overlapped conceptually in Renaissance thought and therefore functioned as semantic twins in the context of talking about different practitioners and their work in the visual arts.[9] For the purposes of this study, however, I shall employ the term *professione* as Vasari largely uses it: to signal the *area of expertise* that incorporates the knowledge—the art/*techne*—that selectively underpins it.

At the same time, it is important to note, Vasari uses the term *professione* in a related but still slightly different way to designate more narrowly a specialized area of expertise *within* a certain overarching profession. Given what we know from scholarly studies by art, cultural, and social historians, it makes perfect sense that Vasari would use the word *professione* in this more restricted manner in the course of thinking about the production of visual art in his time and the value of professional identity. Often enough visual artists were hired to perform a specific task, given their particular area of expertise: one person might be called upon to paint foliage, another grotesques.[10] Vasari drives this point home with particular force when he describes how Raphael, always eager to hire an efficient team of expert workers, benefited from staging a competition among those contracted by him to undertake certain isolated yet integrated tasks as he labored to complete a major commission in Rome:

> Meanwhile Raphael of Urbino had built the Papal Loggie, by the command of Leo X; and the same Pope ordered that Raphael should also have them adorned with stucco, painted, and gilded, according as it should seem best to him. Thereupon Raphael placed at the head of that enterprise, for the stucco-work and the grotesques, Giovanni da Udine, who was very excellent and without an equal in such works, but mostly in executing animals and fruits and other little things [*ma più negli animali e frutti et altre cose minute*]. And since he had chosen in Rome and summoned from other parts a great number of masters, he had assembled together a company of

> men each very able at his own work, one in stucco, another in grotesques, a third in foliage, a fourth in festoons, another in historical narratives/allegories, and others in other things [*chi stucchi, chi grottesche, altri fogliami, altri festoni e storie, et altri altre cose*]; and according as they improved they were brought forward and paid higher salaries, so that by competing in that work many young men attained to great perfection, who were afterwards held to be excellent in their various works. (2.157, G5.112–13)

In this instance, as in so many others recorded in the *Lives*, we are not talking about a radical division of specialized labor within an impersonal art market, with people assigned to perform tasks over and over again as if they were numbly stationed on a fixed assembly line in a modern industrialized factory. Rather, we are talking about a calculated yet still distinctly personal mechanism by which the presiding managerial master of a workshop (*bottega*), typically pressed for time, could efficiently take advantage of different but specific talents to direct them, once thoughtfully combined and decently remunerated, toward a shared goal of quality artistic production (fig. 7).[11] By the same token, a visual artist could be recommended to others and employed specifically because he was known for meeting isolated needs within the art market. In thinking about professions, then, Vasari is consciously reminding us in the *Lives* about the ways in which the art market had been structured in Renaissance Italy, at least for his purposes since the time of Cimabue, who marks the beginning of his narrative of individual Lives and his championed *rinascita* of the visual arts. Masters repeatedly deployed different artists to fulfill specific tasks, given their circumscribed areas of expertise or, as he puts it, *professioni*, and they employed each other in the process. Moreover, patrons, Vasari makes clear, operated under the same assumption: one artist was good for this, another for that, although Vasari certainly values versatility and presumes that good patrons do as well.

Finally, belonging to a profession also meant that one will inevitably be judged by other professionals, just as it meant, inversely, that one necessarily retains the right to cast judgment on others, to literally profess (*profiteri* is the Latin infinitive), in the sense of to speak out on a matter to which you can claim mastery in your working life.[12] As such, you are effectively part of a discerning club because you can readily tell, among other things, if a foreshortening is done correctly, the proportions properly measured, the shading handled just right, the bronze properly cast, the marble chiseled and polished with pumice just so. Professionals thus know each other as such and police the boundaries of what they do, defining "excellence," as Vasari does.[13] At the same time, all these men, who are collectively bound by a group

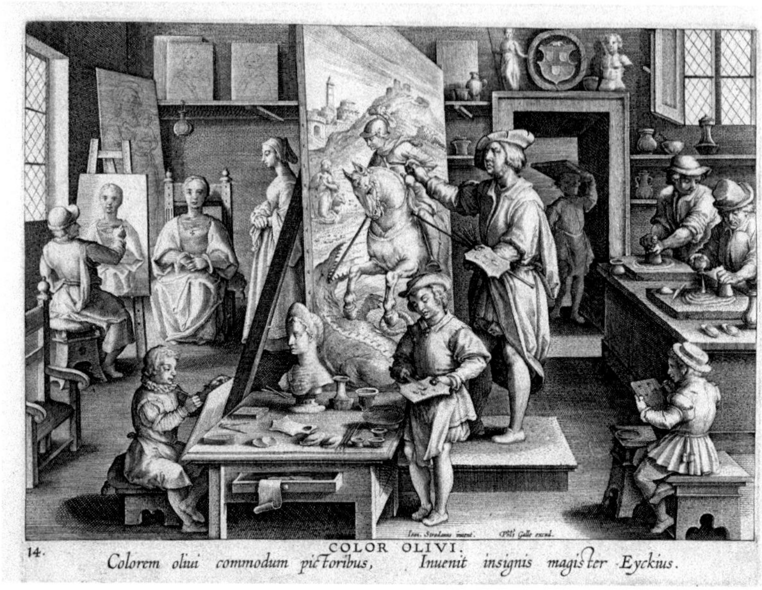

7. Theodoor Galle (1571–1633) after Johannes Stradanus (1523–1605), *Jan van Eyck's Workshop* (ca. 1580–1605). © The Trustees of the British Museum/Art Resource, NY. The image is of a Northern Renaissance workshop, but it nevertheless captures nicely the sorts of activities that would have habitually taken place in an Italian Renaissance workshop. One should perhaps note the *garzoni* to the right, grinding and mixing pigments.

identity insofar as they consciously belong to and police a *professione* as an area of expertise, do not just cast judgment on others in isolation. From time to time we are reminded that the Vasarian judgment delivered to us in his *Lives* is itself couched in terms of a collectivity. In many ways, he is speaking chorally for a profession, or at least for a group of professionals invested in a certain type of visual art that he, along with them, favors—as well as a type of privileged art that would quickly inspire a strong and sustained backlash shortly after the printing of the Torrentiniana edition.[14] By the same token, it is equally significant that outsiders are occasionally seen to confirm what those in the profession already collectively discern and agree upon.[15] Professionals therefore recognize each other as such and painstakingly train each other as such. And they can recognize one style from another, precisely as Vasari aims to teach us, so that we can learn to differentiate one visual "manner [*maniera*]" from another, just as readily as we can distinguish one individual's distinctive handwriting from another.[16] Professionalism, to use contemporary scholarly terms for the subject, requires not just a deontology, an ethics of duty defined by rules. It also requires boundaries, a clearly defined notion of what constitutes a profession as a profession, as a circumscribed field of expertise with its own well-defined "jurisdictional claims."[17] And Vasari is interested in contemplating both in the *Lives*—his particular profession's deontology and its disciplinary boundaries—along with being deeply invested in articulating and constructing both. In sum, part of Vasari's aim in writing the *Lives* is to impress upon the reader that the visual artists whose individual Lives he compiles and describes are "professionals." Or to use a term that Vasari employs in few instances and that will later form part of the very title to Filippo Baldinucci's seventeenth-century history of art, these men are *professori*. That is to say, they are, Vasari means to indicate by using that particular word, expertly trained practitioners who can skillfully do what they profess they can do and whom society routinely credits with mastery over a specific visual art.[18]

Now, if history providentially and organically unfolds for Vasari to direct individual talents toward a collective goal of refining the visual arts until they are fully embodied in a single person, it should hardly be surprising that Leonardo da Vinci (1452–1519), who marks the beginning of the third and final "age" of development of the arts, would occupy a crucial position in the gradual professionalizing of the visual arts grounded in the discipline of *disegno* within the *Lives*.[19] Consider in this light the fact that Leonardo, we learn at the outset of his Life, wished "that his profession [*professione*] should be"—strictly speaking "painting [*la pittura*]" (1.626, G4.17).[20] To this end Leonardo dutifully dedicated himself to drawing all manner of things, from flour mills to fulling mills, doing all this "after nature." Sometimes, to perfect his command over drawing (*disegno*), he also made "models of figures in clay, over which he would lay soft pieces of cloth dipped in clay, and then set himself patiently to draw them [*e poi con pazienza si metteva a retrargli*]" (1.626, G4.17).[21] *Disegno* is thus absolutely essential to Leonardo's process of being a painter and learning the art underpinning his profession. Not only does *disegno* allow Leonardo to capture the world and thereby manipulate it through his compositions with remarkable technical proficiency. It also permits him to understand the world itself. For Leonardo, as for Vasari, the all-important process of drawing—*disegno*—is a cognitive act. It serves as a way of grasping, among other things, the workings of Nature, the deep, hidden causes of things rendered at times expressively through the deft use of line, even to the point where Leonardo innovatively captures through the flow of raindrops or the energetic whirling of winds the passage of time as a compressed sequence of distilled yet integrated moments (fig. 8).[22]

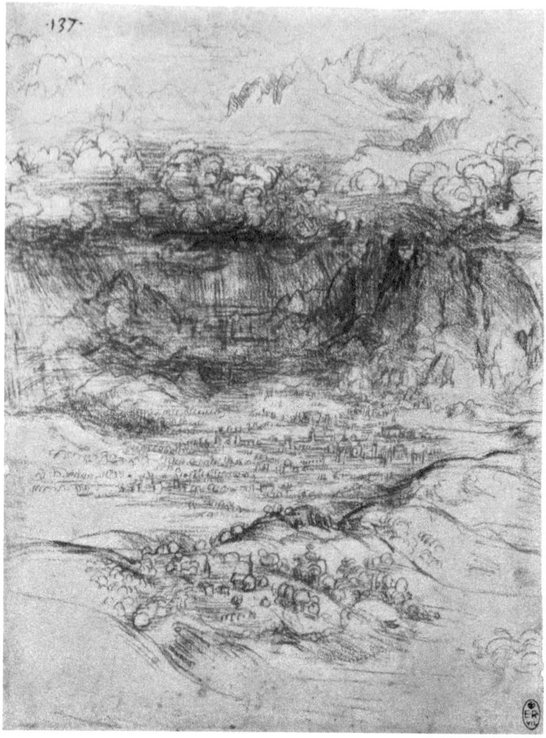

8. Leonardo da Vinci (1452–1519), *Storm in the Alps* (ca. 1503–5). Royal Library, Windsor Castle, Windsor, Great Britain. Photo credit: HIP/Art Resource, NY.

But *disegno* also has a different meaning and function when understood in strictly professional terms. Professionally, *disegno* provides access to, and serves as the foundation of, all sorts of interconnected visual arts as forms of knowledge. For this reason, Leonardo "practiced not one profession," we learn, "but all those in which *disegno* played a part [*e non solo esercitò una professione, ma tutte quelle ove il disegno si interveniva*]" (1.626, G4.17). Thanks to his complete command over *disegno*, Leonardo can prove himself an expert not just as a painter, which he may count his principal profession. He can also prove himself an expert at virtually anything he wants to apply his formidable talents to, which is to say, consequently, virtually any profession, and thus any area of expertise, that interests him within the visual arts. Leonardo can do this not just because he is so very talented and naturally versatile, as Vasari reminds us on various occasions. He can do so because in the end *disegno* is the enabling force behind not only the art of painting but also, among others, the arts of architecture, engineering, goldsmithing, sculpture, engraving, printmaking, woodcarving, manuscript illumination, and stained-glass making. "All these professions [*professioni*] and intellectual arts one sees derive from *disegno*," Vasari announces synthetically at the end of the first part of the *Lives* dedicated specifically to questions of technique, "which is the necessary principle for all things, and without it, one has nothing [*il quale è capo necessario di tutte, e non l'avendo, non si ha nulla*]. Because, although all the secrets and methods may be good, *disegno* is crucial, for by its means everything lost is found again [*ogni cosa perduta si ritrova*], and every difficult thing becomes easy [*ogni difficil cosa per esso diventa facile*], as one can see in reading the lives of the artists, who, aided by their nature and study, have done superhuman things [*cose sopraumane*] solely by means of *disegno*" (G1.172). If you want to be a professional of any sort in the visual arts, much less one who achieves "superhuman things," the linchpin, the lesson of Leonardo's Life conclusively shows us, is unquestionably to master *disegno* as the driving force behind every profession. Accordingly, *disegno* is equally key to every art and every life that Vasari writes about in the process of defining and isolating excellence within the visual arts.

In this context it makes absolute sense that Michelangelo should figure as the epitome of professional, as well as artistic, success in Vasari's triumphant historical narrative.[23] For Vasari, Michelangelo is the greatest master of drawing ever in the history of visual art, bringing to "perfection" the "art of *disegno* in executing the lines, contours, shadows, and highlights." And so Michelangelo is consequently the greatest individual practitioner "in every art and every profession [*professione*]" covered in Vasari's narrative (2.642, G6.3). An emblematic moment that stages Michelangelo's exceptional status in this regard occurs when Vasari describes the competition between Michelangelo and Leonardo. In that major public competition Michelangelo, "desiring to show how much he knew in his profession [*professione*]," designed his cartoon of the *Battle of Cascina* (1504) for the Salone dei Cinquecento in Palazzo Vecchio with such brilliance (fig. 9)—with so "many figures in groups, all sketched in various manners, some outlined with charcoal, some drawn with strokes, others stumped in and heightened with lead-white"—that all the craftsmen who witnessed his massive cartoon, and many indeed came from far and wide to witness it, "were seized with admiration and astonishment, seeing the highest artistic accomplishment [*estremità dell'arte*] revealed to them in that drawing by Michelangelo; and some who saw them, after beholding figures so divine, declare that there has never been seen any work, either by his hand or by the hands of others, no matter how great their genius, that can equal its divine art [*divinità dell'arte*]" (2.657, G6.24). As a result, Michelangelo, we are reminded time and again, "surpassed every

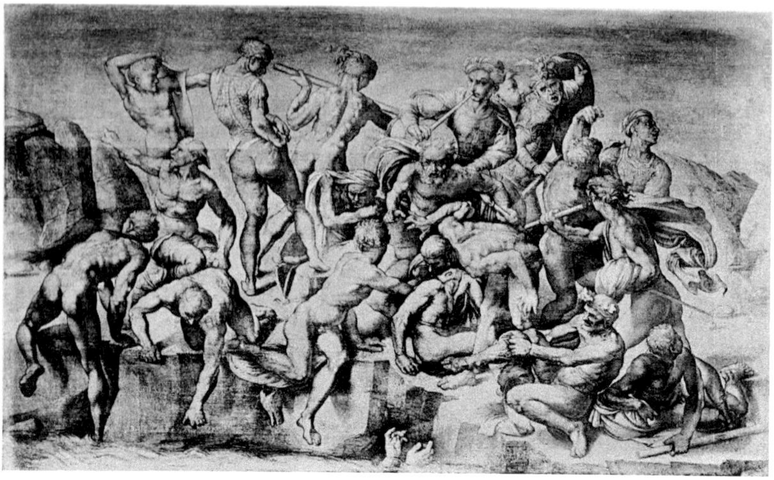

9. Bastiano (Aristotile) da Sangallo (1481–1551), *Copy of the drawing of Michelangelo's cartoon, "Battle of Cascina"* (ca. 1542). Coll. Leicester, Holkam Hall, Norfolk, Great Britain. Photo credit: Foto Marburg/Art Resource, NY.

man in these three professions [*professioni*]" of sculpture, architecture, and painting—the three key professions of the *Lives* (2.681, G6.56).

And yet something changed over time with respect to Vasari's treatment of Michelangelo as the epitome of the professional visual artist. And what had changed over roughly seventeen years, as he revised and considerably enlarged the *Lives* into the Giuntina edition, was that Vasari's overall investment in the notion of professionalism itself intensified markedly.[24] The most compelling historical reason for this intensification is that in the intervening years Vasari had become deeply involved in the founding of the Accademia del Disegno and thus in the academy's overall cultural and social project of institutionalizing the role of the visual artist within a patronage system grounded in a state that arrogated unto itself, with the Duke's blessing, the power and authority to legitimate professions and professional expertise within the visual arts.[25] Moreover, nowhere is this process of institutionalizing the visual arts in the *Lives* made more evident than in the revised and significantly enlarged version of Michelangelo's Life in the Giuntina edition. There, in fact, one of the most obsessive uses of the term *professione* in the entire *Lives* occurs in a letter addressed to "the Lord Duke" Cosimo I from the Lieutenant of the newly formed "Academy and Company of Painters and Sculptors," namely Vincenzo Borghini, who figured so greatly in the creation and formation of the *Lives* itself. In that letter (and here Vasari is drawing his account and language directly from the *Esequie del Divino Michelagnolo Buonarroti* [*Exequies of the Divine Michelagnolo Buonarroti*, printed in 1564], which Vasari himself may well even had a hand in drafting),[26] the Lieutenant of the Academy, charged with the official bureaucratic task of speaking for its members, formally requests that a funeral take place for Michelangelo, with all due pomp and glory. More specifically, recognizing how important it is to champion Michelangelo in a proper and sufficiently dignified way, the letter announces that a tomb must be constructed to honor his memory and trumpet his fame. And this act of commemoration must be done not only because of "the general obligation due from their profession [*professione*] to the extraordinary ability of one who was perhaps the greatest craftsman who has ever lived." It must also be done: (1) because "these professions [*professioni*]" have benefited so greatly from his work; (2) because Cosimo I and his ancestors, who "bestowed extraordinary favors on those excellent in these professions [*professioni*]," would be honored as exalted patrons by the presence of the tomb; and (3) because together the funeral and the tomb would be an inspiration for, among so many people, the *professori* of these arts [*arti*]—that is to say, all the recognized masters of the very professions in question in the visual arts (2.749, G6.124). To ensure the success of the funeral and the execution of the tomb, the members of the Accademia had already divvied up tasks and elected four men, young and old, "each in his own profession [*professione*]," to lead and officially take care of the obsequies and funeral pomp that were to be held (2.748, G6.123)—just as the process of selection is said to have unfolded as it is reported in the *Exequies*. And the monument itself designed to celebrate Michelangelo (fig. 10), which Cosimo I consented to have crafted to honor the acknowledged supreme exemplar of their "profession [*professione*]" (2.751, G6.125),[27] testifies not only to Michelangelo's position as the greatest artist of the key professions of the time, surpassing every man in those and other professions in the visual arts, as Vasari never tires of telling us (2.681, G6.56). It also bears witness to Michelangelo as the foundational hero of the professionalism that the Accademia itself as a corporate body was institutionalizing as something separate from the city's guild system and, as Marco Ruffini has best demonstrated, was commemorating and ritualizing through the funeral—a second funeral, no less, since an earlier and far more modest and pious one had already taken place in Rome. There, from the point of view of the Accademia's members, Michelangelo, the true Florentine apotheosis of visual art of all time, had been prematurely and rather unceremoniously buried.[28]

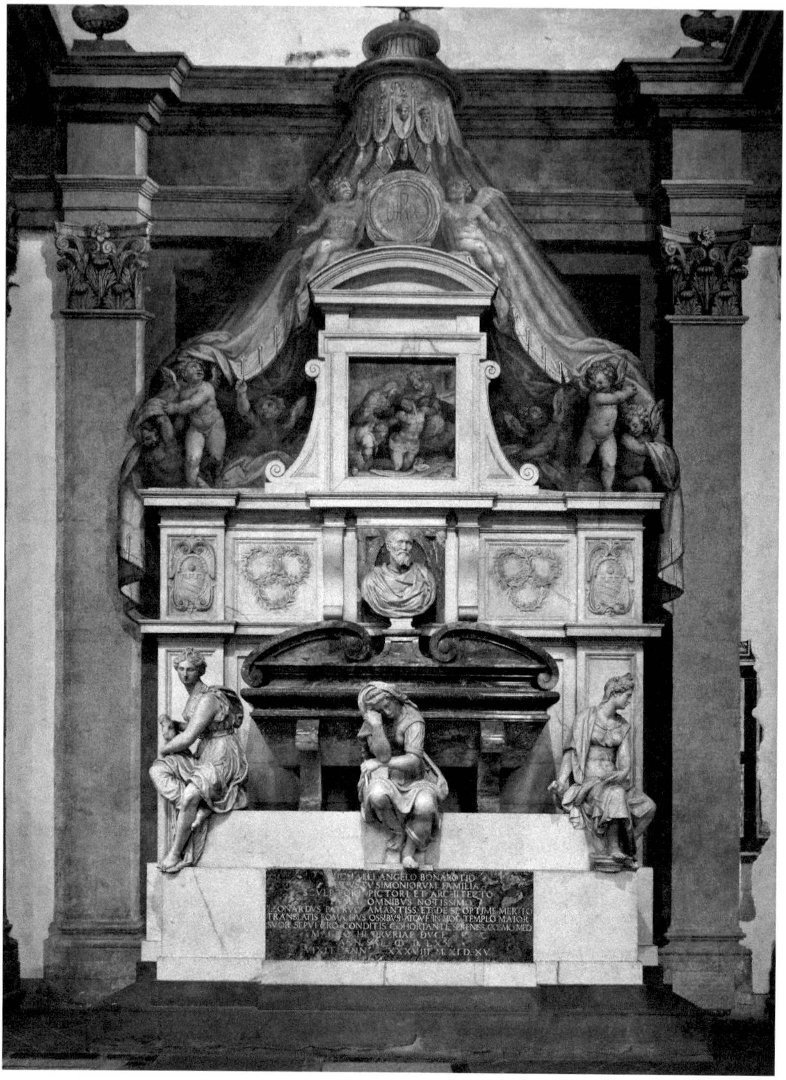

10. Giorgio Vasari (1511–1574), *Tomb of Michelangelo* (1570). Santa Croce, Florence, Italy. Photo credit: Scala/Art Resource, NY.

Hence calculatingly incorporated into Michelangelo's memorial tomb in Santa Croce is the theme of professionalism itself as it is embodied in his staggering achievements, as an artist who possessed, we already know from the first panegyric paragraph of the Life, a heaven-sent "universal ability in every art and every profession [*professione*]" (2.642, G6.3). And so "the device of Michelagnolo," Vasari tells us, as he draws once more on the *Exequies* and expounds upon the allegorical significance of a key portion of the funerary monument, has

> three crowns, or rather, three circlets, intertwined together in such a manner that the circumference of one passed through the center of the two others, and so with each; which sign Michelagnolo used either to suggest that the three professions [*professioni*] of sculpture, painting, and architecture are interwoven one with another and so bound together that each of them receives benefit and adornment from the others, and they neither can nor should be separated; or, indeed, being a man of lofty talent, he may have had a more subtle meaning. But the Academicians, considering him to have been perfect in all these three professions [*professioni*], and that each of these had assisted and embellished the other, changed the three circlets into three crowns intertwined together, with the motto: *Tergeminis Tollit Honoribus* [He bears triple honors]. Which was intended to signify that in those three professions [*professioni*] the crown of human perfection was justly due to him. (2.767, G6.139)

If in the first edition of the *Lives* Vasari emphasizes how Michelangelo marks the end point of a gradual awakening of the visual arts in a process of a punctuated evolution made possible by certain compelling individuals, in the revised and enlarged Giuntina edition Vasari strategically coopts the celebratory language of the *Exequies* and emphasizes how Michelangelo—noticeably no longer placed as the final, culminating Life of the book—stands as the end point in a teleological process of historical awakening of the concept of professionalization itself within the visual arts in Vasari's own time, with Michelangelo now allegorically crowned through his motto as if he were, like Petrarch long before him, a sort of laureate poet masterfully expressing himself. And this historical awakening culminates in its turn with the very monument that celebrates the professionalizing of architecture, sculpture, and painting embodied in the now dead yet transcendent Michelangelo and that the Accademia del Disegno itself organized, designed, constructed, and brilliantly exploited for both its own strategic purposes *and* ducal propaganda in an elaborate, commemorative ceremony devoted precisely to the professionalizing of the visual arts.[29]

How, then, does Vasari's treatment of professions and professional identity differ from that of other writers addressing similar sorts of issues in the Italian Renaissance, and how are we to envision Vasari's own profession (or professions) as he stages himself in relation to it (or them) in the context of the *Lives*? We can begin to answer that question by examining in the first place writings in the Italian Renaissance devoted strictly to the visual arts, as Vasari's book most decidedly was. The Tuscan painter Cennino Cennini (ca. 1370–ca. 1440), whose *Libro dell'arte* (*The Craftsman's Handbook*, ca. 1437) stands as an obvious Renaissance Italian precursor to the *Lives*, does not, for instance, use the word *professione* even once.[30] And a close reading of *The Craftsman's Handbook*, which grew out of and was designed specifically for workshop production, readily reveals that Cennini, as much as he theorized aspects of the development of the arts in terms of the all-important role of *imitatio* in the Renaissance,[31] does not share Vasari's obsession with exploring professional identity, much less Vasari's deep investment not only in tracing historically the process of the gradual professionalization of the visual arts in his own time but in strategically institutionalizing the professionalization of the visual arts. Nor are the words *professione*, *professioni*, *professore*, or *professori* to be found in *Il libro di Antonio Billi* (*The Book of Antonio Billi*, ca. 1487–1537), *Il codice dell'anonimo gaddiano* (*The Codex of the Anonymous Gaddiano*, ca. 1540), and the *Codice Magliabechiano* (*The Codex Magliabechiano*, ca. 1540), three recognized sources for the *Lives*. What is more, none of those texts reveals the slightest concern for the institutionalizing of the visual arts as a profession, any more than does Lorenzo Ghiberti's *Commentarii* (*Commentaries*, ca. 1447–55), another significant source for the *Lives*, which likewise does not deploy the word *professione* or its variants.[32] Nor, for that matter, do the words *professione*, *professioni*, *professore*, or *professori* appear to be a part of Leonardo da Vinci's regular vocabulary in describing or thinking about the visual arts, much less Leon Battista Alberti's in his treatises on painting, architecture, and sculpture.[33] Such as well is the case with respect to Ascanio Condivi's *Vita* (*Life*) of Michelangelo, which appeared in print shortly after the *Lives* came to light, in 1553; Paolo Pino's *Dialogo di pittura* (*Dialogue about Painting*), which appeared two years prior, in 1548; or, for that matter, Romano Alberti's much later *Trattato della nobiltà della pittura* (*Treatise on the Nobility of Painting*, 1585).[34]

Much the same applies to the writings of a variety of non-practitioners thinking about various aspects of the visual arts in sixteenth-century Italy, including those by Benedetto Varchi, Lodovico Dolce, Michelangelo Biondo, Francesco Bocchi, Gregorio Comanini, and Giovanni Andrea Gilio.[35] True, the late Renaissance artists Benvenuto Cellini, Cristoforo Sorte, Pirro Ligorio, Federico Zuccaro, and Gian Paolo Lomazzo deploy the term *professione* and its variants sometimes occasionally, sometimes frequently in their writings, Cellini in his unfinished *Vita* (*Life*), along with his two treatises on sculpture and goldsmithing (both published together in 1568); Sorte in his *Osservazioni nella pittura* (*Observations on Painting*, 1580); Ligorio in his manuscript *Trattato di alcune cose appartenente alla nobiltà dell'antiche arti e massimamente de la pittura, de la scoltura e dell'architettura, e del bene e del male che s'acquistano coloro i quali errano nell'arti, e di quelli che non sono de la professione* ... (*Treatise on Some Things Pertaining to the Nobility of the Ancient Arts and Above All Painting, Sculpture, and Architecture, and on the Good and Bad that Those Exhibit Who Err in the Arts, and Those Who Do Not Belong in the Profession* ..., ca. 1570),[36] Lomazzo in his *Trattato dell'arte della pittura, scoltura et architettura* (*Treatise on the Art of Painting, Sculpture, and Architecture*, 1584); Giovanni Battista Armenini in *De' veri precetti della pittura* (*On the True Precepts of Painting*, 1586); Alberti and Zuccaro in their *Origine et progresso dell'Academia del Dissegno dei pittori, scultori et architetti di Roma* (*Origin and Progress of the Academy of Design of the Painters, Sculptors, and Architects of Rome*, 1604); and Zuccaro in his *L'idea de' pittori, scultori, ed architetti* (*The Idea of Painters, Sculptors, and Architects*, 1607).[37] But in all of these cases, we are dealing, to be sure, with practitioners writing about the profession of the visual arts, as well as in some instances the professional identity of specific visual artists, long after Vasari had already done so at such great length and so thoroughly. Linguistically, then, it would appear that Vasari is doing something strikingly new as he steadfastly thinks about, and noticeably expands our ways of thinking about, professional identity in the visual arts in his *Lives*. Simply put, as far as I can tell, no writer before Vasari—practitioner or not—had paid such meticulous and sustained attention in the Italian Renaissance to articulating such a complex notion of a stratified yet still unified fellowship of a *professione* for those collectively working in the visual arts. And all things considered, this, I contend, is one of Vasari's more significant achievements in his *Lives*. He forged for the first time, as a practitioner himself, a comprehensive vision of professionalism in the visual arts through a singular, repeated emphasis on the very language of what it meant to have, in a word, a *professione*.

For a *professione*, to summarize some of the ground covered so far, could be viewed for Vasari as not just an art but also as a specialized area of expertise within a larger, overarching profession, such as painting, sculpting, goldsmithing, or architecture. Moreover, as in the case of perspective, a *professione* for Vasari could be justifiably considered a "science" in its own right, rendering an artist akin to a philosopher, as in the case of Bastiano da San Gallo, who is tellingly nicknamed "Aristotle."[38] Professionals in the visual arts must be judged and must also judge other professionals. They profit, according to Vasari, from competition and staged rivalries.[39] And they must follow a certain course of conduct and behave accordingly, acting with appropriate decorum within a stratified, hierarchical society, mindful all along of their rank and position within their local cultures.[40] Furthermore, the public itself confers value on the skill of those engaged in the professions of the visual arts. And the public's verdict, along with the patrons' interest and discernment, matters profoundly. Additionally, *disegno* is the animating force underpinning any artist's ability to succeed in a *professione* as well as move fluidly from one profession to another within the visual arts, sometimes with an astonishing capacity for protean versatility. And professionalism in the visual arts of the Renaissance has for Vasari (much as it also has for the first time with Vasari's foundational *Lives*) its own distinguished, fully articulated history, with Michelangelo strategically representing the highest point of perfection within that teleological narrative and the Accademia del Disegno constituting its ultimate, institutionalized culmination in the Giuntina edition. Finally, in both editions of the *Lives* Vasari makes it substantially clear that one of his aims in writing the book is to lift the excellent artist up in stature, transforming him from being a mere craftsman, or even just someone who possesses a science, to one who indeed not only has *a* select profession of some distinction with its own body of knowledge. That excellent artist also now belongs to a single overriding, all-encompassing *professione* with its own impressive, structured history of narrative fulfillment.

Surely it is not happenstance in this regard that in 1550 Vasari ends his first edition of the entire *Lives* in a celebratory manner with, in fact, the very word *professione*, to linguistically remind all those practitioners like him, practitioners whom he at long last addresses and champions with his parting words, that they communally and cooperatively belong to the same single, unifying, interconnected, yet still stratified profession. Thus, even as a diversified and sometimes contentious and rivalrous group, they share the same single, unified vision and goal. This, as he puts it conclusively as his final words (the very words that form the epigraph to this chapter), is "[la] *nostra* professione" (T6.413), which is to say, *our* singular profession, *our* art, *our* area of expertise, *our* form of specialized knowledge, and *our* collective and historically intertwined lives.[41] Or to view Vasari's phrasing as an "illocutionary act," to use the terms of speech act theory favored by certain intellectual historians, the word *professione* in the final sentence of the *Lives* can be said to have the combined force of a command, declaration, and promise. We—which is to say, all of us excellent practitioner *artefici* laboring so diligently in the visual arts—now and forevermore have and will continue to have a unified *professione*. And this command of sorts, as a culminating and celebratory declaration that holds out a promise for the future, comes, as we have seen, at the end of a long line of utterances in the *Lives* about the various ways in which visual artists in Vasari's *rinascita* have indeed always manifestly possessed a so-called *professione*. Read this way, Vasari's performative use of the word *professione* here functions, long before Vasari so persistently concentrates on the idea of professionalization in his discussion of the funeral of Michelangelo in the 1568 edition, as something of a defining moment in both the overall evolution of the *Lives* and, I would submit, the history of art: we "hereby" have a *professione* of visual arts, he seems to be insisting in written rather than oral form, no less and no different than those who have been conventionally understood to possess, say, a *professione* of law, letters, religion, or arms.

At the same time, Vasari's treatment of the concept of professions and professional identity also differs dramatically, it is important to note, when we compare it to the way some Italian Renaissance humanist writers engaged similar sorts of issues. Needless to say, Vasari was not a humanist. Nor would he ever have thought of himself as one or compared himself to one, even if he arguably had some rudimentary training in the *studia humanitatis* in his youth, and certainly more than the average visual artist of his time.[42] However, Vasari's indebtedness to humanism as a cultural and educational program is felt throughout the *Lives*. This is the case not only with respect to his description of how the humanist Giovio initially inspired him to write the book at a convivial gathering at the Palazzo Farnese in Rome (whether or not that event actually occurred in 1546). It is also the case with respect to Vasari's overall handling of such typically humanist topics and areas of interest as exemplarity, rebirth, fame, glory, didactic history, heroic and illustrious biography, nobility of spirit, the dignity of man, friendship, self-fashioning, decorum, and moral philosophy.[43] More important, Vasari interacted closely with humanists in the writing of the *Lives*, just as he did in the creation of the Accademia del Disegno.[44] In this sense a comparison between Vasari's and the humanists' treatment of the notion of professions is entirely apt. And if we look just briefly at two exemplary humanists, one from the beginning and one at the height of the Italian Renaissance—Petrarch (1304–1374) and Castiglione (1478–1529)—we can readily detect a number of similarities as well as salient differences in their and Vasari's respective treatments of professional identity.

Like Vasari, both Petrarch and Castiglione were deeply concerned with matters related to professional identity, Petrarch most conspicuously in his *Collatio laureationis* (*Coronation Oration*) delivered on the Capitoline on Easter Sunday, April 8, 1341, and Castiglione in his landmark *Il libro del cortegiano* (*Book of the Courtier*), begun in roughly 1513, fully revised between 1521 and 1524, and printed in 1528.[45] However, unlike Vasari, both Petrarch and Castiglione—the former writing primarily in Latin, the latter in a highly polished, classicizing vernacular—were not in the least bit interested in institutionalizing the profession they were writing about. In the case of Petrarch, his aim in the *Coronation Oration*, which has often been justifiably taken as a manifesto of humanism and the Renaissance, was to distance himself as much as possible from the "profession of the poet [*poete … professionem*]" as it was institutionalized within the university setting.[46] To this end he purposely staged his crowning not at the University of Paris (where he claimed in his Letter to Posterity to have been invited for just such a watershed event)[47] or, for that matter, the University of Bologna (where Albertino Mussato had recently been "crowned" in 1315).[48] More broadly, Petrarch's aim not only in his *Coronation Oration* but also throughout his life was to establish the profession of the poet as a sort of "professionless profession," as something supremely difficult to pin down.[49] Similarly, Castiglione, not unlike Petrarch, was also deeply invested in the notion of professional identity. And to this effect he announced in the first prefatory letter to *The Courtier* (eventually discarded from the final printed version) that he was writing about the "new profession [*nuova professione*]" of the courtier.[50] But the last thing Castiglione would have ever wanted to do would be to institutionalize officially such a profession in any manner. Quite the contrary, the profession of the courtier, which only in a nominal sense in *The Courtier* was that of "arms," rested for Castiglione on the crucial understanding that courtiers could subtly recognize each other as such: as professionals forming a distinct yet porous group capable of policing each other through daily interactions and elegant conversations.[51] But in Castiglione's refined world dedicated to courtly advice-giving and pleasant banter and idle evening talk rather than to military combat on the battlefield where one ruggedly practiced the "profession of arms [*professione di armi*]," there existed no formal, institutionalized program of training that anyone could possibly pursue systematically in order to practice, day in and day out, the profession of the courtier as a cunning expert skilled in charming people.

Unlike Petrarch and Castiglione, then, Vasari is not interested in advocating the importance of professional identity while simultaneously mystifying what it means to have a *professione* or the process by which one could actually become a professional—or, to use Vasari's term, a *professore*. Far from it. Vasari is insistent and persistent about what it means to be a professional. And instead of parsing subtleties, as Castiglione most assuredly and coyly does, Vasari is bent on being open and forthright about what it takes to be one. Or to use the terms of the opening paragraph of this chapter, Vasari is steadfastly invested in radically *intensifying* our understanding of what professionalism is in the visual arts by bluntly bringing it to our attention time and again in a manner that no one had done before him in the Italian

Renaissance. Consequently, what it means to have a profession and be part of a stratified, complex, competitive, yet unified and collaborative profession in the visual arts with its own distinct body of knowledge is something that we all have to take squarely into account in the process of reading the *Lives* from the very first to last page.[52] To this end, Vasari has created an enormous gallery of visual artists, all of whom, including Vasari, bear abundant witness to the importance of a certain type of training, and many of whom are defined explicitly and linguistically as having a *professione* as he verbally hammers the concept and importance of professional identity into our heads throughout the entire book with a typically Renaissance affection for *copia*.[53] Moreover, unlike Petrarch and Castiglione writing about the professions of the poet and the courtier, Vasari increasingly aims, especially in the revised version of the *Lives*, to *institutionalize* the profession of the visual artist and, what is more, the major professions related to the overarching profession of the visual artist, from the three privileged and nobler professions of painting and architecture and sculpting to those of goldsmithing, engraving, and printing, among others. Indeed, Vasari even aims, as we have seen, to account for what we might call sub-professions within those distinct, overarching professions, from that of reproducing foliage to that of painting animals, crafting book-shelves, and designing grotesques and festoons. Additionally, unlike Petrarch and Castiglione, Vasari eventually provides us in the second version of the *Lives* with arguably what is a fully institutionalized and legitimized, as well as state-sponsored, disciplinary mechanism for training to become, as it were, a "credentialed" professional. In a word, the answer Vasari gives us, if we should ever aspire to be a visual artist of some excellence in his time and thereby be formally elected to the Accademia del Disegno as a *professore*, is that *disegno* is the single, essential key to professional success. And so we must draw.[54] And then we must draw some more. And, yes, when we are done drawing, we must go ahead and draw even more. Or as Michelangelo (in a telling instance not recorded in the *Lives*) admonished his assistant Antonio Mini as he scrawled across a page a stern injunction regarding what he expected out of this rather lackluster draftsman in terms of artistic preparation and professional training, the key to being a visual artist of any merit, simply yet emphatically put, is: "Draw … draw … draw [*disegnia … disegnia … disegnia*]."[55]

Drawing is indeed what Vasari did throughout his own life: he drew and drew and drew (figs. 11 and 12).[56] Or so he gives us to believe in various self-aggrandizing passages in the *Lives*. And when Vasari was done drawing, he drew some more, day in and day out, alone and with others, indoors and outdoors, standing and sitting. He drew in his *bottega*. He drew

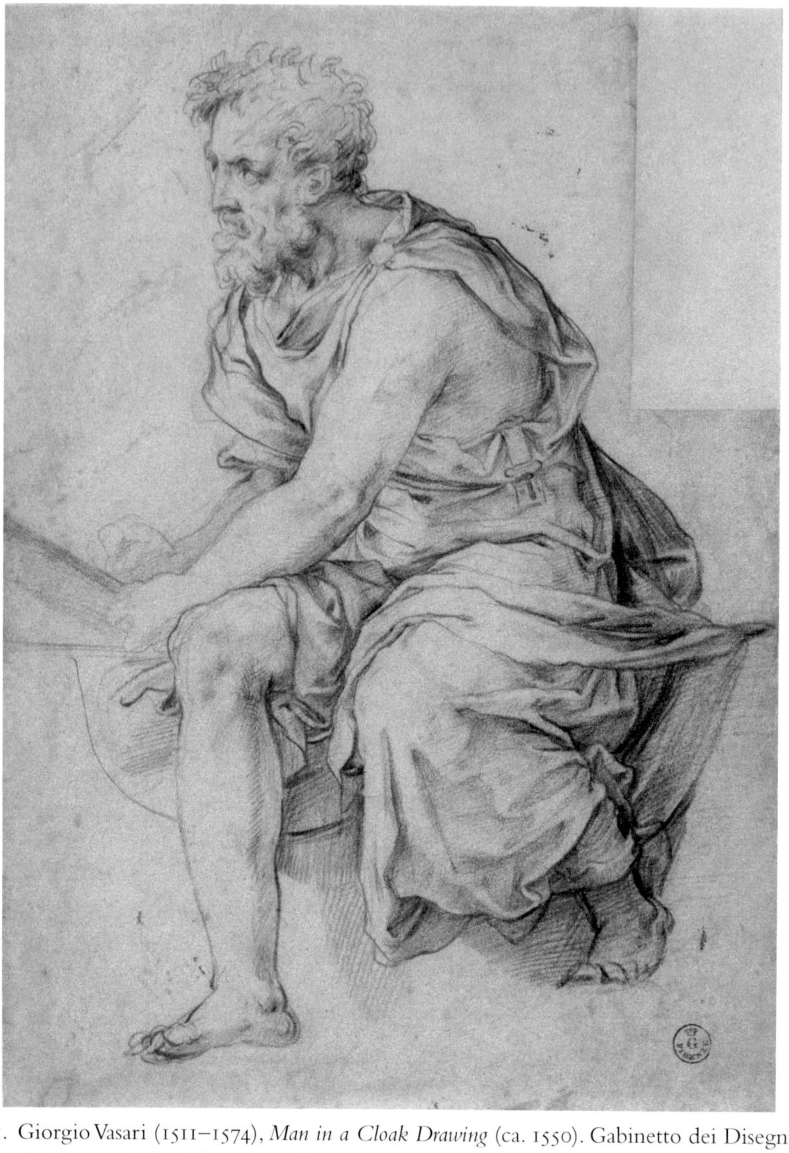

11. Giorgio Vasari (1511–1574), *Man in a Cloak Drawing* (ca. 1550). Gabinetto dei Disegni e delle Stampe, Uffizi, Florence, Italy. N.14274F. Photo credit: Scala/Ministero per i Beni e le Attività culturali/Art Resource, NY.

in churches. He drew at home. He drew early in his career pretty much wherever he could, until there remained, as he tells his story, "nothing notable at that time in Rome, or afterwards in Florence, and in other places where [he] dwelt." And in diligently honing his skills to become a

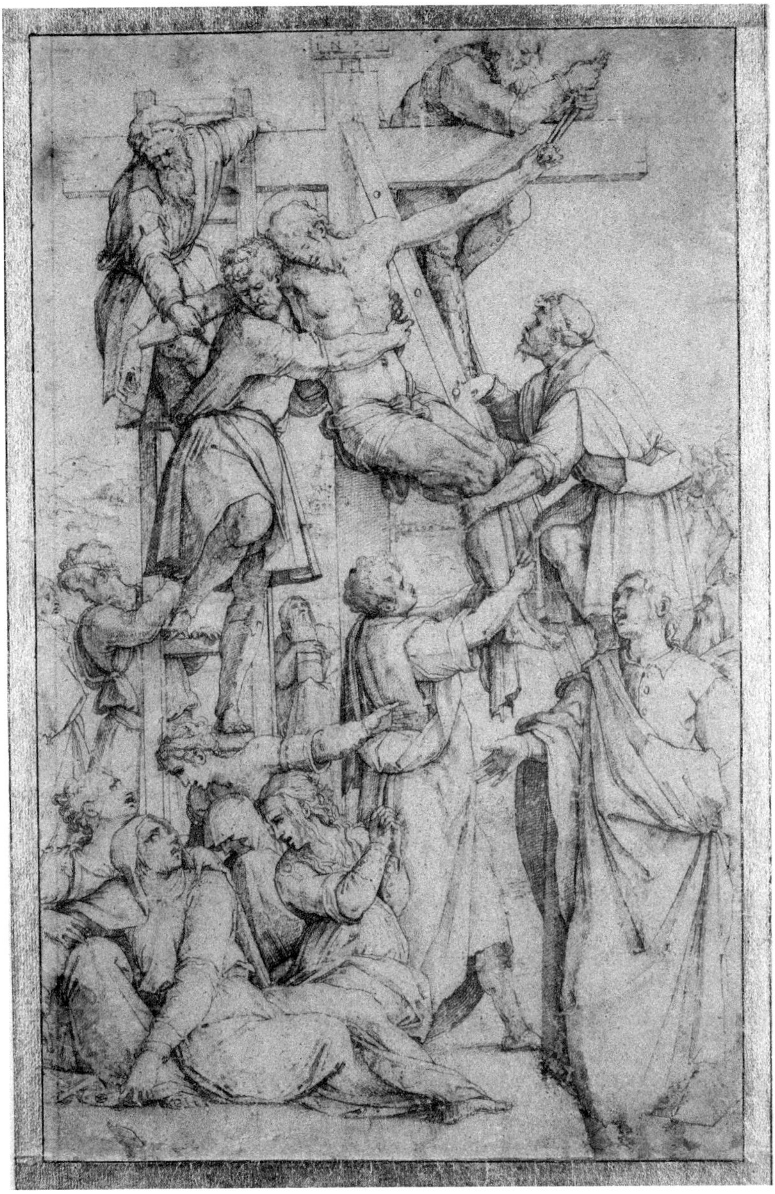

12. Giorgio Vasari (1511–1574), *Descent from the Cross* (1567). Inv. 2194 recto. Musée du Louvre, Paris, France. Photo: Madeleine Coursaget. Photo credit: © RMN-Grand Palais/ Art Resource, NY.

master draftsman, he would not only copy "pictures but also," he insists, "sculptures and architectural works both ancient and modern." Moreover, when he was done "drawing the vaulting and chapel of Michelagnolo," and when there "remained nothing of Raphael, Polidoro [da Caravaggio], and Baldassarre da Siena" to copy, he and his friend and companion Francesco Salviati (1510–1563)—"to the end that each of [them] might have drawings of everything [*d'ogni cosa*]"—would draw different things by day and then swap their drawings and copy each other's by night. By so doing, they were able "to save time and extend [their] studies" together, tirelessly working away in cooperative tandem at every possible moment, even to the point where they would consume their "morning meal standing up, and little at that" in order to keep drawing incessantly, whenever and wherever they could (2.1022, G6.371–2). Indeed, so fascinated was Vasari with *disegno* that he even took the notable step of beginning to collect drawings early on in his career, as testimonials celebrating the significant achievements of others. Often enough he individually framed those collected drawings and created something akin to triumphant collages out of them. And he gathered those artful, ceremonial constructions together in what he repeatedly and affectionately refers to in the Giuntina edition of the *Lives* as his bound "book of drawings [*libro de' disegni*]," which by some scholarly accounts amounted to anywhere from eight to twelve volumes all told and contained approximately one to two thousand images by the end of his life (fig. 13).[57]

But as is evident to anyone holding the multi-volume *Lives* in his or her hands, Vasari also wrote and wrote and wrote, occasionally even at the hurried urging of others. "Write, my brother," Paolo Giovio commanded in a letter from Rome in 1547, "write [*scrivete, fratel mio, scrivete*]."[58] Needless to say, there is no question that Vasari wrote far more than any other visual artist of his time,[59] even if we accept the keen judgment of some discerning modern scholars, above all Charles Hope, Thomas Frangenberg, and Marco Ruffini, that far less than half of the *Lives* (particularly the Giuntina edition) was in fact written by Vasari himself. Instead, it constituted the work of a host of editors, contributors, informants, and colleagues funneling to him stylistic corrections and even lengthy passages, prologues, or entire Lives to be included in his massive, biographical, humanist-inspired history of visual artists.[60] Hence Vasari may rightly insist in his "The Author to the Craftsmen of Design" in the Torrentiniana edition of the *Lives* that his *professione* was "to paint and not to write [*il dipignere et non lo scrivere*]" (T6.410). And indeed we should take that statement at face value, as a candid declaration

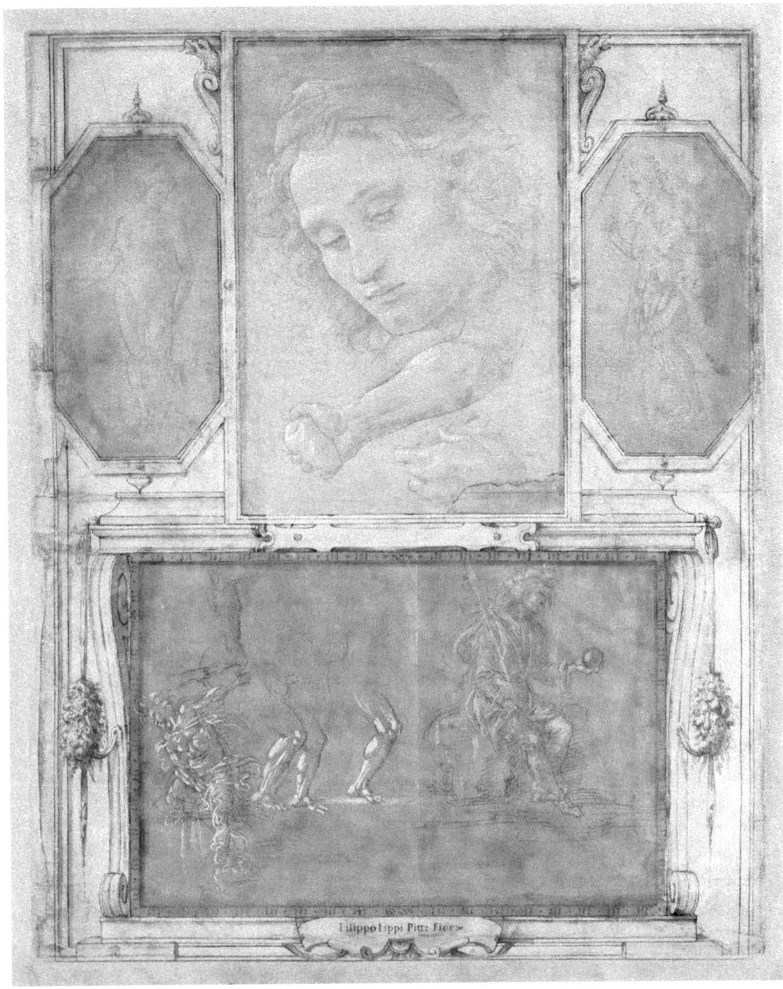

13. Giorgio Vasari (1511–1574), *Page from "Libro de' Disegni," with drawings by Filippino Lippi, Botticelli, and Raffaellino del Garbo* (ca. 1480–1504; mounting and framework by Vasari after 1524). Woodner Collection, Patrons' Permanent Fund. 1991.190.1. Courtesy National Gallery of Art, Washington, D.C.

of professional self-definition delivered with some personal insight. Vasari, whose letters suggest for Hope that he was not exactly a great stylist,[61] was trained to paint, not write. His basic underlying skill was drawing and visual design, not writing and rhetoric. And so there is no reason to think that he was deftly deploying a Castiglione-like *sprezzatura*, grounded as it is in the sleight of hand of irony,[62] to suggest the opposite when he disavows that *lo scrivere* is in fact his profession.[63]

But we may also justifiably consider Vasari a professional writer—taking on "the profession of another [*la professione altrui*]," as Annibale Caro summarily puts it in a congratulatory letter[64]—if indeed we think of Vasari as operating mutatis mutandis within a sort of workshop system of scribal production. In this context Vasari can be seen to have adopted for the purposes of this particular humanist-inspired historical project the dominant model for collaboratively making visual art in his own time and applied it instead to the overall process of writing the *Lives*. And as the sole author on the title pages of both editions, Vasari can thus be reasonably credited with having taken advantage of the collective talents of others far more skilled than he in the profession of writing and having profited from their literary and rhetorical gifts, while no doubt being directed by them on many occasions, even as he collaborated with and directed them, toward a combined, long-term goal. Viewed in this manner, we should no more ask if a massive commissioned painting cycle of sacred or secular history to which Vasari had only marginally put his hands yet conceptually placed his name was "Vasari's" than we should ask if an enormous, multi-volume book of the history of "modern" visual art to which Vasari had only contributed large portions yet placed his name on the title page was also legitimately "Vasari's."[65] Or to put it differently, even if the *Lives* as a work of verbal art was not, like a polished work of visual art coming out of a well-run Renaissance workshop, the product of various contributors uniformly subordinating their unique mode of expression to the single, dominant style of a governing master, Vasari's book, for all that it reads here and there as an uneven and unpolished work of stylistic bricolage, must still be viewed as his book; the *disegno* (in the sense of formal, well-thought-out design) underpinning it should still be construed as his *disegno*; and the ideas laced throughout it should still be taken as his ideas. And in this respect we can retroactively attribute to Vasari the profession of writing, *lo scrivere*, even if he himself believed his talents and training, both as a stylist and as a skilled, entrepreneurial worker, lay elsewhere, no doubt "convinced," as he says he was in the Preface to both the Torrentiniana and Giuntina editions of the *Lives*, that his "labors will delight those who are not engaged in these pursuits, and will both delight and help those who have made them a profession [*professione*]" (1.24, G1.29).

2

INGEGNO/GENIUS

It seems often to happen, indeed, that in their greatest need, when most is expected of them, men become blinded and bewildered in judgment, and do worse work than at any other time; which may result, perchance, from their own malign and evil disposition to be always finding fault with the works of others, or from their seeking too much to strain their genius [*o dal troppo volere sforzare l'ingegno*], seeing that to proceed step by step according to the ruling of nature, yet without neglecting diligence and study, appears to be a better method than seeking to wrest from genius, almost by force, things that are not there [*che il voler cavar le cose quasi per forza dell'ingegno dove non sono*].

—Giorgio Vasari, "The Life of Alfonso Lombardi et al.," the *Lives* (1568)[1]

This chapter examines the professional, pedagogical, creative, and institutional contexts in which Vasari talks about *ingegno*. Significantly enough, the word *ingegno* was used frequently in the fourteenth and early fifteenth centuries in Italy to talk about writers and intellectuals but instead sparingly to characterize visual artists and their powers of "excogitative" invention. Gradually, however, the word *ingegno* acquired greater currency by the mid-fifteenth century when it came to describing visual artists as men of ideas, particularly in the writings of Leon Battista Alberti, and it was certainly part of the regular vocabulary characterizing a number of them by the sixteenth century, which is to say, by the time Vasari began writing the *Lives*.[2] Accordingly, for the most part when Vasari uses the word *ingegno* (and he does so fairly frequently in both editions of the *Lives*), he means, in keeping with the way the word was typically used in his period, that certain fortunate people possess a predisposition and, as it were, "a cast of mind above the ordinary" to undertake select activities in the world with a significant measure of success.[3] We can therefore say, for instance, that Vasari had a genius for crafting a professional identity for himself and other likeminded visual artists, as we saw in the previous chapter, but we cannot say that Vasari was a "genius" (Italian *genio*) in the Romantic, post-Enlightenment sense of the term. Historically, in that context the word "genius" serves to identify a person who for all intents and purposes brings about startlingly original and entirely unforeseen advances in a field of knowledge or practice, thereby effecting in some instances a complete, unprecedented, and permanent paradigm shift in our comprehension of the universal order of things, as Albert Einstein famously did in our own era, so much so that he could be comically billed in at least one instance as having won not just worldly but even cosmic fame.[4]

Moreover, crucial to Vasari's sixteenth-century notion of *ingegno* is the understanding, somewhat similar to our own today, that genius cannot be acquired. Either you have it or you don't. It's as straightforward as that. Accordingly, the word *ingegno*—which derives from the Latin word *genius* meaning the tutelary spirit that governed a person, a family, a people, an entire place (the classical *genius loci*, for instance)—signals for Vasari a quality that is innate, literally in-born (*in-gigno*).[5] It therefore exists, as the *Lexicon of the Academicians of the Crusca* has it, from the outset "without a master [*senza maestro*]."[6] As such, *ingegno*, which is typically understood to mean "talent" or "gift" or "aptitude" or "native intelligence," and which the art historian Martin Kemp has nicely translated as "innate brilliance," freely controls a person by opening up horizons and dictating limitations. Defy it or deny it and you do so at your own peril.[7] *Ingegno* in a sense therefore masters you as a visual artist. But in a real way without *ingegno* you cannot develop into a master within the *professione* of the visual arts. And this is true not just in the social, economic, political, and legal sense of what it meant to be a *maestro* in the visual arts in Vasari's Florence, as someone who juridically possessed the right as a member of a guild to hire, oversee, and train within one's *bottega* the so-called *fattori/fattorini* (apprenticed workers, typically young boys, usually contracted for two to three years to perform a variety of chores, depending on age and experience) and the so-called *garzoni* (advanced assistants of varying ages, abilities, and learning needs remunerated at a higher rate as expert workers engaged under contracts of varying lengths; see figs. 7 and 14).[8] In Vasari's time, without *ingegno*, that innate quality that marks you from birth as especially good at something, you cannot also possibly develop into a "super-artist"—to borrow another of Kemp's felicitous terms—of the order of Brunelleschi, Leonardo, Raphael, or Michelangelo. And this is a key premise for Vasari. You can train all you want and train all the people you want. But without that mysterious, animating, inborn, "natural" gift of *ingegno*, which you must diligently pay attention to as if it were a voice summoning you ineluctably toward a vocation as a literal "calling,"

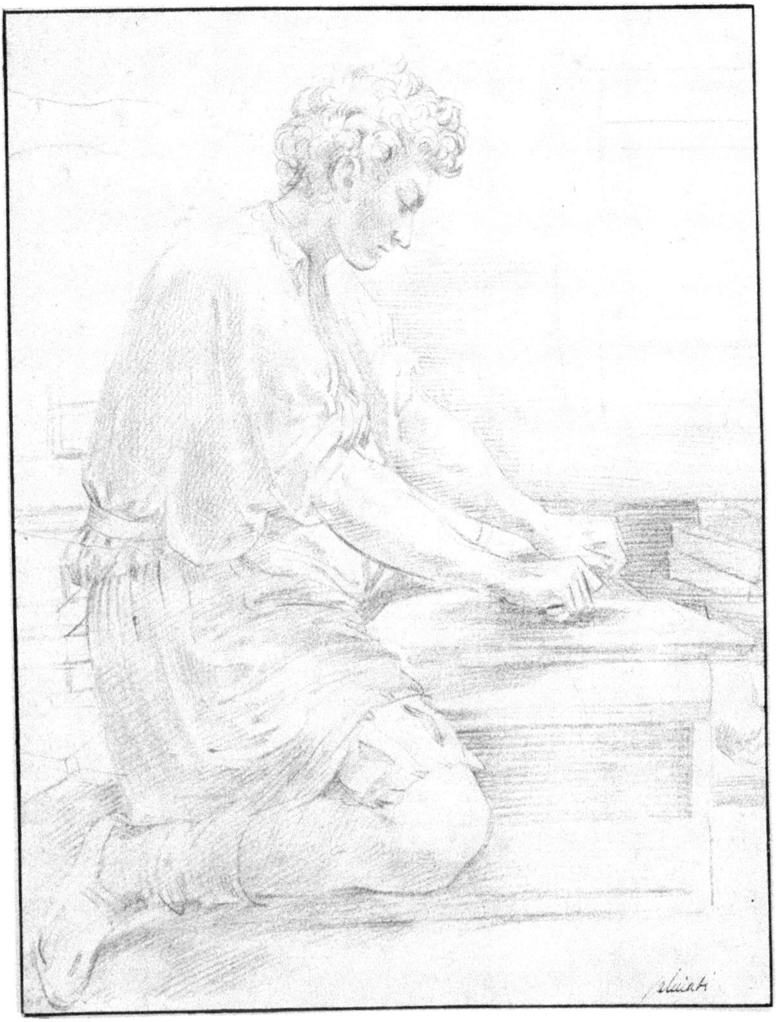

14. Parmigianino (Francesco Mazzola, 1503–1540), *A Painter's Apprentice Grinding Pigments on the Lid of a Chest* (ca. 1530). Victoria and Albert Museum, London, Great Britain. Photo credit: V&A Images, London/Art Resource, NY.

an inherent *vocatio*, you will never truly succeed as a visual artist. Nor, for that matter, will you ever be in a position to contribute to the grand historical development of the arts that Vasari identifies, glorifies, and consciously periodizes as a thoroughgoing *rinascita*, as well as a complete *rinovazione* when considered strictly in terms of the art of painting (1.57, G2.44). So it is that Giotto (ca. 1276–1337), credited with singlehandedly bringing *disegno* back "to complete life [*del tutto in vita*]" and refounding "the true manner of painting [*il vero modo di dipignere*]," is described early in the *Lives* as possessing a "liveliness and readiness of extraordinary genius [*vivacità e prontezza d'ingegno straordinario*]" long before he receives any formal, *techne*-based training in the visual arts, presumably as a *fattore* and then as a *garzone* in a master's *bottega* (1.96–7, G2.95–6; 1.117, G2.122). Giotto's *ingegno straordinario*, at least initially, is what matters most. Everything hinges on that. Without it, we are given to understand, there would have been no Renaissance in the *professione* of the visual arts. No *ingegno*, no Giotto, no Masaccio, no Brunelleschi, no Leonardo, no Raphael, no Michelangelo, and thus, as a result, no Vasarian *rinascita*.

In this context I would like to address the following questions in this chapter, each of which dovetails broadly with humanist thought and concerns. Vasari's book, after all, was inspired by a convivial encounter with a number of humanists in Rome, or so we are told at the end of the Giuntina edition. And Vasari, who was modestly trained in the *studia humanitatis* and thought of himself as a man of ideas, benefited markedly from the input of a number of humanists at various stages of his book's collaborative production, including Giovio, Borghini, Caro, Bartoli, and Giambullari.[9] My questions, then, are as follows.

First, how does Vasari's understanding of *ingegno* in the *Lives* relate to the key humanist assumption espoused in the Italian Renaissance, and predictably enough in humanist pedagogical theory, that people are fundamentally made through a process of education, even if they are selectively born with a certain *ingegno*?[10] Put differently, if history according to humanists teaches through examples, what does the *Lives* as a work of exemplary, didactic, humanist-inspired history teach us about what constitutes a good program (or, for that matter, good programs) of education in the *professione* of the visual arts, specifically when it comes to identifying and training *ingegno*? Moreover, does that professional training thereby account for the success of the roughly three-hundred-year period of rebirth that Vasari embraces and celebrates as a single, coherent, yet still ongoing unit of time?[11]

Second, what relationship, if any, exists between *ingegno* and certain humanist assumptions in the Italian Renaissance about what it means to be a good and virtuous "leader"—a word for which there is, curiously enough, not even an adequate, corresponding term in Italian today? Or to phrase the question in light of the humanist investment in moral philosophy, what specific qualities should we be looking for in a leader, a *capo* or *guida* of some sort, in order to ensure the proper development of men of *ingegno* and thus secure the longevity of a certain privileged, modern style of making visual art?

Third, how do practitioners in the *professione* of the visual arts recognize their own *ingegno* according to Vasari, and what happens if you do not, or cannot, nurture that *ingegno*, or if, for one reason or another, you ill-advisedly work against it by trying to do something you simply are not predisposed to do, given the limits of who you are, your own physiological constitution, and your own specific powers of invention? In other words, does the practice involved in training *ingegno* prepare visual artists to know how to serve their *ingegno* well and know how to instrumentalize it to serve them well within the *professione*?

And, fourth, what happens to *ingegno* in the visual arts once the formal training of it is at least partly institutionalized in an official academic setting? Is the academy, for instance, a good, indeed ideal, place to cultivate *ingegno* in the *professione* of the visual arts? Above all, what in the end is the added value of training *ingegno* in the context of an official, institutionalized, academic setting?

The issues addressed in these four, core, interrelated questions also all come together, we shall see, in the Life of Michelangelo. Nor should this strike us as entirely surprising. The exceptionality of Michelangelo's genius—which served, once more in Kemp's words, as a constant, though routinely contested, "point of reference when [Italian authors writing about visual art in the period] wished to discuss creative 'genius' at the very highest level"—both challenges and reveals the normative structure of Vasari's understanding of what constitutes the virtues and limitations of *ingegno* in the *Lives* and in Italian Renaissance culture generally.[12] Structurally, exceptions may not always prove the rule, but, as anthropologists such as Mary Douglas have long taught us, they can certainly help us understand the nature of the rules that underpin complex systems of thought.

For Vasari, as well as for a variety of Renaissance humanists, including those thinking about an educational program grounded in the classical tradition of the *artes liberales*, certain human beings—with the focus here centered squarely on *male* human beings, as the feminist art historian Linda Nochlin long ago rightfully stressed[13]—have a defined "natural inclination [*inclinazione naturale*]" (1.783, G4.272),[14] a biologically determined, astrologically influenced, and/or God-given "genius."[15] That genius, which emerges in earnest in the early years of a child's development, is first noticed as a general proclivity. In the remarkable but still paradigmatic case of Giotto, for example, who is discovered as a shepherd drawing on the surfaces of flat stones or simply on the ground in the fields near Vespignano, it is viewed early on in the *Lives* as a "natural inclination for the art of *disegno* [*inclinazione della natura all'arte del disegno*]" (1.97, G2.96). Gradually the individual's *ingegno* directs the child toward certain types of fulfilling expertise. In this respect, for Vasari and the humanist pedagogues of the Italian Renaissance, the work of the dutiful and loving parent—and by extension the teacher in the form of the *maestro/magister* of a workshop or a humanist schoolroom—will be to recognize an individual's "genius" and appropriately nurture it. Like a seed (and I use the agricultural metaphor here advisedly), the individual's genius will grow and flourish if properly tended to and thus arrive at a state of perfection through a natural, organic process. Hence, as the famous rhetorician and pedagogue Quintilian long ago imagined in his *Institutio oratoria* (*Institutes of Oratory*, ca. 95 CE),[16] and as Renaissance humanists likewise typically maintained in their treatises, the educational process should be likened to cultivating a garden.[17] Cultivate "geniuses" well and they will bloom, as it were, so that in the end, as Vasari puts in one instance, "excellent and divine elements and marvelous conceptions are seen to issue forth [*si vede uscirne parti eccellenti e divini, e concetti maravigliosi*]" (1.281, G3.62). Cultivate them poorly and, alas, you end up with male artists in a state of arrested development, stunted intellectually and creatively and thereby unable to fulfill the promise of their own particular *ingegno*, that guiding natural inclination and "innate brilliance," as they grow up and eventually take up their position in the social order and assume certain tasks for the greater public good. "No small error," Vasari accordingly observes, "do those fathers of families make who do not allow the talents/genius of their children to run in childhood their natural course [*nella fanciullezza il corso della natura agl'ingegni de' figliuoli*], and do not let them follow the abilities that are most in accordance with their taste; for to try to turn them to something for which they have no inclination is manifestly to prevent them from ever being excellent in anything, because we almost always find that those who labor at something that they do not like make little progress in any occupation whatsoever. On the other hand, those who follow the instinct of nature [*lo instinto della natura*] generally become excellent and famous in the arts that they pursue" (1.393, G3.251).

The precondition for acquiring a *techne*, then, and succeeding as a practitioner in such activities as painting or sculpture or architecture was genius, *ingegno*. The role of the wise leader (a parent, a teacher, a patron, a prince—the last three effectively operating as father figures in Vasari's patriarchal culture) was to recognize the particular genius of an individual in the visual arts and adequately nurture it and guide it, thereby demonstrating desirable qualities of leadership. So it is that we learn that Giotto's father "lovingly [*amorevolmente*]" allows his son to pursue a career in the visual arts away from home and that his teacher Cimabue, known for his "sharp *ingegno* [*lo acume dello ingegno*]" (T2.35), immediately recognizes the young boy's *ingegno straordinario* and dutifully takes it upon himself to ensure that Giotto would be properly "instructed [*ammaestrato*]" (1.97, G2.96–7) as an apprentice—presumably as a *fattore* and/or *garzone*—trained within his workshop.[18] Finally, the function of the *professione* as a whole was to create the economic, social, and cultural conditions whereby those very people with *ingegno* in the visual arts could be cultivated and acquire real mastery over an art, understood as a *techne*, through a program of edification, thus allowing practitioners to become, as we saw in the first chapter, full-fledged *professori*, men who could claim practical, reliable, teachable, and communicable knowledge of a socially valued art.

Now, when examined strictly in terms of demographics, the *Lives* discloses time and again that the vast majority of men of *ingegno* in the visual arts who have successfully mastered the art of *disegno* come, as one might expect, from an artisanal background.[19] Vasari nevertheless also makes evident from the outset that this entirely expected social pattern does not constitute a consistent, absolute rule. Cimabue hails from a noble line, we are told, while his disciple, Giotto, who far surpasses his more socially elevated master and truly ushers in the Renaissance, was merely a shepherd from birth. Thus anyone from any social class, we learn from the outset of the *Lives*, can possess the requisite *ingegno* to succeed brilliantly as a visual artist. *Ingegno* cuts across and through rank and social hierarchy in the *Lives*. Additionally, men of *ingegno* in the *professione* of the visual arts, we learn, have all sorts of innate temperaments, which, according to the medical theory of complexions as a balance of humors, physiologically condition how they behave, think, and feel.[20] But Vasari, it is important to stress, does not subscribe to the notion advanced by philosophers like Marsilio Ficino (1433–1499) that someone with a melancholic or astrologically influenced saturnine humor is decidedly more predisposed to excellence in the creative or intellectual arts and thus has a special *ingegno* in those areas.[21] Were Vasari alive today, he would not accept the widespread notion that manic depressives, say, are more inclined to be great artists or geniuses, any more than he would have subscribed to the Romantic singling out of the diseased, passionate, tubercular artist in the nineteenth and early twentieth centuries as someone particularly predisposed to being a creative genius, a notion that Thomas Mann brilliantly and sometimes hilariously exploited with withering irony in his *Der Zauberberg* (*The Magic Mountain*).[22] Quite the contrary, Vasari recognizes, privileges, and takes some narrative delight in describing the extraordinary variety of individual temperaments associated with a vast array of visual artists: the sweetness of Pietro Perugino (ca. 1450–1523); the genteel, affable, yet sometimes solitary comportment of Leonardo; the choleric, irascible behavior of the pugnacious Pietro Torrigiano (1472–1528); and the moody melancholy of the asocial Pontormo or Vasari's dear friend Francesco Salviati. However, Vasari still acknowledges all the same that, amidst this *copia* of personality traits, it is essential for all artists to know, or better yet to learn to know, how to control their temperament in order to allow for an understanding of how they can use it to their best advantage, thereby realizing their *ingegno*. Michelangelo often enough did this by infusing his works of art with his *terribilità*, just as the elegant and princely Raphael did much the same by imbuing his works of art with his self-evident and socially defining *grazia*. Genius, it is therefore worth stressing, can only exhibit itself in the visual arts through the concrete, material act of making visual objects.

Along with that, visual artists must learn to know how to control their temperaments in order to curb the ways they might undermine them within their *professione*. Exemplary in this instance is the Roman mannerist painter Taddeo Zuccaro (1529–1566), who by his very nature "was sanguine, quick, and very haughty, and moreover given to carnal pleasures, but nevertheless, while he was strongly inclined by nature to these things, he was tempered and knew how to manage them with a certain honest reserve and very secretly [*seppe fare le sue cose con una certa onesta vergogna e molto segretamente*]" (2.618, G5.569). At the same time, visual artists must adhere to the absolute standards of art painstakingly recovered and refined in the Italian Renaissance (above all in the fifteenth century) in order to be sure that "every painter [*ogni pittore*]" does not end up, according to the proverbial wisdom, "painting himself [*diping*[*endo*] *sè*]," thereby involuntarily reproducing one's own self in works of art through an act of "automimesis."[23] Vasarian classicism, with all its unyielding rules and fixed, absolute standards, serves in this way to curtail a visual artist's proclivity to rely on an "innately defective judgment of proportions" grounded not in the universal laws of mathematics underpinning Nature but, rather, a flawed perspective "tainted" by "personal" and physiologically determined prejudices.[24]

Furthermore, genius comes in all shapes and sizes for Vasari, with various degrees of intensity and a plethora of descriptive qualifiers routinely associated with it. Accordingly, just as we would say today that an artist possesses some talent, considerable talent, real talent, a notable talent, a great talent, or a breathtaking talent that staggers the imagination (the last somewhat approximating our everyday, user-friendly notion of "genius"), and just as we would say today that one person demonstrates greater talent than another and for one reason or another, so, too, Vasari distinguishes—with something of a Rabelaisian affinity for variety and *copia*—between those visual artists who have just *ingegno* pure and simple, as well as a mere "weak [*debole*]" or "very weak [*debolissimo*]" or "very small [*piccolissimo*]" *ingegno*, and those who have a "beautiful [*bello*]," "good [*buon*]," "rare [*raro*]," "lively [*vivace*]," "divine [*divino*]," "quick [*spedito/pronto*]," "able [*destro*]," "noble [*nobile*]," "sharp [*acuto*]," "exalted [*alto*]," "sophisticated/clever [*sofistico*]," "wise [*saggio*]," "singular [*singolare*]," "excellent [*eccellente*]," "prudent [*prudente*]," "awesome [*terribile*]," "fierce [*feroce*]," "unique/unusual [*pellegrino*]," "versatile [*versatile*]," "subtle [*sottile*]," "great [*grande*]," "huge [*grosso*]," "marvelous/wondrous [*meraviglioso/mirabile*]," "extraordinary" [*straordinario*]," "inventive/fanciful [*capriccioso*]," "vigorous [*gagliardo*]," or "elevated [*elevato*]" *ingegno*—not to mention those who have, even more impressively, a "very felicitous [*felicissimo*]," "very beautiful [*bellissimo*]," "very good [*bonissimo*]," "very rare [*rarissimo*]," "very lively [*vivacissimo*]," "very divine [*divinissimo*]," "very quick [*speditissimo*]," "very able [*destrissimo*]," "very noble [*nobilissimo*]," "very sharp [*acutissimo*]," and "very exalted [*altissimo*]" *ingegno*.[25] For Vasari, then, there are geniuses and then again there are geniuses, men in some instances of such unparalleled and unprecedented *ingegno* within the *professione* of the visual arts that they can technically do things that others cannot do. Those same remarkable artists, precisely because they have such exceptional talent, can also seem to envision things in the process of invention that others simply cannot see, thus breaking entirely new ground in the arts. Michelangelo's visionary ability, for instance, to extract the unprecedented idea of the *David* (1501–4) out of a marred piece of massive marble is for Vasari yet another obvious case he points to as a "miracle" (G6.20), along with, more generally, Giotto's truly visionary ability to breathe life into images of the human form, so much so that, "helped by nature [*aiutato dalla natura*]," which is to say aided by his own natural inclination and thus by his own particular *ingegno*, Giotto singlehandedly "resuscitated the modern and good art of painting, introducing the ability to draw well and naturally living people, which had fallen out of use for more than two hundred years [*risuscitò la moderna e buona arte della pittura, introducendo il ritrarre bene di naturale le persone vive, il che più di dugento anni non s'era usato*]" (1.97, G2.97).

Moreover, genius does not pass from parent to child in a consistent or predictable manner. Some fathers in the *professione* of the visual arts, for instance, have more talent than their sons (or, in exceptionally rare instances, daughters), while the reverse is often equally true. Giovanni Santi (ca. 1440–1494), described as a man of "good talent [*buono ingegno*]," was certainly capable and gifted as a painter, but his son Raphael far surpasses him as a man deemed possessing a "most beautiful talent [*bellissimo ingegno*]" (G4.156–67). Similarly, the sons of Jacopo Bellini (ca. 1400–ca. 1470), Gentile (ca. 1429–1507) and Giovanni (ca. 1430–1516), profiting from a conscious desire to outdo one another, bested their father through calculated sibling rivalry, "and so on in succession [*e così suc[c]essivamente*]," Vasari adds with an optimistic vision of how the future should indeed unfold as one generation passes on its expertise to the next more accomplished one, always historically gaining in a progressively onward and upward fashion (1.487, G3.428). By contrast, the reverse occurs with the progeny of Taddeo Gaddi (ca. 1290–1366): his son Agnolo (ca. 1350–1396), after auspiciously giving proof of his talent as a painter early on, proved in the end less gifted and proficient than his father as a visual artist. In this respect, Vasari's treatment of the concept of genius resembles the familiar Italian Renaissance understanding about the nature of "nobility" insofar as what primarily mattered for a number of humanists was the so-called "nobility of spirit" of a person, regardless of social origin, rather than "nobility of blood," which was restricted to family line. This is an argument, of course, that dates back to Dante and his poetic interlocutors during a period of some social mobility in the communes of northern Italy and then finds itself rehearsed and debated in a variety of treatises throughout the Italian Renaissance, including, for instance, Castiglione's *The Courtier*.[26] Hence genius for Vasari, like nobility for many humanists invested in the concept of the "dignity of man," is individually tailored and not predictably or reliably, much less evenly, meted out within families or distributed in a progressively uplifting fashion from father to son, always with ever more increasingly positive results over time, successively advancing in stages from one generation to the next within a shared *professione*. What is more, genius does not even necessarily run in families. It can easily skip generations. And at times genius even appears, as in the cases of Cimabue, Giotto, Leonardo, and Michelangelo, spontaneously out of nowhere, occasionally to everyone's surprise and, in some instances, chagrin.[27]

That being the case, the key for Vasari, as for the humanist pedagogues of the Italian Renaissance, is to ensure that someone with laudable leadership qualities is readily available to recognize that *ingegno* in the child whenever and wherever it manifests itself and then take the appropriate steps to see to it that the child's natural inclination is properly nurtured and cultivated, regardless of his (or, in very rare instances, "her") background, humoral temperament, receptivity to astrological influences, and family genealogy. Ideally the father would take on that essential leadership role, as indeed Vasari's own father did in fostering his child's growth in the visual arts in an exemplary way, "with every sort of loving care [*con ogni sorte d'amorevolezza*]." In this manner his father set the young Vasari on the "path of virtue, and in particular of *disegno* [*via delle virtù, et in particolare del disegno*]" to which he was, thanks to his genius, naturally "much inclined [*molto inclinato*]" (2.1020, G6.369). Raphael's father paradigmatically behaves in much the same way, as do a host of other fathers in the *Lives* as they act out the role of good, responsible, parental leaders, setting their children up as *fattori/fattorini* or *garzoni* in the best of all possible workshops. But lacking a father's good guiding hand and example, other factors can just as readily come into play to help nurture a child's genius. Not least of them is the supportive character of culture itself, which can serve as a sort of pervasive social safety net for Vasari when it comes to the recognition and training of *ingegno* within the *professione* of the visual arts. That culture can take on the form of the supportive character of the very people—or in some instances a benevolent, autocratic person—governing the society in question. The appearance of genius in a family line may be unpredictable, albeit providentially explicable for Vasari in retrospect, but the geographical place where genius makes its appearance is not. Historically, certain geographical areas and vibrant, urban centers predictably have men who do a better job than others in cultivating genius in the visual arts. Ancient Athens obviously did so for Vasari, along with its modern avatar: Republican and then ducal—as well as eventually grand-ducal—Florence.[28] There is, then, a deep faith in Vasari that things will work out well in the end in such cultures for those who possess *ingegno* and are willing to put in the effort and labor to nurture it. Or as Vasari succinctly puts it in his Life of Guillaume de Marçillat (Guglielmo da Marcilla, ca. 1470–1529) as an expression of his rather undying, but one might argue not entirely warranted, optimism: "I want to believe that every genius that has a desire to attain perfection can, if he puts in the work, pass beyond the limits of every body of knowledge/science [*voglio credere che ogni ingegno che abbia volontà di pervenire a la perfezzione, possa passare, volendo affaticarsi, il termine d'ogni scienza*]" (1.755, G4.226).

Consider, then, the exemplary and instructive case of Michelangelo, whose Life is so extraordinary in a number of ways, not least because it is the longest in the book, because it was conceived to end the Torrentiniana edition and thus provide structural and thematic closure to the first edition, and because it serves as a crucial turning point, albeit in different ways, in Vasari's historical narrative in both the 1550 and 1568 editions of the *Lives*—a point to which I will return in the fourth chapter dedicated to the concept of "time." To begin with, Michelangelo, we are reminded from the outset of his Life, is Tuscan, and *that* in itself is important, for "Tuscan geniuses/talents [*gli ingegni toscani*]," Vasari observes in a manner that rehearses similar observations scattered throughout the *Lives*, "have always been exalted and raised high above all others, from their being diligent in the labors and studies of every faculty beyond any other people of Italy [*sono stati fra gli altri sommamente elevati e grandi, per essere eglino molto osservanti alle fatiche et agli studii di tutte le facultà sopra qualsivoglia gente di Italia*]" (2.642, G6.4; see also, for instance, G4.397). More important, Michelangelo possesses, we are likewise told at the outset, a genius for the visual arts—specifically and tellingly an *ingegno* for *disegno*. However, Michelangelo, who is consumed with a passion for drawing and secludes himself to feed his love for *disegno* in solitude, finds himself initially thwarted from following the direction in which his genius would otherwise lead him as he materially generates ideas through his visual art. Indeed his male elders, not ones to spare the rod, stubbornly stand in his way, even to the point of actually beating him, largely out of ignorance of the real value of the visual arts as a *professione* (an obvious sign of their social and aesthetic obtuseness for Vasari) and out of an equally ignorant, and consequently misplaced, concern that in becoming a visual artist Michelangelo might end up debasing his family honor by engaging in a mechanical trade: "perhaps considering that to give attention to that ability, which was not known by them, was a base thing and not worthy of their ancient house [*stimando forse che lo attendere a quella virtù, non conosciuta da loro, fussi cosa bassa e non degna della antica casa loro*]" (2.643, G6.5). Fortunately, however, Michelangelo lives in Florence, where so many excellent masters can cultivate the *ingegno* of young males ineluctably drawn to the visual arts by taking them into their workshops and training them as *fattori/fattorini* or *garzoni* through a contractual, guild-regulated arrangement as *dipendenti*, or as Vasari also routinely likes to term them, as *discepoli*. And as Vasari tells us in various instances, Florence itself is the great urban center of the modern age that best cultivates genius in the *professione* of the visual arts, in part because of its historically fierce competitive nature, which itself is fostered and maintained by the nature of the city's environmentally conditioned and locally determined *aria* (air; G2.81, G3.597–8). Simply put, a particular "genius" of Florence, its *genius loci*, in classical terms, fosters the creativity of men of *ingegno* in the visual arts coming from all sorts of backgrounds. Hence others readily intrude into Buonarroti family matters to take up Michelangelo's cause and successfully persuade his father to allow his son to pursue his passion, his natural proclivity to draw (his *ingegno* for *disegno*, that is), despite parental resistance. And that indeed is what happens in Vasari's version of Michelangelo's remarkable life as his father, "advised by friends [*consigliato da amici*]," finally relents and resolves to put his son into apprenticeship in 1488, *di acconciarlo* ("to set him up," 2.644, G6.6) at the ripe age of thirteen.

Finally, last but not least, Michelangelo is providentially blessed because he grows up in a city more or less ruled by Lorenzo de' Medici (1449–1492), a man of exceptional acumen and taste, as well as a man who behaves precisely as an ideal patron of the visual arts should: as a charismatic and amiable father figure for those in need of assistance and guidance. In this manner, Lorenzo resembles his grandfather Cosimo di Giovanni de' Medici (1389–1464), known as the Florentine *pater patriae* (father of the fatherland), an honorific alluding to the great Roman patron Augustus, by exercising the Aristotelian virtue of "magnificence," which is required for sustaining the visual arts in a culture known for valuing them:

> Lorenzo the Magnificent, then, always favored beautiful geniuses/talents [*i belli ingegni*] ... and what is more, he not only gave the means to buy food and clothing to those who, being poor, would otherwise not have been able to pursue the studies of *disegno*, but also bestowed extraordinary gifts on anyone among them who had acquitted himself in some work better than the others; so that the young students of our arts, competing thus with each other, thereby became very excellent ... Truly magnificent was the example thus given by Lorenzo, and whenever Princes and other persons of high degree choose to imitate it, they will always gain everlasting honor and glory thereby; since he who assists and favors, in their noble undertakings, beautiful and rare geniuses [*i belli e pellegrini ingegni*], from whom the world receives such beauty, honor, convenience, and benefit, deserves to live forever in the minds and memories of mankind. (1.693–4, G4.125–6)

The stage is thus set for Michelangelo's genius to be fully realized, despite the formidable family obstacles initially placed in his way, and despite the fact that he was forced to oppose and defy his male elders—something that Vasari emphasizes to stress Michelangelo's undying devotion to his art and indeed even his heroism. Preordained to become the greatest master of the visual arts, whose accomplishments summarize an era and arguably usher in a new one, Michelangelo, who materially generates ideas through the making of visual art, appropriately lives in the right urban center in the right region and in the right society with a strong cultural and economic investment in the visual arts and an equally strong leader. And that leader has dedicated much of his life to ensuring, as a benevolent, fatherly patron should, that the *professione* of the visual arts would always continue to flourish under his guidance, much as they always have under the exemplary magnificence/munificence of Medici rule and patronage.

To this end, it is imperative that Michelangelo is seen to have profited from the economically, socially, and culturally entrenched practice of training visual artists through years of a guild-regulated, contractually arranged apprenticeship in a Florentine workshop, even if Michelangelo would have us believe otherwise in the biography he had his pupil Ascanio Condivi fashion about him shortly after Vasari's book appeared in print—a biography written in part to set the record straight regarding what Michelangelo deemed to be some of Vasari's false assertions about his life.[29] Indeed, Vasari even goes so far as to publish documents the second time around, in the Giuntina edition of 1568, to stress all the more the fact that Michelangelo entered into an apprenticeship with Domenico Ghirlandaio (1448/9–1494), a master artist who maintained one of the largest, most productive, and most successful workshops in Renaissance Florence (G6.6–7).[30] Needless to say, Vasari in the Giuntina edition could have backed down and presented Michelangelo exactly as Michelangelo himself wished to be presented in the Condivi biography. That is, he could have presented him, like Condivi, as someone who appeared on the scene without having benefited in the slightest from his formal training in Ghirlandaio's workshop, pretty much already perfectly fashioned in his own right as a *maestro*, a complete autodidact, a true, untutored "natural," who could and should be able to operate juridically outside the guild-regulated system of artistic production.[31] And in many ways it would have been entirely in Vasari's character to do just that, to defer to the better judgment of the "divine," aristocratic-minded Michelangelo, who preferred to see himself as a man of some breeding, untainted by apprenticeship, as well as a man uninterested later in his career in fostering a *bottega* himself as a master artisan. Needless to say, Vasari was certainly prone to mythologize Michelangelo throughout the *Lives* and thus allow for all sorts of far-fetched stories to be perpetuated about him, such as the story that Michelangelo actually painted the entire Sistine Chapel ceiling—a daunting four-year project—without any assistants. Surely one would think that Vasari, as a practicing visual artist thoroughly versed in the difficult and time-consuming art of fresco painting on such a vast and onerous scale, would have suspected that an extraordinary feat of that magnitude was well-nigh inconceivable by one person acting virtually alone.

Yet Vasari doesn't back down on this occasion. And he doesn't do so—indeed he becomes even more doggedly insistent as he digs up and publishes documents as definitive proof that he was right—in large measure because Vasari needs to demonstrate beyond a shadow of a doubt that Michelangelo unequivocally benefited from the workshop program of training, however briefly, early in his career as a pupil contractually apprenticed to Ghirlandaio (not least by being exposed to, albeit not formally learning, the art of fresco painting during the period when Ghirlandaio was working on the Tornabuoni Chapel in Santa Maria Novella from 1485 to 1490 and thus when Michelangelo served, according to Vasari's own documentation, as one of Ghirlandaio's apprentices from 1488 to 1489/90). For in Vasari's view of things—which is a view consistent with Renaissance attitudes about the relationship between *ingegno* and "the mastery of those rational rules (known collectively as *dottrina* or *disciplina*) which govern such matters as imitation, composition, and decorum"[32]—there can be no purely "natural" undomesticated geniuses capable of achieving great things absolutely on their own, without any prior training whatsoever within the *professione* of the visual arts. Or to draw on Kemp's formulation in his analysis of Giovanni Paolo Lomazzo's views about the concept of *ingegno* as they were articulated in his *Idea del tempio della pittura* (*Idea of the Temple of Painting*, 1590) and *Trattato dell'arte della pittura, scoltura et architettura* (*Treatise on the Art of Painting, Sculpting, and Architecture*, 1584), Vasari shares "the universal insistence with all art theorists during the fifteenth and sixteenth centuries"—from Ghiberti to Alberti to Leonardo—"that rational learning, studious application and manual discipline are absolutely essential if inborn talent is to reach fruition."[33] Michelangelo can therefore be mythologized in the wildest of ways, as someone whose *ingegno* as a sculptor was naturally imbibed from the very beginning of his life as an infant nursed by the wife of a stonemason in an area known for its artisans and rich stone quarries, as if Michelangelo's passion for sculptural *disegno* in the *professione* of the visual arts was thoroughly absorbed into his being with the very milk that nurtured him and then found itself infused into the objects he produced later in his life with such intensity and devotion. But in the end, even though Michelangelo may appear to be a pure, untainted "natural" from his inception, a sort of *senex puer* (wise old boy), to borrow from a literary commonplace deployed in narratives from antiquity on through the Enlightenment,[34] Michelangelo—in all his exceptionality—must still be shown to have been trained in some measure within the workshop system of inculcation and thus ultimately be indebted to the "genius" of Florence as a city that glories in a structured and calculated fashion in the professional creation and cultivation of its men of *ingegno* in the visual arts. Simply put, nothing sublime for Vasari can be achieved in the visual arts, not the Sistine Chapel vault, not the *Last Judgment* wall, much less the *Bacchus*, *Pietà*, *David*, *Moses*, New Medici Sacristy, and the like, unless the artist in question has received some sort of prior formal instruction within his *professione*.

Ingegno, which is given by nature and thus initially knows no master, must nevertheless be fashioned, domesticated, acculturated, and it must be tangibly manifested in the work itself, in the material object of visual art. For Vasari it is really as simple as that. Even the great Michelangelo, who is capable of producing "almost inimitable [*quasi inimmitabili*]" objects of beauty (G6.108), must therefore bow before the demands of the guild-regulated workshop system of training at some point in his life in order to receive at least some rudimentary, practical knowledge of the *techne* underpinning his *professione*, even if he then quickly outshines his master—in this case Ghirlandaio—and thereby outgrows all that being apprenticed in such a major, busy, and well-run workshop can profitably offer him both technically and conceptually.

In the same way, Vasari needs to impress upon us the notion that the fifteen-year-old Michelangelo subsequently participated from 1490 to 1492 in the activities of the sculpture garden of Lorenzo the Magnificent's creation and was welcomed warmly into the Medici household on via Larga. Not only does this observation remind us that Michelangelo received at a formative age, despite the significant obstacles initially put in his path, appropriate parental guidance through the patronage of Lorenzo the Magnificent, who in all his expansive liberality even provided the young Michelangelo with a place at his table, admitting him into his extended *famiglia* as one of his own. It also reminds us that Michelangelo was appropriately "cultivated," to borrow the agricultural metaphor operative in humanist thought about pedagogy, as a fledgling plant in a garden—in this case, literally a sculpture garden (fig. 15).[35] In this bucolic, pedagogical setting located within an enclosed urban space, which is structurally and ideologically meant to evoke the idyllic location in which Plato founded his Academy in a sacred grove near Athens, Michelangelo received some sort of training, albeit not an officially institutionalized one, under the guidance of Bertoldo di Giovanni (ca. 1440–1491), a Medici favorite and pupil of Donatello (1386/7–1466), who presided over the garden and its various edifying activities devoted to Lorenzo the Magnificent's highly valued collection of classical antiquities.[36] At the same time Michelangelo very much benefited intellectually from his participation as an intimate member of the Medici household during these formative years of his growth as an artist, profiting from the insights and ideas of such luminaries as the great humanist Agnolo Poliziano (1454–1494), who provided Michelangelo with the subject matter for his first significant secular project in sculpture, the *Battle between Centaurs and Lapiths*, a bas-relief deliberately designed to rival in conception the carvings on ancient sepulchers, as well as Bertoldo di Giovanni's own *Battle between Romans and*

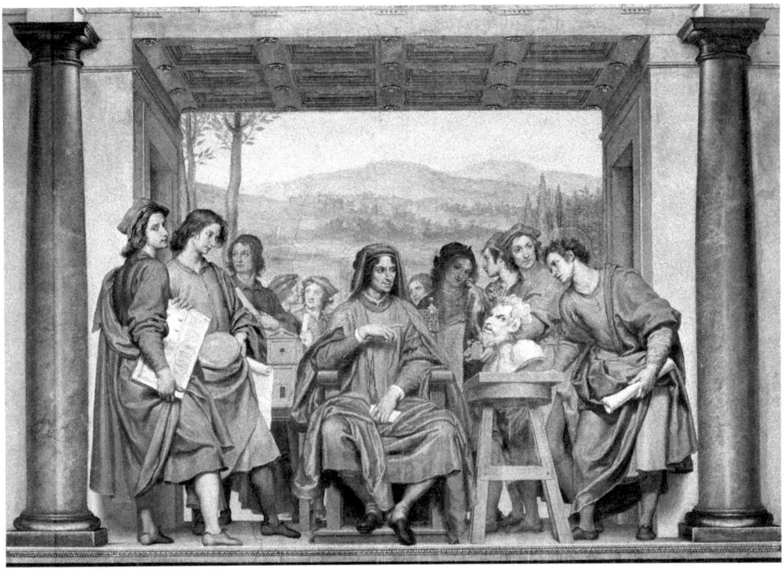

15. Ottavio Vannini (1585–1643), *Lorenzo the Magnificent and the Young Artists in His Garden School* (1638–42). Museo degli Argenti, Palazzo Pitti, Florence, Italy. Photo credit: Scala/ Art Resource, NY.

Barbarians (ca. 1491), a bronze sculpture designed after a Roman sarcophagus located in the Camposanto in Pisa.

Even more important, within the structure of Vasari's narrative we are meant to recognize that the sculpture garden in which Michelangelo received some early training typologically served as a key precursor to the very Accademia del Disegno (1) that Vasari had such a crucial role in creating; (2) that was very much associated in the *Lives* with Michelangelo's genius and a lifelong commitment to the notion that making visual art is a cognitive act grounded in the art of *disegno*; and (3) that did indeed have written, although not extensive, "guidelines binding artists to a prescribed course of study"[37] in a sort of loosely structured *corso di perfezionamento* (advanced course or set of courses, fig. 16).[38] For the Medici sculpture garden located near the Medicean church of San Marco was, as Vasari puts it, "like a school and academy [*come una scuola et academia*] for the young painters and sculptors and all the others who attended to *disegno*, and particularly the young noblemen [*e particolarmente ai giovani nobili*]" (1.692–3, G4.124–5). Roughly seventy years later, however, with the creation of the Accademia del Disegno, Michelangelo does not benefit personally or professionally from such an academic educational program, as he once did as an eager and rather

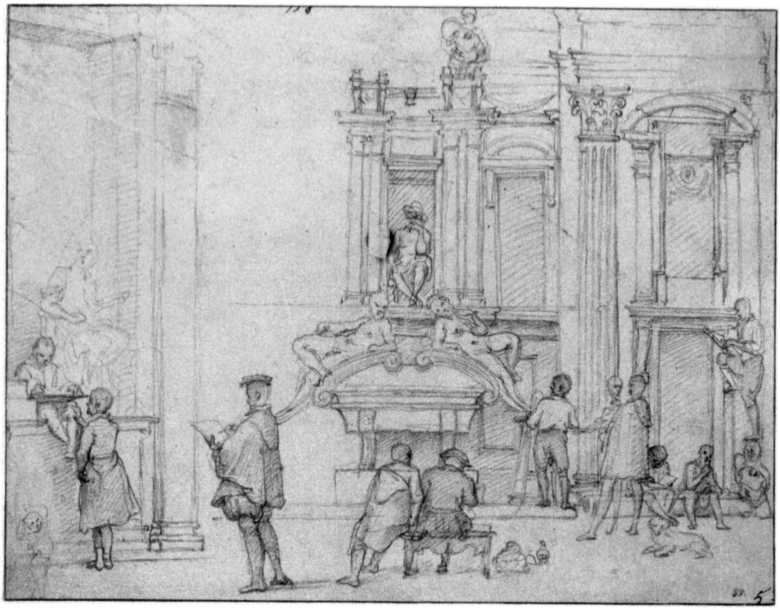

16. Federico Zuccaro (1542–1609), *Artists Studying the Sculptures of the Medici Chapel* (ca. 1564). Musée du Louvre, Paris. © Musée du Louvre, Dist. RMN-Grand Palais/Art Resource, NY. Often taken as an ideal representation of the workings of the Accademia del Disegno.

witty participant in it in his youth.[39] Rather, as a fully recognized master still indefatigably striving for excellence and seeking once more to outdo himself, Michelangelo in his old age lends his name, fame, and authority—in a sense his now legendary, celebrity-like status as a "super-artist"—to the inception and institutionalization of an entirely new educational program sponsored by the Medici and largely initiated and created by Vasari. This new educational program formally makes the Accademia del Disegno the typological fulfillment of the historical process that the sculpture garden, as a sort of early *scuola et academia*, structurally and allegorically prefigured.[40] What is more, this new pedagogical program of the Accademia del Disegno, which eventually took over guild functions for certain visual artists, formally institutionalizes in its approved statutes of 1563 a practical form of instruction. And it did so by officially electing every year a sculptor, a painter, and an architect (collectively dubbed *visitatori*, visitors/inspectors/supervisors) to provide assistance to young men of *ingegno*. But these *visitatori* did *not*, it is important to emphasize, furnish those men with the sort of constant, direct, hands-on, basic training that one putatively received over years as a *fattore* or *garzone* in a guild-regulated workshop.[41] Indeed, the Accademia's loosely structured *corso di perfezionamento* was rooted in a curriculum that united theory and practice in a graded, interlocking study of mathematics, anatomy, and, eventually, natural philosophy. Hence the Accademia's curriculum was not dedicated to furnishing males devoted to the visual arts with the sort of rudimentary training one would normally receive through apprenticeship in a workshop, such as Michelangelo putatively received in that of Ghirlandaio, where one was taught to perform such activities as grinding colors correctly, properly preparing surfaces for paint, and eventually being in a position to be able to imitate perfectly the style ("maniera") of the governing *maestro* (fig. 7). Rather, the Accademia's curriculum was designed to offer its members an Albertian-style, and thus in essence a Vitruvian-style, form of "liberal education" for those invested in succeeding all the more in the *professione* of the nobler visual arts of painting, sculpture, and architecture and equally invested in the crucial notion that making visual art was not just a mechanical but also intellectual act.[42]

Vasari thus clearly wants us to recognize and accept as an indisputable fact that Michelangelo's *ingegno* profited in some significant measure from two important forms of artistic training available to him. First he profited from the long-established apprenticeship program of training in the visual arts, which was overseen and defined by guilds and provided an established form of obvious professional formation for *fattori* as they developed into *garzoni* and thereafter, ideally, into *maestri* running their own *botteghe*, if indeed they had the ways, means, temperament, and businesslike acumen to do so. Subsequently, Michelangelo profited from the newly established and academic-style program of training as a sculptor in Lorenzo the Magnificent's ennobling and classicizing garden, which was overseen by an exalted patron and loosely modeled on the academies of antiquity. In this way, the *Lives* reveals through the life of the greatest exemplar of the visual arts in the period why two key pedagogical programs dedicated to cultivating the *ingegno* of visual artists in late Renaissance Florence are later necessary and, as a consequence, should endure for the benefit of those coming long after Michelangelo has died and long after his lessons as an exemplary but still inimitable artist materially generating ideas through the process of making have been thoroughly absorbed. The Accademia, in the shape of the sculpture garden as a precursor to the institutionalized Accademia del Disegno,[43] does not in any manner permanently replace the longstanding workshop method of artistic pedagogy, which Michelangelo benefited from but outgrew early in his career as an apprentice. And the latter, the workshop, only serves to prepare an artist for the edifying cultural role the former, as a fully institutionalized *scuola et academia*, would play in Vasari's period and beyond by providing a select group of young artists with a sort of *corso di perfezionamento* overseen and undertaken by three academy masters, the so-called *visitatori*, at least one of whom was expected to lecture on Euclid, Vitruvius, and mathematics in general. Above all, both pedagogical programs, as different as they were in practice and conception, helped train Michelangelo and give proper shape to his genius, which is ultimately manifested in the objects he fashioned as works embodying and generating ideas. So too, presumably, the workshop method of artistic training obtained through apprenticeship and the sort of program of supervision advanced through a form of incipient academic training—a program of oversight and *perfezionamento* loosely defined in pedagogical terms in the Accademia's statutes once it was finally realized and institutionalized with Cosimo I's blessing and support—will stand other men of *ingegno* in good stead in Vasari's own time and within his *professione*. Together they will ensure that the remarkable gains made in the visual arts over three hundred years would be consolidated, sustained, and passed on from one generation to another. Read this way, the story of the *Lives* in the Giuntina edition is not only about how the Accademia del Disegno came into being, thanks in large measure to the unremitting efforts of Vasari and his devoted companions committed to the notion that works of visual art generate their own ideas visually. It is also very much about why the Accademia itself is ultimately warranted and necessary in mid-sixteenth-century ducal Medici Florence in order to identify and edify young men of *ingegno*. And in this context Michelangelo's Life can be construed as a crucial case in an underlying cultural and social argument in the Giuntina edition for the existence of the Accademia, or, rather, its co-existence with the workshop practice of cultivating visual artists, with the essential art of *disegno* eventually finding itself thoroughly institutionalized as a state-sponsored discipline dedicated to nurturing precisely the *ingegno* of other such gifted Florentines, binding them together as a new sort of honored, professionalized, male collectivity in the service of the state.[44]

Finally, it is significant and appropriate that with the establishment of the Accademia del Disegno the leader of Florence this time is not the charismatic Lorenzo de' Medici, who oversees a sculpture garden that informally cultivates men of demonstrable genius in the arts; who functions as the father figure and unofficial leader of patriarchal Florence with his impeccable taste in the arts; and who presides over the beginning of Michelangelo's career with his own particular genius as a singularly "magnificent" and therefore liberal, munificent leader of a city so famously and historically invested in the arts.[45] Rather, the leader now is Duke Cosimo I, who is recognized as a nominal "head [*capo*]" (G6.130) of a full-fledged, institutionalized academy that officially cultivates men of recognized genius in the arts through a curriculum of liberal education that unites theory and practice; who functions as their father figure as the now openly legitimated, political leader and ideal, principal patron of Florence with his own demonstrated impeccable taste in the arts; and who can be credited with celebrating Michelangelo as the greatest artist of all time through an elaborate and highly choreographed funeral staged under the aegis of Medicean authority and patronage. The *ingegno* of Michelangelo as a visual artist is thus perfectly suited for the *ingegno* of the Medici as controlling, political leaders in a mutually reinforcing process of cultural exchange and historical fulfillment. One cannot fully exist without the other for Vasari in the new Athens of Cosimo I's ducal Florence.[46] Good, exemplary leaders in politics consequently make for good, exemplary practitioners in the arts, the political *ingegno* of one dovetailing with the artistic *ingegno* of the other. This particular point is conspicuously visualized in one of the ceiling panels in Palazzo Vecchio, in which Duke Cosimo I, who has already been centrally figured as the apotheosis of good leadership (fig. 17), finds himself surrounded by the very artists whose genius he has helped nurture through his patronage and who in their turn have helped fashion his state (fig. 18), not least by representing it, as Vasari has done in the Salone dei Cinquecento itself, as the providential culmination and consolidation of virtuous Medici rule over time, from the first Cosimo to the second even more successful and politically astute one.[47] Moreover, those same artists depicted in the ceiling panel are noticeably configured not in isolation (fig. 18). Rather, Cosimo I's artists collectively form a tightly knit group, each of them represented as individuals contributing to and reinforcing the whole, with Bandinelli and Cellini, for instance, facing each other off in apt, eternal rivalry.

In a number of ways, then, Vasari's understanding of how one must go about detecting and training the *ingegno* of visual artists within their unified yet diversified *professione* resembles ideologically the overall humanist pedagogical project of identifying and cultivating *ingegno*. And there is a very good reason why Vasari periodically turned to that humanist model of edification and incorporated some of its basic principles structurally and rhetorically into his *Lives*. Humanists, who were often called upon to provide artists with the subject matter for their visual inventions, had successfully negotiated for themselves an elevated position in society as arbiters of taste and distinction, operating in a sense as the cultural gatekeepers of polish, elegance, and style. In this respect, the success of humanism as an educational and cultural program provided Vasari with an important model for thinking

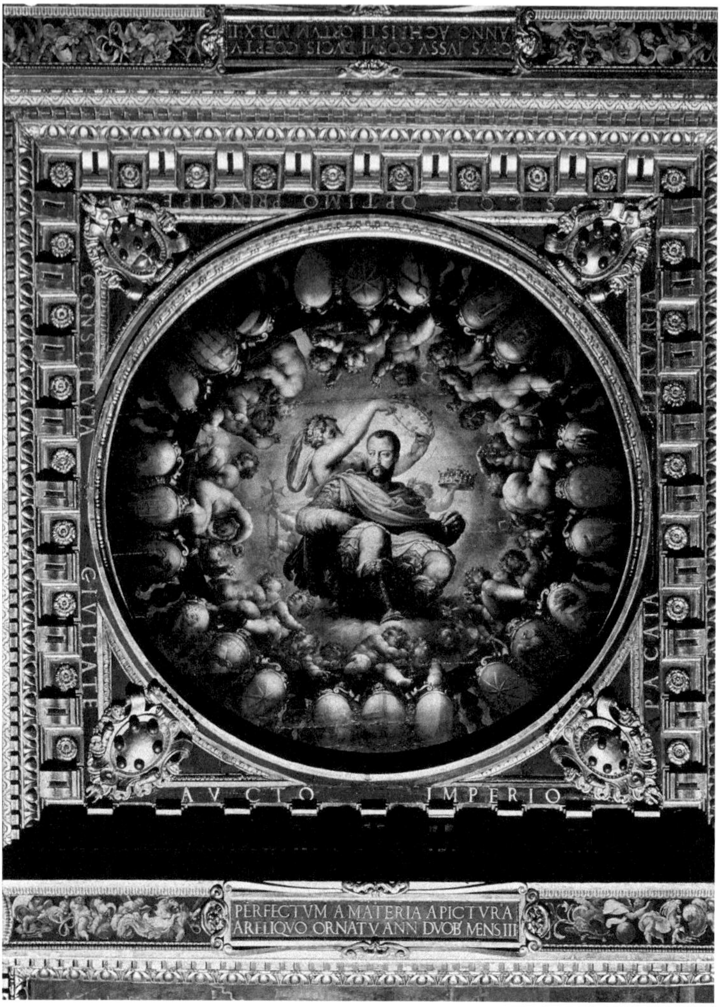

17. Giorgio Vasari (1511–1574), *Apotheosis of Cosimo I* (1563–1565). Palazzo Vecchio, Florence, Italy. Photo credit: Scala/Art Resource, NY.

about the social advancement of all those hardworking, dedicated artists diligently laboring in the *professione* of the visual arts, including Vasari himself. For this reason Vasari has himself conspicuously depicted in his post-1571 portrait (fig. 1) not just as an artist but also as a well-dressed, medal-bearing, honorable gentleman who manifestly executes *and* possesses ideas, with his forehead shining brightly to highlight the centrality of his mind and his well-illumined brush delicately handled as if it were not just being used

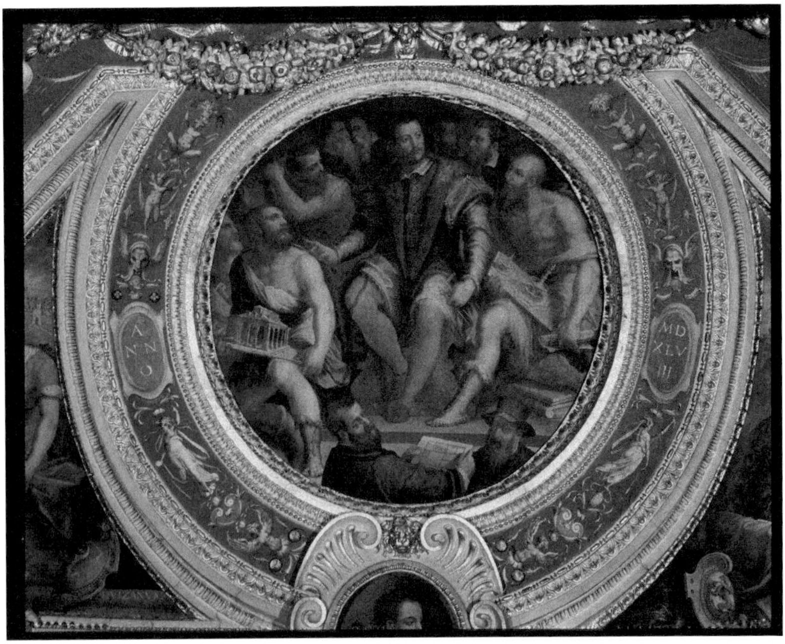

18. Giorgio Vasari (1511–1574), *Cosimo I (1519–1574), Grand Duke of Tuscany, Surrounded by His Artists* (1563–1565). Sala di Cosimo I, Palazzo Vecchio, Florence, Italy. Photo credit: Scala/Art Resource, NY. Bandinelli and Cellini are in profile, fittingly facing one another in close, rivalrous proximity.

to design but also like a stylus manually guided by the Idea in the mind to write. Even Vasari's fingernails, as Philip Sohm has cogently observed, are not soiled by the colors of the painter but instead "rimmed with [the] ink" of a writer, thereby conflating the culturally valued but socially distinct activities of authorship and artisanship that Vasari strategically brings together in writing the *Lives*.[48] Hence what we witness in the portrait of Vasari as a visual artist-cum-writer, much as we do in his representation of himself in the *Lives*, is a man of confident insight about his own character and place in society, as well as a man whose sharp, perspicacious eye has also led him to understand the nature of his own particular genius in the very moment that he offers insights into what constitutes the genius of others within his *professione*. In this respect, Vasari is meant to be viewed once more as exemplary. Not everyone learned how to acquire through training deep, personal insight into his or her own *ingegno*. In particular Pontormo failed miserably in this respect toward the end of his life as he ill-advisedly overstepped the bounds of who he was and what his genius would lead him to be by too egregiously trying to vie with Michelangelo, a man whose works were indeed viewed by Vasari as *quasi inimmitabili*. Know yourself, Vasari thus seems to insist in a Socratic manner over and over again in the *Lives*, interrogate your genius, figure out what makes you tick, as Masaccio, Brunelleschi, Ghiberti, Donatello, Leonardo, Raphael, and Michelangelo, along with so many other exceptional visual artists, most assuredly did, and then do not deviate from it. This is one of the deep, abiding messages of the *Lives*, one of its core ideas, as is evident, for instance, in the epigraph to this chapter. At the same time, this is a core idea that not everyone adheres to within his *professione*, as Vasari also makes evident with some disappointment in the very same epigraph. Hence his stern warning. Be true to your own particular *ingegno*, your own inclination and aptitude, never overextending it beyond its natural, predetermined boundaries so as to *sforzare l'ingegno* ("strain [one's] genius," G4.422),[49] even as you must work studiously against the tendency to paint yourself into every work of art in an act of involuntary automimesis, since every painter, for better or for worse, proverbially "paints himself":[50]

> Every man should be content with doing willingly that work to which he feels himself instinctively drawn by natural inclination [*naturale instinto inclinato*], and should not seek, out of competition, to put his hand to that which has not been given to him by nature [*non gli vien dato dalla natura*], in order not to labor in vain [*faticare invano*], and often to his shame and loss [*vergogna e danno*]. Moreover, when an artist has done enough, he should not seek to overdo it in an effort to surpass [*non si dee cercare di volere strafare per passare innanzi*] those who, with the great help of nature and the particular *grazia* given to them by God [*per grande aiuto di natura e per grazia particolare data loro da Dio*], have produced or are producing miracles of art [*miracoli nell'arte*], because he who is not suited to a thing, will never be able, no matter how he struggles, to arrive where another has easily gone with the help of nature [*perciò che chi non è atto a una cosa, non potrà mai, et affatichisi quanto vuole, arivare dove un altro con l'aiuto della natura è caminato agevolmente*]. There was for example among the older painters Paolo Uccello, who struggled against his abilities to improve, but only slipped back [*tornò sempre indietro*]. The same was done in our own time, and not long ago, by Jacopo Pontormo, and it is seen from experience with respect to many others, as has been said and will be said [*e si è veduto per isperienza in molti altri, come si è detto e come si dirà*]. (1.744, G.4.207–8)

Thus genius, which is a requirement to become an "excellent" painter, sculptor, or architect, is not something that Vasari believes can ever be acquired, the way Castiglione believed, as an accomplished humanist courtier himself, that *grazia* was a quality of character that can be learned, even as he ever-so-cleverly mystifies the very process by which the acquisition of *grazia* can actually occur through some sort of unexplained, and as it turns out entirely inexplicable, process of edification, as I have argued elsewhere.[51] Nor is genius for Vasari something that he surreptitiously or cleverly mystifies. Instead, genius for Vasari is simply the accepted, necessary precondition for what it takes for someone even to begin to be able to become a great visual artist materially producing works that manifestly embody and generate ideas, much less one who will forever alter the course of the history of art. Genius, that driving instinctive, natural inclination and innate brilliance that determines who will be good in one thing or another, has to be there right at the very beginning, baked into the cake, as it were, like the yeast that makes it all rise. But Vasari does not harp on such matters, nor does he wish in the *Lives* to attempt to rationalize what is in all likelihood a mystery to him, much less attempt to ponder its existence as a philosopher might, particularly a sixteenth-century Aristotelian philosopher, for instance, reflecting on the relationship between matter and form. What Vasari does consciously and rather pragmatically do in the *Lives* is offer two different viable pedagogical programs for training *ingegno* within the *professione* of the visual arts and for actively cultivating it. And indeed *ingegno* must, as we have seen, be cultivated, otherwise nothing great will come of it. Not even Giotto, who Vasari at one point indicates miraculously "learned the art [of painting], in a certain manner, without a master [*imparò l'arte, in un certo modo, senza maestro*]" (1.111, G2.114), accomplished what he did as the foundational hero of the rebirth of the visual arts since antiquity without initially receiving and benefiting from some form of significant, technical training—specifically by learning from Cimabue, once Giotto's father willingly and indeed "lovingly" released his son from his filial obligations and allowed him to head off to the grand, commercial city of Florence in order to be properly educated. Giotto may therefore be viewed as an autodidact, naturally producing works of beauty as a solitary shepherd drawing directly from nature in the fields around Vespignano, much as Michelangelo is presented as a largely self-taught, aristocratic-minded artist whose genius for sculpture is naturally imbibed from his birth as he is nursed among the stonemasons in the *contado* (the region surrounding the city). But in the end both artists—the one the first great hero of the Renaissance, the other its supreme, unsurpassed, culminating exemplar; the one socially base in origin, the other far more socially elevated as a member of an *antica casa*—must be conclusively shown in the *Lives* to have received some form of practical, *techne*-based instruction precisely because, it bears repeating, everything "natural" for Vasari must undergo some process of acculturation through a recognized and acceptably channeled social practice of formal training.

Now one longstanding, socially accepted program of education that has obviously stood the test of time, and that has also stood Vasari's period of *rinascita* in good stead, is, as we have seen, the guild-regulated workshop model of inculcation, which the *Lives* consistently demonstrates was successful in training and cultivating a host of young *ingegni*, as *fattori* and *garzoni*, and as a consequence gave rise to a plethora of remarkable artists early on in their careers as they developed into matriculated masters, *maestri*.[52] The story of these men of *ingegno*, trained at least in some measure through apprenticeship within a workshop so that they can eventually develop into master visual artists capable of producing works of sometimes staggering beauty, is in essence largely the story of the *Lives*. All things considered, it is also a great, life-affirming, and triumphant success story as far as prose historical narratives of the period go, as well as a story that has in large measure stood the test of time, despite Vasari's obvious provincialism and somewhat dogmatic preference for all things Florentine and Tuscan. The visual artists Vasari recognizes—and that others in his local culture routinely recognized—as practitioners of remarkable *ingegno* within his unified yet diversified *professione* are indeed for the most part the same ones whose works still prominently grace the walls of major museums and occupy privileged places in coveted, private collections. To be sure, as the early commentators of the *Lives* certainly would have agreed, Vasari's overall hierarchy of value does *not* adequately capture what constitutes a global norm of "excellence" in the *professione* of the visual arts of the period. And we may legitimately wonder why some visual artists do not in fact receive a Life of their own, or are not awarded greater treatment, or are not even mentioned at all.[53] No doubt Benvenuto Cellini (1500–1571) would have felt the same way, presumably with fierce indignation, when he chose to overcompensate, as was also his custom, by obsessively writing, effectively under house arrest,[54] an autobiography that dwarfed even in its incomplete state the length of any single biography in Vasari's *Lives*, including the lengthiest one devoted to Michelangelo.[55]

But even once we have accounted for Vasari's limitations and set aside his obvious biases and acknowledged that he missed this and that, it is still safe to say that when Vasari, in keeping with so many other men of his Florentine and Tuscan culture, isolates Giotto, Ghiberti, Brunelleschi, Bramante, Donatello, Masaccio, Leonardo, Raphael, Michelangelo, and the like as excellent, groundbreaking artists in their time, he has pretty much hit the nail on the head. And when Vasari isolates the fact that the workshop method of inculcating the *professione* of the visual arts was instrumental early on in cultivating these men of *ingegno* and thereby enabling them to become remarkable artists through some sort of disciplined training, he has also, likewise, hit the nail on the head. Which is why, once more, it makes absolute sense that Vasari insisted on calling attention to the fact that the aristocratic-minded Michelangelo, who consciously distanced himself from the *bottega* system of art production, nevertheless unquestionably benefited himself from that very same workshop method of instruction of *ingegno* early on in his life as an apprentice to Ghirlandaio and why Giotto, for all that he was a "natural," also necessarily received formal training from Cimabue and was thus dutifully *ammaestrato*. Vasari vigorously insists on this particular version of events as he constructs his grand, sweeping, celebratory, biographical, and classicizing narrative of the history of art because that tried and true program of training visual artists worked for him at some basic level. Indeed, the workshop model of training worked so well and so reliably and so predictably at times that it could even take some males of rather modest *ingegno* within his *professione* and transform them, it seems, into really quite polished visual artists capable of winning the respect of Vasari and, to their great credit, finding their way into his book by virtue of the fact that they had sufficiently dedicated themselves to prolonged and diligent study and had thereby become true, excellent masters.[56] And one suspects that according to Vasari the underlying desire of every single living or dead painter, sculptor, and architect mentioned by him in his book was in the end to find his place in the *Lives*, much as the tacit yearning of all Homeric heroes, even though they could have never known it as they sought to win everlasting glory on the battlefield, is to be remembered—in essence "named"—in a Homeric poem.

So why the need for the Accademia del Disegno? Why not just leave well enough alone? Why, pedagogically speaking, insist on institutionalizing the *professione* of the visual arts within the context of academic life, which in Florence was principally devoted in Vasari's lifetime to civil conversation, fellowship, and collaboration rather than artisanal pedagogy and formal, practical instruction, with the notable exception, to be sure, of Baccio Bandinelli's *academia* ensconced in his very own workshop (fig. 19)? There are many answers to that question.[57] But one worth mentioning in conclusion and in light of this chapter's focus on the Italian Renaissance cultivation of *ingegno* is that Vasari must have felt that by formally establishing such an academy with the blessings and direct, legitimizing support and patronage of Duke Cosimo I, he could only have helped elevate visual artists culturally and socially by actively seeking to represent them as thoughtful, learned men—in a word, as "academicians"—whose distinctly visual ideas were born out of the very technical *and* intellectual practice of making objects through the now fully institutionalized, state-legitimated art of *disegno*. In effect, with the creation

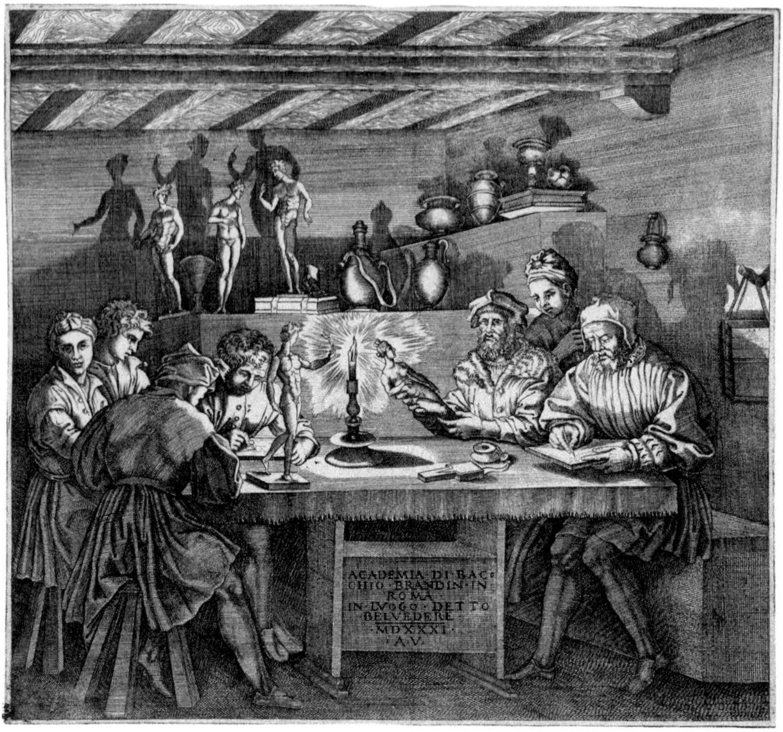

19. Agostino dei Musi (Agostino Veneziano, ca. 1490–ca. 1540), *The Academy of Baccio Bandinelli* (1531). Biblioteca Marucelliana, Florence, Italy. © DeA Picture Library/Art Resource, NY.

of the Accademia Vasari was able to establish an ennobling, learned, unifying, and bounded space for them as Lorenzo de' Medici had once done for a variety of *giovani nobili* in the arts. And in doing so he inevitably sought to present visual artists as recognized intellectual equals to humanists, or at least their near equals, with their own acknowledged discipline, *professione*, and state-sponsored institution. Put differently, if Vasari was looking to acquire prestige and mark visual artists with cultural and social distinction as men of ideas, which was pretty much standard operating procedure for him, then imitating the Accademia Fiorentina (which was dedicated to a sharing of practices in the verbal arts among a privileged group of literati) by founding an Accademia del Disegno (which was dedicated to a sharing of practices in the visual arts among a privileged group of painters, sculptors, and architects) readily presented itself to him as the logical and irresistible mechanism by which he could increase worldly recognition for himself, other likeminded visual artists, and, even more broadly, his *professione*, without in fact ever creating what we would no doubt call today a "professional school." Indeed, the Accademia's statutes in essence prescribed basically an advanced pedagogical program—a sort of loosely structured *corso di perfezionamento*, as we have seen—when it came to the actual training on the part of elected masters of certain young men, "who will be chosen and the most aptly prepared to learn the things belonging to the arts of *disegno* by coming either here [*quivi*]" (which is to say, in the provisional space provided by Cosimo I for the activities of the Accademia)[58] "or to that place belonging to that [particular] master [*o in quel luogo appartenente a quello maestro*]" (which is to say, in the *maestro*'s very own professional space, presumably his workshop).

Accordingly, there is every reason to believe that Vasari assumed, in keeping with the assumptions of others writing after him,[59] that the workshop model of training and supervision would continue to take care of the ongoing, daily, practical, and basic business of training young men of *ingegno* in the early stages of their careers and thus pragmatically serve, as it had for so long, to oversee perfectly well the progress of those capable young men of *ingegno* in the course of their fledgling development. Doubtless Vasari also imagined that some of those young men might then just turn out to be excellent masters in their own right and, in the course of time, be identified as masters worthy of recognition by the so-called *visitatori*, whose job it was to go about visiting the "working premises [*stanze*]" of Florentine *giovani* in search of fresh, young talent to be absorbed eventually into the Accademia's professionalized ranks.[60] However, Vasari also clearly felt the need to create a new sort of pedagogical and conversational space for all those already accomplished and acclaimed artists who lived and worked not only in a Florence brilliantly controlled by an autocratic, repressive duke but also even outside of it.[61] For Vasari it was indeed professionally imperative to establish a more socially elevated and interactive, humanist-style, educational, and confraternal space located eventually beyond the traditional purview of guild oversight,[62] where elected sculptors, painters, and architects of recognized caliber could meet—perhaps not unlike all those bookish philosophers milling about in Raphael's idealized *School of Athens* (fig. 2)?—to collectively improve, collaborate, compete, and ultimately acquire ever more insight into, and thus arguably ever more mastery over, what had originally dictated their limitations, opened up creative horizons, and mastered them before they ever began to set forth on the path of becoming excellent practitioners within the overall *professione* of the visual artists: namely, their underlying and enabling *ingegno*.[63]

3

PRESTEZZA/SPEED

Up to this point, I have discussed the works of others with that greatest diligence and sincerity that I have mastered, thanks to my intellectual talents, and was able to make use of, but now, having reached the end of these labors of mine, I want to gather together and make known to the world the works that Divine Goodness, having bestowed its *grazia* on me, has enabled me to execute. For even though they have not achieved that perfection I might wish, nevertheless, if they were examined by someone who would do so with a sound eye [*sano occhio*], it will be seen that they have been wrought by me with study, diligence, and loving labor [*che elle sono state da me con istudio, diligenza, et amorevole fatica lavorate*], and that if they are not worthy of praise, then they may at least be excused, considering that I cannot hide them since they are out in the open and everyone can see them.

—Giorgio Vasari, "Description of the Works of Giorgio Vasari," the *Lives* (1568)[1]

One reason the art historian Charles Hope has voiced serious doubts as to whether Vasari could have possibly written the entire *Lives* has to do with what we might call the element of speed.[2] Vasari was a busy man during the period in which he worked in earnest on the book, weighed down as usual with pressing commissions. So how, Hope reasonably wonders in a rather amusing manner, could he have also conceivably produced in roughly a year or so the first draft of an extremely lengthy book?

> In short, everything confirms that Vasari ... began systematic research for the book no earlier than the summer of 1546, and that the writing of the text was begun after his return to Florence in October. The bulk of it had been written when he went to Rimini around the end of September 1547. The Torrentiniana amounts to almost 300,000 words. If Vasari wrote it himself, it would mean that, while continuing to work as a painter, he wrote about nine times as fast as a diligent UK doctoral student with a computer, about fourteen times as fast as Cellini, and about twenty times

as fast as Bellori. For someone who had no experience as an author, this is surely unrealistic.[3]

My aim in invoking Hope's position here is not to explore at any length the extent to which Vasari did or did not author much of the book that bears his name—and his name alone—on the title page of both the 1550 Torrentiniana and 1568 Giuntina editions (figs. 5 and 6).[4] Nor is it my principal aim in this chapter to investigate what impact Hope's polemical but entirely warranted questioning of Vasari's role as an author has on our overall understanding of Vasari as a visual artist capable of crafting such a lengthy narrative with its own internal logic and design (something that does indeed beggar the imagination, even if he had been trained modestly in the *studia humanitatis*). Rather, my primary concern here is with the notion of "speed" implicitly raised by Hope, the notion, that is, of *prestezza*, to use the Italian term employed by Vasari and widely current in his period, along with such synonyms as *velocità*, *veloce*, *sollecitudine*, *pronto*, *prontezza*, *spedito*, and *fretta*.[5] My broad claim is that Vasari, who obviously wished to convey to his readers at the end of the Giuntina edition that he originally wrote the first draft of the book with a sort of hurried alacrity, had a significant investment in speed as a topic in the *Lives*. This is particularly true when it comes to investigating how Vasari characterized himself as a painter and, just as important, how he ascribed to speed a considerable role in the development of the history of art from the time of Cimabue to the present, precisely during a period of dynamic social change increasingly fueled by a voracious appetite for quality works of visual art.[6] To see how this is so, I will examine in this chapter why Vasari was so deeply interested in the concept of *prestezza* in the *Lives* and, more specifically, how it resonated with his own sense of self as a professional artist working in a culture of conspicuous consumption.[7] In conclusion I will briefly consider the relationship between Vasari's exceptional output as a fast-paced writer and his equally remarkable work as a fast-paced visual artist, bearing in mind, however, that this was also the very same period in the Italian Renaissance when the *poligrafi* (polygraphs)—those rough-and-ready, commercial, and sometimes crass writers active in Republican, mercantile Venice—were instrumentalizing the printing press and producing voluminous works of literature in the vernacular with exceptional speed. To be sure, visual artists such as Vasari and the *poligrafi* worked quickly for different reasons—the former often to meet the needs of impatient patrons, the latter to make money as swiftly as possible within the expanding print marketplace—but in both cases they did so, it is important to emphasize, in a culture that was already beginning to appreciate speed as a topic so very worthy of discussion, recognition, and even, as we shall see, fascination. Or to put it differently, Vasari once again fruitfully engages a topic of historically determined interest in the *Lives* (a topic that extends itself to such varied areas of cultural interest as fast-paced dueling, swift horsemanship, and rapid mail delivery) and innovatively incorporates it, here for the first time ever, as a significant issue into a history of visual, as opposed to verbal, art.[8]

I begin with what is to my mind one of the more complex uses of the term *prestezza* in the Giuntina edition of the *Lives*, which is an edition about twice as long as the first one—longer, that is to say, than David Foster Wallace's gargantuan *Infinite Jest* but mercifully shorter than Marcel Proust's even lengthier *À la recherche du temps perdu* (*Remembrance of Things Past*). Vasari, as is his wont, is moving fluidly along in his narrative, listing a variety of his accomplishments in the culminating Life of the *Lives*. All of these accomplishments achieved within and for his *professione* are also presented in a manner that keeps our focus on the facts about the art produced rather than the producer of it, as typically occurs more often in the Giuntina than the Torrentiniana edition.[9] But something then happens. Vasari casually diverts our attention from the discussion at hand by closing off his description of a painting with an editorial aside. Since this particular Life, referred to as a "Descrizione dell'opere" ("Description of the works") rather than strictly as a "Vita" ("Life"), is about Vasari, this particular aside is not surprisingly about him. And in his brief, telling digression, Vasari gives us to understand that he completed virtually all his work as a visual artist with the greatest imaginable speed, even though a sense of modesty—a false sense of modesty, to be sure[10]—prevents him from openly saying so. Or to frame the matter slightly differently, as he affects possessing the virtuosity of *facilitas* (a certain facility, *facilità*, in exercising one's expertise), Vasari here presents himself as someone who produced his art nonchalantly, with the unhurried, effortless ease of courtly *sprezzatura*. Gentlemen, after all, should never appear to rush in whatever they do, whatever their profession.[11] But in truth Vasari in the end only calls attention in his calculated digression to the obvious fact that he instead produced his art with, as he puts it, *grandissima prestezza*:

> I will certainly say this because I can do so with truth, that I have always produced my pictures, inventions, and *disegni* [*disegni* here means not just designs and ideas but also drawings], of whatever sort, I will not say with very great speed [*grandissima prestezza*], but truly with an incredible facility and lack of effort [*con incredibile facilità e senza stento*]. As evidence for this, as I have said elsewhere, let me cite the very large canvas [*la grandissima tela*] that I painted in only six days [*in sei giorni soli*] in San Giovanni di Firenze,

> in the year 1542 [*sic*], for the baptism of my lord Don Francesco de' Medici, today the ruler of Florence and Siena. (2.1034, G.6.381)

This is certainly impressive. Six days! An entire canvas! And not a small canvas but a very large one, a *grandissima* canvas done, it would seem, by the quality of Vasari's disavowed yet altogether evident *grandissima* speed. Characterizing himself in this manner, Vasari thereby makes himself appear all the more heroically *grandissimo* in our estimation as he revels in his ability to complete enormous tasks with such facility, effortlessness, and, to be sure, velocity.[12] And that's not all. Vasari, we learn shortly thereafter, also manages to complete work on the ceiling and walls of the massive Salone dei Cinquecento in the Palazzo Vecchio in Florence well ahead of schedule, "not only in much less time [*in molto manco tempo*] than I had promised and the work might be considered to require, but," he vaunts, "in less than even I or his most illustrious Excellency ever thought" (2.1057, G6.401). All this leaves the Duke not only "very satisfied [*sodisfattissim(o)*]" but also "astonished [*maravigliat(o)*]," since the entire complex painting cycle, which was executed "with so much haste [*di tanta sollecitudine*]," was completed in time for a spectacular wedding ceremony (2.1057, G6.401).[13] What is more, Vasari yet again meets the architectural needs of the Duke by expediently building in 1564 "the great corridor" connecting the Uffizi with the ducal palace "under [Vasari's own] direction and after [his] design in five months [*in cinque mesi*], although it is a work that one might think impossible to finish in less than five years [*meno di cinque anni*]" (2.1059, G6.403; see also G6.312). This remarkable accomplishment and a variety of other ones described in the *Lives* were all realized, Vasari assures us, with "something of haste and speed [*qualche fretta e prestezza*]" (2.1059, G6.403). The obvious semantic redundancy here—*fretta* is of course synonymous with *prestezza*—adds rhetorical emphasis. Vasari is not just "speedy" but, as it were, "speedy speedy." Or as modern Italians with their penchant for doubling words would say today, Vasari was *presto presto*. All things considered, Vasari could have easily appropriated the classical adage *festina lente* (make haste slowly), which appeared on so many emblems in the Italian Renaissance, and justifiably transformed it into *festina celeriter* (make haste quickly) as his own personal motto to characterize his longstanding practice of producing works of visual art so rapidly. He certainly demonstrates as much to Giovann' Antonio Lappoli (1492–1552), a rather lazy visual artist for Vasari, by completing, he boasts, an enormous painting full of "more than sixty larger than life figures [*più di sessanta figure maggiori del vivo*]" for the refectory of the Abbey of Sts. Fiora and Lucilla in Arezzo in, astonishingly enough, a mere forty-two days (2.211, G5.185; see the epigraph to Chapter 4 for the relevant, translated passage: the painting in question is the *Marriage of Esther and Ahasuerus*, 1548). And he certainly demonstrates as much all the more categorically in a letter he sent to Cosimo I's secretary, Jacopo Guidi, on June 11, 1557, in which Vasari reports with some self-satisfaction and candor that "being quick will be so much more pleasing to me, given that I get annoyed by all the things that move slowly, in contrast to our life, which is so brief [*tanto mi sarà più caro l'esser presto, quanto io annoio tutte le cose che son tarde di moto, contrarie alla vita nostra ch'è sì breve*]."[14]

Vasari was not the only person of the period to comment on his ability to complete projects quickly. It played a significant role in how others persistently described him, for better or for worse, as a visual artist. In a letter sent to Cardinal Alessandro Farnese in 1543—two years after Vasari's completion of the *grandissima* painting (now lost) executed with *grandissima prestezza*—the humanist Paolo Giovio, credited *within* the *Lives*, as we have seen, with having inspired the writing *of* the *Lives*, describes Vasari as *expedito*, meaning not just expeditious, practical-minded, diligent, and efficient but also, simply put, quick. Three years later, in 1546, the cosmographer Don Miniato Pitti, who maintained close ties with Cosimo I's court and is viewed in the *Lives* as a man "knowledgeable in many sciences and painting" (T6.22),[15] would suggest much the same in a letter to Vasari. Unlike Jacopo Pontormo, Agnolo Bronzino, Francesco Salviati, and Giovanni Battista del Tasso, Vasari knew how to get things done swiftly in his *professione*: "sappiate meglio spacciare la mercanzia vostra" ("you know better [than anyone] how to dispatch your business with alacrity").[16] So it was that others, such as Don Ippolito of Monte Oliveto, characterized Vasari as exceptionally speedy to even Vasari himself,[17] while conversely the Italian mannerist painter and architect Federico Zuccaro (1540/2–1609) viewed this particular aspect of Vasari's craft and character—his signature ability to complete projects of visual art with such noteworthy *prestezza*—far more negatively, as the art historian Phillip Sohm has meticulously documented. "Poor Giorgio," Zuccaro mockingly comments, "who did not know how to do anything except quickly [*il povero Giorgio che non sapeva che far presto*]."[18] Indeed, Vasari's particular talent for working rapidly did not always serve him well in the minds of, say, Benvenuto Cellini, Bronzino, and, much later, the Carracci.[19] And as Vasari even admits in talking about the commission of the Salone dei Cinquecento, perhaps he did not completely satisfy everyone concerned in his haste to complete it in time for the magnificent 1565 wedding celebration of Francesco I de' Medici, the eldest son of Cosimo I de' Medici, and Joanna of Austria, the youngest daughter of the Holy Roman Emperor, Ferdinand I. "The very awesome and grand occasion" of that particular artistic commission, Vasari observes in passing, "will have to serve to excuse me if on account of having been rushed I failed to satisfy [my patron] completely [*doverrà scusarmi se io non avessi per cotal fretta satisfatto pienamente*]" (2.1057, G6.401).[20]

In making this claim, Vasari is no doubt once more adopting the false modesty topos, acting with humility as he simultaneously elevates himself by listing the "variety of great things of war on land and water" he in fact included in the massive painting cycle that he dutifully, as well as expeditiously, completed—things such as "destructions of cities, bombardments, skirmishes, attacks, constructions of cities, public counsels, ancient and modern ceremonies," not to mention "many captains, generals, soldiers, and other leaders" as well as "all the varieties of bodies, faces, vestments, habiliments, armor, helmets, cuirasses, various headdresses, horses, harnesses, caparisons, artillery of every kind, navigations, tempests, rainstorms, snowstorms, and so many other things" (2.1057, G6.401, see also G6.310). And yet, all things considered, Vasari, despite his proclivity to be boastful about his many achievements in his *professione*, may well have been tempted to be somewhat cautious here in talking with too much pride about this specific commission, mindful of the prior occasion when, pressed for time in 1546, the year in which he was effectively engaged to write the *Lives*, he was forced to work with extraordinary *prestezza* on a similarly vast scale. For that commission, which also certainly constituted a "very awesome and grand occasion," Vasari successfully completed an elaborate painting cycle in the restricted time allotted him, a mere one hundred days to cover primarily three walls with elaborate illusionistic frescoes celebrating the life of Paul III and his extensive, groundbreaking patronage in Rome.[21] In the process, however, he pretty much botched the job, not only as far as others were concerned (Michelangelo, legend has it, curtly and disparagingly remarked "It shows [*si vede*]") but also, when all was said and done, as far as Vasari himself was concerned (figs. 20 and 21).[22] As Vasari writes after describing at some length the frescoed panels of the great Salone dei Cento Giorni, "the whole work," which he executed "with the greatest speed possible [*con maggior prestezza che fusse possibile*]" (2.1040, G6.387),

> is full of the most beautiful inscriptions and mottoes by [Paolo] Giovio, and there is one in particular which says that those pictures were all executed in a hundred days; which, indeed, as a young man [*io come giovane*], I did do, being such that I gave no thought to anything but serving that lord, who, as I have said, desired to have the work finished in that time for a particular purpose. But in truth, although I exerted myself greatly in making cartoons

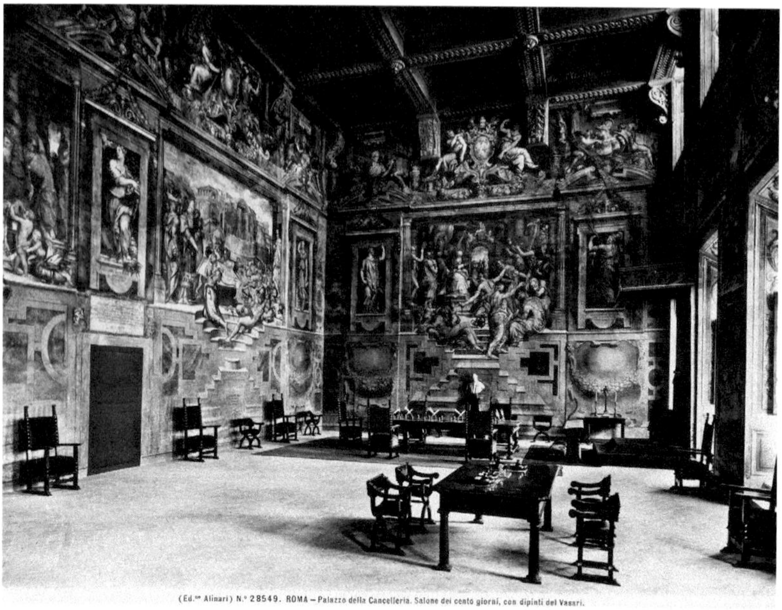

20. Giorgio Vasari (1511–1574), *Salone dei Cento Giorni* (1546). Palazzo della Cancelleria, Rome, Italy. Photo credit: Alinari, Florence.

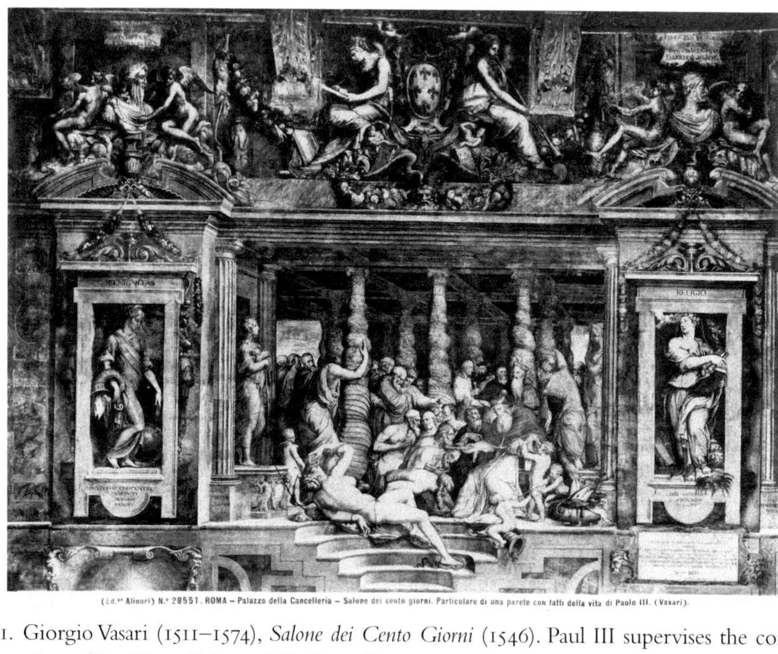

21. Giorgio Vasari (1511–1574), *Salone dei Cento Giorni* (1546). Paul III supervises the construction of San Pietro. Palazzo della Cancelleria, Rome, Italy. Photo credit: Alinari, Florence.

> and studying that work, I confess that I erred putting it afterwards in the hands of assistants [*garzoni*] in order to execute it more quickly [*per condurla più presto*], as I was obliged to do [*come mi bisognò fare*]; for it would have been better to toil over it a hundred months [*cento mesi*] and do it with my own hand, whereby, although I would not have done it in such a way as to satisfy my wish to please the Cardinal and to maintain my own honor, I would at least have had the satisfaction of having executed it with my own hand [*arei pure avuto quella satisfazione d'averla condotta di mia mano*]. However, that error [*errore*] was the reason that I resolved that I would never again do any work without finishing it entirely by myself over a first sketch done by the hands of assistants from designs by my hand. (2.1042, G6.388)

When referring to that particular commission in the autobiographical narrative of his Life, then, Vasari, who apparently chalks up to youthful ignorance (*io come giovane*) whatever flaws the massive fresco cycle seems to contain, takes the opportunity to use the occasion as a teachable moment. Didactically, he presents it as a sort of cautionary tale about what happens when an accomplished visual artist tries to do too much too quickly and with too little oversight. Vasari was a brilliant, multitasking, attentive, entrepreneurial manager who knew how to get things done with exceptional speed. And he could also occasionally create with exceptional speed massive, sophisticated visual programs that required an instructional book for even a learned viewer to use as a handy guide in order to decipher fully the images' hidden allegorical meanings, as in the case of the posthumously printed *Ragionamenti del sig. cavaliere Giorgio Vasari, pittore et architetto aretino, sopra le inventioni da lui dipinte in Firenze nel palazzo di Loro Altezze serenissime, con lo illustriss. & eccellentiss. signor don Francesco Medici, allora principe de Firenze* (*Discourses by the Gentleman Knight Giorgio Vasari, Painter and Architect of Arezzo, on the Inventions Painted by Him in the Palace of Your Most Serene Highnesses in Florence, to the Most Illustrious and Most Excellent Don Francesco Medici, then Prince of Florence*, 1588). However, sometimes—or at least once, Vasari lets us know in the *Lives*—he faltered and committed an *errore*.[23] Of course, in all fairness to Vasari, he does not in truth blame his own *prestezza* for the supposed shortcomings of the frescoes. Rather, he blames the fact that in the interest of *prestezza* he apportioned out the work to other unreliable and inferior hands assisting him, his contracted *garzoni*. That is to say, Vasari himself was not a sloppy worker in those instances when he had to paint ever so quickly. Far from it. He himself can only do excellent work with speed, he insists throughout the *Lives*, but there was not sufficient time in this case for *him* to do everything. So he was forced, unfortunately, to deviate from what he afterwards resolved to maintain as his standard working process in that he did not personally revise those parts of the Salone that were painted by assistants. Vasari drives this point home especially forcefully in the Life of Perino del Vaga when he self-reflexively speaks of the risks a master artist runs in hiring assistants to handle much of the work in one's stead. "Princes," he notes with the self-awareness of someone who has routinely dealt with illustrious men of power and wealth, consistently want their commissioned works of visual art completed "quickly [*presto*]," and this, it stands to reason,

> perhaps benefits the craftsmen who labor upon them, yet, if they were the ablest men in the world, they could never feel that love for the works of others which a man feels for his own. Nor, however well drawn the cartoons may be, can they be imitated exactly and as thoroughly as by the hand of their author, who, seeing the work going to ruin, in despair leaves it to fall into complete destruction. He, then, who thirsts for honor, should do his own painting. This I can say from experience, for after I had labored with the greatest possible pains on the cartoons for the Sala della Cancelleria in the Palace of San Giorgio in Rome, the work having to be executed with great haste in a hundred days [*per aversi a fare con gran prestezza in cento dì*], a vast number of painters were employed to paint it, who departed so far from their outlines and their true form, that I made a resolution to which I have adhered, that from that time onward no one should lay a hand on any works of mine [*d'allora in qua nessuno ha messo mano in sull'opere mie*]. Whoever, therefore, wishes to ensure long life for his name and his works, should undertake fewer and do them all with his own hand, if he desires to obtain that full measure of honor that a man of exalted genius seeks to acquire. (2.182, G5.155)

Two views about *prestezza*, then, each with a clear upside and downside, are set before us throughout the *Lives* as we are invited to trace the labors of the author himself, particularly as his productivity is described in his autobiographical Life, the culminating Life in his book and thus one that Vasari surely meant us to pay particular attention to as a summation of some of his views on how to go about making visual art. On the upside, *prestezza* can signal effortless facility and virtuosity coupled with a remarkable ability to get things done in a timely and businesslike manner. As such it can elicit both wonder and satisfaction, two highly desirable emotions, Vasari makes evident throughout the *Lives*, that a patron wants to feel upon viewing a completed commission and that a painter surely wants a patron to experience when the work of visual art is finally finished.[24] Vasari makes this especially evident when he remarks, in a letter to Francesco I de' Medici, how Pius V responded with satisfied astonishment at the speed with which he was progressing in the completion of the decoration of three chapels. The pope, Vasari observes in his letter of February 10, 1571, "is stupefied [*stupiscie*]."[25] Small wonder, then, that Cardinal Alessandro Farnese commissioned Vasari to paint the fresco cycle for a massive room in the Palazzo della Cancelleria and that Duke Cosimo I similarly hired him a decade and a half later to complete so many vast and impressive undertakings in an effort to enhance the visual splendor of his expanding state. Here is a man—a courtly, well-mannered, fastidious, yet businesslike man—you could always count on. Not only would he meet a deadline, he would sometimes beat it. Tell him to paint a room in a hundred days? Done. Ask him to paint an entire ceiling trumpeting the achievements of a dynasty fashioning itself on the grand scale? Done. Have him bridge the Arno with a novel, elevated, kilometer-long corridor securely linking the newly constructed official state offices with the newly redesigned official ducal residence and its verdant, trellised gardens? Done. This is the right man for the economy of late Renaissance Italy with its booming court culture, its keen investment in nascent state building, and its equally keen appetite for conspicuous consumption.[26] If you want to collect and have constructed more and more quality stuff on an imperial scale, either you need more quality artists working at an average pace to feed your voracious appetite or, conversely, you need a stunningly expeditious artist capable of producing lots of wonder-inspiring things, from fresco cycles to massive building complexes to innovative, suspended corridors, at a seemingly superhuman pace. But therein lies the problem. For *prestezza*, on the downside, can all too easily lead to shoddy workmanship, no matter how excellent the underlying *disegno* is or how dexterous and competent the supervising master artist may be. There are so many risks involved in asking one person to achieve so much. Too many commissions, too little time, not enough reliable hands to cover diligently all the paintings and ensure that things are never done in a slipshod manner. Hence the fiasco of the Cancelleria, the so-called Salone dei Cento Giorni. Hence the cautionary tale. Hence Vasari's success even in failure as he informs us about a single unfortunate, youthful lapse in judgment on his part within the context of the other remarkable triumphs he achieved in his *professione* thanks to his signature *prestezza*.

There is a prehistory to this positive valuing of *prestezza* as it is conceived in the *Lives*, and that prehistory addresses many of its noteworthy rewards, culminating in the figure of Vasari as one of the great, exemplary heroes of speed in the early modern era, as a man who even potentially surpasses the visual artists of recognized speed from classical antiquity recorded in Pliny's *Natural History*, and predictably as well once more in the *Lives*.[27] Such artists from classical antiquity include Pausias, who "finished a painting in a single day in order to give his work the reputation of speed [*celeritatis famam*]," and Nicomachus of Thebes, who was so remarkably quick with his brush that "no other painter was ever a more rapid worker [*nec fuit alius in ea arte velocior*]" (35.124), along with his pupil Philoxenus of Etreria, who, in the process of imitating "the rapidity of his master [*celeritatem praeceptoris*]," eventually "executed [paintings] with still more rapidity of technique."[28] However, Vasari's particular narrative of fulfillment with regard to *prestezza* effectively begins in the *Lives* not—oddly enough—with Cimabue or Giotto, when the revival of the visual arts, as Vasari articulates it, was in its childhood and visual artists according to him were only starting to break off the shackles of artistic ignorance and thereby acquire competence in producing art in the "modern," as opposed to the clumsy and rough "Greek" (meaning Byzantine) or "German" (meaning Gothic), styles. Instead, Vasari's narrative about the tripartite historical development of speedy art production in his *rinascita* begins in earnest at the very *end* of the first "age" (running roughly from 1250 to 1430), when the revival of the visual arts is about to advance from childhood into the second age, the period, that is to say, of adolescence (running roughly from 1400 to 1500). Historically, at this point, according to Vasari, visual artists are starting to experience a much greater sense of confidence, freedom, and control in their *professione* because they have mastered certain techniques and more thoroughly grasped the classicizing rules of visual art that govern how they should use them.[29] And one of the essential techniques mastered was the art of fresco painting on wet, rather than dry, plaster (*buon fresco*, true fresco, as opposed to *fresco secco*), a technique, we already know from the introductory section of the *Lives*, that requires "a dexterous, resolute, and swift hand [*una mano dèstra, resoluta e veloce*]" (G1.129). Simply put, speed is essential in painting *buon fresco* because the hand applying pigment needs to work with self-assurance and alacrity before the plaster dries and crystallizes into the chemical compound of hardened, colored limestone—something that painters later working quickly in the medium of oil did not have to concern themselves with. This, then, is the context in which Vasari introduces Lorenzo di Bicci (ca. 1350–ca. 1427), the very last figure mentioned in the period designated as the first "age," whose quick wit is readily matched by his equally quick hand. Called to dinner at the precise moment in which he has just applied the *intonaco* (wet plaster) to the wall, the clever Lorenzo whimsically calls out to the Prior of the Convent of Santa Croce, without missing a beat, that they should go ahead and pour his bowl of soup since he plans to finish the task soon enough and will therefore presumably be sitting at the table with everyone else before his hot dish turns cold. "Wherefore it is with good reason," Vasari comments, "that men say that Lorenzo had such speed with his hands [*tanta velocità nelle mani*], had such great practice in coloring, and had such resoluteness, that no other man ever had more" (1.237, G2.318).

It is hardly surprising, then, that Domenico Ghirlandaio, who labors in Vasari's second "age" of the development of the *professione* of the visual arts but also on the cusp of the third, is said to have become "so prompt and speedy and adept [*sì pronto e presto e facile*]" as a draughtsman that, while at his father's (Tommaso Bigordi's) goldsmith shop where he happened to have worked at that point early in his career, he sketched every person that passed by and "rendered a likeness of them right away [*li faceva sùbito somigliare*]" (1.516, G3.476). In just the same way, but in more general terms, it is entirely significant that the gradual perfection of various artistic techniques, progressively refined through an enhanced understanding of the rules and absolute standards underpinning the *professione* of the visual arts, has in the end allowed the artists of the third and final age of Vasari's narrative (those liberated artists of the sixteenth century, that is to say, who belong to the period of adulthood running from roughly 1480 to 1550/68) to be able to produce remarkably accomplished works of visual art with extraordinary facility, efficiency, and, most importantly for our purposes, velocity as they now achieve more reliably and consistently a certain supreme *grazia* in everything they do:

> For what most concerns this art is that they have now brought it to such perfection, and made it so easy for someone who possesses *disegno*, invention, and coloring, that, whereas those early masters took six years to paint one panel, today our masters can paint six in one year [*che dove prima da que' nostri maestri si faceva una tavola in sei anni, oggi in un anno questi maestri ne fanno sei*], as I can testify with the greatest confidence both from what I have seen and done; and our pictures are clearly much more highly finished and perfect than those executed in former time by masters of account. (1.621, G4.10)

The Venetian artist Sebastiano del Piombo (ca. 1485–1547), just to drive home the same point and clinch the matter in the *Lives*, is said to have made a similar sort of observation once he put down his brush and, flush with income as the Keeper of the Papal Seals and shamelessly indolent, no longer feels the need to paint any more in order to earn a living. "There are now men in the world of genius/talent," Vasari records Sebastiano as having remarked, "who do in two months what I used to do in two years [*sono oggi al mondo ingegni che fanno in due mesi quello che io soleva fare in due anni*]" (2.151, G5.101).[30]

Accordingly, by the time we have arrived at the third period in the history of the development of the *professione* of the visual arts, a variety of painters, sculptors, goldsmiths, and architects—each as diverse as Giuliano San Gallo (ca. 1445–1516), Andrea da Fiesole (Andrea Ferrucci, ca. 1465–1526), Giovanni Antonio Licinio (ca. 1515–1576), Polidoro da Caravaggio (Polidoro Caldara, ca. 1500–ca. 1543), Maturino Fiorentino (ca. 1490–1528), Giovanni da Castel Bolognese (Giovanni Bernardi, 1494–1553), Valerio Belli (Valerio Vicentino, ca. 1468–1546), Niccolò di Raffaello di Niccolò dei Pericoli (Il Tribolo, ca. 1500–1550), and Ridolfo Ghirlandaio (1483–1561)—all can freely glory in the unharnessed speed of their astonishing productivity.[31] So the exceptional Donato Bramante (ca. 1444–1514) constructs an entire building in Milan "both speedily and perfectly [*e prestamente e perfettamente*]" (1.661, G4.77). All the more impressive, he completes the construction in Rome of the massive and imperial Cortile Belvedere, despite all the faults that are later discovered to be part of it, with "very great speed [*grandissima prestezza*]" (1.663, G4.78) at the behest of the characteristically impatient and imperious Julius II (1443–1513). What is more, Bramante even completes much of the foundation of the new St. Peter's with his "customary speed [*solita prestezza*]" (1.666, G4.82), thereby ensuring that the core, structural conception of his design as a distinctly visual idea would endure long after he has died and therefore could not be easily bowdlerized—something that so often happened to large-scale building enterprises, since architecture, as Vasari well knew, was the one area of the visual arts where major projects notoriously dragged on for lifetimes and beyond (G4.78–9; see also G6.96).[32] For that matter, even the malicious, conniving detractors of Francesco Salviati, who seek to undermine his favor with Cosimo I by repeatedly finding isolated things to censure in his paintings in a petty, discrediting manner, must still recognize and rather grudgingly praise "the excellence of the art that was in him, and the facility and speed [*prestezza*] with which he executed his works so well and completely" (2.569, G5.523). These ambitious, well-trained men of the third "age," the adulthood of the arts, who can produce a variety of artifacts in size and shape with exceptional speed—in the case of Antonio Sangallo (1484–1546) with nothing less than a "wondrous speed [*prestezza maravigliosa*]" (2.113, G5.47)—have arrived on the scene in Italy just in time to meet the burgeoning needs of keen consumer demand. Most notable of them all is the young Michelangelo. He is recognized for having sculpted his formative and groundbreaking *Pietà* in Rome (ca. 1498–1500) in such a brief a span of time that personified Wonder itself marvels at his achievement in the creation of such a miracle of visual art: "in truth stupor [*lo stupore*] itself marvels [*si meraviglia*] that the hand of a craftsman should have been able to execute so divinely and so aptly in very little time [*in pochissimo tempo*] something so wondrous [*sì mirabile*]: certainly it is a miracle [*miracolo*] that a stone without any shape at the beginning should ever have been reduced to such perfection as Nature is scarcely able to create in the flesh" (2.652, G6.17). These eager-to-please men may not be as extraordinarily fast as the prolific seventeenth-century baroque artist Luca Giordano (1634–1705), nicknamed Luca-fa-presto (Luca-makes-it-quickly) for the noteworthy speed with which he produced his paintings in oil—a medium that, of course, only accelerated the pace of production—but they are nevertheless surely swift practitioners of the arts capable of completing things of supreme *grazia* with impressive alacrity.

To be sure, Vasari appreciates true excellence wherever and whenever it occurs, even if it takes the practitioner in question ages to complete a single work of visual art. Leonardo's *Last Supper* (1495–8) is an obvious case in point. In that particular instance Vasari memorably exemplifies the value of a visual artist taking his time to ensure that the work is just right. In the context of working on the *Last Supper*, for example, Leonardo deliberately chose to unburden his mind at length, we are told in the Giuntina edition, and "reasoned much with the Duke [Ludovico Sforza] about the art of painting [*gli ragionò assai de l'arte*]" (1.632, G4.26), shunning the foolish prior who had actually commissioned the fresco in the first place and who kept urging Leonardo to hurry up, not realizing that profound invention always requires extended deliberation and, above all, the requisite time to meditate on how best to convey visually the underlying idea.[33] Diligent forethought for this sophisticated painter who worked out ideas through the process of making visual art is consequently more important than swift action, Vasari leads us to believe, for indeed the time spent on contemplating and refining the underlying idea serves to bring the work of art and its invention as an object to absolute perfection. In the case of the *Last Supper*, in fact, Leonardo uses the time productively to work out the best and most innovative way to fashion visually through posture, gestures, physiognomy, *sfumato*, and *chiaroscuro* the image of shadowy evil embodied in Judas as the "true portrait of betrayal and inhumanity [*il vero ritratto del tradimento et inumanità*]" (1.632, G4.26).[34]

For this reason speed is sometimes construed as terrific, but sometimes it most assuredly is not in the context of thinking about how time is spent on the production of visual art. And more often than not in the *Lives* it all seems to depend on what Vasari deems, admittedly in a highly partisan and prejudicial manner, to be the underlying quality of the artist in question. Consequently, Vasari has largely positive things to say about Ghirlandaio and his recognized ability to produce works with speed as evidence of his acknowledged genius, despite some of his apparent shortcomings as a visual artist. But since Vasari has largely negative things to say about Pinturicchio (Bernardino di Betto, ca. 1452–1513), in part because he is taken as an artist lacking in visual ideas, *prestezza* in his case is viewed as a symptom of his pandering to the art market and his jeopardizing of quality to please his patrons: "Pinturicchio, who among other things satisfied greatly many princes and gentlemen, because he finished his works quickly, as they so desire, albeit far less well as a result than whoever does them slowly and painstakingly [*Pinturicchio, il quale fra l'altre cose sodisfece assai a molti prìncipi e signori, perché dava presto l'opere finite, sì come disiderano, se bene per avventura manco buone che chi le fa adagio e consideratamente*]" (1.576, G3.578). Better in the end to go slow and steady, *adagio e consideratamente,* and get the job done perfectly, as the contemplative Leonardo obviously did, than to go quickly and make a mess of it, so long as one is not wasting time in the process. So Simone del Pollaiuolo (Il Cronaca, 1457–1508), otherwise praised for his exceptional and admirable speed, should have taken more time in the construction of the "Great Council Chamber of the Palace of the Signoria in Florence," which turned out be unappealingly "low, dark, gloomy, and out of square" (1.762–4, G4.241–2) as a result of the haste—*prestezza*—with which he felt constrained to design and execute it. And yet in the end, if a visual artist can do both—constantly innovate *and* exercise his talent quickly in the context of never wasting time while bringing works of visual art to ripe perfection—he is viewed in the *Lives* as being all the better and thus all the more excellent in his *professione*. Hence Sebastiano del Piombo, who eventually ceases to paint in part because he proves unwilling to compete with those who produce works in far less time than he can, does indeed finish things to perfection. And those accomplishments all redound to his credit. But in one case Vasari somewhat diminishes Sebastiano for taking so much time to complete just a minor commission, as excellent as the painting in the end proved to be: "And although he labored painstakingly for six years to do this little work [*a far questa piccola cosa*], when works are executed to perfection, one should not consider whether they have been finished quickly or slowly [*se più presto o più tardi sono state finite*], albeit more praise is due to him who carries his labors to completion/perfection both quickly and well [*se ben è più lodato chi presto e bene conduce le sue opere a perfezzione*]" (2.143, G5.90).

Vasari, it goes without saying, was not the only Renaissance Italian writer to think about matters of speed in the visual arts, not only before the *Lives* came to light but also just shortly after it was printed. Alberti, for instance, comments in passing on such matters in the context of talking about technique in both his *On Painting* of 1435 and *On Architecture* of 1452 (Italian translation by Cosimo Bartoli in 1550), largely arguing that one must "bring together diligence and speed [*congiugnere la diligenza con la prestezza*]" in the process of making visual art, while also seriously cautioning against the habit of crafting objects with excessive, undisciplined speed.[35] Translating almost word for word Pliny's observations about Nichomacus and his pupil Philoxenus, Ghiberti briefly characterizes their notable speed in antiquity in his unfinished *Commentaries* of 1447–55.[36] Following Alberti, Leonardo dutifully warns visual artists about working with speed at the expense of "diligence" but then, significantly, goes one step further and urges artists to "sketch subjects quickly [*il bozzar delle storie sia pronto*]." In making this statement, Leonardo—as Ernst H. Gombrich long ago observed—emphasized for the very first time in the visual arts the importance that must be placed on the formative process of invention (in rhetorical terms *inventio*) as a means of imaginatively exploring ideas as they evolve on paper in a still fluid, inchoate state.[37] "What concerns the artist first and foremost," according to Gombrich as he explores Leonardo's novel method of rapidly working out compositions on paper, "is the capacity to invent, not to execute; and to become a vehicle and aid to invention the drawing has to assume an entirely different character—reminiscent not of the craftsman's pattern but of the poet's inspired and untidy draft. Only then is the artist free to follow his imagination where it leads him and to 'attend to the movements appropriate to the mental states of the figures which make up his story.' He needs the most pliable of mediums which allows him to write down quickly whatever he sees in his mind."[38] Like both Alberti and Leonardo, Paolo Pino (*fl.* 1534–1565) rather guardedly reflects on the upside and, above all, downside of speed in a few instances in his *Dialogo di pittura* (*Dialogue about Painting*) of 1548.[39] And Lodovico Dolce (1508–1568), writing a few years after Vasari, and partly in polemical response to his *Lives*, takes note twice of the value of speed by briefly applauding Titian (his particular hero of the visual arts, as opposed to Vasari's Michelangelo) for producing works not just "vigorously [*gagliardamente*]" but also "with much speed [*con molta prestezza*]." In this manner Dolce—yet another advocate of the importance of the "inspired and untidy draft" as an essential feature of the exploratory process of making visual art—effectively identifies Titian as a sort of latter-day

Apelles, who in one instance, he observes as he elaborates on an observation recorded in Pliny's *Natural History*, "drew quickly [*prestamente*] on a wall the face of [an] enemy."[40]

But even if Alberti, Ghiberti, Leonardo, Pino, and Dolce do indeed consider the topic of *prestezza* in various instances and sometimes in influential ways,[41] they certainly give far less emphasis to it than Vasari, who persistently does so, as we have seen, in a sustained, self-evident, elaborate, and calculated fashion, with *prestezza* serving throughout his master narrative—and especially in the 1568 edition—as an awe-inspiring sign of how visual artists increasingly acquire absolute control over their *techne* and, as a consequence, emerge all the more in the sixteenth century as spellbinding professionals capable of meeting the demands of their clients, come what may. For unlike any author writing about the visual arts before him in the Italian Renaissance, or even about the visual arts in antiquity, such as when Pliny writes his *Natural History* or Vitruvius his *De architectura* (*On Architecture*, ca. 30–15 BCE), Vasari stands as the first great lover and promoter of speed when it comes to celebrating the swift execution of works of visual art. And for Vasari, the sixteenth century stood out developmentally in his mind as indeed the great period of *prestezza*, the very period when "princes," he observes, "like to have their works delivered quickly [*si faccia piacere a' prencipi per dar loro l'opere presto*]" (2.182, G5.155). Not surprisingly, for a man widely recognized for his ability to complete jobs quickly in his own time and who was obviously extremely proud of that fact in his *Lives*, speed appropriately emerges as an essential quality that only sixteenth-century writers like Vasari, much less sixteenth-century practitioners or consumers, can adequately appreciate. It is, it would seem for Vasari, a time-sensitive issue peculiar to the mid-sixteenth century and on, whatever the visual medium in question, be it oil painting, fresco painting, tempera painting, marble sculpting, bronze casting, or, for that matter, silver goldsmithing. Speed may therefore not be visible in the completed, purchased image itself. Indeed, for Vasari a completed and purchased work of quality art, in all its perfection as the visual embodiment of ideas, should never betray the speed with which it was either originally sketched out imaginatively in a fluid, exploratory, and untidy fashion or, for that matter, with which it was finally realized and produced. Nevertheless, Vasari selectively makes speed visible to us through his *Lives* by relentlessly bringing it to our attention as something of immense social and cultural value.

Needless to say, this same period also witnessed the advent of the printing press, with its well-recognized (but not always admired) capacity to proliferate ever so rapidly books that had once been disseminated far and wide only in manuscript form.[42] By the same token this same period also witnessed the rise of the professional "adventurers of the pen," the so-called *poligrafi*, a group of fast-paced editors, copyeditors, translators, plagiarizers, commentators, and (often hack) writers who aggressively sought to imitate Pietro Aretino by instrumentalizing the printing press in a popularizing manner in mid-sixteenth-century Italy; who lived and worked primarily in and around Venice, the printing capital of the world, exactly as Pietro Aretino did; and who churned out one printed book after another in the vernacular, sometimes in multiple editions, in an effort to capture an audience and earn a living, although they typically often just barely eked out one.[43] "I had no sooner shat out [*scacazzato*] a page or a tale than I slipped it under a press to be printed, so that they came out as they did," one such *poligrafo*, the blustery, self-promoting Anton Francesco Doni somewhat characteristically confesses in a rather crass mode in a book that appeared in print in precisely the same year as the first edition of the *Lives* saw the light.[44] To be sure, Vasari would never have been an advocate of the *poligrafi*'s commercial-based and frequently unpolished writings, much less their often aggressive, at times even belligerent, uncouth, anti-courtly manners that rendered them, by extension, the apt cultural and literary heirs of Pietro Aretino as the universally recognized and feared "scourge of princes." Rather, Vasari's modern linguistic and literary models and advisors were his refined, humanistic, courtly collaborators and editors, such as Giovio, Borghini, Caro, Bartoli, and Giambullari. These men were far more inclined to adhere to the Horatian, classical ideal of *limae labor et mora* (the labor and delay of the file) to characterize the desired slow, steady artistry required to polish leisurely a work of poetry or prose. Nevertheless, as a dedicated, contemplative practitioner widely recognized for his *prestezza* as a painter and architect, and as a writer himself invested in completing a book as quickly as possible in order to meet the needs of others and potentially win significant recognition for himself in his *professione*, Vasari, I think it is safe to say, could have only been impressed with the voluminous productivity achieved by the *poligrafi* through their astonishing speed. In any event, Charles Hope may justifiably find it completely "unrealistic" that Vasari, a courtly, gentleman artist with no prior rhetorical training as a writer, completed the first edition of the *Lives* entirely on his own in roughly a year while also working on a host of commissions. But the *poligrafi*, as professional adventurers of the pen wedded to the fast-paced printing press in Venice, would not have batted an eye at the thought of producing such a lengthy book completely on their own in such a brief span of time. Indeed, Doni, in his typically self-aggrandizing and provocative manner, even boasted that he wrote his *I mondi* (*The Worlds*, 1552), all two hundred and forty pages of that particular book in its first edition, in a mere twenty days.[45] All of which would make the apparent dazzling speed with which Vasari completed his massive fresco cycle in the Cancelleria in just one hundred days seem positively slow by comparison. The sixteenth century in Italy was from time to time a period, at least midway through it, so very fascinated with the concept of speed when it came to thinking about the commercial production of *both* verbal and visual art. Or to put it differently, and in comparative literary terms, Boccaccio's Florentines and Tuscans of the thirteenth and fourteenth centuries in his *Decameron*—including painters such as Giotto—were often enough the heroes who could speak with exceptionally quick verbal wit; Vasari's Florentines and Tuscans of the sixteenth century in his *Lives* were often enough the enduring heroes who could materially produce things of notable, polished visual quality with, at least in part, exceptional, artisanal speed.

That said, there is yet another, and perhaps even more important, positive, emotionally charged quality associated with speed as a category of thought in the *Lives*. And that quality emerges most conspicuously in the Life of Giulio Romano (ca. 1499–1546), a High Renaissance artist who, as a particularly gifted disciple of Raphael, "always expressed his conceptions," which is to say his visual solutions to expressing ideas, "better in drawings than in finished work or in painting." Sometimes, Vasari informs us, Giulio was even able to finish those drawings in just an "hour." Consequently, he was able to transmit the initial passion of a project, when he was "all intense and aflame in the work [*tutto fiero et acceso nell'opera*]," to a single sheet of paper in a manner that simply failed him when he turned to complex projects that sometimes took "months, and even years, so that, growing weary of them, and losing that lively and ardent love that one has at the beginning of something [*quel vivo et ardente amore che si ha quando si comincia alcuna cosa*], it is no marvel that he did not give them that absolute perfection that is to be seen in the drawings" (2.121, G5.60). Speed produces, or just as likely is a direct byproduct of, the ardent glow of inspiration that dedication to an extended time-consuming project can easily dim or even entirely extinguish, thereby depriving Giulio's work of the supreme *grazia* in the finished, perfected product earlier glimpsed in the rapidly dashed off—yet still in its own way conceptually complete—drawing. More broadly, Giulio's skill as a draftsman is closely linked to the emergent value associated in the *Lives*, as well as sixteenth-century Italian artistic culture, with the swift, fluid, confident markings of the masterfully produced *schizzo*, *macchia*, and *abbozzo* (jotting, splotch, sketch) as an essential part of the *furor*-inspired, process-oriented, inventive working out of an elaborate, grand, visual idea. This was an essential skill that Leonardo in all his pathbreaking genius, as we have seen, first developed and perfected as an ongoing means for imaginatively working out visual inventions, much as a poet initially worked out verbal inventions, in a rapid, untidy, and unfettered manner, swiftly sketching things in here and there on the page in an exploratory "draft form" before committing them, admittedly after much time-consuming elaboration, to the final phase of polished, artistic production.[46] "In this technique," Gombrich has cogently written, "the inner vision, the inspiration, is 'thrown' on to the paper as if the artist were anxious to strike the iron while it is hot." Hence, what we come to value as informed and appreciative viewers of any one of these brilliant, rapidly rendered and fluid drawings done in the impassioned heat of the moment is arguably not the finished product per se as a visual object contracted for purchase by some sixteenth-century patron but the inquisitive process of invention itself, the residual trace of the master's hand swiftly giving shape to visual ideas in a searching, creative, imaginative state of flux.[47]

Not everyone, however, was so fortunate in being able to work as quickly and consistently as, say, Giulio Romano, much less Leonardo or Raphael or Michelangelo. And this is especially true when it comes to thinking about the matter of producing fully executed works of visual art. A case in point for Vasari is the mannerist Florentine painter Jacopo Pontormo (Jacopo Carucci, 1494–1556). On the upside, early in his career, "being carried away by the wish to make a name, by his desire in working, and by nature, which had endowed him with a *grazia* and fertility of very great genius/talent [*d'una grazia e fertilità d'ingegno grandissimo*], he executed [a painting], with incredible speed [*con prestezza incredibile*] and with such perfection as could not have been surpassed by an old, well-practiced, and excellent master" (2.342, G6.309). On the downside, however, as Pontormo aged, this peculiar, often solitary man would then lock himself up with onerous projects not just for months but even years—in one case for no fewer than eleven years—with the result that, as he all too openly and ill-advisedly vied with Michelangelo, his projects as visual ideas became confused in conception, overworked, overwrought, incoherent as a program, and ultimately even left unfinished. As a consequence, Pontormo's late muddled works, according to Vasari, reveal little of the "*grazia* and fertility of very great talent" that he was able to transmit to his earlier painting produced with such astonishing *prestezza*.[48] Here was a man, it would seem, who conceptually stood on the opposite end of the spectrum from Raphael, who, according to the later art historian and academic Giovanni Battista Armenini (1525–1609) in his *On the True Precepts of Painting* (1586), "used to set out many drawings [*molti dissegni*] he'd done with his own hand, and of those that seemed to him to be closest to the subject matter and for which he had already conceived the idea [*idea*], he would look now at one and then at another, yet all the while continuing to draw with great speed [*velocemente dissegnando*], he thus succeeded in giving shape to his entire invention [*così veniva a formar tutta la sua invenzione*], which seemed to be borne straight from his mind, in such a manner that the invention itself was helped and enriched from the multitude of those designs."[49] Needless to say, Raphael's well-trained, industrious assistants laboring in a highly efficient workshop (including, among others, Giulio Romano himself) then rapidly produced a variety of stunningly fresh, vibrant paintings from those earlier rapidly drafted designs.[50] And much of what Armenini has to say about Raphael as a fast-paced draftsman also, predictably, holds true for his great appreciation for Michelangelo's stunning ability to produce "in a short time [*in breve tempo*]" a completely finished drawing that "others," in all their amazement, "would have judged could be made only with a month's effort [*altri avrebbe giudicato dentro la fatica di un mese*]."[51]

Ultimately the key for Vasari, as it was largely for Armenini writing in response to Vasari eighteen years later,[52] is to find a way to retain that initial passion detected in the swiftly rendered drawing (be it even just an unfinished *schizzo*, *macchia*, *abbozzo*) or the rapidly and masterfully produced painting, so that the artist does not grow weary along the way and fail to complete a particular, onerous commission and thus bring it to fully executed perfection, no matter how time-consuming and arduous the task. How, then, does one do this? How do you keep the initial, emotional spark alive? How can you imbue a single work with all the longing and passion of youth, that life-enhancing, vigorous "vivo e ardente amore," even as the project grows old and both the body and mind grow weary? And how do you manage to complete a truly massive artistic project, for that matter, in a specified time without mismanaging and therefore somewhat botching the job, as Vasari did in his zeal to satisfy his demanding, autocratic patron and complete the task of painting the entire Salone dei Cento Giorni with such dazzling speed? The answer, at least at one level for Vasari, is that you need to be Michelangelo. For Michelangelo's *terribilità*, as a sort of fierce, nourishing, *furor*-inspired emotion, can sustain him, it would seem, over several years as he works on a single complex project as quickly as possible. Similarly, he has the ability, facility, and stamina to work both meticulously and quickly while engaged in a time-consuming commission at the behest of an irascible and hyper-demanding patron. Likewise, he possesses the presence of mind even to stand up in an insubordinate manner to an autocratic, insistent patron when periodically ignored by him in his demands for financial assistance just to complete the commission in the first place. And, finally, Michelangelo certainly does not make the sorts of egregious mistakes that Vasari did when, pressed for time, he once poorly managed his affairs and relied too heavily on his rather lackluster assistants to give proper shape to his underlying pictorial idea. Hence in 1510, the mercurial and powerful Julius II, having already demonstrated his impatience with Bramante for not having completed things rapidly enough in his construction of the massive Cortile Belvedere, immediately pressures Michelangelo to finish the taxing work of painting the Sistine Chapel as quickly as possible now that half of it has been unveiled to him and, thoroughly amazed at what sees as he gazes at the vault about seventy feet above his head, is all the more impatient to see it completed as soon as possible. Here, then, is the story as Vasari tells it:

> Michelagnolo complained at times that on account of the haste that the Pope imposed on him [*per la fretta che li faceva il Papa*] he was not able to finish it in his own fashion, as he would have liked; for his Holiness was always asking him importunately when he would finish it. On one occasion, among others, he replied, "It will be finished when I shall have satisfied [*satisfatto*] myself in the matter of art." "But it is our pleasure," answered the Pope, "that you should satisfy us [*satisfacciate a noi*] in our desire to have it done quickly [*di farla presto*]." And he added, finally, that if Michelagnolo did not finish the work quickly [*se non la finiva presto*], he would have him thrown down from the scaffolding. Whereupon Michelangelo, who feared, and had good reason to fear, the anger of the Pope, straightway finished all that was wanting without losing any time [*finì sùbito senza metter tempo in mezzo quel che mancava*], and, after taking down the rest of the scaffolding, threw it open to view on the morning of All Saints' Day, when the Pope went into the chapel to sing Mass, to the great satisfaction of the whole city [*con satisfazione di tutta quella città*]. (2.668, G6.37)

If Michelangelo is consistently presented as the greatest exemplar of the visual arts, here he is notably cast—even though he is often remembered in the *Lives* as a ponderous yet industrious worker—as one of the greatest masters of what me might well call "deliberative speed," arguably surpassing even Vasari, whose expeditiousness, as we have seen, characterized much of his artistic production.[53] Indeed, Michelangelo, even as he completes the monumental undertaking of the Sistine Chapel vault (1508–12), can withstand the pressures of a needy and ill-tempered patron in order to produce a work of visual art worthy of his own name, design, and conception, as the embodiment of a sophisticated idea conceived through the actual, generative process of making art. Thus in the end, as self-critical as Michelangelo notoriously was about his own visual art, even to the point where he would abandon certain projects that he could not bring to perfection, surely he can claim, Vasari would nevertheless have us believe, that he was still largely "able to finish it in his own fashion." By contrast, Vasari, to his own sorrow, was unable to withstand the pressures of a needy and powerful patron in the execution of the Salone dei Cento Giorni, even though he certainly managed to get the job done in a speedy fashion. And in the end he failed to produce a work of visual art that fully satisfied him. He should have devoted far more time to it, he confesses with the clarity of professional insight and hindsight, or have been more careful in overseeing his assistants and reworking their mistakes. What is more, Michelangelo not only satisfies his patron in executing the massive fresco, as Vasari likewise did when he acted with breakneck speed in his large-scale commissions for Cosimo I and Cardinal Alessandro Farnese. Michelangelo actually even satisfies an entire city, we are told. All of Rome rejoices in Michelangelo's spectacular triumph, not just the pope. And, of course, for all that Michelangelo, according to Vasari, may have demurred and deemed the Sistine Chapel ceiling to be unfinished, the final product quickly becomes a school for visual artists, a veritable place of homage for anyone wishing to study, imitate, and emulate the finest example(s) of *disegno*, much less witness how the human form can be conceived and rendered in seemingly endless and stunning variations, with all the clothed and naked bodies imaged on the vault profoundly inspired by, but also at the same time surpassing, the visual models surviving from classical antiquity, including such recently unearthed ones as the *Laocoön*.

Consequently, time and again throughout the *Lives* Vasari consciously draws an analogy between his own labors in his profession and those of Michelangelo. To compare big things to small, he even deliberately reveals that he understands intimately the physical suffering Michelangelo endured while painting the Sistine Chapel ceiling for his autocratic patron (Julius II), standing for hours with his neck achingly bent back and his face dripping with pigment. Vasari, we learn in the *Lives*, evidently had to experience much the same agony while working on various "vaulted chambers" in the ducal palace in Florence for likewise his autocratic patron (Cosimo I), even though he ingeniously rigged up a mechanism to relieve him of some of the stress and pain he experienced while laboring over that particular commission:

> I can bear witness, having painted five vaulted chambers in the great apartments in the palace of Duke Cosimo, when, if I had not made a chair on which I could rest my head and lie down at my work, I would never have finished it; even so, it has so ruined my sight and injured my head, that I still feel the effects, and I am astonished that Michelagnolo endured all

> that discomfort so well [*e stupisco che Michelagnolo reggessi tanto a quell disagio*]. But in truth, becoming more and more kindled every day by his fervor in the work [*accesso ogni dì più dal desiderio del fare*], and encouraged by the proficiency and improvement that he made, he felt no fatigue and cared nothing for discomfort [*non sentiva fatica né curava disagio*]. (2.668–9, G6.38)

In the end Vasari, predictably enough, will always inevitably pale in comparison with Michelangelo, indisputably the greatest artist of the *Lives*, despite, or precisely because of, the parallels he repeatedly draws between the two of them. And this is true with regard to how they respectively undertake monumental achievements when *prestezza* is required of them. If, on the one hand, Vasari needs assistants to complete immense, taxing jobs with speed (and in one instance he even botches the commission in part because of the ineptitude of his own *garzoni*), Michelangelo, on the other hand, can accomplish something even far more staggering while working with all deliberative speed and, as Vasari would have it, completely by himself, without a single assistant to aid him in his daunting, painful task, not even with someone present "to grind his colors" (2.668, G6.37), since, as it turns out, Michelangelo had the foresight to send his ignorant and incompetent assistants packing once he realized early on that these so-called helpers did not, and could not, reliably serve him.[54]

How, then, are we supposed to understand Vasari's role as a practitioner of the visual arts capable of working with such speed in the mid- to late sixteenth century when the professional bravura associated with speed itself was beginning to become so highly valued, as it was, say, for the Portuguese court artist Francisco de Holanda (1517–1585), when he declares in his 1548 dialogue *Da pintura antigua* (*On Ancient Painting*) that a work of visual art, while meticulously labored over, should appear in the end "as if done as if quickly [*quasi depressa*]," or when he insists earlier in the very same Neoplatonic treatise that "the vigilant and most excellent painter," once taken over by a "divine *furor* [*divino furor*],"[55] should "put his idea and conception very rapidly into execution [*porá velocissima execução à sua idea e conceito*], before it is lost to him or diminished by any disturbance"?[56] Or Dolce in 1557 in his *L'Aretino ovvero Dialogo della pittura* (*Dialogue on Painting*), when he observes that Titian "couldn't stand following that dry and labored [*secca e stentata*] method of Gentile [Bellini] but drew vigorously and very quickly [*con molta prestezza*]"?[57] Or for the baffled Frenchman Blaise de Vigenère (1523–1596), who recollects in 1566 how he stood in awe earlier in 1550 at Michelangelo's ability to "knock off more chips of a very hard marble in a quarter of an hour than three young stone carvers could have done in three or four, an almost incredible thing to one who has not seen it [*chose presqu'incroyable qui ne le verroit*]"?[58] Or twenty years later for the art historian and academic Armenini, who marvels in his *On the True Precepts of Painting* at the "incredible speed [*incredibil prestezza*]" with which the ambidextrous Genoese artist Luca Cambiaso completes paintings in oil—in an almost comical but still fascinating fashion—with "both hands" working simultaneously, "holding a brush full of color" in each?[59] Or, for that matter, for the late Renaissance cartographer Cristoforo Sorte (ca. 1510–ca. 1595), who in his *Osservazione nella pittura* (*Observations on Painting*, 1580) takes great delight in Jacopo Tintoretto's "velocity and speed, which is a wonder to see him handle [*velocità e prestezza, ch'è una meraviglia vederlo operare*]" as he likewise produces his canvases in oil?[60] And what, perhaps even more important in the context of thinking about the value and significance of the concept of *prestezza* in the *Lives,* makes Vasari's specific Life itself in some way truly worthy of being the final, exemplary biographical entry in his book, so as to serve within the narrative as a sort of crowning summation of the "excellence" that he persistently wishes to identify, describe, exemplify, and explain?

After all, Vasari is not only *not* the greatest visual artist of them all. He even positions himself occasionally in his own narrative as something of an underdog within his *professione*. He is talented, to be sure, unbelievably quick no doubt, dutiful and loyal and precise and deferential, as well as being a dedicated man of exceptional business acumen most assuredly and a devoted practitioner who was deeply committed to his *professione* and the notion that visual artists expressed distinctly visual ideas through the process of making art itself. But for all his self-ingratiating, careerist bluster on occasion,[61] Vasari certainly does not portray himself in the *Lives* as a man self-evidently worthy of being the subject of the sort of triumphant, self-aggrandizing biography that Benvenuto Cellini in all his unrestrained hubris wrote about himself or that Michelangelo in all his strategic self-mythologizing and chutzpah had his pupil Ascanio Condivi (1525–1574) write about his life and unsurpassed achievements (albeit not always even to the vainglorious Michelangelo's satisfaction).[62] No doubt Vasari could have written that sort of divinely inspired biography of his own life had he wanted to and no one would have ever been the wiser, or perhaps even cared. But he doesn't. And that is truly significant. Instead, what Vasari offers his reader when it comes to authoring *his* autobiography—and Vasari himself deliberately makes this evident from the very first sentence of his Life—is not his personal investment in the power of *terribilità* or the *furore* of rapturous inspiration (two key features of both Cellini's and Michelangelo's often hyperbolic biographies, for instance). Rather, what animates Vasari, he gives us to understand, is a deep, abiding appreciation for the longstanding, quotidian practice of "study, diligence, and loving labor [*istudio, diligenza et amorevole fatica*]" (2.1019, G6.369). Those are indeed key issues for Vasari, the very issues that underpin his ability to perform and produce things with such dazzling speed when necessary. And they are also the issues that his individual, culminating Life of the book steadfastly exemplifies and highlights from beginning to end.

For Vasari, being an accomplished artist is not about doing things with "effort" (*stento*), as crucial as effort is in getting things done both well and on time in a competitive art market, or even when exceptional *prestezza* is absolutely required of the artist to meet the needs of an impatient and needy patron. Nor is it only about being exceptionally gifted by nature, as absolutely essential as it is for any particular artist aspiring to excel in the *professione* of the visual arts to possess a certain, inexplicable *ingegno* that then gets perfected over time through socially accepted forms of training and dedicated, daily "study" (*istudio*), as we saw in the second chapter to this book. Instead, being an accomplished artist for Vasari, whatever the medium in question, is all about *diligenza*, which should be understood as the willingness to dedicate oneself fully to a task, to meet a patron's demands come what may. Moreover, the artist in question is expected to do all that and more with "delight," as the word *diligenza*, derived from the Latin verb *deligere* (to respect, esteem, love), would seem to suggest. At the same time, for Vasari being an accomplished artist is also very much about the ongoing, quotidian practice of doing things with *fatica*, with the tacit understanding that the labor involved in the creation of the well-crafted object of visual ideas must be cleverly hidden, so that the art of making a beautiful work of visual art, be it a painting, sculpture, or magnificent and massive building, even when done with exceptional *prestezza*, is deftly concealed through the discipline of art, thus revealing not effort or struggle but instead the artist's *sprezzatura*-like *facilità*.[63] However, if in fact you fail for some reason to exert *fatica* in the process of producing excellent visual art, if you perchance dash something off without having painstakingly built up the ability to do so with absolute control through long and dedicated *istudio*—as Jacopo Tintoretto (1519–1594), for instance, seems to do for Vasari with his puzzlingly incomplete and all too rapidly sketched oil paintings[64]—then you are also in some significant way cheating your patrons of what is owed them. And by extension you are cheating yourself of being fully recognized as a true professional, as a master painter, sculptor, or architect generating visual ideas. In a very real sense, then, to produce a work of high-quality visual art with *fatica* is for Vasari to give patrons their due. It represents for Vasari the true value delivered for the money spent. It is the real, underlying currency of exchange. Consequently, the actual act of painting quickly is one thing. That potentially anyone can do after some rudimentary training. But the *fatica* of years of patient, unyielding, dedicated *istudio* is quite another: *fatica* ultimately ensures that the speed of production in the creation of a perfectly finished work of truly excellent visual art tangibly grounded in visual ideas is enabled by years of exacting preparation. This is particularly true for Vasari when it comes to developing the essential skill of *disegno*, which should be understood not only as the technical art of drawing but also, as Vasari makes evident early on in the *Lives*, the intellectual skill of conceptualizing an idea long before it has actually been visualized materially and then giving shape to it through the material process of actually making art itself. Lastly, for Vasari being an accomplished artist is also all about the love of *fatica*—the very "love" that inspired Jacopo Pontormo and Giulio Romano to dash off beautiful works of visual art in the first flush of inspiration but that then no longer seems to have sustained them in their final products as they got too bogged down in their onerous projects. It is the sort of empowering "labor of love"—*amorevole fatica*—that propels Vasari forward in his career and compels him with such resolve to take on one commission after another, no matter how big they are and no matter how quickly the patron wants to see them completed.

Vasari's commitment to his profession extends no doubt to his willingness to consider taking on the task of writing the *Lives*, or at least initially consider assembling preparatory material for the writing of it, while working with unprecedented alacrity and *fatica* on a monumental and heroicizing fresco cycle commissioned by Cardinal Alessandro Farnese for his Palazzo della Cancelleria. The completion of the Salone dei Cento Giorni and the first stirrings of the idea to write the *Lives*, we are thus told twenty-two years after the fact in the Giuntina edition, tellingly occur in precisely the same period (1546), in precisely the same urban space (Rome), and with precisely the same illustrious patron (Cardinal Farnese) presiding over both the hurried commission and the fashionable dinner gathering in which various distinguished humanists and poets pass time together chatting over an edifying evening meal. Yet in setting out to write such a book, which grew into the Torrentiniana edition so quickly and then eventually into the much, much larger Giuntina, Vasari still obviously had to overcome all sorts of obstacles, just as he did when he started out as a painter in the important yet still provincial town of Arezzo with Guillaume de Marçillat, a good but not great artist, as his first teacher. In the most obvious sense, Vasari had to overcome the truly notable obstacle that he was not at all trained to write books, much less big books that go on for roughly 300,000, and then 600,000, words. He was trained to paint pictures, often big pictures, and he developed, as we have seen, a widely recognized ability to complete them quickly, occasionally with dazzling *prestezza*. And yet despite all the obstacles he has to face as an author of a massive book, and indeed as someone who certainly does not self-evidently possess the literary credentials of those distinguished humanists and poets dining and conversing with him when the idea of the book is first broached in Rome in 1546, much less the literary credentials of those fast-paced and sometimes pugnacious *poligrafi* operating in Venice at the same time, Vasari still takes on the onerous task of writing the *Lives*. No doubt he does so in part because he labored under the illusion that no task could be too great for a man of such conviction and dedication to his *professione*, as well as for a man who could impressively complete during the very same period a large fresco cycle in merely a hundred days (even if in reality it took him perhaps twice as long to complete).[65]

And therein, I would like to suggest in conclusion, lies one of the great ironies of Vasari's career if, at least for a moment, we pause to judge his book solely on the basis of his own aesthetic standards and thus consider the *Lives* specifically in the context of how Vasari professionally sought throughout his life to articulate, visualize, and disseminate an aesthetics based on his own view of the presumed classicizing principles of "rule," "order," "proportion," "*disegno*," and "measure," not to mention "delicacy," "refinement," "polish," "sweetness," "charm," "liveliness," and, ideally, "supreme *grazia*"[66]—an aesthetics, it is worth mentioning, drawn for the most part from classical rhetorical theory.[67] For as structurally thought out as the *Lives* may be in its deliberate and studied *disegno*, with one part often echoing another so that there is indeed some internal coherence to its narrative and themes and overall rhetorical strategy, and as accomplished a storyteller as Vasari can occasionally be,[68] Vasari's book—so rapidly and unevenly produced with the assistance of others in a sort of modified workshop model of scribal production—conspicuously lacks from beginning to end a confident, effortless polish that marks the best of Vasari's own highly finished and perfected mannerist paintings, such as the very frescoes adorning his own home in Arezzo.[69] All of which is to say that from a purely Vasarian standpoint, the *Lives* as a stylistically hybrid work of verbal art created through a fast-paced mode of shared literary production has become a classic of art history somewhat despite itself. Or, to put it differently, the *Lives* has become a classic of art history despite the fact that as a work of verbal art it does not conform—admittedly in a far different manner than the hurried and often unpolished, anti-conformist writings of the *poligrafi*—to the aesthetic, classicizing norms that its author demands stylistically within the *Lives* from excellent and polished works of visual art produced in his own time, much less the truly massive, excellent, and polished works of visual art produced by Vasari himself at his very finest with such "istudio, diligenza et amorevole fatica" and, to be sure, "grandissima prestezza."

4

TEMPO/TIME

With respect to increasing fame and reputation, it can be seen to be true that among all things writings have both the greatest force and the longest life, considering that books readily travel everywhere [*i libri agevolmente vanno per tutto*] and win trust everywhere [*per tutto*] as long as they are truthful and without lies; by these means any country can know of a person's worth, talent, and admirable virtues more effectively than by means of manual works [*le opere manuali*], which can only rarely move from where they have been placed [*che rare volte posson mutarsi da quel luogo ove elle son poste*].

—Giorgio Vasari, "The Life of Alberti," the *Lives* (1550)[1]

Finally, recognizing that perfection in this art consists in nothing else but seeking early on to become rich in invention and to study the nude continually, and thus to render facile the difficulty of execution, Giovann' Antonio repented that he had not spent in the study of art the time [*tempo*] that he had given to his pleasures, perceiving that what can be done easily in youth cannot be done well in old age. But although he was always conscious of his error, yet he did not recognize it fully until, having set himself to study when already an old man, he saw a picture in oils, fourteen braccia long and six braccia and a half high, executed in forty-two days by Giorgio Vasari, who painted it for the Refectory of the Monks of the Abbey of San Fiore at Arezzo; in which work are painted the Nuptials of Esther and King Ahasuerus, and there are in it more than sixty figures larger than life. Going therefore at times to see Giorgio at work, and staying to discourse with him, Giovann' Antonio said: "Now I see that continual study and work [*continuo studio e lavorare*] is what lifts men out of laborious effort, and that our art does not come down upon us through the Holy Ghost."

—Giorgio Vasari, "The Life of Giovann' Antonio Lappoli," the *Lives* (1568)[2]

One of the reasons why Vasari wrote the *Lives*, he reveals only at the very end of the Giuntina edition, was to please a group of humanists and poets gathered together in Rome at the Palazzo Farnese in 1546, where the idea for the book—at least as Vasari imagines the story, and as I have rather fancifully retold it in the Introduction—was first formally concocted. Friends help friends, we are given to understand in the Giuntina edition, and gathering information for a novel history of art, as well as venturing forth to write it without being a trained professional writer, seems to be the amicable as well as dutiful thing to do. At the same time, Vasari makes evident in the *Lives*, but particularly the opening prefaces and dedicatory letters, that he wrote the book to please not just friends but also patrons, particularly Duke Cosimo I. Acts of kindness require obligation in a courtly world where reciprocity is the name of the game. And Vasari, well versed in the established social graces of gift-giving, is no doubt hoping for some sort of return in investment for all his hard work, although not in the crude form of receiving cash. Indeed, it would be too crass and mercantile for Vasari to hope for just a simple monetary reward as a direct form of compensation in these particular circumstances, the way the *poligrafi* commercially sold themselves—prostituted themselves, according to some[3]—for their literary labors within the printing industry. Rather, Vasari presumably aims to be remunerated in the far more decorous, indirect, and socially acceptable form of being awarded significant commissions as a visual artist that will potentially win him fame or, just as important, offered a stable position at court, perhaps with a house, workspace, and monthly allowance thrown in for good measure. Winning everlasting glory is wonderful, but gaining some worldly recognition and reward is, practically speaking, good too.[4] All of this, of course, is standard operating procedure within the established economic, social, and cultural practices of Italian Renaissance patronage strategies, particularly for court artists.[5] Finally, yet another—and, for my purposes, much more important—reason that Vasari wrote the *Lives*, or so he claims toward the outset of the book, has to do with what he calls the "voraciousness of time [*la voracità del tempo*]" (1.13, G1.9). In keeping with the Ovidian commonplace "time is the devourer of things [*tempus edax rerum*]," Vasari's *la voracità del tempo* renders all people and things "prey" to the eventuality of "death" and "oblivion," precisely as we are told in the first paragraph of the book's proemium (G1.10).[6] In this light, one of Vasari's overall aims in writing the *Lives* is to try to rescue from that *voracità del tempo* every last artist and work of visual art that he finds of particular value.

It is that issue of time in general, not just its specific *voracità* but also the way it is conceived and represented more broadly in Vasari's *Lives*, that

I would like to investigate in this penultimate chapter (the final chapter will instead address more narrowly a particular span of time—the night—and how it is visualized materially). To this end, in the first section of this chapter I initially explore how the issues of loss, death, and memory figure into Vasari's ongoing efforts within the *Lives* to cope with the destructive onslaught of time, its relentless *voracità*. Above all Vasari does so by providing for posterity verbal descriptions of excellent artists and their works of art, commemorating those artists and their sometimes astonishing productions within a narrative history designed as a collective biography and disseminated far and wide in the enduring form of hundreds of mechanically reproduced, printed copies. Yet underneath it all, what especially exasperates the hyperproductive, resourceful, and indefatigable Vasari, I contend at the end of the first section, is that so many noteworthy, excellent artists dedicated to the speedy and often profitable production of visual art have simply wasted precious time in a competitive and industrious age. As a result, those same artists, who have inexcusably managed their time so poorly, have deprived the world and posterity of potentially even more inspired works of excellent visual art designed in the modern style that Vasari champions throughout his book. In the second section of this chapter I then shift focus and turn to explore not how time is used and abused by professional artists over a broad historical period. Rather, I explore how Vasari conceptualizes the passage of time as it is structured in narrative form within works of visual and verbal art in light of the Italian Renaissance *paragone* (comparison/competition) of *ut pictura poesis*—a phrase that is drawn from Horace's *Ars Poetica* (*Art of Poetry*, ca. 15 BCE) and can roughly be translated as "just as it is in painting, so it is (will be, or should be) in poetry." In the context of this particular Renaissance *paragone*'s concern with how temporality functions differently in the visual and verbal arts, I consider how Vasari makes certain works of visual art, which he has sought to preserve for posterity through the printed word, appear to be—and thus experientially *feel* to be on the part of the reader—timeless through a form of vivid, affective narration. Lastly, at the end of the second section I demonstrate how Vasari calculatingly configures the passage of time into his overall narrative of the development of visual art in different and sometimes innovative ways, not least by intermittently designing his secular history to be read not just literally but also, as one might a divinely inspired religious text, figurally. And here, once again, the "divine" Michelangelo will have an important role to play in Vasari's complex narrative.

I The Uses and Abuses of Time in the *Lives*: Loss, Memory, Print, Preservation, and the Benefits of Productivity for the Present and Posterity

Let us begin, then, by reflecting on how the concept of *tempo* resonates with a particular feeling expressed throughout the *Lives*: namely, the feeling of loss ineluctably associated throughout much of Vasari's book with the twinned concepts of time and memory. For memory, which is essential to the wholesale rescue operation of the visual arts that Vasari is engaged in as he personally and professionally battles *la voracità del tempo*, can be a tricky thing, rendering it at once a boon and a bane. Simply put, the more you work hard to resuscitate people from the past by exercising your memory and toiling to collect all sorts of information to aid and sustain it, the more you gradually become aware, and thus in a peculiar sense remember, that you indeed *had* to resuscitate those people in the first place and therefore had to work so very hard, with such "great labor [*fatica grande*]," to do so (G1.10). And that nagging awareness in its turn only fuels the grim realization that things will in all likelihood, if not inevitably, slip back into oblivion again as they are swallowed up once more by *la voracità del tempo*. The all-consuming power of forgetfulness is simply more powerful than the power of memory, a point certainly not lost on Sigmund Freud, who centuries after Vasari was far more impressed with the human capacity to forget (and, to be sure, deny and repress and distort) than to remember accurately.[7] And that fact troubles Vasari, both as an author taking on the role of the historian and as a practicing artist reflecting on the lives and works of others in his *professione*. Hence, even when his friend and editor Vincenzo Borghini urges him in a letter to not focus on the lives of artists in the second edition of his book but to talk just about what they actually produced,[8] Vasari nevertheless feels compelled to go ahead and somewhat defiantly tell all sorts of stories about many of the artists who deeply interest him.[9] By doing so, Vasari is giving his tale some novelistic color by imaginatively fleshing out the people, so that they can and should be viewed as individuals within larger collectivities that make up their societies, sodalities, local cultures, and day-to-day professional experiences. In this manner Vasari intermittently brings these people back to life in verbal form, endowing them with that naturalized *vivezza* (lifelikeness and vivacity) he finds so essential in works of visual art, where people can and should be portrayed not just in their ideal form, as humans sometimes theatrically and regally staged as heroic players in a grand historical event but, conversely, in their very real bodily form, as humans who are sometimes visualized with all their intimate, corporeal peculiarities, from warts to broken noses.[10]

Needless to say, so many of the people whom Vasari labors to bring back to life, in defiance of *la voracità del tempo* as he steadfastly exercises his memory, are also unmistakably dead. This is a fact that any author self-consciously addressing issues of temporality has to contend with when writing about people's lives in a narrative that not only treats the past as something that indeed took place in a period that is self-evidently complete and done with but that also, with one artist "following after another [*di mano in mano*]" (G1.10), unfolds methodically and for the most part chronologically toward some end point in an undisclosed future when everything will in fact be complete and done with, when everyone mentioned in the book who is still living at the date of its composition and printing will finally be, in a word, dead. And mortality is certainly something that Vasari renders all the more evident by including memorials at the end of many individual Lives. By doing so, he transforms the *Lives* intermittently into a sort of graveyard filled with tombstones containing epitaphs of the dead that serve to remember them and synthetically encapsulate their lives, especially all those visual artists whose untimely deaths, such as Raphael's, evoke great pathos.[11] So conceived, the *Lives* as a sort of "paper cemetery," in Maia Wellington Gahtan's felicitous phrase,[12] can and should be construed as a narrative full of commemorative moments, some of which are no doubt indebted to the classicizing practices of Renaissance humanists engaged in crafting highly rhetorical funeral orations, not to mention the considerable humanist investment in composing saints' lives and collecting epigraphic texts, epitaphs, and commemorative poetry. Nevertheless, inasmuch as the commemorative moment in the *Lives* is distinctly allied to the grave and, as such, makes us only too aware that these people are indeed dead (and, what is more, that even those living artists described in Vasari's book, including the author himself in the Giuntina edition, will one day die as well), each commemorative moment in the *Lives* also has a distinctly life-affirming function. It offers Vasari, as a practitioner-cum-historian, the opportunity to tell the story of how the end of a particular person's life confers meaning on the whole and how and why a particular life was worth living and should not only be remembered but also viewed potentially as a model for others. Along with that, each commemorative moment in the *Lives* offers Vasari the opportunity to show how and why an artist's legacy was or should be carried on for future generations through the life-enhancing work of his followers, those very survivors who will genealogically perpetuate and divulgate the artist's style and achievements through their own individual works in the *professione* of the visual arts.

Hence one way of memorializing the dead, keeping them present in our minds, is to eulogize them and recognize the ways in which their gifts have survived through their artistic progeny, their "disciples [*discepoli*]." And it is through that process that Vasari additionally seeks to keep them alive, present in our imagination while we read. The commemorative moment in the *Lives* in this way seeks to take something distinctly time-bound and, in defiance of *la voracità del tempo*, render it timeless—perhaps never so conspicuously, as we saw in the first chapter, with the magnificent mythologizing of Michelangelo as a transcendent figure of artistic perfection celebrated in an elaborate, state-sponsored funeral, as the epitome of success "in every art [*ciascheduna arte*] and every profession [*ogni professione*]" (2.642, G6.3). And there is every good reason to think that Vasari was right to be concerned about how *la voracità del tempo* would eventually erode memory and confine so many people about whom he writes to a "second death" (1.13, G1.10), not Dante's religious "second death" (*Inf.* 1.117) of being relegated to a punishing Hell of everlasting pain and damnation but the putative second death of being forgotten as time increasingly passes by and thereby leaves so many "in prey of death and of oblivion [*in preda della morte e della oblivione*]" (1.4, G1.3).[13] Even today, to be sure, we readily remember all those canonical figures of the Italian Renaissance who appear in anthologized versions of the *Lives.* But few, aside from a handful of specialists, recall a large number of the visual artists discussed in Vasari's book, some of whom exist only in the historical record thanks to the *Lives* itself. "Hac sospite nunquam hos periisse viros victos aut morte fatebor" ("While this [history] lives never shall I say that these men have perished nor been conquered by death"), Vasari declares in an inscription that is inspired from the eighth book of Virgil's *Aeneid* and borders the central image of the new title page to the Giuntina edition—an image in which, as T. S. R. Boase has observed, "fame awoke with a blast of horns the dead from their graves."[14] Vasari's book is thus not only about rebirth but resurrection. In a Virgilian, and thus heroicizing, epic mode, he is conferring on the dead, as well as those mentioned in the book who will one day die, eternal life through his words.

At the same time, the *Lives* makes us all too keenly aware that not just people but things themselves—all that material culture produced by visual artists since the time of Cimabue—will likewise succumb to *la voracità del tempo* and eventually be forgotten, cast into "death" and "oblivion" and thereby fall "prey to dust [*preda della polvere*]" and serve in the end as mere "food for worms [*cibo de' tarli*]" (1.13, G1.10). This elegiac awareness on the part of Vasari grows out of a familiar Renaissance sensibility, one that typically finds expression as a mournful longing for all those valuable works of ancient material culture either destroyed in the period after the fall of the Roman empire; simply left buried and waiting, like the *Laocoön*, to be fortuitously dug up and resurrected in a literal groundbreaking process of "unearthing the past"; or, worse, actively destroyed even in Vasari's own time to make way for the arguably new and improved classical and classicizing structures of "modern" Renaissance art.[15] But in Vasari's case the sense of loss experienced on his part is perhaps all the more acutely felt. For the loss he often talks about when it comes to reflecting on the transitory nature of art objects has to do with the very works produced in the "modern" period that he is seeking to memorialize in words and consciously mark as constituting a *rinascita*. So many of those works, indeed even things produced in the very recent past, are bound to get lost, he reveals to us, and thus likewise succumb to *la voracità del tempo*. For this reason, Vasari repeatedly calls attention to the fact that so many splendid works of art, including those he had once observed in person, have now been destroyed for one reason or another. Sometimes they have been destroyed simply as a consequence of the inevitable hazards of unforeseen accidents: storms, fires, earthquakes, and the like. But also, far worse, they have been destroyed because they have fallen victim to what we would today call the "collateral damage" of battles and the plunder of wars, not to mention how they have simply been left prey to human stupidity and avarice; ill-advisedly been created through experimentation with non-durable materials; had to be demolished to make way for other more desirable works of visual art that would eventually take their place; were in fact consciously constructed for private and public festivities so that they would purposely not survive beyond the short-lived duration of those sometimes lavish celebrations; or suffered deterioration from the natural forces of a local, corrosive, salt-saturated climate. The *voracità del tempo* has a habit, it would seem, of doing away with all sorts of art objects in so many different ways. Some of those objects are great ones that will be sorely missed, such as Michelangelo's bronze statue of Julius II demolished by the Bolognese after the conquering papal army retreated, or Leonardo's massive equestrian statue destroyed by the French troops sacking Milan. Others, by contrast, are just incidental and somewhat ephemeral works of art, such as the transitory writings placed beneath the coats of arms and emblems of families pictured on household facades, which, as Vasari observes, "have been eaten away by time [*per esser consumate dal tempo*]" (1.191, G2.232).[16]

Vasari was not alone in expressing a desire to capture the material culture of the present or recent past for the future in print, since books, unlike manual works (*le opere manuali*), which are so often stuck in place, can—as the first epigraph to this chapter makes plain—travel far and wide: *i libri agevolmente vanno per tutto*. In precisely the same year in which the Torrentiniana edition of the *Lives* appeared in print, the popular Florentine writer Anton Francesco Doni published in Venice at the Giolito press a somewhat novel book titled *La libraria* (first edition 1550). In it he provides a rather long list of books composed in the vernacular for people to read or collect, with the primary aim of preserving for posterity the various works of a wide array of authors who might otherwise, as he phrases it, "witness the death of their writings [*la morte de' loro scritti*] for various reasons."[17] The books Doni then lists, as he arranges them alphabetically by author, somewhat like the art objects that Vasari talks about as he arranges them in rough chronological order in the *Lives*, might well be left, we are given to understand, "in preda alla morte e della oblivione" and thus likewise fall "prey to dust" and serve as "food for worms." Yet unlike Vasari, Doni writes a very short, compact book, with hardly any descriptive account of the contents of the books themselves that he lists, much less any substantive, credible, or useful information about the lives of the authors who wrote them. And there is a very good, practical reason why Doni, a fast-paced professional writer with an unusual gift for gab, feels free to give us just the bare, necessary, and sometimes quirky information rather than go on and on about the books he means to highlight, as Vasari sometimes does about certain paintings or sculptures he finds of extraordinary value. For ex-printer that he was, Doni—who assumed as early as 1547 he was initially slated to print the first edition of the *Lives* at his Florentine press[18]—is acutely aware that his own dynamic culture has constructed a hyper-efficient mechanism that will help ensure the survival of many of the printed books he hopes to bring to light and preserve, along with all those books in manuscript form (listed in the enlarged, second edition of his *Libraria*) that, as a self-anointed arbiter of taste, he deems should be preserved by being disseminated in print. And that innovative mechanism, the printing press, effectively relieves Doni of the responsibility of having to dutifully describe those writings at any length in his novel book about books. Doni, in other words, does not need to provide substantive accounts of those books because so many of them, if not all, will presumably survive thanks to their dissemination far and wide in the form of identical printed copies, some of them running into the thousands if they have successfully managed to go, once printed, through multiple editions. Doni thus merely needs to bring those books listed back to memory, keep them from falling prey to the death and oblivion of forgetfulness by just mentioning them and, in the process, sometimes bizarrely identifying and attesting to their content and value, as he does particularly in the *Libraria*'s second edition of 1551 (printed by the Marcolini press) and then in the fully enlarged edition of 1557/8 (printed, once more, by the Giolito press). In this way Doni's primary job in the *Libraria* is not so much to conserve or preserve but, as an ex-printer and professional writer himself, to record and canonize. Simply put, his principal job is to jog the memory, not to create a descriptive substitute for it.

But for a man whose chief focus in the *Lives* is on the arts of painting, sculpting, and architecture, as well as the lives of so many excellent practitioners of those three nobler arts, Vasari as a writer cannot possibly operate in the same way as Doni did, for all that Vasari as a visual artist recognized the ways in which print itself could be instrumentalized to disseminate far and wide a vocabulary of visual style through woodcuts, etchings, and engravings.[19] Put differently, Vasari's model for the survival of the material works of art he primarily writes about in his wholesale rescue operation against the inevitable, destructive force of *la voracità del tempo* was not Doni's printing press with its ingenious mechanism for mechanical reproduction. Instead, it was the visual artist's workshop, the traditional artisanal space where workers used their hands and long-established tools of their trade (not some newfangled, fast-paced machine) to generate collectively and systematically works of visual art or, for that matter, excellent and highly valued copies of works of visual art (fig. 7). To be sure, no matter how adept they had become in producing works with extraordinary *prestezza*, painters and sculptors could never even begin to dream of possibly matching, much less competing with, the power of the printing press with its uncanny ability to manufacture perfect duplicate copies. And this is the case within a culture in which the copy of a work of visual art could be said to be, as Vasari himself attests, as valuable as the original.[20]

What, then, is Vasari to do? Time and again, wherever he goes in his search to identify objects of visual value, Vasari bears witness to all sorts of works of art getting destroyed bit by bit, occasionally even at the hands of a competitive and irascible fellow visual artist, such as Baccio Bandinelli (1493–1560), when he rips apart Michelangelo's cartoon of the *Battle of Cascina* in an act of bellicose, professional envy, according to at least one explanation in the *Lives* of his rash, destructive behavior (G5.241). Needless to say, one thing Vasari can do is to preserve some material portion of that visual art himself wherever and whenever he can, including even a surviving piece of that very same destroyed cartoon of the *Battle of Cascina*.[21] In that light, it is hardly surprising that Vasari, an avid, life-long collector (and indeed one of the first great early collectors) of drawings on the grand scale, somewhat obsessively reminds us in the Giuntina edition of the *Lives* that he has a precious book full of designs. Arguably that book also contains the very sorts of designs that would potentially allow him to reconstruct a work of visual art, at least in terms of its essential conception as an invention, if, like so many durable things in the world, the works of visual art upon which those designs were based were to get destroyed by falling victim, along with virtually everything else, to *la voracità del tempo*. But as a unique object of visual art referenced time and again within the Giuntina edition of the *Lives* as a sort of companion volume to the *Lives* itself and, more specifically, as a sort of mnemonic device for some of the works of art described in it, Vasari's precious, eventually multi-volume thesaurus of drawings can also, alas, easily disappear, get lost, or end up destroyed, we need to keep in mind. So what, it bears repeating, is Vasari to do? In the absence of the modern technology of photography, much less the ability to incorporate into his book hundreds, if not literally thousands, of printed illustrations in the form of engravings, woodcuts, or etchings perfectly duplicating the major works of visual art mentioned in the *Lives* (a nightmarish, labor-intensive business venture for a writer or printer to take on at an irrecuperable expense in sixteenth-century Italy), there is only one thing Vasari can do. He must write about every work of visual art he deems truly exceptional and in the process try to preserve those works for posterity by describing them.[22] And he must do so specifically with the aim of preserving both the form and the content of paintings, since those particular objects—as Vasari well knew, given that so few paintings had endured from antiquity—were the least liable to survive through time.[23]

Hence we find ourselves subjected occasionally to lengthy *ekphrases* of works of visual art, above all paintings, in part because Vasari desperately needs to keep a precise record of them so that he can reveal to the world what was done even in light of the fact that surely over time many of them, with presumably the notable exception of those widely available through prints, would not survive.[24] Just as important, Vasari must labor to ensure that his own words will survive by disseminating them through the medium of mechanical reproduction. For that is the medium that can provide him with the secure foreknowledge that at least some of those works of visual art described will be remembered in some measure precisely because his book, printed in so many identical copies, will itself in all likelihood endure, even when so many of the unique artifacts themselves recorded in it will not. Conceivably, then, one day, if and when his own civilization falls by the wayside as surely as the Roman empire did (and this assumption about the organic life-cycles of civilizations as they come and go was indeed a commonplace of the Italian Renaissance, just as it was of classical antiquity),[25] some curious and intrepid persons may come upon an object forgotten in a dark and stuffy attic and, marveling at it, recognize it for what it was. Indeed, they will recognize it precisely because Vasari will have provided them with an accurate description of it in his book, just the way artists of his own culture had come upon the unearthed *Laocoön* in Rome in 1506 and, in all their excitement, recognized that celebrated, excavated work of visual art for what it was from even just the brief description of it contained in Pliny's *Natural History*. The *Lives*, that is to say, is no doubt written as a work of history that aims to capture the past and preserve it for those in Vasari's own present, such as, for instance, the humanist collector Paolo Giovio, who effectively commissioned the book, we are led to believe. But as Vasari openly vies in his own time with Pliny and the memorial function of the *Natural History*, he is also heeding a familiar Renaissance humanist impulse by writing for *us*: his presumed, interested, and enlightened readers in the future. Or, rather, we might say that Vasari is arguably writing for all those connoisseurs or excellent, informed practitioners who will one day desperately need his book to identify works of visual art fashioned during the period that he lavishly praises for constituting a true *rinascita*.[26] In the process of doing so, Vasari, as Paolo Giovio insists in a letter, has himself created something that will remain immortal in printed form, while rendering the author himself also "immortale" by defying the voraciousness of time: "non lo consumera il ladro tempo" ("the thief, time, will not devour it").[27] It is entirely fitting, then, that Doni, who was likewise eager to forestall the destructive power of time through the publication of his *Libraria*, was originally slated to print the first edition of the *Lives*.

Nevertheless, as devastating as the destructive force of the passage of time was for Vasari, nothing in the end perhaps bothered him so much as simply wasting time. Not the loss of visual art over time. Not the forgetting of visual art over time. Not even bad visual art: the uncouth, *goffo* (clumsy) style of the "Greeks" or the *rozzo* (rough) style of the "Germans."[28] Not even, for that matter, his cantankerous, thorn-in-the-side rival Cellini, whom, all things considered, he treats fairly well in the *Lives*, even if the rather mean-spirited and pugnacious Cellini has only nasty things to say about Vasari in his autobiographical *Life*, calling him names, ridiculing him for having long, dirty fingernails, and generally heaping contempt upon him whenever he could.[29] No, what seems to bother Vasari the most is that an able artist of some stature, especially a truly excellent one, wastes precious time, just as Giovann' Antonio Lappoli somewhat belatedly recognizes he did when he finally comes to term with his longstanding indolence and "error," as recorded in the second epigraph heading this chapter. How wonderful Paolo Uccello (1397–1475) would have been as an artist, Vasari therefore gives us to believe, if he just hadn't spent so much time idly swept up in a trance over perspective, oohing and aahing about it day in and day out and sometimes through the night, even to the point where he neglects (or purposely avoids) his conjugal bedtime duties (G3.72). Perspective is good, but for the moderate and temperate Vasari, for whom "in all things one must observe a certain mean and avoid extremes," too much of a good thing can be very bad.[30] This is especially true if a particular artistic fixation keeps you, as it does Uccello with his obsessive attention to perspective, from focusing on larger issues of *disegno*, much less settling down to focus on your work in a studious and sustained way. The same can be said about Fra Filippo Lippi (1406–1469), Filippino Lippi (1457–1504), and Daniele da Volterra (ca. 1509–1566),[31] as well as a variety of other artists of some significant stature. All of them possess various good qualities that recommend them to us as valuable visual artists, marking them as "excellent," if not truly exceptional, within their *professione*. But one negative feature they all seem to share to varying degrees at one point or another in their distinguished careers is that they somewhat inexplicably for Vasari wasted time. Worst of them all was Parmigianino (Girolamo Francesco Maria Mazzola, 1503–1540), a brilliant, unique, and pathbreaking artist, whose enviable style so many others wished to imitate, but who wasted so much time absorbed in the vain pursuit of alchemical riches, Vasari wistfully observes, that he not only destroyed his health but also undermined his potential to become one of the great luminaries of the visual arts (1.932–3, G4.531–2; see also G4.543–4). Doubtless in Vasari's mind, for someone like the extraordinarily talented Parmigianino to waste time (*perdé il tempo*, G4.532) on fruitless pursuits, while periodically abandoning what should have been his singular and honorable focus of professional devotion, simply means that the world has potentially been deprived of yet another masterpiece—something that might well have moved the history of art ever onward and upward in an even loftier trajectory of historical fulfillment.[32] And that is deeply troubling for Vasari as he reflects on the history of art, both as an accomplished practitioner invested in valuing excellence and as a writer authoring a book about its very *rinascita* over a three-hundred-year period.

Consequently, not just diligence and speed are praised in the *Lives* but industriousness, the ability to apply oneself to assigned tasks on an ongoing basis, with the right sort of "work ethic," we might say today in a neoliberalist mode of thought, and still find ways of maximizing efficiency to enhance productivity while exhibiting true excellence in the completed work of visual art. This is in large measure the story of Luca della Robbia (1399/1400–1482), about whom Vasari prepares the way for an account of his excellence with the moralizing observation delivered toward the beginning of his Life that "it is not by sleeping but by waking and studying continually [*non dormendo, ma veg[g]hiando e studiando continuamente*]" that real progress in the arts is made (1.273, G3.50). And, to be sure, Luca was extraordinarily industrious as well as inventive and resourceful. First, he astutely recognized that the amount of time he dedicated, or that indeed anyone else in the visual arts for that matter dedicated, to fashioning sculptures in bronze and marble was inefficiently spent. Then, in a calculated effort to optimize his time, he invented an ingenious method by means of which he could take clay, a readily available and malleable substance that "could be worked easily and with little labor," and transform it, thanks to his own newly invented and secretly devised glazing procedure, into a hardened material that allowed him to preserve the molded artifact "for a long time [*lungo tempo*]," with the net result that he was able to cleverly "defend [these newly crafted objects] from the injuries of time [*ingiurie del tempo*]" (1.275, G3.53). If time is money, why waste time, Luca seems to reason in a pragmatic manner, on something that takes so much effort and yields so little profit? Of course, there is something of the practical, competitive businessman at work here as Luca, good merchant-minded Florentine that he is, seeks to produce more and more long-lasting, innovative objects of exceptional quality for a dynamic art market and, as a consequence, accumulate substantial personal wealth in the process. In any event, one of the morals of the story of Luca della Robbia's Life is, in large measure, that one should value inventiveness and industriousness, as well as versatility, curiosity, adaptability, resourcefulness, and experimentation, at the service of mercantile efficiency and artisanal excellence within a vibrant, competitive marketplace: "Luca, then, while passing from one method of work to another, from marble to bronze, and from bronze to clay, did this not by reason of laziness or because he was, as many are, capricious, unstable, and discontented with his art, but because he felt himself drawn by nature to new things [*cose nuove*] and by necessity to an exercise according to his taste, both less fatiguing and more profitable [*di manco fatica e più guadagno*]" (1.280, G3.58).

Like the hyper-industrious Luca, or for that matter Perino del Vaga (1501–1547), who went about tirelessly "stealing time from time itself [*rubando al tempo il tempo*]" (2.156, G5.111) early in his career to learn and master the art of *disegno*, burning the proverbial candle at both ends by working constantly (and even indiscriminately taking on far too many commissions later in his life as a master artist overseeing his own busy and highly profitable workshop), Vasari was never one to waste time.[33] That is a fact he means to impress upon us in a variety of ways. In part he does so by just telling self-ingratiating stories about himself, such as the one recorded in the epigraph to this chapter, in which Vasari chastises Lappoli for wasting so much time in his career yet boasts instead how he, in stark contrast, conscientiously completed in an exemplary manner a massive painting full of larger-than-life figures in a mere forty-two days, thus once more with his signature *prestezza*. But Vasari also impresses upon us the fact that he never wasted time, whether he happened to be working slowly or quickly, by just overwhelming his readers with accounts of his seemingly endless and various achievements. Indeed, were he coming up for promotion in any particular studio art program in an institution of higher learning today, Vasari's c.v. would be impressive by any reasonable standard of measurement on the basis of the sheer quantity of objects of visual art that he managed to produce during his illustrious career (the entire issue of the consistency of the quality of his work is a much different matter altogether and, admittedly, somewhat questionable in Vasari's particular case, although both he and his defenders would have no doubt protested otherwise). Go ahead and count all the things he lists in just his Life, although bear in mind that Vasari only registers the ones worthy of being mentioned, thus leaving out, for instance, all those "little things in oil of not much importance [*alcune cosette a olio di non molta importanza*]" (2.1021, G6.370; see also G6.382, 387, 391, 393, and 399).[34] What is more, Vasari actually *completed* virtually all the works of visual art he ever started. And he makes a point of persistently calling attention to that fact time and again, whereas some favored artists, such as his rival Bandinelli, left behind so many unfinished commissions—an array of things unpardonably abandoned in an inchoate, *imperfetto* state.[35] And that perplexes Vasari. He simply cannot fathom how master artists, from Pontormo to Bandinelli, cannot reliably get things done on schedule. Time management consequently seems to be an absolutely essential component for artistic success, where one of the functions of the *dipendenti* in a *bottega* was in fact to move things along swiftly in a calculated, fluid fashion. And whoever fails in properly managing time in such pressing, businesslike affairs as a visual artist therefore typically comes in for some chastising on his part, whether or not they happen to be particularly slow or fast painters, sculptors, or architects. How, Vasari seems to wonder with barely restrained disdain, can the Florentine painter Giuliano Bugiardini (1475–1577) spend twelve years on an altarpiece and still not complete it (G5.281)?

Not surprisingly, Michelangelo, as always, is an important exception in the *Lives*—something that traditionally goes hand in hand with him being a foundational figure who at once reinforces and escapes, as a structurally recognized exception, the accepted rules of the game. And that is once more true when it comes to contemplating the completion of works of visual art. For as is well known, and as Vasari repeatedly makes evident, the great Michelangelo left a number of extraordinary projects—almost exclusively sculptures—unfinished. Vasari nevertheless gives us to understand that all of this occurred not because Michelangelo ever voluntarily wasted time. Quite the contrary. It occurred for any number of acceptable reasons, according to Vasari. One obvious reason is that Michelangelo simply took on too many oversized commissions in the first place and thus could not feasibly complete them all in the allotted time frame. In the end some of his assigned projects were just too staggering in conception for any one person to complete in a single lifetime, so he understandably felt compelled to abandon them, or his grand and terrible conceptions outstripped even his own unparalleled skill to fully realize them, and so they had to remain unfinished. In other instances Michelangelo's mercurial patrons periodically interrupted his progress and diverted his attention to other equally, if not more daunting, time-consuming projects, while on other occasions he discovered an unexpected flaw in the marble he was working on and therefore set the project aside in his relentless search for absolute perfection. Political or military misfortunes, moreover, not to mention the death of a patron, at times prevented him from ever finishing specific projects. And even when Michelangelo, for one reason or another, left certain sculptures in an unfinished state, such as his enigmatic *non-finito* "slaves" or the reclining, curvilinear figures of *Dawn*, *Dusk*, *Night*, and *Day* ensconced in the New Medici Sacristy (1520–34), Vasari still indicates that one can appreciate and learn from the brilliance of their underlying *disegno*.

Michelangelo—along with, for different reasons, Leonardo da Vinci[36]—is thus excused in the *Lives* for not completing many of his projects. What is more, even in the one instance when Michelangelo can be said to have marginally wasted time (*perdeva tempo*, 2.650, G6.14) while sojourning for nearly a year in Bologna as the honored guest of Giovanni Francesco Aldovrandini (where he nonetheless completed a few sculptural commissions), he quickly returns to work once he departs and then, thereafter, never ceases to amaze people in all his productivity and industriousness, perhaps never so much, as we have seen, as when he completes the *Pietà* so rapidly and then, later, the Sistine Chapel for Julius II in just four intense years, despite all the unnecessary delays imposed upon him by a periodically negligent and difficult pope. In any event, it certainly distresses Michelangelo when patrons force him to waste time for one reason or another (2.677, G6.52; 2.708,

G6.86). In large measure this is the case because, as Vasari tells his life story, he was a man who simply could never stop working, always employing his time productively in the service of his visual art: "The spirit and virtue/power of Michelagnolo would not [let him] rest without doing something [*Non poteva lo spirito e la virtù di Michelagnolo restare senza far qualcosa*]" (G6.77). Indeed, often enough, according to Vasari (and Condivi), he would forget to eat, so absorbed was he in the task at hand. Lying about idly and wasting time, whether one happened to be working quickly or slowly, constituted not just something of a nightmare for Vasari in the *Lives* but also, it would seem, the divine Michelangelo.[37] Hence his injunction to his pupil Antonio Mini, not mentioned in the *Lives* but nonetheless worth recalling once again: "Draw, Antonio, draw, Antonio, draw, and don't waste time [*Disegnia Antonio disegnia Antonio disegnia e non perdere tempo*]." Unmistakably both Vasari and Michelangelo, like Luca della Robbia and Perino del Vaga and so many others in the *Lives*, are viewed as exceptionally industrious, constantly filling up their valuable time with work. And for Vasari this makes all the difference in the world, for "continual study and work is what lifts men out of laborious effort," he has Giovann'Antonio Lappoli retroactively admit with some lament over his own personal *errore* and lack of professional foresight.

II The Structures of Time in the *Lives*: Visual and Verbal Art, *Ekphrasis*, Emotional Investment, and Narrative Configurations

If time is so very important to Vasari as an author-practitioner invested in recapturing the past, preserving it for the future in printed form, and never, ever wasting it in the here and now, what, then, can we say about the way he actually represented and manipulated time in the *Lives* as a verbal narrative describing the historical development of the visual arts? Or, rather, how does Vasari, as a professional painter who has simultaneously taken up the role of the professional author for the purpose of writing the *Lives*, deal with the crucial issue of temporality as it is explored, for instance, in the context of the so-called Renaissance *paragone* of *ut pictura poesis*, a *paragone* that selectively pits the verbal and visual arts against one another? For Italian Renaissance artists and art theorists, beginning most famously with Leonardo, carefully differentiated between the way time is structured and experienced phenomenologically when it comes to the way narratives develop in verbal and pictorial forms. And the emphasis should indeed be placed here on the viewer's *experience* of an object of visual art. On the one hand, the narrative produced by writing in manuscript or book form, which is composed of sequentially ordered words moving from left to right and then downwards on the page as well as laterally from page to page, ineluctably unfolds in time and is thus fundamentally diachronic in nature. On the other hand, the visual art of painting presents the viewer with a moment seen all at once and is thus, according to this temporal model, fundamentally synchronic in nature. Hence we "read" a painting—especially, but not exclusively, a Renaissance painting that represents or relies on a narrative—by situating those moments into a sequence. Or as Rensselaer W. Lee summarized the issue roughly a half century ago in his *Ut Pictura Poesis, The Humanistic Theory of Painting*:

> the poet must render things piecemeal as "if a face were to be revealed bit by bit, with the part previously shown covered up, so that we are prevented by our own forgetfulness from comparing any harmony of proportions, because the eye cannot embrace the whole simultaneously in its field of vision," whereas a painting would represent all the parts of the face at the same instant, like so many voices joined together in sweet harmony. The passage [from Leonardo's notebooks] recalls Lessing's famous comment on the distinctness of Ariosto's long and detailed description of Alcina [in the *Orlando furioso*], which Dolce ... praised as a model for painters to follow—a comment in which Lessing illustrates his view that since the successive addition of details in description cannot result in a clear and definitive image of coexistent forms, descriptive poetry is not the province of the poet, and cannot challenge painting in depicting the beauty of the external world. And in pointing out the painter's capacity, which the poet does not share, to represent figures or details that one apprehends in a single moment of time, Leonardo clearly anticipates Lessing's virtually identical definition of painting as an art of figures coexistent in space that has for its province the depiction of objective reality. Furthermore, when he observes that "the only true office of the poet is to invent the words of people, who are conversing together," [Leonardo] seems to have in mind something that approximates Lessing's definition of poetry as an art of words succeeding one other in time in which, as the German critic was to add, the poet must deal not with description, but with progressive human actions and emotions. Leonardo thus anticipated by two and a half centuries Lessing's famous distinction between poetry and painting.[38]

As professionals with a vested interest in telling stories, painters in the Italian Renaissance devised all sorts of strategies to convey temporality, given the limitations of their medium and the constraints imposed upon it by narrative pictorial conventions, all the more after the invention of perspective allowed them to fashion a verisimilar, illusionary space on a two-dimensional surface.[39] One familiar and widely diffused narrative pictorial

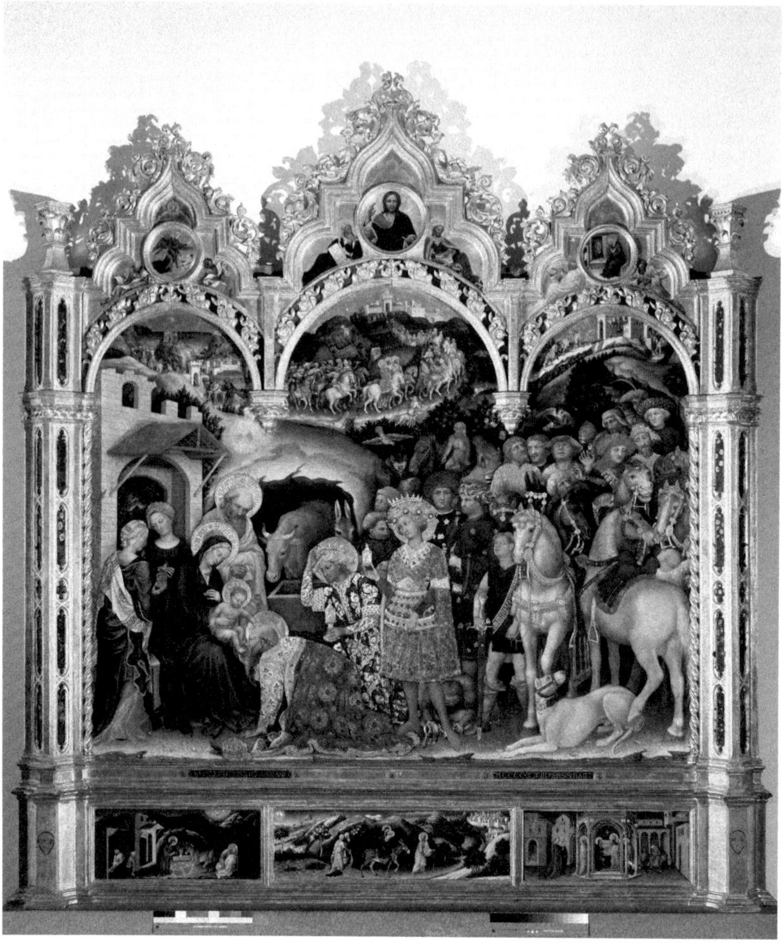

22. Gentile da Fabriano (ca. 1370–1427), *Adoration of the Magi* (1423). Galleria degli Uffizi Florence. Photo credit: Scala/Ministro per i Beni e le Attività Culturali/The Art Archive at Art Resource, NY.

convention included the creation of composite objects, polyptychs or triptychs or paintings with *predelle* (small chronologically arranged panels placed at the base of altar pieces), each designed to be read in a manner that recalls, but does not necessarily duplicate, the orderly temporal flow of verbal narratives (figs. 22 and 23). The painting so conceived and structured as a narrative thus functioned as a sort of visual book that could be read serially. However, it is important to emphasize that there was no codified set of strategies that articulated how one should go about reading a painting,

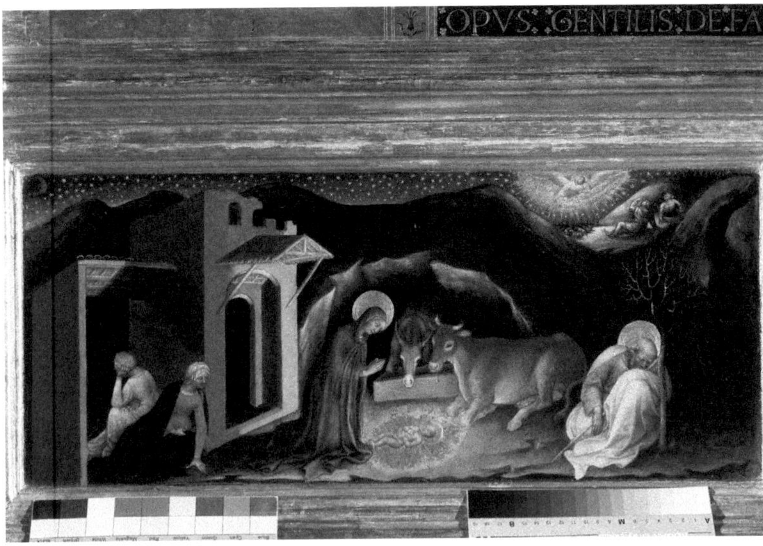

23. Gentile da Fabriano (ca. 1370–1427), *Adoration of the Magi* (1423). Galleria degli Uffizi Florence. Detail of the *Nativity* (followed by the *Flight into Egypt* and *Presentation at the Temple*, on which see fig. 22). Photo credit: Scala/Ministro per i Beni e le Attività Culturali/The Art Archive at Art Resource, NY.

much less, for that matter, a fresco cycle,[40] the way there existed highly developed and clearly articulated strategies dictating how one should go about reading a book.[41] Another pictorial convention adopted by artists to capture the passage of time in a painting included incorporating distinct moments represented in a "continuous narrative mode." In this case the same figures appeared more than once, "performing various actions of various episodes of the story" within the illusory depths of the painting, and time can be seen to compress or expand within the visualized story (fig. 22). As such, the viewer, potentially overwhelmed by visual *copia* incorporated into a painting but also probably taking pleasure in it, must spend some time—what Jack M. Greenstein has called "perusal time"[42]—decoding the images in a manner that perhaps even begins to approximate the amount of time it might take for those moments themselves to have actually occurred as they are dramatized in the fully realized fictive world contained within the picture frame—the Albertian window that opened up onto a plausible extension of our own real world or an entirely different, alternative, perhaps even fantastical otherworld. Yet another related pictorial convention employed during the period included depicting two or more chronologically separate moments together, all at once, in a "polyscenic narrative mode."

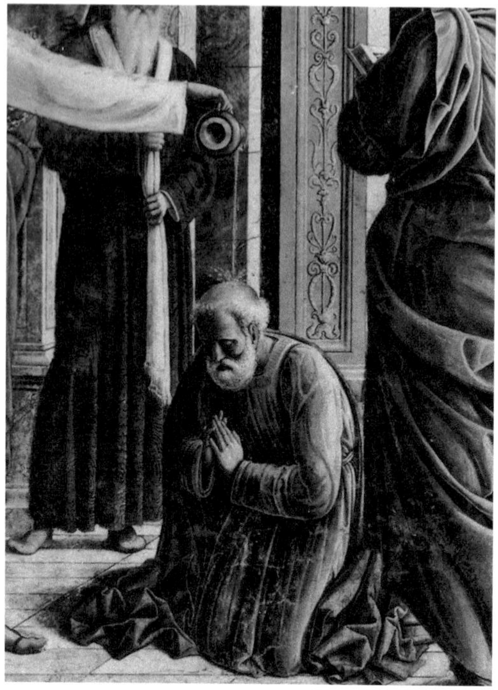

24. Andrea Mantegna (ca. 1431–1506), *St. James Baptizing Hermogenes* (ca. 1450–6, destroyed). Chiesa degli Eremitani. Padua, Italy. Detail. Photo credit: Alinari/Art Resource, NY.

In this case "the figures are shown once but are doing more than one thing, moving the story ahead by more than one episode," and space and time find themselves conflated within the visualized narrative to create a complex narrative experience that exploits illusionistic effects to engage, delight, and involve the viewer both intellectually and emotionally. Finally, painters recorded the passage of time in a "monoscenic narrative mode." In this case "the main elements of a story are concentrated into one framed scene" and "the main figures are shown once in a defined space, performing a single action that telescopes much of the story."[43] Hence the droplet splattering on Hermogenes' head in a painting by Andrea Mantegna (ca. 1431–1506) determines the length of time it took for him to be baptized (fig. 24), while the differing lengths of coagulating blood trickling down St. Sebastian's body in yet another of Mantegna's paintings register how he was pierced at different moments by different arrows shot from distinctly different angles over a harrowing span of time (fig. 25).[44] Again and again, sophisticated painters of the Italian Renaissance, trained to capture naturalized forms

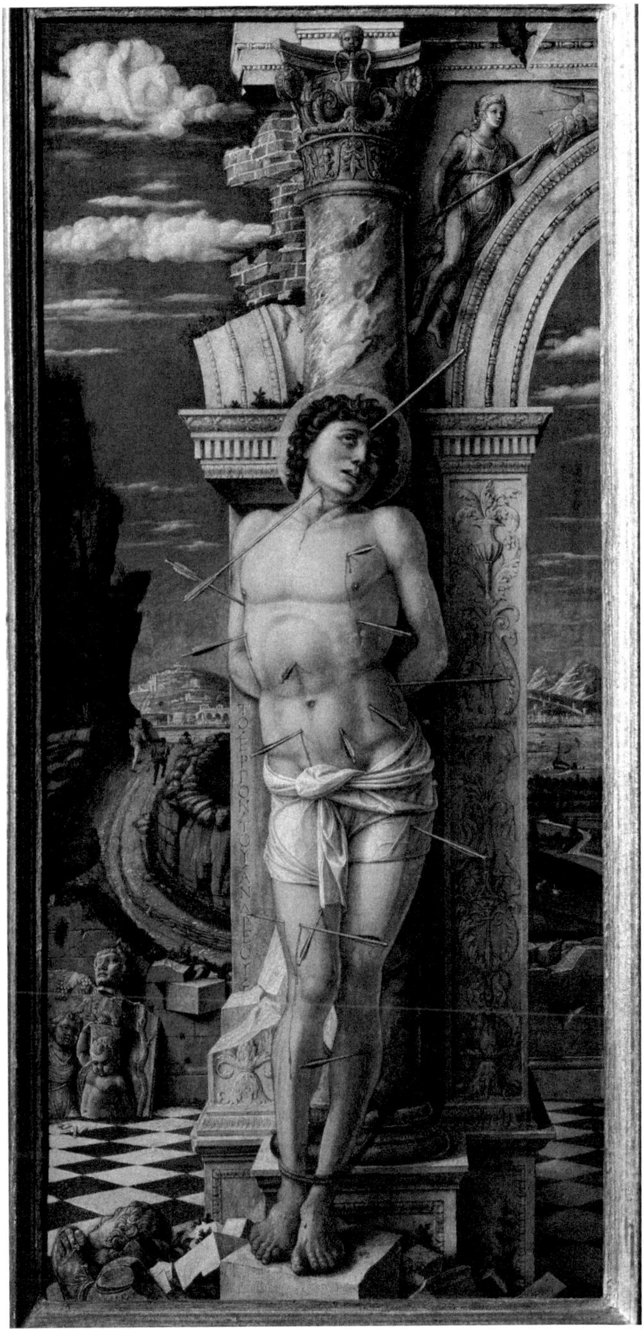

25. Andrea Mantegna (ca. 1431–1506), *St. Sebastian* (ca. 1457–9). Kunsthistorisches Museum, Vienna, Austria. Photo credit: Erich Lessing/Art Resource, NY.

in a realistic, illusory, perspectival space, ingeniously encoded the passage of time in their paintings as a sequence of blended, integrated moments and not as an absolutely single, frozen moment in time, a *punctum temporis*. Perhaps the most remarkable instance of this occurs in Leonardo's iconic *Last Supper*. There, what Leonardo accomplishes with *sfumato*, the technique of visually blending spatial relations, so that light and dark dissolve into one another to create the illusion of realistic volumes positioned in a perspectively organized setting, resembles—Leo Steinberg has observed[45]—what Leonardo brilliantly does with time, as he innovatively blends temporal relations, so that one moment of the Eucharist story in Leonardo's polyscenic/monoscenic narrative dissolves into another to create the illusion that a series of closely related events has somehow taken place all at once. Put differently, the technique of *sfumato*, which allows Leonardo to represent volumes in space through the art of *disegno*, provides Leonardo as a master draftsman with the narrative solution to how he can go about representing visually moments unfolding in time on a single picture plane.

Now, as a highly trained professional painter who takes up the profession of the author for the purposes of writing the *Lives*, and as someone who has obviously thought a good deal about matters of pictorial technique, composition, and *disegno*, Vasari does not seem particularly concerned, interestingly enough, either in the Torrentiniana or Giuntina editions, with explicitly examining at any length how temporality figures into the *paragone* of the Horatian *ut pictura poesis* as it was revised, elaborated upon, and explored in the Italian Renaissance.[46] But that does not mean that temporality does not play an important role in how Vasari treats his narrative descriptions of works of visual art in the *Lives*. Rather, as Svetlana Alpers observed in her seminal study of the function of *ekphrasis* in the *Lives*, Vasari's descriptions of works of visual art, which for the most part focus on paintings, serve two separate yet interrelated functions.[47] On the one hand, in a number of descriptions in the *Lives*, Vasari picks out key items of interest but does not display in the process any deep concern for the overall narrative unfolding in time as the visual artist captures a distinct moment or series of moments embedded within a full-fledged story that has a recognizable beginning, middle, and end. Vasari, that is to say, is only partly invested in retelling the story visualized or in observing how a particular artist achieved certain goals as a storyteller communicating distinctly visual ideas through the very elements he finds so essential to works of visual art: rule, order, proportion, *disegno*, and measure. Instead, what typically interests Vasari and what sticks in his memory are the key emotive moments of the story represented, the most affective parts that grab him as an involved and caring viewer. Nor should this strike us as entirely surprising. For Vasari, as for Leonardo and so many other visual artists of the period, every motion depicted in a painting, from a nimble gesture to a shifting glance to an expressive twisting turn of the body, was expected to convey, and was designed to be read as conveying, a corresponding emotion.[48] Hence Vasari looks for and responds to the emotional impact conveyed through actions, postures, gazes, facial expressions, and gestures as an underlying, principal goal of any work of visual art. On the other hand, accompanying those descriptions of paintings in the *Lives* is often a running editorial narrative about the artifact, in which Vasari vividly describes the flow of his own emotional responses to the work described in the form of *ekphrasis*. As a result, what we read is not just a verbal depiction of the (decidedly partial) story represented within the picture frame but a sort of secondary narrative—a metanarrative, if you will—about Vasari reacting emotively, at times even viscerally, to aspects of the story resuscitated by his memory.[49] An emblematic case in point seized upon by Alpers to bolster her argument is Vasari's *ekphrasis* of Raphael's *Entombment* (fig. 26), a painting completed in 1507 for Atalanta Baglioni as part of an altarpiece erected in the family chapel in San Francesco al Prato in Perugia to commemorate the death of her slain son, Grifonetto.[50] "In this most divine picture," Vasari writes, conscious that he is discussing an important and transformative work constructed at a point when Raphael was demonstrating how he had thoroughly surpassed Pietro Perugino and had selectively absorbed the visual lessons of Leonardo and Michelangelo:[51]

> there is a Dead Christ being carried [*portato*] to bury, executed [*condotto*] with such freshness and such loving care that it seems to the eye to have been only just done [*pare fatto pur ora*]. In the composition of this work, Raphael imagined to himself [*immaginossi*] the sorrow that the nearest and most affectionate relatives of the dead one feel [*il dolore che hanno i più stretti et amorevoli parenti*] in laying to rest the body of him who has been their best beloved, and on whom, in truth, the happiness, honor, and welfare of a whole family depends [*consista il bene, l'onore e l'utile di tutta una famiglia*]. Our Lady is seen [*si vede*] in a swoon; and the heads of all the figures are very gracious in their weeping, particularly that of St. John, who, with his hands clasped, bows his head [*china la testa*] in such a manner as to move the hardest heart to pity. And in truth, whoever considers [*chi considera*] the diligence, love, art, and *grazia* shown by this picture, has great reason to marvel, for it amazes [*ella fa stupire*] all of us who behold it [*la mira*], with the air of the figures, the beauty of the draperies, and, in short, the supreme excellence that it possesses in every part [*ch'ell'ha in tutte le parti*] (1.716, G4.164)

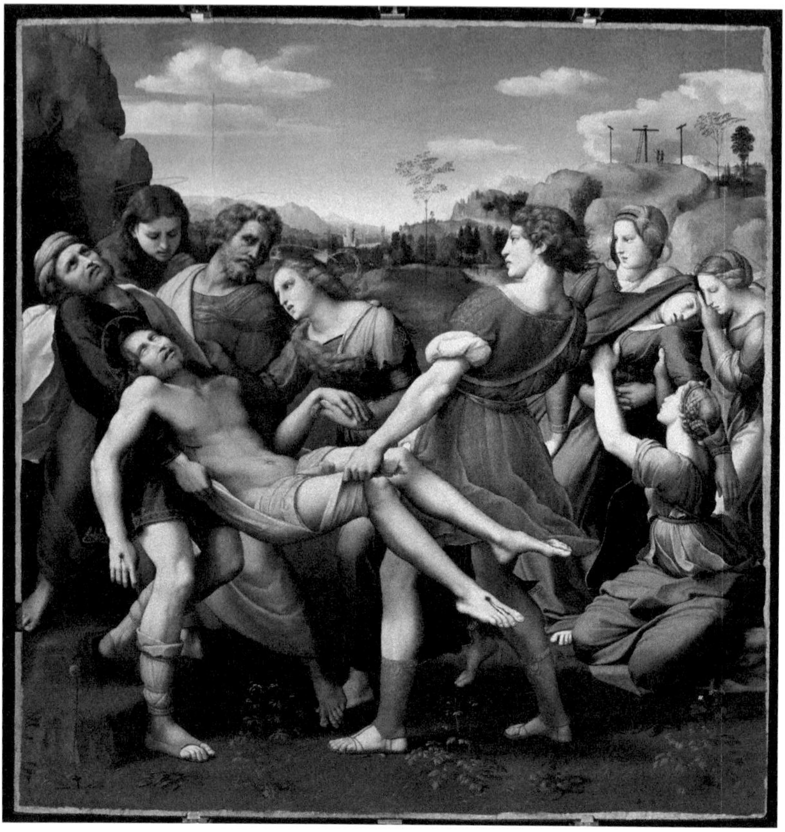

26. Raphael (Raffaello Sanzio, 1483–1520), *Entombment* (1507). Galleria Borghese, Rome, Italy. Photo credit: Scala/Ministero per i Beni e le Attività Culturali/Art Resource, NY. The image, designed in the *all'antica maniera*, is also aptly based on an ancient Roman sarcophagus relief of Meleager, the hero from Greek mythology.

Much can be said about this passage in terms of Vasari's overall desire, as Alpers observes, "to gather together the total force of the picture by relating both the artist and the viewer to the scene at hand," as well as how Vasari's overall handling of the technique of *ekphrasis* tells much about his own "aesthetics" as an artist generally privileging certain types of emotionally charged moments as they are staged in his own mannerist paintings (fig. 27).[52] In the same way the passage tells us much about how informed viewers in the Italian Renaissance, such as Vasari himself, were spiritually trained to respond to and meditate upon images of veneration

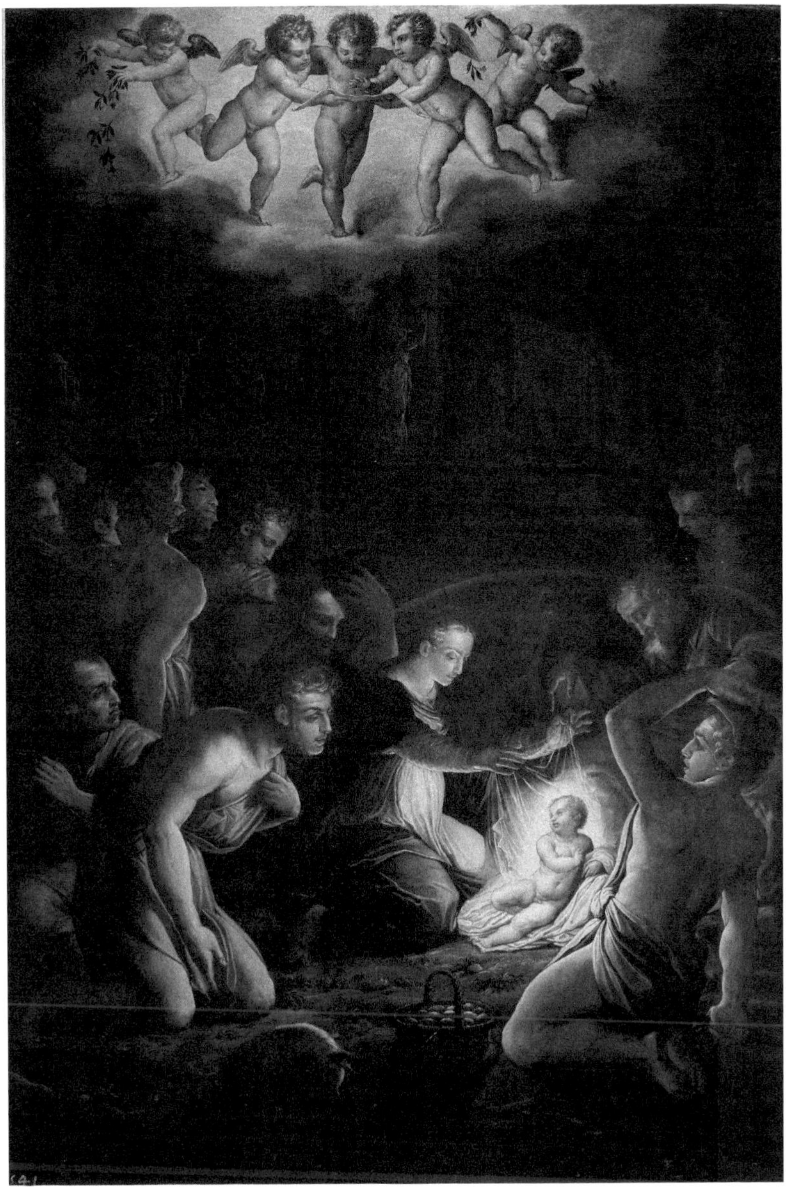

27. Giorgio Vasari (1511–1574), *Nativity of Christ* (ca. 1546). Galleria Borghese, Rome, Italy. Photo credit: Scala/Art Resource, NY.

emotionally, even to the point where those images could be vividly recalled as instructive mental models that could then be contemplated at will. Lodged deep in the memory, those interiorized images could serve as personalized visions that the viewer appropriated and summoned up as his or her own at any given moment in time, as something he or she always, in a word, "owned."[53] In this regard, Vasari's ability to recall Raphael's painting and reproduce it in his—and by extension our—"mind's eye" through *ekphrasis*, without the object ever presumably being in front of him as he writes, is indeed noteworthy. It is all the more noteworthy when considered in the context of the well-developed and increasingly important Renaissance investment in the "art of memory" (*ars memoriae*), which can be construed in this particular instance as the ability to train oneself systematically to remember and rhetorically reconstruct things vividly, with the appropriate *enargeia*, through visual recall. But for our purposes, what is so striking about Vasari's description of the *Entombment* are the temporal shifts of focus and how they relate to one another as they blend together and, in the process, conflate the subject with the object in a manner not entirely unlike the subtle braiding of perspectives in the nineteenth-century novelistic technique of *style indirect libre* (free indirect discourse).

On the one hand there is the narrative of the story depicted and the actual technical rendering of it, both of which are placed in the past tense. The painting is "executed." It is "imagined." It seems to have been just "done," a sure sign of its immediacy and freshness and intensity in the moment of it being viewed. Something has happened, we are told, not only in terms of Raphael's labor in crafting the work of visual art at a specific moment in time with praiseworthy facility. Something has also happened in terms of the action suggestively depicted in the dramatized story that once took place in the past—a distinctly distant past. Both of these events—Raphael's actual act of rendering the painting and the realized act of the deposition itself depicted realistically within the highly staged, dramatic *mise-en-scène*—are unmistakably over and done with, even if the painting itself may seem to have been completed just now, *pur ora*.[54] As such, they remind us, to draw from the prior observations of this chapter, that if someone with the perspicacious eye of a connoisseur were to find this remarkable painting somehow stored away and lost in an attic, that absurdly fortunate person would (or could, or should) be able to identify the painting for what it actually was: Raphael's magnificent lost altarpiece, the *Entombment*. Vasari has given us at least that much information for posterity's sake as he arguably draws on the language of devotional handbooks and the art of epideictic rhetoric, a ceremonial rhetoric of praise and blame fashionable in Renaissance oratory and so brilliantly developed in the *ars praedicandi* (the art of preaching).[55]

On the other hand, there are all the emotional observations that reveal how Vasari as an informed practitioner responds to the painting. And Vasari's responses, which signal to us how we are expected to react to the painting as sympathetic subjects viewing an object of sublime visual art, are often, but not always, presented in light of what the characters presumably experience in the present tense of the story. They "feel" sorrow, and so should we. Everyone "depends" on Christ, and so should we as sinners liberated through Him. One figure "bows" his head in pity, and so should we as penitent and pious Christians who empathetically experience the kindred emotion of devotion. And anyone who "considers" the painting must marvel over its pathos and beauty because it simply "amazes" everyone, much as, mutatis mutandis, we must every day, at every moment, in every place, be amazed at Christ's sacrifice, which, like the completed painting itself, took place in a localizable past but must still be experienced as if it had just occurred in the present, *pur ora*. This affective metanarrative about the psychological reactions provoked by the movements of the figures within the picture plane captures responses to a work of visual art not just in the present tense of Vasari's own time but in a sort of vivid, sempiternal present. It tells us how to experience that work at any given moment, just as it tells that absurdly fortunate connoisseur, who happens to come upon the well-preserved *Entombment* in a dark, stuffy attic, how he or she should respond emotionally to Raphael's painting. He or she should respond to it and thus emotively experience it not like so many "real" people on PBS's popular *Antiques Road Show*, who remain stunned by the astonishingly high sticker price attached to a recovered masterpiece and shriek or swoon at the recognition of the wealth they have unexpectedly acquired. Rather, he or she should respond to it and emotively experience it like an informed, sensitive, sympathetic, contemplative, and indeed pious Renaissance viewer of visual art, who remains stunned by the painting's vibrant beauty and finds himself or herself reacting to the passions of sorrow and pity and amazement that the painting is designed to evoke as it depicts for Vasari a matter of intense devotional interest with a dazzling sense of timeless freshness and immediacy. Put differently, what is arguably extraordinary here is that Vasari draws on a somewhat familiar rhetoric of medieval and Renaissance sermons and devotional handbooks in order to manipulate the emotional responses of the spectator as he or she recalls Raphael's image and renders it so vivid to others through his descriptive prose; yet in doing so Vasari simultaneously turns that same passionate, affective rhetoric into a sort of swooning over not just Christ's death but also, by extension, Raphael's astounding achievement of technical and conceptual excellence. The professional mastery exhibited in Raphael's gripping painting full of pathos has here become something—not to sound to coy about it—"to die for."

By the same token, the overall structure of the *Lives* as a work of verbal art describing visual art exists on distinctly different temporal planes as a large-scale narrative that employs various interconnected strategies, to borrow Hayden White's term, of historical "emplotment."[56] At the most obvious level, the *Lives* as a form of goal-oriented history is openly cyclical yet teleological in nature, with the visual arts being providentially reborn even as they develop sequentially over time, often in a recursive fashion but always with a driving, underlying direction toward an ideal end point of ever greater perfection. That much we can readily glean at the outset from the book's preface, which traces the development of the arts of painting, sculpture, and architecture from antiquity up to the time when Vasari's narrative officially commences as a full-fledged sequence of individual Lives. At that point the rebirth of the visual arts as a circular yet enhanced return to "classical" origins and ancient practices also begins. Then again, there is the linear, biological model of time, which, as we have seen, defines the period of *rinascita* that formally makes up the bulk of the (for the most part) chronologically arranged narrative. That period of *rinascita* starts with the "age" of childhood, beginning with Cimabue, when the forms of visual art start to appear naturalistic, lifelike, balanced, and stylistically apt but still lack proportion and do not reliably reveal a complete and proper understanding of measure, order, and the rules of constructing visual art *all'antica*. As a consequence there is often a certain lingering awkwardness (*goffezza*) and roughness (*rozzezza*) to them. That period of *rinascita* then progresses on to the "age" of adolescence, beginning with Jacopo della Quercia (1374/5–1438), when the forms of works of visual art begin to acquire *grazia* yet nevertheless often appear to the viewer as labored, affected, and stilted both in their conception and construction. Finally, the period of *rinascita* reaches its fulfillment with the "age" of adulthood, beginning with Leonardo. From that point on truly excellent works of visual art reveal on the part of the artist who has designed them a thorough understanding of measure, proportion, *disegno*, order, and rule. They regularly and naturally exhibit richness, delicacy, aptness, refinement, sweetness, charm, liveliness, and polish. And at long last they are also more consistently imbued with a certain "supreme *grazia*."

Yet again, there is a form of "static" time conceptualized in the *Lives*. That form of time, as the art historian Alina Payne has cogently analyzed it, is characterized by the permanence that the architectural orders had obtained in Vasari's mind in the context of his appropriation of writings about architecture in the Italian Renaissance, from Leon Battista Alberti's *De re aedificatoria* (*On Architecture*, 1452) to a variety of treatises written by sixteenth-century practitioners of architecture and commentators of Vitruvius' *De architectura* (*On Architecture*, ca. 30–15 BCE).[57] Accordingly, for Payne, architecture, as it was theorized in the Italian Renaissance, provided Vasari with the best and most useful model for thinking in general terms about the historical and teleological evolution of artistic development in the *Lives*. After all, the three architectural orders (the Doric, Ionic, and Corinthian) had all once gone through their own appropriate and paradigmatic process of evolution in classical antiquity and had thus finally arrived over time at their predestined and organically determined *telos*. At the same time, architecture as it was theorized in the Italian Renaissance provided Vasari with the best and most useful model for thinking about the ahistorical, "static" status of eternal principles of visual art. After all, the three architectural orders had acquired a sort of permanence, although those very same orders, albeit fixed in terms of their perfected historical progression, could, of course, be then reworked and recombined selectively at one's will to create new, innovative works of visual art, as Michelangelo so famously did in his entirely unconventional yet masterful design for the vestibule to the Laurentian library. As such, the ways in which architecture was seen to have developed over time lay, for Payne, conceptually at the heart of Vasari's conflicting notions of time, with one notion being fundamentally progressive, teleological, and evolutionary in nature, the other static, permanent, and transcendent.

Once more, at yet another level, there are the historical nodal points that plot how the period in question ends over time and consequently provide some sense of formal closure to the *Lives* as a structured narrative. One such historical nodal point, which is emphasized in the Torrentiniana edition, has Michelangelo as the final goal of the entire teleological process of the development of the arts. Hence Michelangelo is the last life dealt with at any length in the *Lives*. Moreover, with the exception of Benedetto da Rovezzano, who is considered artistically dead because he is physically blind, Michelangelo is the only living, active visual artist who has a Life exclusively dedicated to him. Yet another historical nodal point, which is emphasized in the Giuntina edition, has the now dead, twice-buried, and elaborately celebrated and commemorated Michelangelo functioning as the legendary, mythified figure of consummate artistic perfection and professionalism. Accordingly, Michelangelo has a twofold function within this narrative as time is structurally configured into it. In one instance, Michelangelo functions as a pivotal figure who sums up an entire era of accomplishment, in whom all the absolute rules of visual art have been gradually resuscitated, codified, familiarized, interiorized, and then surpassed. In another instance, he functions as a foundational figure who has paved the way for an entirely new era of visual art production, in which all the absolute rules of art have now been placed at the service of an institutionalized, state-sponsored, professionalizing academy devoted not just to "artists" but, as Marco Ruffini has suggested, to a form of anonymously authored and collaboratively crafted art production. Either way, whatever way we look at it, Michelangelo in both the Torrentiniana and Giuntina editions functions structurally as the crucial figure in terms of the temporal development of the plot that makes up the *Lives* as a teleological narrative.[58]

Finally, Michelangelo's role as a historical "figure" of critical importance in the temporal unfolding of the *Lives* must be read in terms of the age-old Christian concept of *figura*, which itself ineluctably structures how time can and should be perceived in narrative terms.[59] In one sense, there is, of course, the literal, real, flesh-and-blood Michelangelo, whom Vasari characterizes as all-too-human, a man who lived and breathed and suffered for his art with wondrous devotion and talent and sometimes even headstrong anguish, defiance, passion, piety, immodesty, irascibility, and determination. But in another sense, which is distinctly allegorical in nature, there is the "divine," heaven-sent Michelangelo, whom Vasari characterizes as the providentially ordained man who has effectively divided the world of visual art since his coming into largely two distinct historical periods, with a clear before and after. As such, everyone before Michelangelo in Vasari's narrative seems to strive, as if seeing things through a glass darkly, to do what Michelangelo can masterfully do on such a monumental scale and with such variety and perfection and technical finesse as he overcomes every manner of difficulty and every problem of *disegno* within his *professione*. By the same token, everyone after Michelangelo similarly seems to yearn, like committed believers in a devotional cause, to replicate in some measure what he was able to do in a manner that surpassed even the greatest achievements of the greatest visual artists of classical antiquity:

> While the most noble and industrious spirits were striving, by the light of the famous Giotto and of his followers, to give to the world proof of the ability that the benign influence of the stars and the proportionate admixture of humors had given to their intellects, and while, desirous to imitate with the excellence of their art the grandeur of Nature in order to approach as near as possible that supreme knowledge that many call understanding, they were universally toiling, although in vain, the most

> benign Ruler of Heaven in His clemency turned His eyes to the earth, and, having perceived the infinite variety of all those labors, the ardent studies without any fruit, and the presumptuous self-sufficiency of men, which is even further removed from truth than is darkness from light, and desiring to deliver us from such great errors, was minded to send down to earth a spirit with universal ability in every art and every profession, who would be able, working by himself alone, to show what manner of thing is the perfection of the art of design in executing lines, contours, shadows, and highlights, so as to give relief to works of painting, and what it is to work with correct judgment in sculpture, and how in architecture it is possible to render habitations secure and commodious, healthy and cheerful, well-proportioned, and rich with varied adornments ... And since He saw that in the practice of these rare exercises and arts—namely, in painting, in sculpture, and in architecture—the Tuscan intellects have always been exalted and raised high above all others, from their being diligent in the labors and studies of every faculty beyond no matter what other people of Italy, He chose to give him Florence, as worthy beyond all other cities, for his country, in order to bring all the talents to their highest perfection in her, as was her due, in the person of one of her citizens (2.642, G6.3–4)

In approaching Vasari's book in light of the temporal structure that a figural reading unavoidably imposes on the historical narrative of Vasari's *Lives*, with one event prefiguring another and necessarily being fulfilled by it in the process, I do not wish to overstate the case. Typologically, Michelangelo is no sustained *figura Christi* (figure of Christ) in the *Lives* as both the wayfarer and Beatrice are in Dante's *Divine Comedy*.[60] And there is no reason to believe that one can profitably apply four-fold, theological allegory to the *Lives* in a consistent manner as one can to Dante's extraordinarily complex and intricately fashioned poem, which was designed to attract such intense forms of scholarly exegesis, as Dante himself makes plain in his Letter to Can Grande.[61] But the temporal structure that necessarily underpins the concept of *figura* does help explain a few curious aspects about how time is providentially configured in the *Lives*, with Michelangelo creatively construed as divine in more than just the purely nominal sense that flatters and mythologizes him, as when Ludovico Ariosto in the *Orlando furioso* refers to him as "Michael, more than mortal, divine angel [*Michel, più che mortale, angel divino*]" (33.2).[62] At the very least it helps us understand how the period after Michelangelo does not necessarily constitute in the *Lives* a period of decay and decline, any more than the period following the advent of Christ did.[63] Quite the contrary. Michelangelo's life, which at once functions as an immutable end point and as a decisive turning point, heralds a new beginning as it captures everything good about the past in terms of the invention, disposition, and execution of exceptionally high-quality visual art and transmits it through Michelangelo to the future—and thus to a future of labor-intensive and studious academicians in the Accademia del Disegno at the service of Cosimo I's increasingly bureaucratic, behavior-monitoring state.

But more important, at least in light of the themes of this chapter, it helps explain why it makes perfect sense that Vasari, who is relentlessly cast in the role of Michelangelo's longstanding friend and ongoing correspondent and most devoted enthusiast, appears at the very end of the Giuntina edition of the *Lives* as a pivotal, testimonial figure in his own right. For Vasari, if not a truly great artist, does make for a superb disciple, figurally if not literally. Hence, while he can never measure up to Michelangelo and will inevitably pale in comparison to him as a visual artist, even as he participates sympathetically in some of Michelangelo's agonizing pain as he constructs in one instance his own elaborate painting cycle on a grand ceiling and therefore likewise suffers physically in the process of working at the behest of his autocratic patron, Vasari can still take up the pen and, as *both* a professional writer and a professional painter, bear witness to the greatness of Michelangelo's coming into the world in the fullness of time. In any event, as a practitioner-writer spreading the word, Vasari can rest assured that this particular Florentine artist, whose life and genius he describes at extraordinary length and with such loyalty and veneration, will not be left prey to death and oblivion, *preda della morte e della oblivione*, in large measure because of the formidable brilliance of Michelangelo himself, to be sure, but also in part because of the durability of print and, of course, Vasari's own lionizing efforts as he exercises his memory and does everything he possibly can to defy the destructive and implacable force of *la voracità del tempo*.

5

NOTTE/NIGHT

Art in itself is difficult [*l'arte in sé è dificile*]

—Giorgio Vasari, "Description of the Works of Giorgio Vasari," the *Lives* (1568)[1]

Alfonso di Tommaso Cambi, who was then a very beautiful youth, well-lettered, accomplished, and most gentle and courteous, had himself portrayed nude and at full length in the person of the huntsman Endymion beloved by the Moon, whose white form, and the fanciful landscape all around, receive their light from the brightness of the moon, which in the darkness of the night makes a vision/view/effect very apt and natural [*che fa nell'oscuro della notte una veduta assai propria e naturale*], for, being as diligent as possible, I did my best [*perciò che io m'ingegnai con ogni diligenza*] to counterfeit the particular colors that the pale yellow light of the moon usually gives to the things it strikes.

—Giorgio Vasari, "Description of the Works of Giorgio Vasari," the *Lives* (1568)[2]

I The *Difficultà* of Visually Representing the Night in the *Lives*

Time and again Vasari's "excellent" visual artists are seen in the *Lives* to have faced complex visual challenges within their *professione*, what he refers to often enough as *difficultà* (difficulties), many of them self-imposed, but also many of them imposed upon them by demanding patrons.[3] And time and again those very same visual artists are seen in the *Lives* to have steadfastly overcome those *difficultà* by coming up with distinctly visual solutions to specifically material, visual challenges. In the *Lives*, no one did so as brilliantly, we have seen, as the incomparable Michelangelo Buonarroti, who was always seeking to outdo himself and others, according to Vasari, including the hallowed ancients with whom he aggressively vied in the three nobler arts of painting, sculpture, and architecture. To this end, for instance, Vasari describes the *Last Judgment* as a work that can never be praised enough, in part because Michelangelo reveals in it an ability to represent the human form in so many different, expressive, and affective ways without ever once repeating himself, but also in part because the *Last Judgment* itself serves as such a great "example of foreshortenings and all the other difficulties of art [*tutte l'altre difficultà dell'arte*]" (2.760, G6.133). As a convenient catchword, then, the term *difficultà* signaled historical progress for Vasari insofar as excellent visual artists—in rivalry with one another, classical antiquity, and/or their own past achievements—demonstrated how they could take on more and more impressive visual challenges and, in a sense, conquer them, thereby manifestly revealing how they, unlike anyone else, had competitively achieved certain remarkable, if not entirely always unprecedented, results within and for their *professione*. Emblematic in this regard is Bramante's extraordinary ability "to demonstrate the strength of his talent/genius and mastery over those artistic difficulties that he showed in architecture [*mostrare il valore dello ingegno suo e quelle arteficiose difficultà che nella architettura mostrò*]" (1.659, G4.73–4) or Jacopo Sansovino's ability to fashion a statue of the ribald Greek god Bacchus in a manner that allowed him to overcome a "difficulty never yet attempted [*una difficultà, non più usata*]" (2.808, G6.181). To be sure, a far-too-excessive and single-minded attention to "difficulties" could lead in certain cases to all manner of dreary sterility in the visual arts, Vasari warns when examining the case of Paolo Uccello. His paintings, according to Vasari, in the end devolved into unimaginative, mechanical demonstrations of visual problem-solving in the newly invented and codified art of geometric, analytical perspective (1.281, G3.61). But for the most part, incorporating and overcoming difficulties in works of sculpture, painting, and architecture is deemed in the *Lives* to have unquestionably furthered the history and *professione* of the visual arts as a whole. For this reason, Vasari claims that he himself was always searching in his own work to display and overcome, as he puts it in his Life, "the difficult in art [*il difficile dell'arte*]" (2.1031, G6.379). Truly excellent visual artists of the order of Michelangelo or Bramante or Sansovino (or arguably Vasari) thus deserved to be recognized and congratulated for overcoming certain *difficultà* when they managed to do so.[4] And by extension each of them deserved to be recognized and congratulated for contributing to the overall historical development of the *professione* of the visual arts. By tracing how painters, sculptors, and architects as visual artists of ideas masterfully overcame certain *difficultà* on the small and grand scale, Vasari could, at least in part, tell a compelling, teleological narrative about the individual and collective development of the visual arts in Italy over the roughly three-hundred-year period he characterized as a full-fledged *rinascita*—and, presumably, well beyond into an era that included the creation, establishment, and eventual rise of the Florentine Accademia del Disegno.

By the same token, the term *difficultà* signaled for Vasari what consumers invested in commissioning and/or purchasing works of visual art should learn to appreciate when looking at paintings, sculptures, or buildings of real, lasting, material quality crafted by visual artists deeply committed to their *professione*. "Difficulties," conceived as things to be valued, were sometimes cunningly incorporated into works of visual art, such as when Michelangelo managed to take the prophet Jonah—a familiar, allegorical figure foreshadowing Christ's harrowing of hell and resurrection—and make him appear to lean backwards within a pendentive that physically curves forward toward the viewer, precisely where the wall meets the ceiling at the far end of the Sistine Chapel and, appropriately enough, right above Perugino's altarpiece that depicted the redemptive power of the Virgin Mary in a chapel devoted to her ascension and glory (the altarpiece was later destroyed to make way for the *Last Judgment*). Only a trained eye could adequately recognize how extraordinarily difficult Michelangelo's feat of illusionism and foreshortening technically was, especially when one considers how he had to determine well in advance how Jonah in the pendentive would appear to the eye when viewed from the floor, roughly seventy feet beneath him. Suspended on a scaffold, Michelangelo flawlessly had to paint it without the benefit of being able to see it from its ideal vantage point below. Difficulties were thus aesthetic qualities that inhered in the works of art themselves, consciously placed there by the hand of the visual artist, created, that is to say, through the mechanical and intellectual art of *disegno*. So the untutored viewer needed to be indoctrinated into those "difficulties" through what we might call object lessons and thereby trained to detect them in order acquire an informed "period eye," to borrow and adapt Michael Baxandall's famous phrase.[5] In acquiring such an informed period eye, moreover, a viewer arguably acquired at the same time cultural and social distinction.[6] For difficulties effectively served as signaling devices: being able to detect and decode them in a sort of competitive game of recognizing the underlying artistic ideas separated the more sophisticated and cultured viewers from the others.[7] Either you saw those difficulties or you didn't, were part of an "in" group that acknowledged them or weren't. In reading the *Lives*, non-practitioners were therefore repeatedly invited to learn to see, and accordingly appreciate, what expert practitioners saw and valued as they overcame one more *difficultà* after another and, in the process, both individually and collectively furthered the development of the *professione* of the visual arts, charting its path forward in an upward and uplifting trajectory. Overcoming difficulties consequently marked significant achievements, at once artistic, intellectual, and historical, on the part of the visual artist who labored on behalf of consumers increasingly invested in learning more and more about works of visual art in a culture of conspicuous consumption and in seeking social mechanisms for distinguishing themselves within a highly stratified world. At the same time, inquisitive producers and consumers of visual art were presumably expected to strive to better themselves by continuously working to overcome and/or understand difficulties. In this way difficulties had, in a phrase, complex cultural value.

One such artistic, intellectual, and historical achievement in Vasari's eyes, which this final chapter is dedicated to exploring at some length, was how certain visual artists of his trumpeted *rinascita* had developed the ability to capture pictorially not just light but also, to adopt John Milton's memorable phrase, the "darkness visible" of the night.[8] This was an extremely difficult thing to do, as Kenneth Clark succinctly remarked in his *Landscape into Art*, precisely because "night," as a distinct span of time, "is not a subject for naturalistic painting"—and naturalistic painting was in part for Vasari what his *rinascita* was all about, albeit not when it comes to thinking specifically about representing landscapes or the emerging genre of landscape painting itself.[9] Leonardo da Vinci, a sometimes crepuscular artist who never produced a full-fledged nocturne himself, seems to have had something of this in mind when he self-consciously explored the difficulty of "how one ought to represent a night [*come si dee figurar una notte*]" and arrived at the following practical solution in the course of articulating his thoughts in what would develop into a fragmented, unfinished, and often repetitive but still groundbreaking treatise on painting compiled posthumously by his former pupil and assistant, Francesco Melzi. "Whatever is entirely devoid of light," Leonardo observes,

> is all darkness. Since the night is such a condition [*essendo la notte in simile conditione*], and you wish to represent a scene in darkness, do it with a great fire, for that which is nearest to the fire is more tinged with its color, since that which is nearest to the object opposite takes on more of its nature. By painting the fire tending toward red, you will make all the things illuminated by it also reddish and those which are farther away from the fire will be more tinged by the black color of the night [*tinte del colore nero della notte*]. The figures that are against the fire will seem dark in the brightness of the fire, because the part of what you see is tinged with the darkness of the night [*è tinta dalla oscurità della notte*] and not with the brightness of the fire, and those that are at the sides are half dark and half reddish, and those which can be seen beyond the outlines of the flames

will be all illuminated by ruddy light against a dark background. With regard to their actions, show those that are near protecting themselves with their hands and mantles, to guard against the excessive heat, their faces in the contrary direction showing an inclination to move away. A large part of those more distant will protect their eyes with their hands, hurt by the intolerable brilliance.[10]

As Leonardo recognized, the seemingly boundless darkness of night robs objects of definition, form, texture, and color. "In the shadows on a cloudy night," Leonardo also observes elsewhere in the same collection of thoughts that make up the Vatican's *Codex Urbinas 1270*, "no shape or color of a body is perceived [*nelle tenebre di una notte nubillosa nella quale niuna figura o colore di corpo si comprende*]."[11] In the same way, the darkness of night robs objects of the hard outlines associated with the art of *disegno*, as opposed to the soft, blurred contours and gradual building up of form through the studied and expressive application of paint associated with the art of *colorito*. Accordingly, linear perspective, one of the great inventions of the Italian Renaissance, for instance, arguably has no great purchase on the imagination when everything is cast in deep, dark shadow and orthogonals are barely visible and shapes and outlines become so blurred that they easily dissolve into atmosphere. Hence Filippo Brunelleschi's groundbreaking lesson in catoptrics, conceived in order to demonstrate his command of linear perspective, would be pretty much a disaster if performed at twilight.[12] By contrast "light," as Paul Hills has observed, "illuminates as much as there is to be seen."[13] Or at least as much as the visual artist wants us or allows us to see, as Leonardo clarified yet again in his unfinished treatise on painting, this time in the context of talking extensively about different sorts of shadows: "An object seen in places that have little light, or at twilight [*in sul principiare della notte*], also shows little difference between its lights and shadows, and if the time be complete night [*et se sia intera notte*], for the human eye the difference between light and shadows is imperceptible, to such a point that the object entirely loses shape, and is then apparent only to the keen eye of the nocturnal animals [*e solo si dimostra alle sottili viste delli animali notturni*]."[14] Being able to represent what the human eye can see at twilight, much less what a nocturnal animal alone can see once darkness has completely descended on the world and everything is shrouded *nelle tenebre di una notte nubillosa*: that, in a nutshell, is a notable *difficultà* that sixteenth-century painters began to address in earnest. In the process a number of artists also arrived at all sorts of clever visual and compositional solutions worthy of some recognition, not just for us, as we look back to the past and admire how some painters managed to solve certain complex artistic problems, but also for Vasari, who was actively shaping for posterity how readers in the future should appreciate the accomplishments that make up the legacy of his triumphant *rinascita*.

In this regard it is hardly accidental that Cardinal Alessandro Farnese, apparently concerned with visual matters related to the niceties of verisimilitude, is described in the *Lives* as having demanded the following from the mannerist painter Taddeo Zuccaro, who was commissioned to paint the subject of "night" in a room devoted specifically to sleep in the Villa Farnese at Caprarola:

> Now to declare my conception first in general, I would have a Night painted there [*vorrei che vi si facesse una Notte*], because, aside from the fact that it would be appropriate for sleep, it would be a subject not very customary and different from those of the other rooms, and would give you an occasion to execute rare and beautiful works in your art, since the strong lights and deep shadows that go into such a subject are wont to give much grace and relief to the figures [*perché i gran lumi e le grand'ombre che ci vanno soglion dare assai di vaghezza e di rilievo alle figure*]; and it would please me to have the time of this Night approaching dawn, so that the things represented there may be visible in a verisimilar manner [*E mi piacerebbe che il tempo di questa Notte fosse in su l'alba, perché le cose che vi si rapresenteranno siano verisimilmente visibili*]. (2.627, G5.576)[15]

Mindful of these sorts of concerns, Vasari himself, he affirms in the *Lives*, seems to have also taken on the significant visual challenge of painting the night naturalistically three different times (G6.377, 394, and 398), once to great praise even early on in his career, when he represented for the hermits of the Abbey of Camaldoli "a night illumined by the splendor of the newborn Christ [*notte alluminata dallo splendore di Cristo nato*], who is surrounded by some shepherds adoring him" (fig. 27), or, some years later, when he captured with great diligence the subtle, luminous effects of the moon "in the darkness of the night [*nell'oscuro della notte*]" (as recorded in the epigraph to this chapter).[16] So, too, the contemporaneous Titian (ca. 1488–1576) capitalized on his ability to articulate different kinds of competing light sources (torchlight, lamplight, firelight, candlelight, and celestial lightening) when he "fashioned a night [*ha finto una notte*]" with "beautiful art, talent, and judgment" in at least one case recorded with praise in the *Lives* (2.795, G6.167), in this instance the extraordinary *Martyrdom of St. Lorenzo* made for Santa Maria Assunta (otherwise known as the Church of the Jesuits, I Gesuiti; fig. 28). Similarly, the Venetian painter Lorenzo Lotto (ca. 1480–1556/7) rendered a "very beautiful" Nativity scene "as a night [*finta in una notte, che è bellissimo*]" (1.947, G4.552), Antonio da Correggio (ca. 1489–1534)

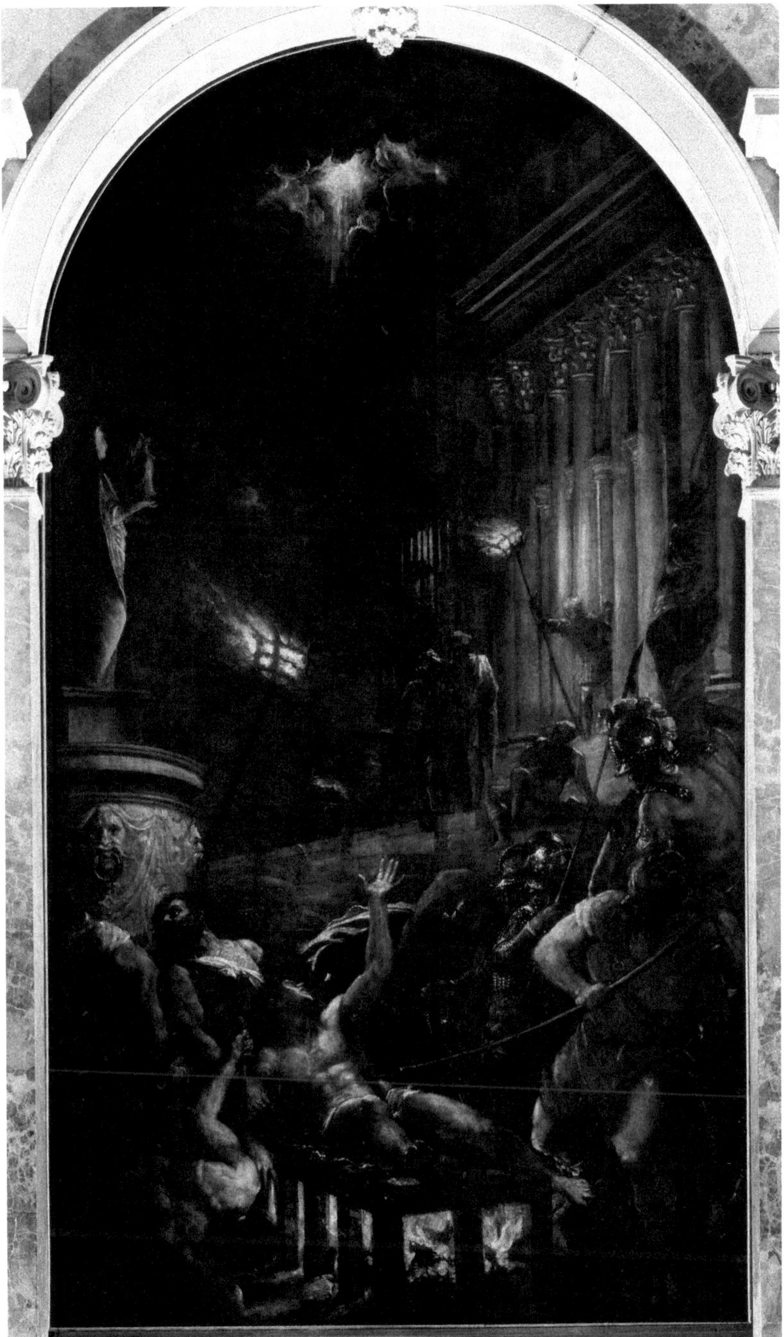

28. Titian (Tiziano Veccellio, ca. 1488–1576), *Martyrdom of St. Lawrence* (1558). Chiesa dei Gesuiti (S. Maria Assunta), Venice, Italy. Photo credit: Cameraphoto Arte, Venice/Art Resource, NY.

captured Christ in the garden at night in much the same way (G4.53), and the Brescian Girolamo Savoldo (ca. 1480/5–after 1548) produced "four pictures of night and fire, which are very beautiful [*quattro quadri di notte e di fuochi, molto belli*]," along with a "Nativity of Christ," with "a very lovely rendered night [*finta di notte, molto bella*]" (2.470, G5.430).[17]

Yet Vasari's great hero who proves most capable of handling the particular visual *difficultà* of painting the night both naturalistically and on the grand scale in fresco turns out to be a rather unexpected one, especially if we take into account the notion articulated throughout the *Lives* that pictorial subject matter typically conforms to the character of the artist, a deeply engrained notion proverbially encapsulated, as we saw in a previous chapter, in the familiar Renaissance adage that "every painter paints himself [*ogni dipintore dipinge se*]." Vasari's hero in this case is not, as one might reasonably anticipate it to be, Leonardo, who routinely painted in a "dark manner" with figures ringed by an encroaching blackness of smoky, atmospheric shadows,[18] or, by the same token, Michelangelo, who crafted a sculpture of "Night" (fig. 29) for the New Medici Sacristy—a work to which I will later return very briefly.[19] Indeed, the melancholic Michelangelo, whose lyric poetry could wax nocturnal at times,[20] in fact made no attempt in his long and illustrious career to paint a credible nighttime scene, even though he obviously dedicated a panel of the Sistine Chapel vault to God's separation of light and dark and could certainly set one against the other in dramatic pictorial contrast, as in the corner pendentive devoted to Judith victoriously bearing aloft Holofernes' gigantic head on an oversized platter. Rather, Vasari's hero in this particular case turns out to be the graceful, princely, charming, rather libidinous, contemplative, and presumably cheerful—by no means moody, dark- or nocturnal-tempered—Raphael Sanzio. As it turns out in the *Lives*, no one before Raphael—the philosophical painter of the luminous *School of Athens* (fig. 2)—had displayed such mastery in overcoming the singular *difficultà* of representing the night as a distinct span of time on the grand scale in fresco form. And as the art historian Costanza Barbieri has cogently observed, "in the early Cinquecento, thanks to the newly achieved subtle effects of oil painting, the nocturne theme represented challenges and potentialities"—which is to say a complex visual *difficultà* to overcome—"previously inconceivable," thereby bringing about in Italy "a new emphasis [in the 1520s] on tonal painting, dramatic outcomes by using different sources of light, new possibilities with painting local colors, the exploitation of *sfumato*, a more effective chiaroscuro, and a unifying dark tonality."[21] In a similar fashion, no one before Vasari himself had focused so intensely on the importance of materially capturing the idea of the night *in* the visual arts in a narrative

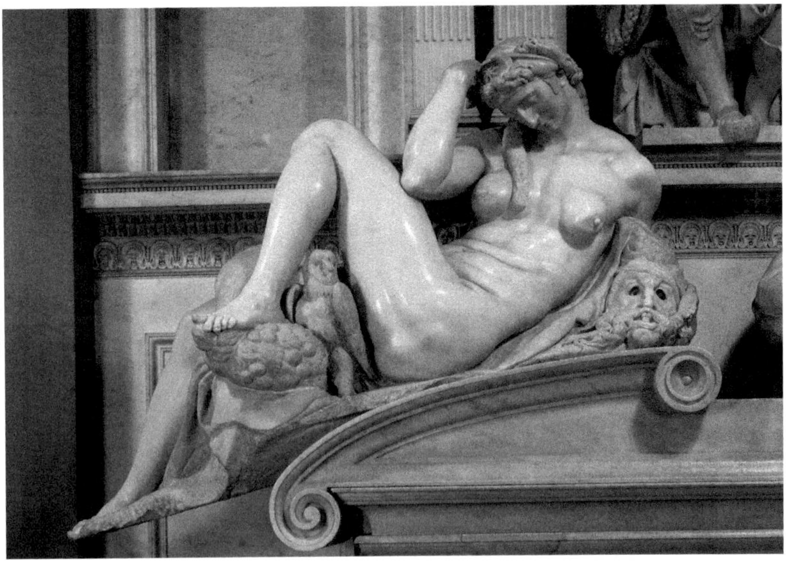

29. Michelangelo Buonarroti (1475–1564), *Night* (1526–31). Medici Chapels (New Sacristy), San Lorenzo, Florence, Italy. Photo credit: Scala/Art Resource, NY.

dedicated strictly *to* the visual arts. Not Pliny the Elder in his formative and influential *Natural History*, not even when he talks about Apelles' habit of using the tonally darkened "black varnish" of *atramentum* to lend "an austere somberness [*austeritatis*] to colors."[22] Nor, with the notable exception of Leonardo, did any other writer thinking seriously about the visual arts in the Italian Renaissance do so before the *Lives* first appeared in print in 1550, from Cennini, Alberti, and Ghiberti in the fifteenth century to Giovio, Pino, the Anonimo Magliabechiano, and the Anonimo Gaddiano in the sixteenth.[23]

II The Visual Matter of Time: Raphael and the Conquest of Naturalistically Representing the Night in the *Lives*

The year is 1514. Raphael takes on an enormous pictorial challenge as he paints the *Deliverance of St. Peter*, a work topically linked to its original patron, Julius II, who had previously been cardinal of the titular church of San Pietro in Vincoli (St. Peter in Chains). The *Deliverance of St. Peter* is also a work thematically designed to remind everyone concerned that God had guaranteed heavenly protection to the papacy and by extension to the now deceased, determined warrior pope who had so aggressively sought to regain the papal states (the relevant text underpinning the story

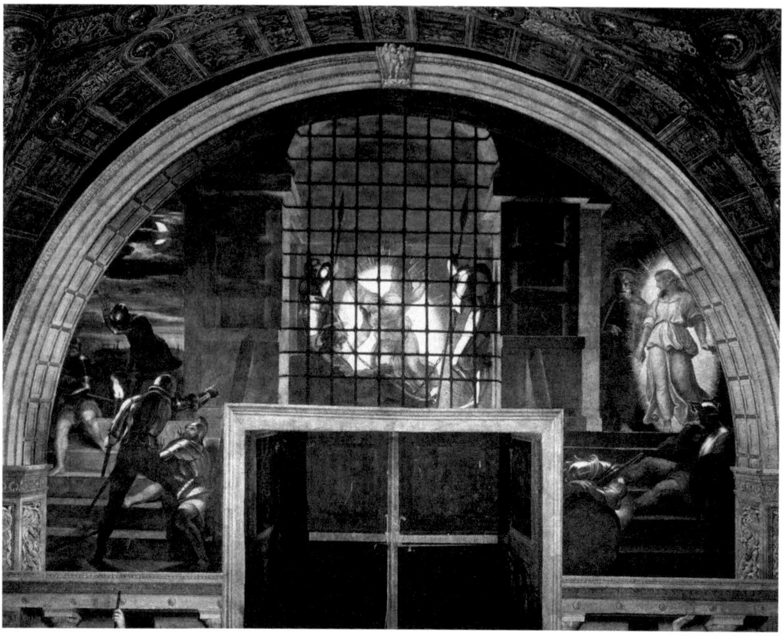

30. Raphael (Raffaello Sanzio, 1483–1520), *Deliverance of St. Peter* (1514). Stanza d'Eliodoro, Vatican Palace. Alinari/Art Resource, NY.

comes from the Acts of the Apostles 12.13).[24] In the process of painting the *Deliverance of St. Peter*, Raphael overcomes a host of visual and compositional difficulties within his *professione* (fig. 30). Or so Vasari gives us to believe. Capturing the sheen on the armor of the guards keeping watch over St. Peter is one such obvious difficulty. Indeed, in one instance examined toward the very end of the *Lives*, Vasari describes how he himself struggled to duplicate perfectly with paint the way the light strikes Alessandro de' Medici's glinting, silver armor and how, thanks to Jacopo Pontormo's fortuitous intervention, he came to realize that mimesis cannot always duplicate the thing being represented no matter how hard one tries to match or surpass Nature (fig. 31). Yet Raphael overcomes that particular pictorial *difficultà* in an altogether astonishing fashion in the *Deliverance of St. Peter* by making "his armor shine most resplendently [*vivacissimamente risplendere l'armi*] … in such a way that their luster seemed more burnished than if they were absolutely real rather than painted [*in modo che i lustri paiono bruniti più che se fussino verissimi e non dipinti*]" (1.725, G4.180). In this respect, as in so many others, Raphael—envisioned as a second Apelles in the *Lives*[25]—is a far more accomplished painter than any other visual artist, with the exception of the divine Michelangelo. In Raphael's hands representation can predictably be

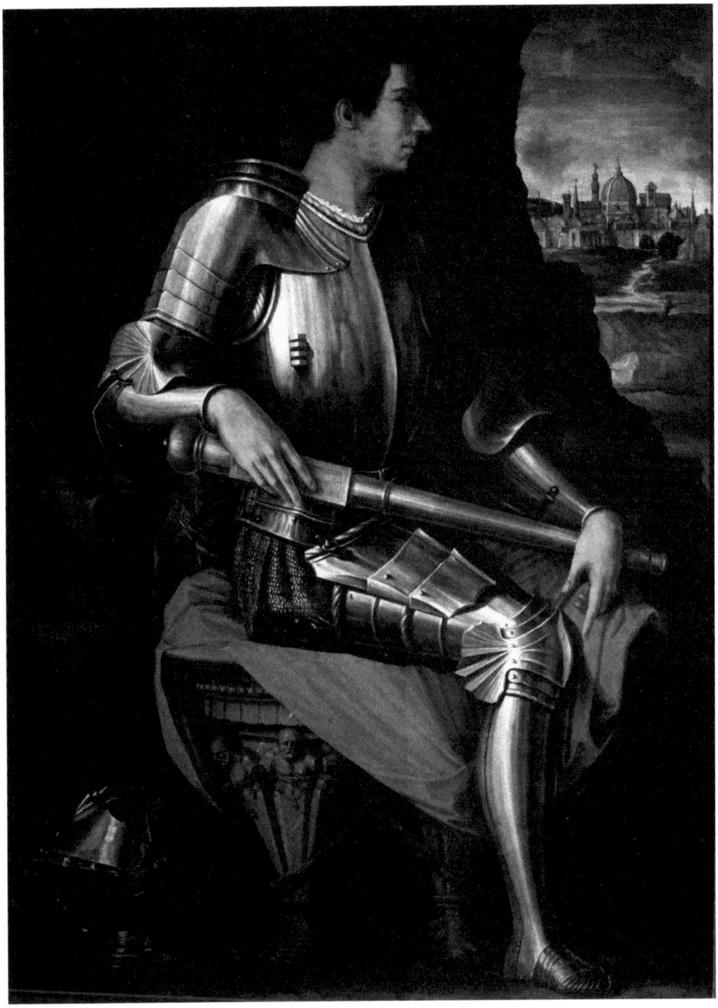

31. Giorgio Vasari (1511–1574), *Portrait of Alessandro de' Medici* (1534). Uffizi, Florence, Italy. Alfredo Dagli Orti/Art Resource, NY. As Vasari tells the story, Pontormo, seeing the frustrated Vasari struggling to duplicate perfectly the sheen of Alessandro's armor, advised him to take the actual, physical armor away and he would then recognize that, compositionally, the light within the painting already worked on its own terms as a highly successful, mirror-like representation of reality—all of which constitutes yet another object lesson within the *Lives* about, among other things, *mimesis*.

mistaken for the thing itself, painted light seeming more like real light. In making this claim, Vasari is here of course rehearsing commonplaces about hyper-realism in the visual arts familiar to readers of Pliny's *Natural History*, where painted grapes or curtains are mistakenly taken for the real things, or, for that matter, Giovanni Boccaccio's *Decameron* (ca. 1353).[26]

What is more, Raphael, we learn, overcomes yet another *difficultà* by proving himself to be a masterful storyteller in the still vital, evolving, and complex form of the continuous narrative mode. Hence, as Vasari looks at the *Deliverance of St. Peter* or recalls it for us through the verbal art of *ekphrasis*, he can imagine hearing the heavy, iron gates creaking open, just as he can sense, as he absorbs the meaning of various gestures, body postures, and facial expressions, the weight of the "very deep slumber [*gravissimo sonno*]" (1.725, G4.180) of the guards and the eerie quality of the liberated St. Peter's oneiric state of mind as he, too, wakes up and experiences his own miraculous liberation in a sort of trance, struck with "the belief that it is rather a dream than visible reality" (1.725, G4.180). Moreover, the whole fresco is painted vividly, with the appropriate *enargeia*, to draw on the rhetorical terms that both Vasari and Raphael were familiar with, so that it would appear "so natural and true/lifelike that you would never say that it was painted at all [*sì naturali e sì vere che non diresti mai che ella fussi dipinta*]" (1.726, G4.181). Simply put, Raphael demonstrates for Vasari the remarkable ability to realize within this particular painting a "difficult conception [*difficile imaginazione*]" (1.726, G4.181).

Yet what is most remarkable about the painting as Raphael overcomes every manner of *difficultà* in the process of realizing this *difficile imaginazione* is how he manages to paint a full-blown nighttime scene in fresco on the grand scale. And Raphael almost seems to have designed this nocturne in a manner that reads in parts like a visual realization of Leonardo's pragmatic solution to painting the night by strategically using a fire (in this case a small fire isolated off to the left, rather than a "great" centrally located one) to illuminate figures positioned in different, naturalistic, and somewhat colorful poses amid the pervasive, atmospheric darkness. Needless to say, this is by no means the very first worldly nighttime scene ever painted in the Italian Renaissance, so many of which typically boast stylized (often deep blue) skies, as in any number of Giotto's nighttime scenes, such as *The Kiss of Judas* or *The Raising of Lazarus* in the Scrovegni Chapel (1304–6), or, for that matter, any number of religious representations of the Nativity, the Annunciation to the Shepherds (fig. 32), the Crucifixion, the Transfiguration, the Flight into Egypt, the Betrayal, the three Magi bearing gifts to the newly born Christ child (fig. 23), and the like.[27] And nighttime scenes do predictably figure from time to time in a variety of engravings of the period,

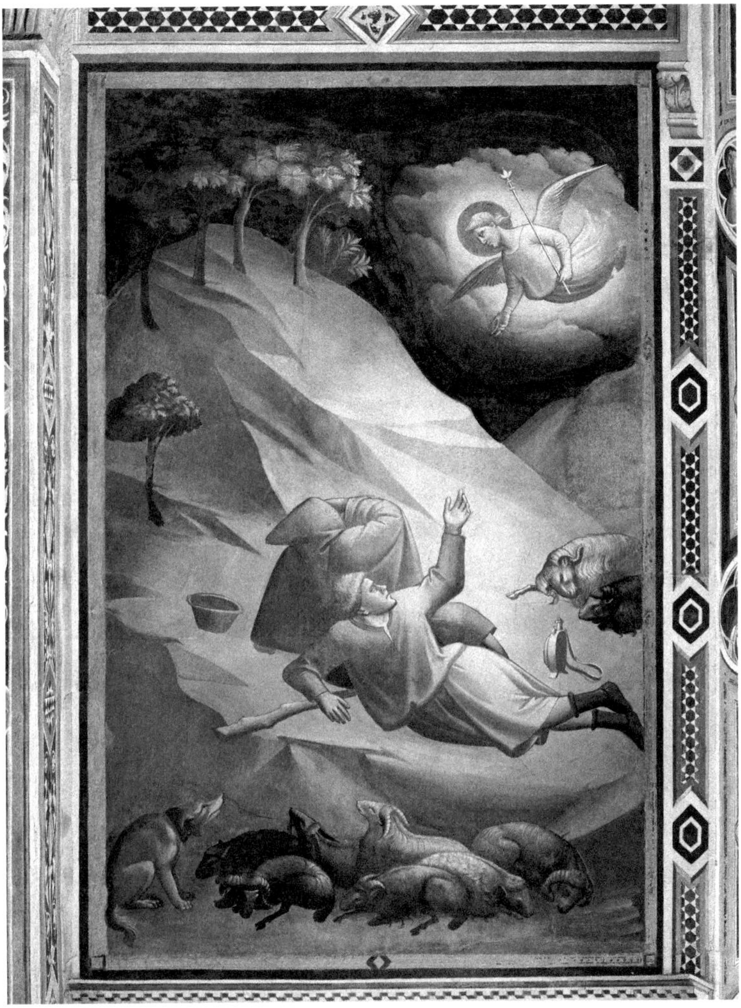

32. Taddeo Gaddi (ca. 1300–1366), *Annunciation to the Shepherds* (ca. 1330). Cappella Baroncelli, Santa Croce, Florence, Italy. Photo credit: Scala/ Art Resource, NY.

perhaps, we might expect, because engraving itself as a medium necessarily relies so heavily upon light and darkness, without the help of color, that its tonal emphasis becomes a natural vehicle for chiaroscuro compositions. Prints like Marcantonio Raimondi's *The Dream of Raphael* (ca. 1508/9), for instance, and arguably Agostino Veneziano's *Lo Stregozzo* (ca. 1515–25) are engraved nocturnes that parallel the rise of the nighttime theme in Roman painting and surely helped to spread its innovations abroad. What is more, Albrecht Dürer, the most famous northern Renaissance artist, may well have played a role in establishing the nocturne theme as an important one in the early sixteenth century in Italy through the wide dissemination of such famous prints as his *Melencolia* (1514), a print that memorably captures a resplendent sun before it sets, sparkling, behind a placid sea. And there were other northern Renaissance artists who had explored the nocturne theme well before Raphael did, such as the Netherlandish painter Geertgen tot Sint Jan in his *Nativity at Night* (ca. 1490). Likewise, miniaturists in the European Renaissance also produced a variety of nocturnes, albeit on the small scale, as one can see in the *Christ in Gethsemane* in the early fifteenth-century French Gothic *Très Riches Heures* (ca. 1412–16). But for Vasari, it is important to stress, Raphael's painting in the *Lives* represents the first such image in which darkness is seen to dominate the nighttime scene in a recognizably realistic sublunary world and, above all, one in which nocturnal darkness completely and convincingly pervades a large pictorial space in fresco. And for Vasari that particular, complex pictorial problem, as he finds it so magisterially resolved in the *Deliverance of St. Peter*, constituted a major *difficultà* that only the great Raphael—envisioned in the second edition of the *Lives* as virtually second to none—could face and satisfactorily overcome on the grand scale in fresco form.

To be sure, Piero della Francesca's *Dream of Constantine* (fig. 33), which forms the most obvious precursor to the *Deliverance of St. Peter*, is, like Raphael's fresco, unmistakably dark, with both sharp and soft shadows capturing a worldly nighttime frescoed scene. And significantly enough, Vasari considers Piero's fresco to be a representation not just of a prophetic dream of the True Cross but also in some measure of "night" itself: "But above every other consideration, whether of genius or art, there is his painting of night [*la notte*] and an angel in foreshortening who is flying with his head downwards, bringing the sign of victory to Constantine, who is sleeping in a pavilion" (1.400, G3.262). Two "men-at-arms," placed on either side of Constantine's bed, are thus appropriately "obscured by the darkness of the night [*oscurati dalle tenebre della notte*]," Vasari observes, and Piero (ca. 1415–1492), as if providing us with a sort of object lesson by focusing on the subject matter of night, "makes us understand in this darkness how important it is to copy things as they truly are [*fa conoscere in questa oscurità quanto importi imitare le cose vere*] and to take them always from the true model, which he did so well that he enabled the moderns to attain, by following him, that supreme height which is seen in the art of our own time" (1.400, G3.262). But in truth much of Piero's painting is dominated by light, not nocturnal darkness—something that is rendered immediately evident to the eye when one squints at the image. And the darkness dramatized in the fresco seems to be largely restricted to isolated sections: the one impenetrably

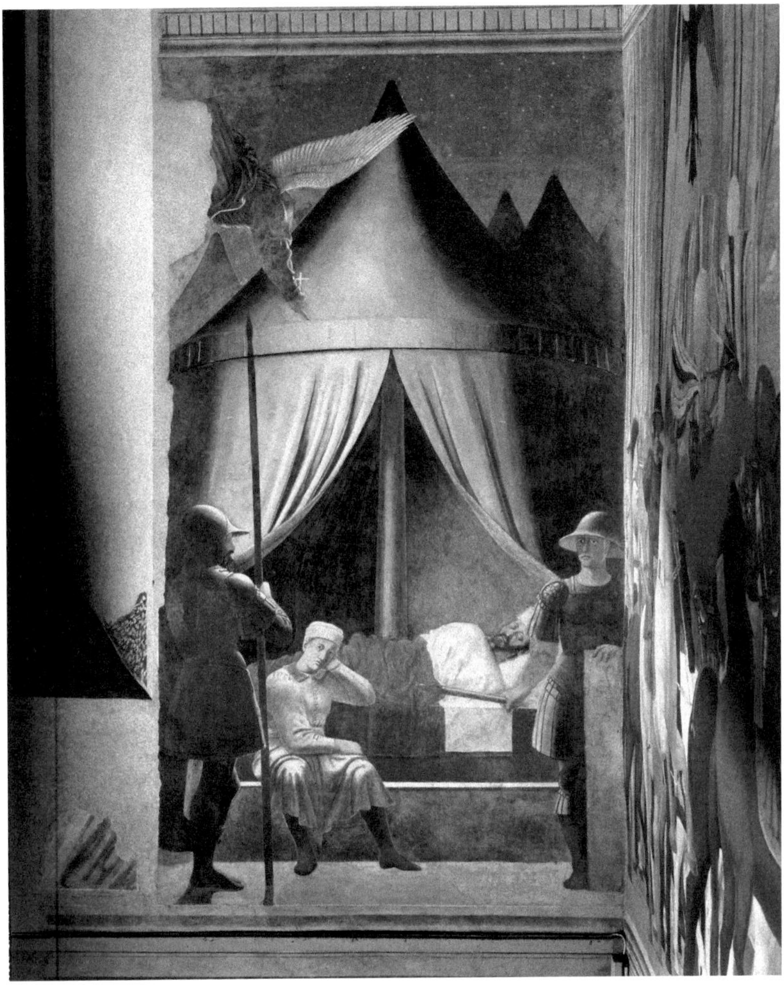

33. Piero della Francesca (ca. 1415–1492), *Legend of the True Cross: Dream of Constantine* (ca. 1450–65). San Francesco, Arezzo, Italy. Photo credit: Scala/Ministero per i Beni e le Attività Culturali/Art Resource, NY.

opaque, visually flat, blackened interior section of the tent where Constantine sleeps soundly; the tips of the receding, depthless, conical tents fading into the distance; the sweeping, dark, contoured folds of the brightly lit central tent; and the single, standing, silhouetted guard keeping watch over Constantine with a vertical spear in hand, while the cloudless blue sky above, albeit perhaps paled over time, suggests an hour of dawn or dusk rather than full-fledged night. Indeed, dawn would have been the time, appropriately enough, when a truly prophetic dream, such as Constantine's, would have conventionally taken place.

By contrast, Raphael's fresco, which captures a moment when the low crescent moon is partly occluded by a thin, dark cloud, is full of what Vasari calls "le scure tenebre della notte" (the dark shadows of the night, 1.726, G4.180). And there are indeed different kinds of layered shadows to the painting—"primary," "derivative," and "compound" shadows, to borrow Leonardo's terms[28]—that make up varied tonalities of darkness: a blackened darkness around the edges of the twisting flames of a torch, a reflected darkness of shadow upon shadow cast upon the armor of the guards, a nebulous darkness within the arched stone prison, and varied shades of darkness defining the steps and surfaces of the outside columns and textured walls. The overall impression is thus of a patterned, materialized darkness that covers the entire painting from edge to edge and illusionistically from the background to the foreground, atmospherically engulfing virtually everything in its path. As a consequence, the darkness in Raphael's painting (unlike that in Piero della Francesca's, where it is largely flat and depthless) requires from the viewer a demanding, pressured gaze in order to grasp the nuances of how one shadow plays upon another in deep space and how, as a result, one sort of darkness visually interacts with another, fades into another, overlaps with another, gives shape to another. "Here are seen shadows," Vasari observes, "on the armor [*si scorgono nell'arme l'ombre*], other shadows projected, reflections, and a vaporous glare from the lights [*i riflessi e le fumosità del calor de' lumi*], all executed with darkest shade, and so well, that it may be truly said that he was the master of every other master [*lavorati con ombra sì abbacinata che invero si può dire che egli fosse il maestro degli altri*]" (1.726, G4.181). All the more extraordinary, Raphael captures this patterned darkness by placing the fresco directly over and around a "window [*finestra*]," precisely where the "wall [*facciata*]" is itself "darker [*più scura*]" (1.726, G4.180). "Thus, when you look at the picture," Vasari observes, "the light strikes you in the face [*ti dà il lume nel viso*], and the real light conflicts so well with the different lights of the night in the painting [*e contendono tanto bene insieme la luce viva con quella dipinta co' diversi lumi della notte*]" (1.726, G4.180). Squint at the composition and it becomes readily apparent that this is a painting of night—illuminated within by both worldly and otherworldly sources of light and rendered atmospheric by a combination of opaque and transparent shadows—in a way that Piero's *Dream of Constantine* never fully was.

At one level, for Vasari, Raphael's *Deliverance of St. Peter* is thus very much about the remarkable technical accomplishment of depicting, in the difficult and taxing medium of fresco,[29] a light that seems more real than real light itself amid a patterned darkness that has an astonishing density, depth, and beauty to it. At the same time for Vasari this is self-evidently a painting

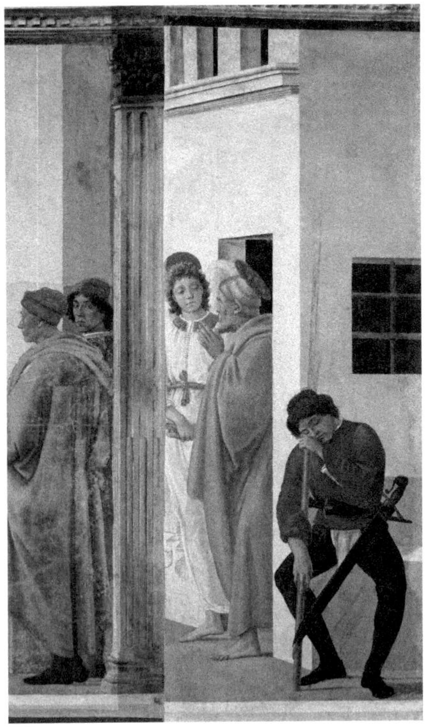

34. Filippino Lippi (ca. 1457–1504), *Deliverance of St. Peter from Prison* (ca. 1485). Brancacci Chapel, S. Maria del Carmine, Florence, Italy. Photo credit: Scala/Art Resource, NY. Detail.

about the spiritual meaning of light and dark, capturing in the process, as Paolo Giovio had put it, "an uncertain light in the shadow itself of the night [*in ipsa noctis umbra dubia quadam luce*]."[30] The darkness that pervades the picture and that demands so much from the viewer in order to sort out its varied features is indeed all about what it means to be in a state of terror, ignorance, and sin, like the guards who sleep through the miraculous event, oblivious to the heavenly light associated with the liberation of St. Peter, or the awakened guards who remain frightened, astonished, and dumbfounded by the presence of the angel, perhaps suddenly seeing things now for the first time, in Pauline terms, and not through a glass darkly. Nothing of this sort, for instance, even remotely appears in Filippino Lippi's bright and colorful rendition of St. Peter's liberation in the Brancacci Chapel, which strangely enough seems to stage the event during the day and not, as it should be, at night (the sitting somnambulant guard seems to have simply taken an early afternoon nap, fig. 34). Additionally, Raphael's *Deliverance of St. Peter* is very much for Vasari a painting about the light's dominion over the shadowy pervasiveness of night. There is the ethereal, angelic light that invades the darkness and seems to punch a sparkling hole in the center of the wall, while the moonlight and torchlight serve to illuminate dimly the surroundings, rendering the imprisoning darkness, in Milton's oxymoron, "visible." At the same time there is the real, natural light that "strikes you in the face" as it pours through a window facing out onto Bramante's newly constructed imperial Cortile Belvedere, at the far end of which stands the Vatican's prized possession of the Apollo Belvedere occupying its prominent place in Julius II's sculpture garden. That light—arguably an Apollonian light in its association with the celebrated Roman copy of a Greek sculpture—fills the room and illuminates not only the thoughtful viewers who contemplate the painting as they sort out the various kinds of shadows that intricately define it, but also the painting itself. And that painting, Vasari observes, stages a *paragone* between the fictive and the real, the material and the immaterial: between the mandorla of light created by the guiding hand of the professional artist and the framed natural sunlight filtered through a rectangular window positioned directly below it, as well as between the haunting, cavernous darkness of the painted mise-en-scène and the real, ambient darkness of the room in which the painting is placed.

When it comes to thinking about matters of technique, then, both light and dark certainly have positive valences for Vasari in the *Deliverance of St. Peter*, much as do the terms *chiaro* and *scuro* when he thinks more generally about matters of technique, modeling, and *disegno*. One is by no means privileged over the other in the *Lives*, since both are materially required to create the credible illusion of three-dimensional volume and depth by bringing people and things into low and high relief (in a word through "chiaroscuro"), although Vasari, like Leonardo and others before him, recognized that optically it is light that actually gives objects concrete, material definition in the real world. Overcoming the *difficultà* of painting light in the *Deliverance of St. Peter* is thus just as important, technically speaking, as overcoming the *difficultà* of painting darkness. And both light and darkness are equally meaningful for Vasari as a practitioner himself, although clearly the former is privileged over the latter when it comes to thinking about moral, theological, and spiritual matters. The darkness of evil for Vasari, as for Augustine long before him, surely signaled the absence of the good and thus conceptually had no material essence, *but it nevertheless had to appear materially and recognizably in a painted image that captured night as a distinct span of time.* When understood strictly in terms of what it means in the *Lives* to paint a credible, naturalistic, nocturnal scene, the *Deliverance of St. Peter* is therefore singularly important because it represents the one moment when Vasari consciously emphasizes a visual artist's material conquest of the night, or what some scholars of the early modern period have called "nocturnalization," a concept defined by the cultural historian Craig Koslofsky in his *Evening's Empire* as "the ongoing expansion of the legitimate and symbolic uses of the night" as a distinct, circumscribed span of time.[31] For no one up to then had done anything of this sort before when it came to taking on the notable challenge of painting a realistic, worldly night scene in fresco on the grand scale, we are invited to glean from the *Lives*. Not Giotto, Masaccio, Piero della Francesca, Leonardo, or even Michelangelo, who had already completed his monumental Sistine Chapel, which included a panel dedicated to God's cosmic separation of light and dark. For the first time in the Italian Renaissance, Vasari leads us to believe in his discussion of Raphael's *Deliverance of St Peter*, night as an idea of distinct cultural value and as a distinct time of the day has legitimately become the primary, material subject of an entire large fresco, physically occupying—in all its density, complexity, and atmospheric depth—the full extent of the wall. Even the sky, far from being painted in the conventional mode of a stylized, nocturnal blue, is an ashen gray, rimmed by just a fading, dusky pink at the horizon, while mostly dark clouds loom overhead and obscure some of the light from the low-hanging moon. Put differently, night in Raphael's fresco is not simply the background for Vasari: it is instead the all-encompassing ground from which everything else springs visually to life. Hence what is being captured in Raphael's fresco is arguably not just darkness per se but the distinct span of time in which darkness all-encompassingly envelops, and thus at one and the same moment seemingly dissolves into boundless atmosphere, the "real" material world—the time, that is to say, of night as a visually rendered idea.

Now Raphael was not a visual artist invested in materially capturing the night as a distinct span of time through paint, at least not until this moment in his career, and so he can be deemed an unlikely hero in accomplishing this feat as it is described in the *Lives*. Quite the contrary, he was a painter whom one would much more readily associate today, looking back over his overall artistic output, with the transparent luminosity of the day, not the thick, sometimes impenetrable opacity of *le scure tenebre della notte*. Emblematic in this regard were the series of thematically integrated frescoes he had just completed in the Stanza della Segnatura, covering four walls and the ceiling, all of which speak to various forms of illumination (juridical, poetic, theological, moral, and philosophical) handled technically in a soft, muted, luminous tone dominated by an overall "*unione* manner of coloring" (figs. 2 and 4)—as opposed to the "chiaroscuro mode" of coloring that characterizes the more theatrical and dramatic frescoes of the Stanza di Heliodoro, where the *Deliverance of St. Peter* itself is in fact placed.[32] The same can be said for Raphael's early works fashioned in the manner of his teacher, Pietro Perugino. They include, among other paintings: a large number of his portraits capturing members of the male and female elite posing indoors or outdoors during the day as well as his various religious scenes of the Madonna with the Christ child, and the radiant frescoes for the Villa Farnesina, such as the vibrant *Triumph of Galatea*, completed about the same time as the *Deliverance of St. Peter*. In short, Raphael, a master artist seemingly capable of overcoming any manner of *difficultà* within his *professione* and widely commended for his supple, balanced, unifying, and sensitive handling of color,[33] was by no means predisposed to being darkly crepuscular in his painting, any more than he was in his temperament. And for the most part that remained the case throughout his career,[34] albeit with one notable exception conceived on the grand scale after the completion of his *Deliverance of St. Peter*.

Just before he died, Raphael created his monumental *Transfiguration* (fig. 35), a painting commissioned originally by Cardinal Giulio de' Medici (the future Clement VII) for his cathedral in France, Saint-Just, at Narbonne. This was Raphael's last great challenge, his last great painting, and, as it turns out, one of the great nocturnal scenes of the High Renaissance. The painting also marked the occasion for Raphael's last *paragone* with another major visual artist. This time the *paragone* was with Sebastiano del Piombo, a Venetian artist who had already painted his tonally subdued and wistful *Polyphemus* (ca. 1512) in the Farnesina in direct contrast with Raphael's far more color-saturated and upbeat *Triumph of Galatea* (likewise ca. 1512). Sebastiano del Piombo was then receiving support and encouragement from Michelangelo in Rome and, like Raphael, was known as a subtle and sensitive colorist who just a few years earlier had also produced, following Michelangelo's design, yet another great nighttime painting of the High Renaissance. The painting in question, which constitutes "an attempt to unify Florentine *disegno*, or even sculpture itself, with Venetian *colorito*,"[35] is Sebastiano's magnificent, somber, nocturnal *Pietà of Viterbo*, a painting recognized by Vasari himself as a "much praised dark landscape [*un paese tenebroso molto lodato*]" (2.142, G5.89) and described in our own time by Michael Hirst as indeed the first such nocturnal altarpiece of the Italian Renaissance (ca. 1517; fig. 36).[36] Hence, by the time Raphael turned to paint his monumental *Transfiguration*, there was yet another eminent visual artist already working in and about Rome who had become deeply invested in the *difficultà* of painting nighttime scenes. To be sure, as Barbieri has demonstrated, "Sebastiano was, by then, the acclaimed master of night scenes and their theatrical lighting effects, considered second to

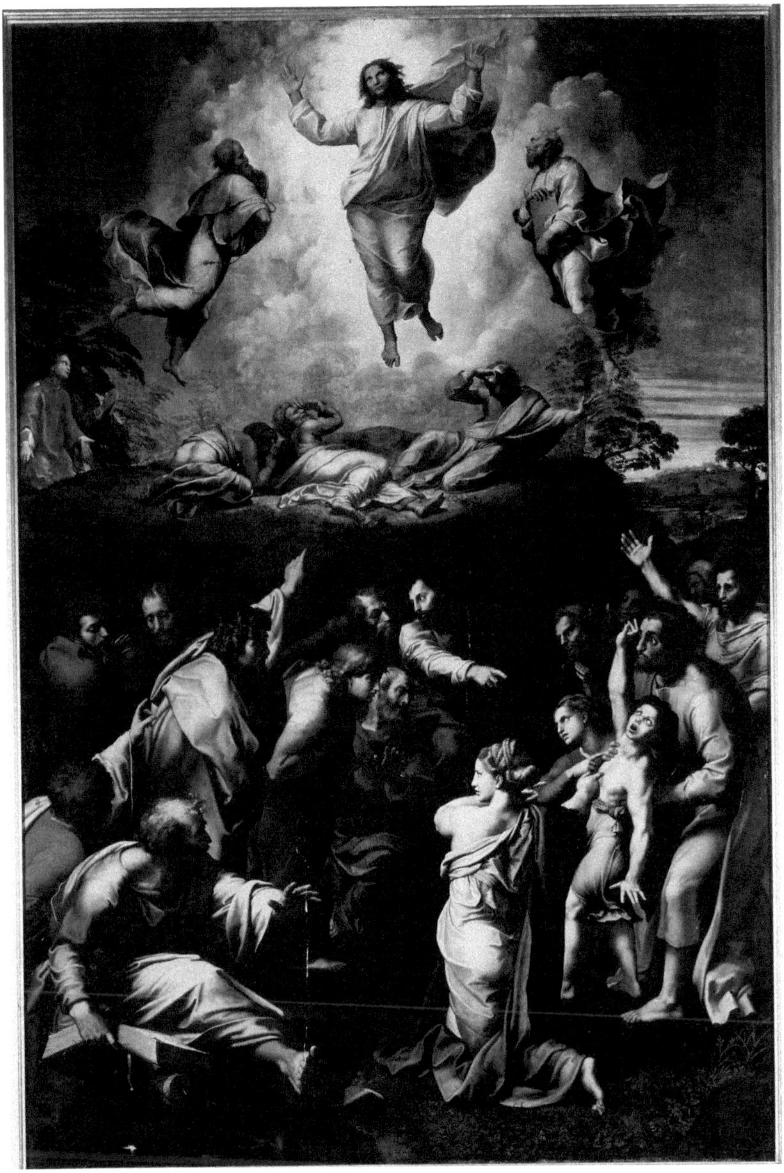

35. Raphael (Raffaello Sanzio, 1483–1520), *The Transfiguration* (1517–20). Pinacoteca, Vatican Museums, Vatican State. Scala/Art Resource, NY.

none," or "at least," she gingerly adds, "after the death of Raphael." And nighttime scenes, Barbieri goes on to observe, had become "the latest trend in painting" by the 1520s, so much so that not long after producing the magnificent *Deliverance of St. Peter*, a work roughly contemporaneous

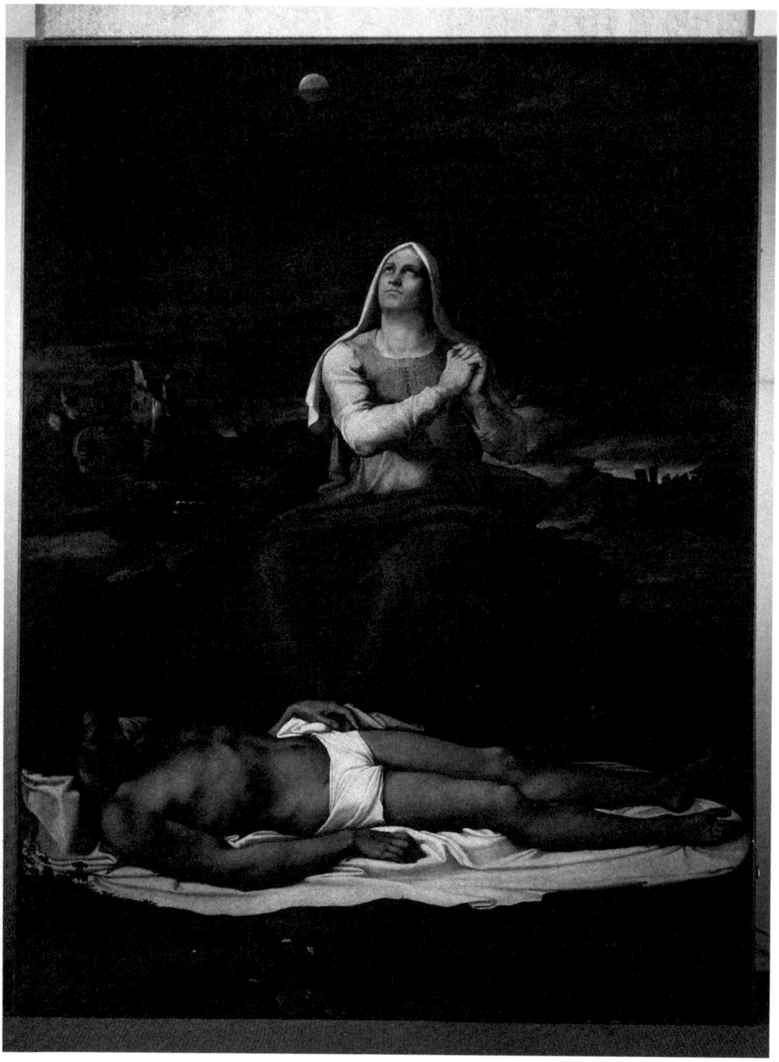

36. Sebastiano del Piombo (ca. 1485–1547), *Pietà of Viterbo* (ca. 1513). Viterbo, Italy. Photo credit: Scala/Art Resource, NY.

with Sebastiano's *Pietà of Viterbo*, "Raphael had been effectively entrusted with the [never-completed] commission for a nocturne representing the *Resurrection of Christ* for Agostino Chigi's funerary chapel in Santa Maria della Pace."[37] Consequently, these two great High Renaissance artists—one coming from central Italy, the other from the north, one deeply influenced by Leonardo's art of *sfumato*, the other deeply influenced by Giorgione's art of *colorito*,[38] and both profoundly influenced in Rome by Michelangelo's sculptural mode of painting and his innovative, muscular treatment of the human body on the Sistine Chapel vault—both found themselves in precisely the same city focusing on precisely the same pictorial problem in what turns out to have been a carefully staged rivalry orchestrated precisely by the very same patron. As Vasari writes in the process of explaining the origins of Raphael's *Transfiguration*, Michelangelo indeed made strategic use of Sebastiano as a sort of proxy in his ongoing artistic rivalry with Raphael:

> Sebastiano also executed at the same time an altarpiece of the same size, as it were in competition with Raphael, of Lazarus being raised from the dead four days after death, which was fashioned and painted with supreme diligence under the direction of Michelangelo, and using some parts of his design. These altarpieces, when finished, were publicly exhibited together in the Consistory in competition [*in paragone*], and were greatly extolled, both the one and the other, and although the works of Raphael had no equals in their perfect grace and beauty, nevertheless the labors of Sebastiano were also praised by all without exception. One of these pictures [Sebastiano's] was sent by Cardinal Giulio de' Medici to his episcopal palace at Narbonne in France, and the other [Raphael's, too beautiful to be sent away] was placed in the Cancelleria, where it remained until it was taken to San Pietro a Montorio. (2.143–4, G5.91)

In that landmark work "of perfect grace and beauty," which every artist must consult, according to Vasari, if they wanted "to know how Christ Transfigured and made Divine should be represented in painting" (1.740, G4.204), Raphael once more returned to capture the night materially in paint on the grand scale as a distinct span of time of the day. On this occasion he did so, however, in the medium of oil, rather than fresco, the latter being a medium inherently not suited to "the representation of translucent darkness."[39] And thanks to working with the elaborate and difficult technique of glazing in oil, Raphael was able on this occasion to make the darks appear even darker than he was ever able to do in the *Deliverance of St. Peter.* To this end, perhaps inspired by Pliny's story of Apelles' invention of *atramentum*, a technique of unifying a painting with a blackened varnish that tonally lent a "subtle darkness to overly bright colors,"[40] Raphael ill-advisedly meddled with the medium of oil itself, Vasari notes, which unfortunately had a deleterious effect on the whole painting over time by darkening it more and more. "And if," Vasari observes, "he had not employed in this work, as it were out of a caprice, printer's smoke-black [*il nero di fumo da stampatori*], the nature of which, as had been remarked many times, is to become ever darker with time [*di sua natura diventa sempre col tempo più scuro*], to the injury of other colors with which it is mixed [*et offende gl'altri colori coi quali è mescolato*], I believe that the picture would still be as fresh as when he painted it; whereas it now appears to be instead tinged [in darkness] rather than anything else" (1.744, G4.207).[41] Here, somewhat like the English Romantic J. M. W. Turner (1775–1851), who reportedly remarked that he only wished he had possessed the colors to make the mournful black sails even darker in his nocturnal *Burial at Sea*, Raphael sought in his *Transfiguration* to paint in a mode that would capture fully the dramatic effect and natural, atmospheric experience of the night in a sublunary world, whether or not he intentionally mixed his colors with *il nero di fumo da stampatori*, as Vasari claimed he did, to make the painting all the more unifyingly somber, dark, and austere. And trying to capture that unifying depth of nocturnal darkness by painting in a so-called "dark manner"—by actually mixing *il nero di fumo da stampatori* into his pigments rather than just applying a final "black varnish" to the overall image as Apelles had done in antiquity—may in truth have been a key feature in Raphael's ongoing *paragone* with Sebastiano del Piombo in Rome. After all, Sebastiano's painting, *The Raising of Lazarus* (fig. 37), itself partly designed but not crafted by Michelangelo, was markedly dark from edge to edge, with the darkness atmospherically engulfing virtually everything in its path to give visual, material expression to the pervasive depth and power of the night, not unlike his earlier *Pietà of Viterbo*, for which Michelangelo, according to Vasari, had also provided the cartoon.[42] In this context, Raphael in his *paragone* with Sebastiano sought to demonstrate how he, as the recognized prince of painters and as an equally sensitive colorist, could paint all the more convincingly than Sebastiano a nighttime scene in oil on the grand scale. And this was no small achievement, it is important to bear in mind, during a period in the history of art when nighttime scenes had become something of a vogue. Indeed, only gifted artists of a certain caliber—those truly great ones who had thoroughly absorbed all the lesson of the past and could now forge ahead by taking on all the more complex visual problems—could adequately overcome that particular *difficultà*, thereby contributing to the triumphant, historical advancement of the *professione* of the visual arts in the third and most accomplished age of Vasari's *rinascita*.

But to vie successfully with Sebastiano, a deft visual artist and nuanced colorist who would prove capable of painting in so many different tonalities of black in his portrait of Pietro Aretino ("a truly stupendous picture," Vasari

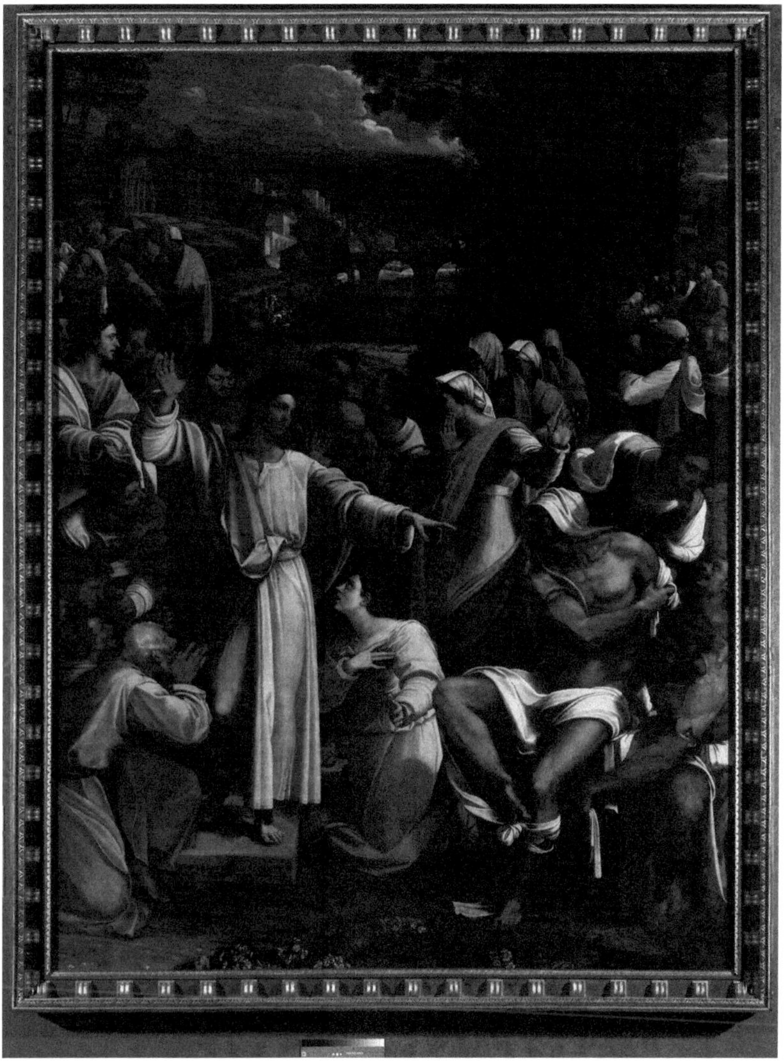

37. Sebastiano del Piombo (ca. 1485–1547), *The Raising of Lazarus* (ca. 1517–19). National Gallery, London, Great Britain. © National Gallery, London/Art Resource, NY.

admiringly writes, "in which there may be seen five or six different kinds of black in the clothes he is wearing—velvet, satin, ormuzine, damask, and cloth—and, over and above those blacks, a beard of the deepest black, painted in such beautiful detail, that the real beard could not be more natural," 2.146, G5.94–5), Raphael had to paint not so much like Michelangelo, who was the true, underlying rival in this particular instance, and whose heroic, muscular, and indeed sculptural figures on the Sistine Chapel vault had so influenced Raphael in Rome when he painted, for instance, Heraclitus in the *School of Athens*, the sibyls adorning the interior of Santa Maria della Pace, and the prophet Isaiah in the Basilica of Sant'Agostino. Raphael instead here had to paint like Leonardo da Vinci,[43] Michelangelo's greatest early rival, who, according to Vasari, "added … to the manner of painting in oil a certain darkness [*una certa oscurità*]" (1.639–40 G4.37), thereby suppressing color in favor of the subtle, tonal modeling of *sfumato*, and, as a consequence, taught other visual artists how to articulate through chiaroscuro a dark shadow that seemed light night itself.[44] "It is an extraordinary thing,"Vasari in fact notes, as he reflects on Leonardo's ability to paint in the darkest of all possible manners,

> how that genius [Leonardo], in his desire to give the highest relief to the works that he made, went so far with dark shadows, in order to find the darkest possible grounds [*andava tanto con l'ombre scure a trovare i fondi de' più scuri*], that he sought blacks that might make deeper shadows and be darker than other blacks [*che cercava neri che ombrassino e fussino più scuri degl'altri neri*], that by their means he might make his lights the brighter; and in the end this method turned out so tinged/darkened [*et infine riusciva questo modo tanto tinto*], that, no light remaining there [*non vi rimanendo chiaro*], his pictures had more the form of things made to represent an effect of night, than the clear quality of daylight [*avevon più forma di cose fatte per contrafare una notte che una finezza del lume del dì*]; which all came from seeking to give greater relief, and to achieve the final perfection of art. (1.630, G4.23–4)

In a strikingly similar manner, the *Transfiguration*, or rather the bottom half of it, should be viewed as a work of sharp, powerful chiaroscuro relief, with figures emerging out of an enveloping, velvety darkness with dramatic intensity (fig. 35), not unlike the huddled figures caught in a state of interconnected, pious wonderment and surprise within the all-absorbing *sfumato* and chiaroscuro shadows of Leonardo's unfinished *Adoration of the Magi* (fig. 38)—a formative painting that markedly influenced Raphael's design for the *Transfiguration*.[45] And like Leonardo, Raphael proved himself a darkly crepuscular painter with his *Transfiguration* in that he could make, as a "consummate master of optical effects," dense shadows seem as impenetrably thick as night. The *Transfiguration* thus served Raphael as "an ideal demonstration piece in which the possibilities and advantages of a Leonardoesque dark manner could be fully realized," as Kathleen Weil-Garris Posner has aptly

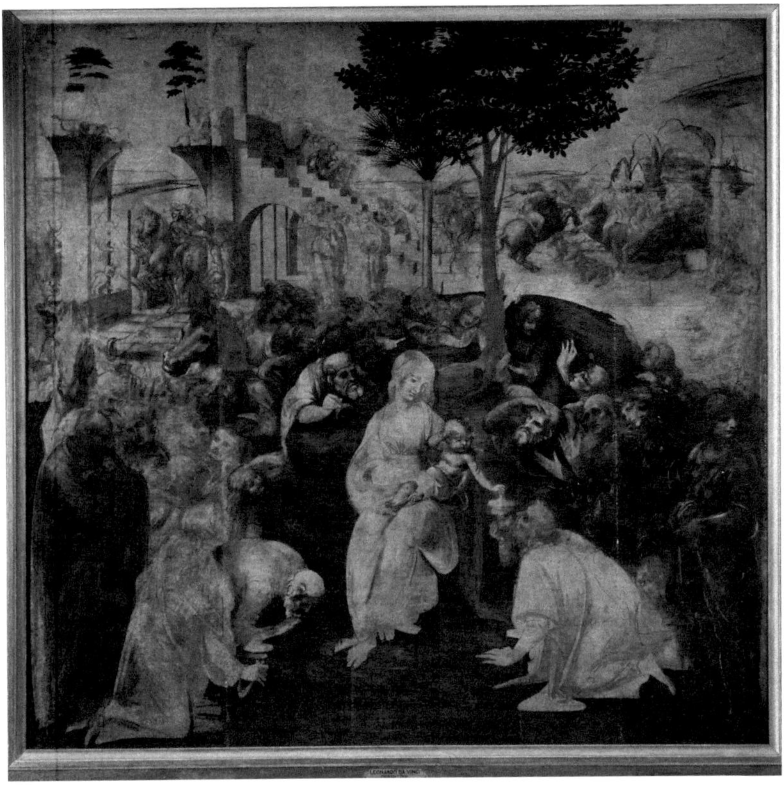

38. Leonardo da Vinci (1452–1519), *Adoration of the Magi* (ca. 1481). Galleria degli Uffizi, Florence, Italy. Alfredo Dagli Orti/The Art Archive at Art Resource, NY.

observed,[46] even as Raphael demonstrated once more wth the *Transfiguration* how deft and supple a colorist he could be. But as Raphael appropriated and perfected that Leonardoesque dark manner in the *Transfiguration*, he also dramatized the conquest of light over dark by concentrating on a distinctly nocturnal span of time in a manner that Leonardo, as a recognized master of chiaroscuro *and* as an art theorist who had thought about "how one ought to represent the night," had never sought to do through his innovative *sfumato* technique.[47] In this respect, Raphael not only aimed to surpass Sebastiano del Piombo, or for that matter Michelangelo, as the supreme visual artist of all time as he labored to overcome the pictorial *difficultà* of painting the night in the *Transfiguration*.[48] As the greatest Zeuxis-like synthesizer in the *Lives* of other artists' visual styles and pictorial innovations, Raphael with his nocturnal *Transfiguration* aimed to surpass Leonardo as well. As such, when it comes to capturing a credible, naturalistic nighttime scene, the noble art of painting—with its capacity to construct alternative worlds by contrasting light and dark—understandably trumps the noble art of sculpture in the ongoing Italian Renaissance *paragone* between those two privileged forms of visually representing the world. And Raphael, predictably enough, trumps everyone else within the *professione* of the visual arts—at least, until Michelangelo comes along and, transforming lifeless stone into apparently living, breathing matter, materially crafts a sculpture of *Night* as a lyrical figure *not* of nocturnal darkness as a distinct span of time but, instead, of immortalized, funereal sleep (fig. 29):

> And what can I say of Night, a statue not rare only, but unique [*E che potrò io dire della Notte, statua non rara ma unica*]? Who is there who has ever seen in that art in any age, ancient or modern, statues of such a kind? For in her may be seen not only the stillness of one sleeping, but the grief and melancholy of one who has lost a great and honored possession; and we must believe that this is that night that obscures all those who thought for some time, I will not say to surpass, but to equal Michelagnolo in sculpture and design [*quella Notte la quale oscuri tutti coloro che per alcun tempo nella scultura e nel disegno pensavano, non dico di passarlo, ma di paragonarlo già mai*]. In that figure is infused all the somnolence that is seen in sleeping forms [*Nella qual figura quella sonnolenza si scorge che nelle imagini adormentate si vede*]; wherefore many verses in Latin and rhymes in the vulgar tongue were written in her praise by persons of great learning, such as these, of which the author is not known:
>
> The Night that you see in such sweet poses
> Sleep was by an angel sculpted
> In this stone; and because it sleeps, it has life.
> Wake it, if you don't believe it, and talk to it.
>
> To which Michelangelo, speaking in the person of Night [*in persona della Notte*], answered thus—
>
> This sleep pleases me, and even more being of stone;
> While danger and shame endure,
> It is a great fortune to me not to see or feel.
> So do not wake me; rather, speak softly.
>
> (2.682, G6.58–9)

III Conquering the Night in the *Lives* and Early Modern Italy

Night, Koslofsky teaches us in *Evening's Empire*, was an important period of the day dominated by a host of familiar activities—and, to be sure, in some instances inactivities—in the early modern period.[49] Naturally enough, as a distinct span of time, night was a period of the day characteristically associated with restorative sleep, both "first sleep" and "second sleep," and so it is in the *Lives*.[50] What is more, night was the time of mischief, both playful and injurious. This, too, is the case in the *Lives*. Giovanni Boccaccio's and Franco Sacchetti's happy-go-lucky Buonamico Buffalmacco (ca. 1290–ca. 1340), whose roguish antics in the *Decameron* and *Trecentonovelle* (*Three Hundred Tales*, ca. 1385–92) were occasionally adapted for storytelling in the *Lives*, typically privileges the night as the period when he can delight in exploiting others and play his trickster's pranks. Here again in the *Lives*, as in Boccaccio's and Sacchetti's stories, the devilish, fourteenth-century painter Buffalmacco takes advantage of gullible people in the dead of night, perhaps most hilariously when he cleverly fools and terrifies his first master, Andrea Tafi, just as he does in the *Three Hundred Tales*,[51] but also when he ingeniously dupes his bothersome, noisy neighbors who simply will not allow him to sleep as soundly as he wished.[52] Likewise, night was the time of thievery. Master's drawings and designs are said in the *Lives* to have disappeared during the night (G4.396), and a hanged man is stolen in the dead of night, soon thereafter to be dissected in an anatomical investigation (G4.260). Night was also the privileged time to escape from others, as is the case when Parmigianino, having "deserted his profession of painting" to pursue an ill-advised obsession with alchemy, covertly flees "one night [*una notte*] with some of his friends to Casal Maggiore" after a suit is brought against him in Parma for having abandoned work at the Chapel of the Steccata (1.941, G4.544), or when Giovann'Antonio Lappoli fearfully takes to flight "in his shirt one night [*una notte*] with some other prisoners" to liberate himself from the clutches of Charles V's ruthless Spanish and Lutheran forces occupying and terrorizing Rome during the traumatic Sack of 1527 (2.208, G5.182). And of course night was the perfect time to plan a murder, much less deviously bring it to fruition while insidiously profiting in the process, as happens in the *Lives* when two unsuspecting individuals end their lives, one with a throat cut, the other strangled.[53] Last but not least, night is the period when rituals took place in antiquity, much as they did in Vasari's own time, in an ongoing battle against the powers of darkness in a dynamic world teeming with hidden, demonic forces: "Che usavan fare di notte per cacciare i mali spiriti di casa" (It was customary to drive evil spirits at night from their houses, 2.633, G5.581).[54] In a similar manner, Cellini would likewise speak in his autobiography of demonic rituals taking place in the Coliseum during the dead of night.

But as Koslofsky also teaches us, night gradually acquired different functions and associations as a distinct span of time as it became increasingly "colonized" in the early modern period. It became not just a period of the day associated with such things as sleep, rest, knavery, mischief, exorcisms, flight, mysticism, murder, thievery, and the demonic, much less romance and spiritual agony and travails—as in the so-called dark night of the soul so powerfully dramatized in enduring literary form in Dante's *Divine Comedy*. It also increasingly became a distinct span of time associated with highly productive labor and what would have traditionally been deemed daylight professional activities and chores. And so it is as well in the *Lives*. Indeed, time and again we read in the *Lives* of devoted painters, sculptors, architects, goldsmiths, silversmiths, potters, and other visual artists of singular merit who dedicated themselves so persistently and diligently to their *professione* that they studied or worked through the entire night, tirelessly burning the midnight oil. Other artisans may be ordinarily bound temporally to the hours of the day to work. The great Renaissance architect Donato Bramante, always forced by the impatient Julius II to move things quickly along, in fact makes a point of ensuring that "the builders of the foundations" of St. Peter's "brought the sand and the solid foundation-clay by night [*portavano di notte la sabbia e il pancone fermo della terra*]" (1.663, G4.78) so that other forms of work could be done by the light of day. But Vasari's dedicated visual artists, heedless of time and deeply concerned with wasting it, willingly labor through the entire night, intensely focused and productively engaged, fueled by their own initiative. As a result, these men, as we saw in the previous chapter, collectively come off in the *Lives* as the great, committed, restless, professional heroes of an industrious age, none of whom ever seem to have to be forced to work through the night but instead so often passionately do so out of their own accord. Most conspicuous in this regard was the indefatigable Michelangelo, who "often got up at night [*spesso la notte si levava*]" (2.740, G6.112) to get back to work, even to be found well into old age with a lone candle propped on his head so that he could properly see and labor through the long, late hours and the ambient, nocturnal dark. But a host of other visual artists behaved in a kindred fashion in the *Lives*, including Perugino, who "made the day out of the night [*fece de la notte giorno*], and with very great fervor continually attended to the study of his profession [*professione*]" (1.583, G3.595), or the unflagging Luca della Robbia, who by day devoted himself to sculpting and "by night to design/drawing [*la notte disegnare*]"—"and he did this," Vasari goes on to say, "with so great zeal that, feeling his feet very often freezing at night [*sentendosi di notte aghiadare i piedi*], he took to keeping them in a basket full of shavings, such as carpenters strip from planks when they shape them with the plane, in order to warm them without giving up his drawing" (1.272, G3.49). The list of likeminded, tireless artists productively engaged in nocturnal work indeed goes on and on in the *Lives* to include, not surprisingly, Vasari himself.[55] Once again, then, the passage of time is irrelevant for these indefatigable artists, especially the passage of time during the night, a period by no means customarily associated with intense, productive labor.

At the same time, Koslofsky shows, night as a distinct span of time was being "conquered" in the early modern period through "artificial" light itself—eventually in the seventeenth century and on by gradually illuminating entire European cities through streetlamps. And so, to be sure, something of that sort happens in the *Lives* when, mindful of the metallurgist Vannoccio Biringuccio's treatise on pyrotechnics, Vasari describes how a *girandola*—"a contrivance full of fire-trumpets, rockets, and other fireworks"—is typically constructed for festive occasions "in such a manner that the lights that burn in certain vases may last the whole night and illuminate the piazza [*in modo che i lumi, che ardono in certi vasi, durino tutta la notte e faccino la piazza luminosa*]" (2.250, G5.222),[56] thereby artificially transforming the night, a period primarily confined for most people to sleep and rest, into a lively, luminous, urban day. Similarly, the night was increasingly the time set aside for convivial and edifying conversations, not unlike the crucial, determining evening conversation that putatively inspired the writing of the *Lives* itself at the magnificent Palazzo Farnese. Ideas are born in the night, innovative visual and verbal projects planned, and friendships and collaborations formed through "civil conversation," to borrow the title of Stefano Guazzo's late Renaissance treatise on manners and decorous, gentlemanly conduct. And all these conversations took place, no doubt, in well-illuminated social spaces designed for the cultural elite, not unlike the exemplary conversations that memorably occurred over four evenings in Castiglione's *Courtier*, with the final one tellingly lasting the entire night without anyone even being aware of the hours passing until the windows are thrown open and sunlight issues into the room at the break of dawn.

Now if the night was more and more being productively colonized in the early modern period economically, socially, and culturally, so too, it would seem from a reading of Vasari's *Lives*, artists effectively began to colonize it visually as well, giving concrete shape and expression to it as an object, which is to say as a materialized idea consciously developed through the process of making and the mechanical and intellectual art of *disegno*. And therein lies part of the broader historical and cultural importance of Vasari's attention in the *Lives* to Raphael's exemplary ability to overcome the *difficultà* of representing the night so completely and credibly on the grand scale in his fresco of *The Deliverance of St. Peter*, as well as Leonardo's ability to craft a deep, dense shadow through chiaroscuro that was as impenetrably dark as night itself. For as the night as a distinct, circumscribed span of time was being conquered in so many different ways in the early modern period, with people bending its dominion to their sway and making it serve different individual and communal and professional needs, artists in their turn began to visualize—and thus successfully conquer—the night by materially representing it all the more accurately, completely, naturalistically, and persuasively in pictorial form. To be sure, we may rightly claim with the clarity and charity of hindsight that Vasari was fundamentally wrong when he envisions Raphael as such a key, transformative figure in that historical process of visually colonizing the night, both in Raphael's ability to capture on the grand scale "le scure tenebre della notte" and, at one and the same time, powerfully disrupt that pervasive, atmospheric darkness with a dazzling, material, painted light that seems more real than light itself. In retrospect the great artists in Vasari's own period most dedicated to capturing nocturnal scenes in pictorial form in Italy were arguably not the Tuscans or the Umbrians or, more generally, those from central Italy but, instead, their northern rivals, namely, the Venetians, who favored the art of *colorito* over *disegno*, such as Giorgione (fig. 39),[57] Titian (fig. 28), and Tintoretto (fig. 40), as well as, of course, Sebastiano del Piombo, with his innovative nocturnal *Pietà of Viterbo* and equally remarkable *Raising of Lazarus* (figs. 36 and 37).[58] But that is not the important point here. What is important is not that the philo-Florentine and ever-so-loyal Tuscan Vasari got it wrong—he got many things wrong in the *Lives*, including mistaking Pythagoras for St. Matthew in Raphael's *School of Athens*, as we have seen. What is important instead is that Vasari successfully recognized, in a manner that no one had effectively or persuasively done before him, the historical significance of what it meant to overcome within the *professione* of the visual arts the *difficultà* of naturalistically representing the night as a distinct, materialized span of time on the grand scale in fresco. Most important of all, as both a practitioner who had labored to paint nocturnal darkness himself *and* as a historian laboring to teach visually generated ideas through examples, Vasari deemed that achievement of naturalistically representing the night

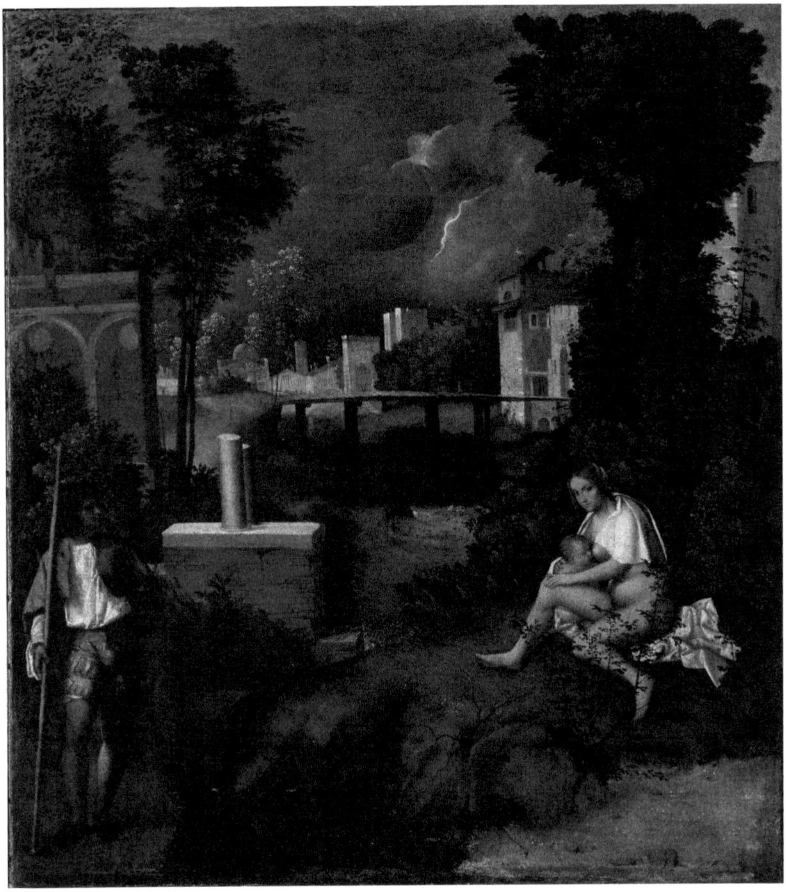

39. Giorgione (da Castelfranco, ca. 1477/8–ca. 1510), *The Tempest* (ca. 1508). Gallerie dell'Accademia, Venice, Italy. HIP/Art Resource, NY.

to be a meaningful one—admittedly not the most notable achievement of his trumpeted *rinascita* but a noteworthy one nonetheless within and for his *professione*.

For Vasari, it may have therefore been Raphael who plausibly taught us all how to visually conquer the night as a distinct span of time in a dramatic and naturalistic way and to find cultural value in doing so, but for us, as historically distanced and informed readers of his *Lives*, it was ultimately Vasari himself who helped demonstrate through his nocturnal reflections how important that particular achievement was as a pictorial problem solved in the third age of his glorified *rinascita* and thus as a significant *difficultà*

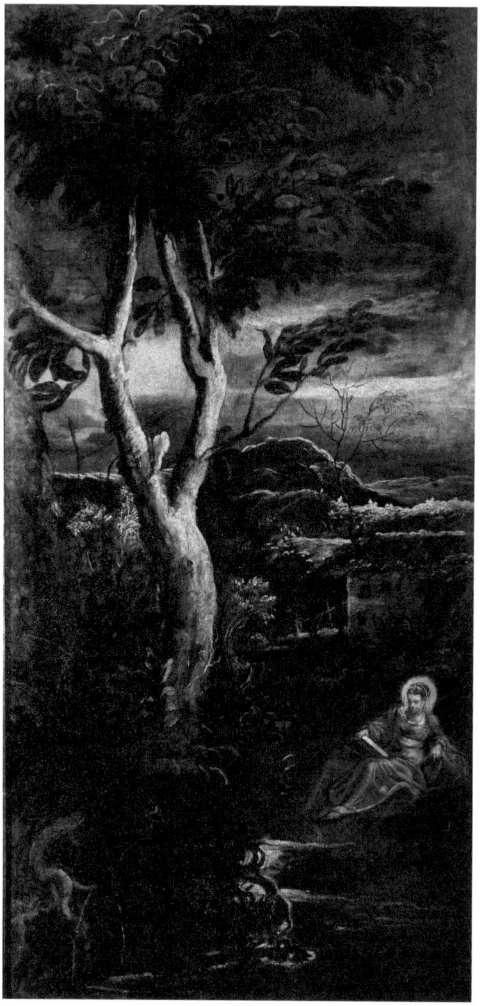

40. Tintoretto (Jacopo Robusti, 1519–1594), *St. Mary Magdalen* (1582–7). Scuola Grande di S. Rocco, Venice, Italy. Photo credit: Scala/Art Resource, NY.

overcome once more through his cherished art of *disegno*. Or to stress the point once more, night was not just colonized economically, socially, and culturally at the dawn of the early modern period in Europe but—Vasari reminds us by focusing on Raphael's *Deliverance of St. Peter*—visually as well in the pictorial arts. And all of this occurred, it is worth noting in conclusion, shortly before Adam Elsheimer (1578–1610), a German artist living and working in Rome, painted in the early seventeenth century his influential

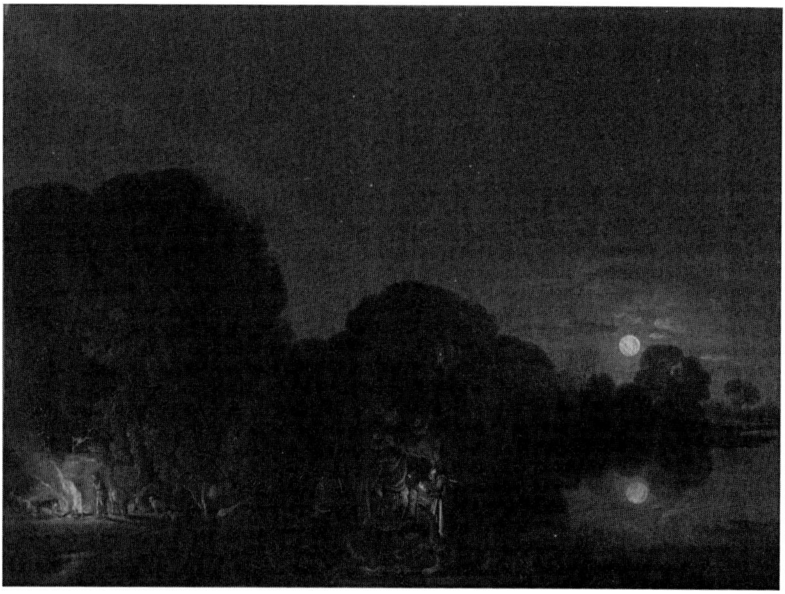

41. Adam Elsheimer (1578–1610), *Flight into Egypt* (1609). Alte Pinakothek, Bayerische Staatsgemaeldesammlungen, Munich, Germany. Art Resource, NY.

landscape of a large, moonlit, evening sky in his *Flight into Egypt* (fig. 41), after which tenebrism took hold of the European cultural imagination in the age of the baroque—an age so often deeply invested in visually representing, in admittedly a rather dark and brooding fashion, the varied, atmospheric, and boundless *tenebre della notte*.[59]

CONCLUSION

And one winter, when a lot of snow fell in Florence, he [Piero de' Medici] caused him [Michelangelo] to make in his courtyard a statue of snow, which was very beautiful [*una statua, che fu bellissima*], and he honored Michelagnolo on account of his talents in such a manner that his father, beginning to see that he was esteemed among the great [*che era stimato fra i grandi*], clothed him much more honorably than he had been wont to do.

—Giorgio Vasari, "Life of Michelagnolo," the *Lives* (1568)[1]

Like so many authors writing about various types of professional expertise in sixteenth-century Italy, Vasari sought to make a case for the value of what he and likeminded men in the visual arts did *in* their *professione* and what they had individually and collectively accomplished over time *for* their *professione*. In the process, Vasari sought to elevate their status as professionals of recognized *ingegno* who, thanks to their dazzling accomplishments, deserved a new, state-sponsored form of training. Viewed in this context, Vasari's *Lives* is not only a book about elevating certain excellent visual artists and recognizing their cultural and social value as men of unparalleled *ingegno*. It is also very much a book, at least in its second edition, about the importance of institutionalizing the visual arts, or more precisely the three nobler arts of painting, sculpture, and architecture, through the creation of the Accademia del Disegno, and thus about distinguishing men of *ingegno* with an ennobling, elevated space in which they can study, develop, collaborate, hone their skills, and socialize as practitioners belonging to a unified yet still diversified *professione*. By extension, the works of visual art produced by academicians, who were officially trained in a state-sponsored program rooted institutionally in the liberal arts and grounded in *disegno* as an intellectual as well as mechanical art, were now necessarily seen to generate ideas in much the same manner as works of complex verbal art—like all those bound volumes of philosophy represented in Raphael's *School of Athens*—had always been expected to do. Finally, thanks to their combined work as professionals, these men of *ingegno* in Vasari's own time had also gradually learned to produce a variety of excellent works of visual art with ever-increasing speed, whatever the medium in question, whether it be tempera, oil, wax, chalk, fresco, brick, stone, wood, bronze, clay, gold, copper, enamel, or silver. And this, for Vasari, was no small professional achievement. Indeed, it was perhaps one of the greatest and most astonishing achievements of his age in the overarching *professione* of the visual arts. In Vasari's sixteenth-century Italy, you could now purchase not just brilliantly executed and brilliantly conceived works of visual art in the "modern" style, some of them quite staggering in size, such as vast works of imperial architecture. You could also purchase them quickly. And quickly produced works of visual art were also aesthetically appealing for Vasari, so long as they were done by someone who had acquired his expertise through long and dedicated *fatica* and *istudio*. Moreover, quickly produced works of visual art often enough exhibited a freshness that made them appear, in all their polish and perfection, as if they had been completed in the heat of the moment, dashed off with a sort of cool, detached ardor, a peculiarly impassioned form of *sprezzatura*.

No other writer had ever accounted for the historical development of the visual arts—or for that matter any art—in this manner by focusing so relentlessly on speed. And no other writer had so valued *prestezza* in the visual arts. Not Pliny. Not Vitruvius. Not Cennini, Ghiberti, Alberti, Leonardo, or Pino. To be sure, as in our own historical period, Vasari's *rinascita* was by no means the product of a mechanized "industrial age." But it should very much be conceived as an extraordinarily "industrious" one in the *professione* of the visual arts, and not just when it comes to thinking about matters of *prestezza*. Yet therein lay one of the problems that occasionally tinges Vasari's otherwise triumphant narrative with a lingering sense of melancholy as he traces the development of this extraordinarily industrious age. For one nagging issue that bothers Vasari from the beginning to end of the *Lives* is that so many wonderful, celebrated, and gifted visual artists of ideas—some of whom were no doubt capable of producing works of art with remarkable speed—were wasting time. Worst of all, once precious time was wasted, it was irrecuperably lost. As a result certain painters, sculptors, and architects not only failed to realize their natural, inborn, God-given, and/or astrologically influenced *ingegno* and develop into remarkable, thought-provoking artists. They also failed to advance the overall *professione* of the visual arts the way they could have had they dedicated themselves to their work with constant *istudio, diligenza, et amorevole fatica*, precisely the way Vasari did himself, relentlessly, over the course of his exemplary, industrious career. What is more important, by wasting time, these artists simply failed to produce—let alone diligently complete—more works of excellent art. And excellent, ennobling, idea-generating, and sometimes groundbreaking art completed in the modern style by trained practitioners with a masterful command of *disegno* was just what Vasari as a professional artist *and* as something of a professional writer needed and wanted. Moreover, when he looked to the past and saw how many works of quality art from classical antiquity had disappeared, Vasari became all the more painfully aware how many works of quality art from his own age had likewise disappeared. It was therefore inevitable that many works of material culture produced by him and his fellow practitioners of *ingegno* in his *professione* were also bound to disappear in the future—disappear just like Michelangelo's "very beautiful" snowman that once upon a time melted to the ground and vanished from sight. As a result, the more excellent visual art there was, the more likely a greater portion of it would survive.

The *Lives* is consequently a book decidedly at odds with itself, much as a good deal of humanist culture, which Vasari would have us believe informed the writing of the book, was also decidedly at odds with itself when it comes to thinking about issues of temporality. Like many humanists in sixteenth-century Italy, albeit not necessarily all those dining together in the Palazzo Farnese where the idea of the book was putatively first conceived, Vasari believed that classical antiquity did and should have a powerful and lasting claim upon the present. And like many humanists in sixteenth-century Italy, he also believed that, although much of classical antiquity was lost, what had survived still allowed men of *ingegno* to forge ahead and build upon the past—or what they individually and collectively considered to be the best elements of the past—in a way that permitted them to create within and for his beloved *professione* even greater works in the period he labeled a *rinascita*. Finally, Vasari was also attuned to the notion that posterity would inevitably be deprived of some of the greatest accomplishments of his own age, including the works of such spectacular visual artists as Raphael, who had taken on, for instance, a notable *difficultà* by capturing the depth and darkness of the *notte* as a distinct span of time. And Vasari was right to be so concerned. For when we read the *Lives* almost five hundred years after its first and second editions were printed, we necessarily become painfully aware that much of what Vasari lists or describes when he talks about works of art is irrecuperably lost. His book in one sense thus serves to account for the origins of the originality of his own celebrated era and the ideas that animated both it and his *professione*, a few of which have been examined in this book. But in another sense it does so with the foreknowledge that much of the material culture he talks about with such enthusiasm and care and concern would not be available in the future and that the only traces of it that will remain would be what he offers us in his widely disseminated, printed words—or rather, we might say in closing, "Vasari's" words, to frame the matter one last time in terms of the collaborative nature of his grand historical project.

NOTES

PREFACE

1 Payne 2001, 51.
2 Rowland and Charney 2017, 16 are only among the most recent to insist on this.
3 Williams 2015. For additional crucial inspirations, see Introduction, n. 12.
4 Those in need of just such a basic knowledge as background can do no better than consult, in English, Ruggiero 2015. For art history, standard studies in English are Paoletti and Radke 2012, Freedberg 1993, Welch 1997, and Campbell and Cole 2011. For a recent lively account of Vasari's life, see Rowland and Charney 2017, although the finest study devoted to his life and work in English remains Rubin 1995.
5 Hall 1999.

INTRODUCTION

1 2.1050–1, G6.396.
2 My thoughts on Raphael's *School of Athens* and the Stanza della Segnatura in general are indebted to Rowland 1997 and 2005, Rosand 2000, Joost-Gaugier 2002, and Kleinbub 2011.
3 Hall 1997, 11 and Bellori 1751, 29.
4 Kleinbub 2011, 51, for instance, states it succinctly: "The meaning of the Euclid group must have been self-evident to contemporary viewers, who would have understood that Raphael's self-portrait and signature proclaimed the alliance of painting and philosophy through perspective."
5 I use the word "visionary" advisedly in light of Kleinbub 2011.
6 A point emphasized in Rosand 2000, among others.
7 Bellori 1997, 48–9.
8 Hall 1997, 25. See also Rowland 1997, 154 and *passim*.
9 Hall 1997, 33–4, Chastel 1961, and Rowland 1997, 153 and n. 61. See also Wittkower 1971, 101–61 on the importance of Pythagorean influences on the visual arts. For a recent treatment of Vasari and typological thought, see Blum 2013.
10 Kleinbub 2011, 46–69 (I cite from 50 and 53–4 below) has developed this theme most recently in a close reading of the fresco. The *School of Athens*, he argues, "is

a painting about thinking in subject *and* form. The process by which our vision traverses horizontal space by means of the perspectival *veduta* [by which Kleinbub means 'the emphatic horizontality of the forceful display of perspective that divides the composition down the center, drawing the viewer's eyes through the building of the Academy to the vista of the celestial blue sky beyond it'] is itself tantamount to a contemplative journey through the image, the dialectical unfurling of an idea in time. In the perspectival *veduta* of the Academy, Raphael has visualized the operations of thought, a mute route formerly occupied by the strolling and debating figures of Plato and Aristotle and now wandered by our eyes in contemplation of their journey. In retracing the philosophers' movement through the building, we thus imagine not only the harmonization of their ideas developing in time but also perceive the ultimate object of their thinking. Though moving in opposite directions, our eyes and the philosophers arrive at the same intellectual destination: whereas our visual journey culminates with the *veduta* of the sky symbolizing the heavens, the philosophers finish their debate facing the *Disputa*."

11 As opposed to the way the term was used to describe narratives in the visual arts, on which see Greenstein 1992, 14–58 and Grafton 1999. For classic studies of the rhetorical nature and structure of Italian Renaissance history writing, see Gilbert 1965, Cochrane 1981, and Struever 1970.

12 Wierzbicka 1997, 16. I am referring to Greene 2013, Jay 1998, and Williams 2015 (first edition 1976, revised 1983), but see also, in a different vein, the earlier Lewis 1960. For thoughts on new approaches to thinking of keywords, see Scholar 2013, along with the essays collected in Mac Carthy 2013a, as well as her own Mac Carthy 2009, 2013b, and 2014. For a different take on a semantic analysis of the *Lives*, see Le Mollé 1985 and 1988.

13 Wierzbicka 1997, 16.

14 For the *Lives* having a design to it, see, for instance, Alpers 1960, Barocchi 1984, Barolsky 1991 and 1992 (in particular), Rubin 1995, Pozzi and Mattioda 2006, Ladis 2008, Cast 2009, Ruffini 2011, and Agosti 2013.

15 Hope 1995, 2005, and 2014, Frangenberg 2002, and Ruffini 2011, but see the strong case for discrediting that reading and claiming Vasari as the sole author, Carrara 2015. On Vasari as a stylist, see Scoti-Bertinelli 1905, 157–223 and Nencioni 1952 and 1965. A number of the more recent studies (Frangenberg 2002, for instance) tend to be limited in number and largely devoted to demonstrating linguistic inconsistencies in the text as scholars parse out different voices belonging to different possible authors collaborating in the making of the *Lives*. On the issue of the "mannerist" style of Vasari, see Nencioni 1965. For my part, Rubin 1995, 120 captures it succinctly with the observation that "there are a variety of voices in the text"—voices that belong to many of the sources that Vasari had diligently "gathered together unsystematically over a number of years," "as a hobby," and then later, in an effort to impose a "deceptive unity and authority" on the material collected, "subordinated to his scheme."

16 G3.5 as well as G2.13. Much has been written about what exactly Vasari means by the word *rinascita*, on which see, for instance, the different arguments of Garin 1974, Campbell 2008, and Burioni 2010.

17 On the *Transfiguration*, see, for instance, Bertini 1961, Mellini 1963, Weil-Garris Posner 1972, Calvesi 1984, Brown 1986, and Cranston 2003, but in particular Kleinbub 2011,

for a reading of vision and the "visionary" in the altarpiece, and Preimesberger 2011, for a thoughtful study of how the Aristotelian concept of tragedy is encoded into the painting.

18 Baxandall 1985, 1.

19 As Alpers 1960 has best observed in discussing *ekphrases* in the *Lives*.

20 This is among the latest appreciative evaluations of the *Lives* as a "project," this time by Vasari's most recent biographers in English, Rowland and Charney 2017, 237.

21 On Vasari as a narrator with significant literary talent or as writer with a truly sophisticated rhetorical strategy at play, see Maginnis 1993, Watts 1995, Bartoli 1997, Land 2005, Ladis 2008, Phillips-Court 2011a, Goodchild 2014, and virtually all the articles collected in Barriault et al. 2005 (in particular Ahl, Barriault, James, Freiberg, and Oettinger), but above all Barolsky 1990, 1991, 1992, 1994, 1999, 2005, 2010, and 2014. Vasari also certainly made notable strides himself as a narrator describing art as we move from his earlier *Libro di ricordanze* to his *Lives*, on which see, for instance, Stimato 2005a.

22 Maginnis 1993, 385–6 asserts, as do others, that this was how the book was traditionally read, cumulatively, from beginning to end. By contrast, Rowland and Charney 2017, 16 maintains that its format "is designed for dipping" and is thus hardly to be read from "cover to cover."

23 Grafton 2006. I have also found of value McMahon 2014, Bavaj 2010, and, for a prehistory of intellectual history, Kelley 2002.

24 McMahon 2014, 26.

25 Ginzburg 1980.

26 For reflections on "centers" and "peripheries" in the context of the visual arts, see Campbell 2014. Rowland and Charney 2017, 144 are among the most recent to remind us that Vasari would not have been characterized as Florentine in his own time, for all that he worked hard in the *Lives* to be associated with Florence, characterize himself as something of an "insider" rather than a provincial outsider, and self-consciously labored to be viewed as part of what he constructs as a long, ongoing, and unifying tradition of Florentine art by completely disregarding, or at least selectively glossing over, wide variations in style over time: "As Vasari realized, some of the animosity he generated was a matter of local patriotism. Although Arezzo and Florence are less than forty miles apart, they were (and remain) two separate societies. Since the late Middle Ages, Florence had become the leading city in the region of Tuscany, Arezzo a local capital in the system of dependent cities the Florentines called their *Dominio*. To some Florentines, therefore, Vasari was an outsider and something of a provincial, even though he was a fellow Tuscan."

27 On Giovio, see Zimmermann 1995. On Caro, see Mutini 1977, on Molza, see Pignatti 2011, and on Amaseo, see Avesani 1960.

28 Zimmermann 1978.

29 On Pliny's role in the *Lives*, see McHam 2011, along with the cogent observations in Emison 2004, 19–58, and for the Renaissance more generally, see McHam 2013. On the importance of consulting practitioners in the visual arts when writing about those very arts, see, for instance, Vasari's discussion of Giovanni della Casa (G5.545).

30 That said, Annibal Caro, it is worth noting, wrote iconographical programs for painted programs with "ideas" for sites like the Villa Giulia in Rome (much in the way that many humanists provided artists with visual programs), but I am not aware that he argued for

the making of visual art as a distinctly cognitive act (in the way, say, that Vasari—like Leonardo in his writings—does throughout the *Lives*, as he seeks to transform painters such as Leonardo, Raphael, and Michelangelo, among others, into intellectuals who are capable of articulating those very same sorts of complex visual programs for themselves). On Giovio and his writing of a history of art in miniature, see Zimmermann 1976 and 1995. On Renaissance visual artists as the repositories of information about the places and substance of art objects and the "climate of ignorance of modern art" among non-practitioners, right on up to the time of Vasari, see Hope 2008.

31 Rowland and Charney 2017, 235.

32 See on this most recently Sohm 2000; all scholars note that Molza was dead in 1546. Rubin 1995, 144 judiciously deems it all a "demonstrable fiction ... intended to give distinct and distinguished literary pedigree to Vasari's book."

33 Cast 2009, 1–34. On the dialogue form generally in Renaissance Italy, see Marsh 1980, Snyder 1989, and Cox 1992. For conversational spaces, see Tribby 1991 and 1992a/b, and Findlen 1994 and 1998. For the convivia of humanists in Rome, see Zimmermann 1978 and Rowland 1998. Summers 1981, 11–13 reminds us how vibrant artists' *botteghe* must have been as sites of conversation and debate, as does Cast 2009, 45–8, while Franceschi 1999 explores them as spaces of sociability. More generally, on classicizing discourses about the Italian Renaissance "art of conversation," see Quondam 2007.

34 There is an extensive bibliography on the so-called *questione della lingua*. For the purposes of this book I have benefited particularly from De Gaetano 1967, Vitale 1978, Pozzi 1996, Sherberg 2003, and Moyer 2006.

35 The order of their publications is as follows: (1) Giambullari's *Origine della lingua fiorentina, altrimenti il Gello* appeared in 1546 (I have consulted the 1549 edition); (2) Gelli's *I capricci del bottaio* appeared in 1546 (I have consulted the modern edition in Gelli 1967); (3) both Giambullari's *Della lingua che si parla e scrive in Firenze* and Gelli's *Ragionamento* appeared in 1551, the two published in the same volume (I have consulted the modern edition, Gelli 1967 for the latter, while the original for the former); and (4) Lenzoni's *Difesa della lingua fiorentina e di Dante* appeared in 1556 (edited by Giambullari after Lenzoni's death). Not all three academicians shared precisely the same views all the time. On Gelli, who did not think a Florentine grammar could be reliably produced, since for him all spoken, living languages were in a constant state of flux, see De Gaetano 1967. By contrast, Giambullari aimed to fix that language in his *Della lingua*, the first formal grammar of the Florentine vernacular. These three men also differed markedly in social station. Gelli was a shoemaker and hosier who aspired to be accepted by the elite, Giambullari a humanist who worked often enough as a secretary. On Gelli, see De Gaetano 1976; on Giambullari, see Pignatti 2000; on Lenzoni, see Mammana 2005. On their interactions in relation to the Accademia Fiorentina, see Plaisance 2004, and on their interactions with regard to the *questione della lingua*, see Sherberg 2003 and Moyer 2006.

36 See Plaisance 2004 and Sherberg 2003.

37 On Borghini, see Woodhouse 1967 and 1971, Williams 1988 and 2014, Rubin 1995, and Ruffini 2011, esp. 72–103 and 137–60. On Bartoli, see Bryce 1983, Frangenberg 2002, and Ruffini 2011. On their thoughts on the *questione della lingua* and interactions with Lenzoni, Giambullari, Gelli, and Varchi, see the synthetic observations in Vitale

1978, 80–100 and Moyer 2006. On their influence on Vasari in the context of a discussion of the historicizing of art, see also Payne 2001 and Burioni 2010.

38 Ruffini 2011, 5. Frangenberg 2002 in fact argues that Giambullari wrote the first preface and that Lenzoni wrote with Bartoli the second and third prefaces.

39 Ruffini 2011, 141.

40 I have translated the word "numerosa" as "rhythm," although Lenzoni is concerned in musical terms here with metrics, as observed by Moyer 2006.

41 The questions are not idle in terms of the sixteenth-century concern for producing aulic writing in a classicized vernacular. As is well known, Ariosto, for instance, substantially revised and polished the language of the *Orlando furioso* after the printing of Bembo's *Prose*, refining his diction as he reworked the 1521 version into the final, amplified, and lexically more classicized 1532 edition, although Ariosto was by no means slavish to Bembo's dictates. Castiglione, conversely, quite consciously refused to alter his mode of writing to suit the lexical pronouncements of others, as he openly declares in the preface to his *Courtier*. On the *fiorentinità* of Vasari's style, which is nevertheless marked by "una leggiera tinta dialettale aretina che le dà, talvolta, un carattere un po' ibrido," see Scoti-Bertinelli 1905, esp. 161 and 223.

42 The matter is intricately viewed in Ruffini 2011, 137–60, as well as, more specifically, when it comes to matters of orthography (144–5).

43 Giambullari 1551, 7–8 makes it clear in his prefatory letter to his reader that he is writing a grammar of Florentine, not Tuscan.

44 Gelli 1967, 53. Lenzoni 1556, 17–19 was of the same mind, as observed by Sherberg 2003, 37 and 46; see also Vitale 1978, 89.

45 Gelli 1967, 306.

46 "Resterebbemi a fare scusa de lo avere alle volte usato qualche voce non ben toscana, de la qual cosa non vo' parlare, avendo avuto sempre più cura di usare le voci et i vocaboli particulari e proprii delle nostre arti, che i leggiadri o scelti della delicatezza degli scrittori. Siami lecito adunque usare nella propria lingua le proprie voci de' nostri artefici, e contentisi ognuno de la buona volontà mia" (G1.29). As much as these statements can be, and have been, and up to a point should be, construed rhetorically as part of the longstanding self-modesty topos, they can also be conceived on the face of it as straightforward, sincere, and insightful recognitions on Vasari's part about his own self-conscious limitations as a practitioner-writer being assisted by established *scrittori* in the formal editing and writing of the *Lives*. Note as well the use of the word *Toscana* rather than *Fiorentina*.

47 See, for instance, Frey 1923, 210 (December 15, 1947): "Solo vi desidero che se ne levino certi trasportamenti di parole e certi verbi, posti in fine, che si fanno talvolta per eleganza e a me generano fastidio. In un'opera simile vorrei la scrittura apunto come il parlare; e questa è così veramente, se non in pochissimi lochi, i quali rilegendo, avvertirete subito, e s'emenderanno facilmente." For Vasari's own pronouncements on this matter in the *Lives*, see 1.25, G1.29; 2.1067, G6.412–13. When it comes to citing from Vasari's letters, I have followed throughout the bibliographical referencing of Memofonte for easier reference and access: www.memofonte.it/autori/carteggio-vasariano-1532–1574.html.

48 Hope 1995, 2005, and 2014, Frangenberg 2002, and Ruffini 2011, 137–60, but see also Nencioni 1952, 1965, as well as Boase 1979, 46–7. It is by no means uniformly

accepted (especially among Italian scholars) that the actual writing of the book was the product of multiple authors, with strenuous objections most recently voiced by Carrara 2015. But it is well documented that it is the product of extensive collaboration, on which see, yet again, most recently Carrara 2015.

49 Tolomei, one of the more innovative participants in the *questione della lingua*, was a devoted subscriber to the notion that Tuscan, not Florentine, should constitute the universal standard for the vernacular, on which see Vitale 1978, 80–3.

50 A key difference, of course, is that an assistant is supposed to paint, say, in precisely the style of the master of the workshop, so that there would, in theory, be no detectable difference in the style of one or the other. Or to put it differently, the work coming out of a workshop should never—yet again in theory—appear as a work of stylistic bricolage.

51 Bakhtin 1981.

52 While everything else described in this paragraph is, of course, fictive (but still in its own way entirely plausible), this particular paperback edition of the *Lives* is not: see Vasari 2009, which is part of the "Grandi tascabili economici I Mammut" series.

1 *PROFESSIONE*/PROFESSION

1 T6.413, translation mine.

2 Characteristic of the growth of interest in this area of study generally in Italy, across a variety of periods also focused on Europe, are the volumes produced by the Milanese academic publishing house FrancoAngeli, each with the telling titles *Formare alle professioni*, and each with a different subtitle directing readers to the specific professions covered across broad periods, on which see Becchi and Ferrari 2009a, Rota 2009, Ferrari and Mazzarello 2010, Ferrari and Ledda 2011, Ferraresi and Visioli 2012, and Morandi 2013. See as well the earlier significant contributions of Malatesta 1995 and 1996. For a variety of scholarly interests in professions in the Italian Renaissance (as well as the Middle Ages and early modern period), see, for instance, Alford 1979, Bec 1983, Biow 2002, 2010, and 2015, Bragantini 1996, Bullough 1966, Cipolla 1973 and 1976, Eamon 2010, Filippo Bareggi 1988, Fiorato 1989, Fragnito 1998, Gilmore 1979, Grendler 1969, Kempers 1987, Long 2001 and 2011, McClure 2004, Merrill 2017, Park 1987, and Zuccolin 2010. For the changing meaning of the words *professioni*, *professionisti*, *professionalizzare*, see, for instance, Becchi and Ferrari 2009b.

3 Consider, for instance, Nigro, 1983, 1984, 1987, and 1991, Watkins 2008, Hampton 2009, Biow 2002, 2010, and 2015, Kennedy 2016, and Kiséry 2016.

4 McClure 2004.

5 Comanducci 2014, 66. On the structure of the workshop in Renaissance Italy, see Rossi 1980, Thomas 1995 and 2006, and Comanducci 2000, as well as the synthetic discussion by Welch 1997, 83–101, on artistic training and workshop collaborations, O'Malley 2013, 126–71, for quality control, and Reilly 2014.

6 On the importance and function of *ekphrasis* in the *Lives*, see Alpers 1960, along with Land 2005, 158–76 and Ruffini 2011, 104–36 for additional insights. It should be stated that Webb 1999 and 2009 have demonstrated that the ancient concept of *ekphrasis* had little to do with the modern notion of it as strictly a verbal description of a work of art, much less the modern concern with it as a literary device that

raises a variety of thorny issues about the relationship between the verbal and the visual. Rather, *ekphrasis* was understood in the classical period as a form of narration that could focus on anything, including actions, people, and places, but certainly not exclusively works of art. The key was vividness, *enargeia*, and the desire to bring oratorically such things as battles to life in the "mind's eye" of the listeners, so that they feel as if they were present at the event. For the purposes of this book, however, I draw on both "classical" and "modern" conceptions of the term *ekphrasis* and treat it, as Alpers 1960, for instance, does, as way of critically designating, for the lack of a better word, a familiar poetic and rhetorical practice of describing works of art. At the same time, those very descriptions of works of art, thanks to the way they were occasionally presented with great vividness (*enargeia*), were also designed, in keeping with the classical notion of *ekphrasis*, to seem all the more real and forceful as they were experienced by readers in their mind's eye, thus allowing readers to feel as if they were indeed present before the work of art.

7 See Biow 2015, 21–92 for a historical tracing of the concept of *techne* to *ars* from ancient Greece to Renaissance Italy and its relationship to professions. Rubin 1995, 235–6 has key things to say about an "art" in Vasari's period, distinguishing it, as Boccaccio had, between "an art ('arte') and a trade ('mestiero')."

8 Accessed online http://vocabolario.sns.it/html/index.html.

9 Along with those listed in the notes of this chapter, and those indicated in the body of this chapter itself, the following artists are deemed to be experts in a *professione* within the visual arts in the *Lives*: Cimabue (1.52, G2.36); Donatello (G1.95); Andrea Pisano (1.134, G2.149); Ugolino Sanese (Ugolino di Nerio, T2.140); Andrea di Cione Orcagna (1.179, G2.217; 1.184–5, G2.222); Giovanni dal Ponte (1.195, G2.241); Lorenzo Ghiberti (1.290, G3.77; 1.293, G3.81); Brunelleschi (1.326, G3.141); Michelozzo Michelozzi (T3.229); Alessio Baldovinetti (1.432, G3.317); Vellano da Padova (Bartolomeo Bellano, 1.434, G3.322–3); Francesco di Giorgio (1.464, G3.383); Maestro Mino (Mino da Fiesole, 1.477, G3.407); Paolo da Verona (T3.508); Benedetto da Maiano (T3.523; 1.548, G3.531); Lorenzo Costa (1.480, G3.415); Giovanni Bellini (T3.430); Andrea Verrocchio (1.551–2, G3.537); Pietro Perugino (1.583, G3.595); Pietro Torrigiano (1.691, G4.123; 1.694, G4.126); Guglielmo da Marcilla (Guillaume de Marçillat, 1.753, G4.223); Domenico Puligo (1.771, G4.251); Baldassare Peruzzi (1.813, G4.322); Girolamo Santacroce (1.867, G4.418); Antonio Floriani (1.874, G4.428); Polidoro da Caravaggio (1.898, G4.470–1); Francesco Mazzuoli (Parmigianino, 1.934, G4.534); Giovanni Giocondo (2.3–4, G4.559); Bastiano da San Gallo (T4.515); Francesco dai Libri (elder and younger) and Girolamo dai Libri (2.50, G4.599); Marcantonio Raimondi (2.101, G5.25); Sebastiano del Piombo (2.140, G5.85); Perino del Vaga (2.155, G5.109–10; 2.156, G5.112); Giovanni Battista Belluzzi (2.395, G5.357); Giovanni da Udine (Giovanni Nanni, 2.497, G5.456); Giovanni Francesco Rustici (2.517, G5.476); Nanni di Prospero delle Corniuole, Francesco di Girolamo dal Prato, and Nannoccio da San Giorgio (2.555, G5.511); Michelangelo (2.642, G6.3); Girolamo Siciolante of Sermoneta (2.857, G6.220); Jacopino del Conte (2.860, G6.222); Benvenuto Cellini (2.884–5, G6.245); and Vincenzo Danti (2. 889, G6.249).

10 Maso Finiguerra (G1.166); Francesco Pesellino (1.459, G3.371); Domenico Puligo (1.771, G4.251); Tommaso di Stefano (Giottino, 1.802, G4.302); Polidoro da Caravaggio (1.894, G4.463); Morto da Feltre (1.924, G4.517; 1.925, G4.518); Andrea

Feltrini (Andrea di Cosimo, 1.927, G4.521); Girolamo dai Libri (2.47, G4.596); Cosimo da Trezzo (2.72, G4.629); Dello Delli (2.267, G3.38); (Battista dal Borro, 2.570, G5.524); Cristofano Gherardi (Doceno, 2.335, G5.301); Battista del Cinque and Ciappino (2.687, G6.65); Giovanni [?] (2.825, G6.195). The term *professione* is used in this sense also in G1.152, G1.157, G1.170, T4.628, and G4.229.

11 See, for instance, Thomas 1995 and 2006. On time pressures, see O'Malley 2013.

12 In this sense, Vasari also adopts the equally conventional and longstanding usage of the phrase *fare professione* in a strictly religious context to talk about someone taking sacred vows, to "profess," speak out, as in the cases of Lionardo Dati (1.297, G3.89), Savonarola (1.673, G4.92), Giovanni Angelo Montorsoli (2.534, G5.492), and Giulio Clovio (2.850–1, G6.214).

13 Bramante (1.665, 4.80–1), along with Andrea Sansovino (1.782, G4.271), Perino del Vaga (2.156, G5.112), and Girolomo Genga (2.383, G5.348).

14 See, for instance, Barocchi 1976, Fanti 1979, Dempsey 1986, Goldberg 1988, Hochman 1998, Roskill 1968, Spagnolo 2007, and Ruffini 2009 and 2010, among the many works that have traced responses to the two editions of the *Lives* after their printings.

15 Consider, for instance, Perino del Vaga (2.160, G5.119) and Baccio Bandinelli (2.298, G5.267).

16 "così riconosce le varie maniere degli artefici come un pratico cancelliere i diversi e variati scritti de' suoi equali" (2.1066, G6.411).

17 Abbott 1988 and Larson 1977.

18 The term *professori* is used three times in the *Lives*, the two most important occasions being in the first letter from Vasari to the Duke and in the Giuntina edition, both addressed in this chapter. I am referring to Filippo Baldinucci, *Notizie de' professori del disegno da Cimabue in qua* (1681–1728). See also Dempsey 1980, 554 n. 11.

19 On *disegno* in the *Lives*, see the observations of Barzman 1991 and 2000, Rubin 1995, 241–6, and Williams 1997, 29–72. On the semantic range of the word *disegno* in the Renaissance, see the synthetic discussion in Thomas 2013.

20 "la professione sua volle che fusse la pittura."

21 "modegli di figure di terra, et adosso a quelle metteva cenci molli interrati, e poi con pazienza si metteva a ritrargli."

22 On Leonardo and his art, along with *disegno*, as a science, I have benefited from Kemp 1981, 1990, and 2006. On Leonardo theorizing about and capturing through line the passage of time, see Greenstein 2012.

23 For a somewhat analogous semantic function of Michelangelo embodying the new conception of the term *artista*, see Comanducci 1999. Studies of Michelangelo are legion. I have found Summers 1981, Hibbard 1998, Goffen 2002, and Wallace 2010 to provide the best introductions.

24 This does not at all mean that Vasari's investment in professions and professional identity was not already strong in the Torrentiniana version of the *Lives*. Indeed it was. And this is perhaps most evident if we begin by looking at the opening paratextual materials to both editions. For in the dedication to the 1550 edition, which is reproduced word for word in the 1568 edition, Vasari emphasizes not just the value of professions but also the value of all those practitioners who have been brilliantly engaged in them. Moreover, in the same dedication, which reminds Duke Cosimo I how he and his ancestors have always proven to be guiding patrons of "these professions" (1.4, G1.3), Vasari claims that he hopes to

help, by compiling all these Lives and by writing the book, the living *professori*—the masters, that is, who can profess knowledge over their art—and, perhaps, profitably please those *professori*, so long as they have "taste and pleasure" (1.4, G1.3). Moreover, in both editions Vasari indicates at the end of the preface to the whole work that before he recounts the history of the individual Lives themselves he will offer an "introduction" in the form of an exposition of the various arts "to the end that every gracious spirit may first learn the most notable things in their professions [*professioni*]" (1.24, G1.28). See also G1.2. More to the point, the Torrentiniana edition contains a plethora of examples of artists whose art is defined as a profession, many of which survive into the Giuntina edition, but some of which remain specific to that first edition. The second sentence of Vasari's letter to Cosimo I for the Giuntina edition is perfectly consonant with his interest in professions in the Torrentiniana (1.7, G1.6). For studies that have traced some of the salient differences as Vasari reworked his *Lives*, see Brizio 1952, Bettarini 1976, Rubin 1995, 187–230, Simonetti 2005, Pozzi and Mattioda 2006, 1–24, and Ruffini 2011.

25 I am indebted here to Barzman 2000, but on the Accademia and its creation, see also Goldstein 1975 and 1996, Jack 1976, Dempsey 1980, Hughes 1986a/b, Bolland 2006, Ruffini 2011, and Williams 2014. I cite from Comanducci 2014, 68. See Waźbiński 1987, 2.471 for the ducal acceptance of the petition, and Hughes 1986a/b for the relationship of the Accademia to the guilds.

26 Vasari is either drawing throughout on the *Exequies of the Divine Michelagnolo Buonarroti* or working from the same source, from which much of that material is drawn, on which see Wittkower and Wittkower 1964, 59, 60, 64, 89, 109, and 120.

27 Again, Vasari draws on the *Exequies*, Wittkower and Wittkower 1964, 60.

28 Ruffini 2011, 11–38. For a narrative of the funeral, see Wittkower and Wittkower 1964.

29 I am indebted once again to Ruffini 2011. For the significance of the emblem and its revision, see also Barolsky 1990, 130–4 and Stack 2000, 169.

30 Cennini 1933, 1971. On his life, see the synthetic observations of Bacci and Stoppelli 1979.

31 Bolland 1996.

32 Anonimo 1969, Billi 1969, and Ghiberti 1947. For the sources generally, see Kallab 1908, Schlosser 1977, 295–7 and *passim*, as well as Tanturli 1976. Merrill 2017, 30 nonetheless perceptively argues that the concept of the *professione di architetto*, formatively present in Alberti's treatise, was already somewhat developed in that of Ghiberti and "entirely absent from the two primary vernacular architectural treatises of the fifteenth century: those of Filarete and Francesco di Giorgio," even though "these two authors unquestionably considered architecture as a profession." By contrast, in the sixteenth century, when the concept of *professione* comes into its own (see Biow 2002, McClure 2004) and intensifies, the *professione di architetto* also emerges more forthrightly as a means to "cement the parameters of [an] occupation," as also argued in Merrill 2017; and yet the term *professione* does not appear to have been used in the vernacular in a widespread fashion until after Vasari's monumental *Vite* appeared in print.

33 I have consulted Leonardo 1970 and 1996, and Alberti 1804, 1833, 1960–73.

34 The word *professione* appears in this context only a few times in Condivi's *Life* (1998, 1976), the first, for instance, at the outset, when Condivi declares himself an "amator

de la professione e della bontà sua [the 'bontà' of Michelangelo, his 'teacher']" (5). In sum, Condivi's *Life* does not highlight the significance Michelangelo's professional identity, as Vasari's most emphatically does (all the more so in the Giuntina edition); rather, Condivi's *Life* emphasizes Michelangelo's aristocratic disdain, excellence, and inimitability as an artist. Pino's *Dialogue* only contains two references to the word *professione*, neither of them relevant to the issue at hand (Barocchi 1960–2, 1.101, 1.137), and it is scarcely used in Vincenzo Danti's *Trattato delle perfette proporzioni*. Cellini's use of the terms can be readily consulted in Cellini 1568 and 1960.

35 Consider Varchi's *Lezzione della maggioranza delle arti* (Barocchi 1960–2), for instance, which makes few mentions of the word *professione* (or its variants) in the context of discussing visual art or artists. Nor does the concept of *professione* have any purchase in Dolce's *Dialogo di pittura*, where it is scarcely used (as in Dolce in Roskill 1968, 128–9).

36 See Merrill 2017, 24.

37 As Merrill 2017, 24 observes, the term *professione* is repeated quite frequently in particular in Alberti and Zuccaro's *Origine et progresso* (Zuccaro 1961). It appears a few times in Ligorio (accessible in Barocchi 1971–7, 2.1412, 2.1416, 2.1417, and 2.1418, including the title itself); only rarely in Lomazzo 1974, 2.220, 2.305, and 2.363; a few more times in Sorte: see Barocchi 1960–2, 1.275, 1.278, 1.282, 1.285, and 1.299 (three times); and almost obsessively, even from the first paragraph, in Alberti and Zuccaro 1961, 13 (four times), 15 (twice), 16, 17 (twice), 19, 20 (three times), 21 (three times), 37 (twice), 39 (twice), 42, 48, 50 (twice), 53, 58 (three times), 60, 61(twice), 63, 66, 69, 70, 71, 73, 75, 80, 83, and 91. The word *professione* (and its variants) has virtually no purchase, however, in Alberti's *Trattato della nobiltà della pittura* (1585), which can be consulted in Barocchi 1960–2, 3.195–235. The word is used often enough in Armenini's *De' veri precetti della pittura*, and once quite emphatically, it strikes me, when placed as the final, ringing conclusion to the end of the second book (not unlike the way it appears at the end of Vasari's 1550 edition): "Procuri dunque ciascuno, con ogni studio, che siano nelle sue opere, acciò piacendo ad ogni genere di persone, siano notate sempre per cosa singulare e degna di ammirazione e non solo notato egli, ma onorato ancora et amato come uomo singolare di questa bellissima professione" (Armenini 1988, 164–5).

38 Bastiano da San Gallo (Aristotle, 2.432, G5.395; T4.515). See also Paolo Uccello (1.283, G3.64); Pietro Perugino (1.589, G3.603); and Franciabigio (T4.515). On the discovery of perspective and its impact as a science grounded in mathematics, see Edgerton 1975.

39 As is made evident in the case of Masaccio (1.317, G3.123). On competition in the *Lives*, see Clifton 1996.

40 As is made evident in the case of Alfonso Lombardi of Ferrara, whose Life's moral message is summed up in the Torrentiniana version: one needs to labor at a *professione* and not be sidetracked by enticing distractions (T4.407).

41 On the *Lives* offering a sort of family of collective Lives, see Barolsky 1992 and Stack 2000.

42 On Vasari's education, see Rubin 1995, 57–70.

43 See, for instance, Cast 2009. For the issue of whether or not the gathering with Giovio ever occurred, see Sohm 2000, as well as how Vasari's participation as narrated in his own Life can be construed in the context of Renaissance self-fashioning.

44 Cast 2009 and Williams 2014.

45 This reading of Petrarch and Castiglione in terms of professions, here rapidly synthesized, is developed at length in Biow 2002 (for Petrarch, 27–44), 2010 (for Castiglione, 35–59), and 2015 (yet again for Castiglione, 57–72).

46 For Petrarch's formulation of the "profession of the poet" in the *Coronation Oration*, see Petrarch 1975, 9.2, 9.4, and 9.6–8.

47 I refer, of course, to the last letter in Petrarch 1992, 672–80.

48 On Mussato, see Witt 2000, 117–73. On Petrarch's crowning, see Calcaterra 1942, Wilkins 1951, Godi 1970, Gensini 1980, Trapp 1982, Biow 2002, 27–44, and Looney 2009.

49 Biow 2002, 44.

50 See Biow 2002 and 2015, as well as Saccone 1978 and 1987. For Castiglione's first preface, eventually discarded, see Castiglione 1769, 1.193.

51 Castiglione 1929 and 1959, where the author occasionally refers to the courtier as having the "profession of arms."

52 This is all the more conspicuously the case with the Torrentiniana edition, where the word *professione* is used in the third sentence of the very first page of the opening dedicatory letter (T1.2) and then strategically placed as the final word of the final sentence of the final page of the entire book (see the epigraph to this chapter and my discussion of it herein).

53 Vasari's insistence is all the more noticeable given the paucity of its occurrences as a term in his letters, as in Frey 1923, 7.

54 Barzman 1991 and 2000 has important things to say about *disegno* in the Accademia, of which "drawing," to be sure, was only a part—a key, foundational part, of course (145, 150–1, and 156 in particular), but only a part—of what was understood to constitute the notion of *disegno* for Vasari and others associated with the Accademia. Rubin 1995, 214 succinctly describes the centrality of *disegno* for the Accademia as having "received state approval with an academy to promulgate it. It had been given official status as the basis of Tuscan excellence in the arts, meant to flourish under Cosimo's reign."

55 See the discussion of this drawing and Mini in Barkan 2011, 188–96.

56 See now Härb 2015 on Vasari's drawings.

57 On Vasari's collection of drawings, whose volumes as integral collections we have in fact lost, see Ragghianti Collobi 1974, 12 and 17, which estimates that the total number was between one and two thousand contained in anywhere from eight to twelve tomes. As Boase 1979 observes, and others have similarly maintained, Vasari's book of drawings was conceived in some measure as an appendix to the *Lives*. See also most recently Tempesti 2014. According to Vasari himself (G3.104), he began acquiring drawings in 1528, well before he would have even begun assembling materials for the *Lives*.

58 Frey 1923, 198: Paolo Giovio to Giorgio Vasari, letter dated May 7, 1547, from Rome.

59 In this way, the tensions that Ruffini (2011) locates conceptually at the heart of the *Lives*—tensions between heroic individualism, say, and group identities fashioned in terms of professionalization through institutional formation—are formally developed within the book that "Vasari," as the nominal sole author, writes.

60 In particular Hope 2005 (slightly amended in 2014), Frangenberg 2002, and Ruffini 2011, as well as the important observations of Nova 2013, esp. 59–63, 65, and 70. Not

everyone (such as Ackerman 1997, Pozzi and Mattioda 2006, 22, Ginzburg 2007, Scapecchi 2011, and most emphatically Carrara 2015) shares Hope's view, while some, such as Barolsky, who is invested in reading the *Lives* as a complex literary narrative (see Introduction, n. 21), do not address issues related to who wrote the *Lives* and how many people were involved in the writing of it. The entire issue of authorship is, of course, a complex one in the medieval, Renaissance, and early modern periods. See, for instance, the claims and insights of Ascoli 2008 regarding Dante as the harbinger of the modern notion of the author. See also Rubin 1995, particularly 184 and 216, but also more generally 148–86, 231–85, 403–12.

61 A point stressed in Hope 2014. Rubin 1995, 50–1 and 116–20, by contrast, finds the letters to be rhetorically apt.

62 See Saccone 1983 on *sprezzatura* deriving from notions of irony in classical rhetoric.

63 Rubin 1995, 148 sees this as a characteristic rhetorical strategy of affected modesty, in which Vasari effectively employs a self-modesty topos (on which see Curtius 1990, 83–5) to ingratiate himself with his readers. On the other hand, he routinely signed himself in his letters as a painter, although on occasion he was addressed by others as *storico*.

64 Frey 1923, 210. Annibale Caro to Giorgio Vasari, letter dated December 15, 1547, from Rome: "Del resto mi rallegro con voi, che ne la professione altrui habbiate fatta sì bella e sì utile fatica."

65 Frangenberg 2002, 258 draws the same analogy. See also the observations of Nova 2013, who attributes to Vasari, even as the *Lives* was the product of multiple authors, control over the "unità di quell'impresa" and thus "la sostanziale coerenza e unità delle *Vite*" (63, 70, and *passim*).

2 *INGEGNO*/GENIUS

1 1.869, G4.421–2.

2 Kemp 1977, 385–7. See also Panofsky 1962 and Murray 1989. On "excogitative" invention and how it constitutes "a power of the artist's *ingenium*," which is a concept developed in the Quattrocento, see also Kemp 1977, esp. 348–61. On its function for Lomazzo, see Kemp 1987; for Dürer, see the concise observations in Panofsky 1968, 121–5. For a "historiography of *ingegno*," see Emison 2004, 321–48 and *passim* for its complex evolution in the Italian Renaissance from Villani and Alberti on as it is associated with visual artists and, in particular, its ties to the concept of the "divine." For the intellectual life of the Renaissance artist in Italy, see Ames-Lewis 2000.

3 Lewis 1960, 89. Occasionally, as Emison 2004, 344 observes, Vasari can employ the word to mean something akin to "an inhibiting critical acumen, a sign of intelligence" or just "mind," but for the most part he tends to restrict the meanings of the term to those indicated in my chapter.

4 For the concept of genius in the Italian Renaissance, see Klibansky et al. 1964, Summers 1987, 99–101, Kemp 1977, 1987, and 1989, Brann 2002, and Emison 2004, 321–48 and *passim*; on the classical period, out of which the Renaissance notion grows, see Murray 1989, as well as Lewis 1960, 89–92. For an attempt at a general history of it, see the collection of essays in Murray 1989, the lively synthesis of Robinson 2011, and, above all, the engaging McMahon 2013.

5 See the synthetic observations of Murray 1989, 2–3, 9–31.
6 I cite from *Vocabolario degli accademici della Crusca, ad locum*. http://vocabolario.sns.it/html/_s_index2.html.
7 Kemp 1977, 351 n. 14.
8 Comanducci 2000 provides a synthesis of the legal, contractual, social, political, and economic structure of the *bottega* in Renaissance Florence. Pozzi and Mattioda 2006, 354–92 usefully sketches out how Vasari traces the roles and development of visual artists from their initial formation on, including those who choose to become or not become *maestri*, along with what Vasari perceives to be the positive and negative experiences of *garzoni*.
9 See Cast 2009 in general on the *Lives* and humanism, along with Williams 1988 and 2014, and Ruffini 2011.
10 On humanist pedagogy in Renaissance Italy, which is an enormous topic, see Grendler 1989, Black 1991 and 2001, and Grafton and Jardine 1986.
11 See Hampton 1990 on exemplarity and history as teaching by example. Stimato 2005b, 89–90 has helpful observations on Vasari's views on the overall pedagogy of visual artists.
12 Kemp 1989, 46. Pon 1996, 1016 further argues that the concept of the exceptional genius artist emerges fully with Vasari, with a principal focus on Michelangelo, while Condivi and then the authors of the *Exequies*, according to Pon, elaborate upon the Vasarian concept of the unique genius embodied in Michelangelo. On Michelangelo's genius, see also Summers 1981.
13 For a now classic, early feminist treatment of this issue, see Nochlin 1971. The literature on this topic is understandably large. See recently, for instance, McIver 2005 and Och 2012.
14 I take this precise formulation from the Life of Andrea dal Monte Sansovino, but different versions of it appear throughout the *Lives*.
15 On the *artes liberales*, see Marrou 1938 and 1956. Translations of Italian educational treatises can be found in Woodward 1963 and Kallendorf 2002. More generally, on humanist pedagogy in the Italian Renaissance, see Grafton and Jardine 1986, Grendler 1989, and Black 1991 and 2001.
16 Quintilian 2001, 2.19.
17 Rebhorn 1976, 151, along with Bushnell 1996.
18 See Barolsky 1992 on fathers and sons and family structures in the *Lives*. That Vasari maintained that Giotto was indeed apprenticed to Cimabue for narrative purposes, see Maginnis 2004.
19 As indeed was the case, on which see the brief comments of Reilly 2014.
20 For a concise description of the notion of complexion and humors in the medical theory of the period, see Siraisi 1990. For its application to the *Lives*, see Britton 2003 and 2008, and more generally for Renaissance artists, Klibansky et al. 1964.
21 Wittkower and Wittkower 1963, Klibansky et al. 1964, Steptoe 1998, and Brann 2002.
22 Jamison 1996. Essential as well on this topic in general is Sontag 1989.
23 Kemp 1976.
24 Kemp 1976, 317–18.
25 For an array of adjectives associated with the word *ingegno* in the Italian Renaissance, see Emison 2004, 63 n. 9.

26 This is fairly standard part of the humanist view of the "dignity of man," on which see, for instance, Garin 1965.

27 On this as a topos culminating with Michelangelo, of fathers who wish to block their children from becoming visual artists, including Filippo Brunelleschi, Sandro Botticelli, and Domenico Ghirlandaio, along with those who foster their development early on, see Pozzi and Mattioda 2006, 356–9.

28 As well as, to be sure, Venice (G4.565).

29 See the comments of Elam in Condivi 1998.

30 Cadogan 1993 furnishes archival evidence that Michelangelo was indeed apprenticed to Ghirlandaio well before the date that Vasari gives, and that Michelangelo during that period of apprenticeship would have also learned fresco painting while Ghirlandaio was working on the Tornabuoni chapel in Santa Maria Novella. On Ghirlandaio's workshop, see Cadogan 2000.

31 Condivi 1976 and 1998.

32 Kemp 1989, 38.

33 Kemp 1989, 49. See also the germane observations in Dempsey 1980, 566.

34 Curtius 1990, and for its application to Vasari's Michelangelo, see Barolsky 1990, 30.

35 Elam 1992.

36 Interestingly, Bertoldo is completely written out by Condivi and barely mentioned in Vasari's Life of Michelangelo, as if to erase his impact.

37 Barzman 2000, 7.

38 I borrow the term from Jacobs 2005, *passim*, but see also Waźbiński 1987, 281.

39 On Michelangelo's wit, see Barolsky 1978.

40 The recently revived medieval confraternity, the Compagnia di San Luca, serves the same typological function as a precursor of the Accademia within the context of Vasari's *Lives* (G5.506–7).

41 There is some debate regarding how extensive the Accademia's newly institutionalized educational program actually was in terms of the practical, hands-on teaching of the *technai* of painting, architecture, and sculpture. Dempsey 1980, Waźbiński 1987 (who nevertheless reminds us that the Accademia fundamentally served as a form of "perfezionamento professionale," 281), and Barzman 2000 highlight the importance of that sort of training, whereas Pevsner 1973, 45–48, Goldstein 1975 and 1996, 21–29, and Rossi 1980, esp. 171, downplay it somewhat. It is substantially clear, as Barzman 2000, 151–3 indicates, that the Accademia's educational program emphasized how Euclidean mathematics lay at the heart of teaching *disegno*, but it is not at all clear how systematic the actual instruction was on the part of the three members elected to attend to the needs of young men, or, for that matter, how well realized it actually was in practice. From what I can glean, the *visitatori* by no means took over the role of the *maestro* of the workshop where young men were traditionally apprenticed in various and by no means consistent ways (on which see in particular Thomas 1995 and Comanducci 2000), and in some instances the *visitatori*, as inspectors, served as what we might call "scouts" of talent. As Barzman 2000, 152 observes, teaching initially "may have taken place, although archival sources documenting such activities have not come to light," and as Waźbiński 1987, 281 also points out: "Non si occupava per nulla, o quasi, di tecnologia: questo genere di scienza spettava alla bottega" (see also *idem* 49, 275, 292, 298–9, and 322). In essence, then, there was clearly an educational program to the Accademia, with its focus on mathematics

and *disegno* (as well as more generally the "liberal arts"), along with anatomy classes, staged competitions, and lectures, as Dempsey 1980, Waźbiński 1987, and Barzman 1989 and 2000 have emphasized. But there was *not*, from what I can tell (or Pilliod 2001, 195 can tell), a systematic program of practical, technical training. As Pevsner 1973, 48 summarily puts it: "no replacement of workshop training by something that could be called academic training was considered"—a point confirmed as late as 1591 in a letter by Giovan Battista Paggi (1554–1627), who "non negava certo l'importanza dell'apprendimento in bottega," even as he balks at the typical length of it (Waźbiński 1987, 275). Hughes 1986 a/b focuses more on the Accademia's relationship to the guilds, but also places in question the positions of Waźbiński, Dempsey, and Pevsner.

42 Barzman 1989.

43 A point alluded to also in the *Exequies*, on which see Wittkower and Wittkower 1964, 92. The connection, of course, is a staple of scholarship on Vasari; see, for instance, Chastel 1952.

44 See also Jacobs 2005 for an exploration of how Bronzino figures into this argument as well, as the first artist treated in the section devoted to "Degli Accademici del Disegno." Ruffini 2011 identifies Raphael in particular as being characterized as a proto-academician in the Giuntina edition.

45 See Trexler 1980 on Lorenzo as a charismatic figure.

46 Consider, for instance, the observation in describing Cosimo I more generally in terms of his patronage, "il quale, come è in tutte le cose e nel governo de' suoi popoli di felicissimo ingegno e di grandissimo giudizio" (G4.243).

47 On the strategy of depicting Cosimo I as the culmination of Medici rule through pictorial programs, see Cox-Rearick 1984.

48 On the portrait as the work of a follower of Vasari, see Giordani 2011, 104. On the nails "rimmed with ink," see Sohm 2015, 81–2 n. 78.

49 Consider also, in a related manner (even if the word *ingegno* is here not employed), the following from the Life of Franciabigio: "Non volle mai uscir di Firenze, perché avendo vedute alcune opere di Raffaello da Urbino, e parendogli non esser pari a tanto uomo né a molti altri di grandissimo nome, non si volle mettere a paragone d'artefici così eccellenti e rarissimi. E nel vero, la maggior prudenza e saviezza che possa essere in un uomo *è conoscersi, e non presumere di sé più di quello che sia il valore*" (G4.513–14; emphasis mine).

50 Kemp 1977, as well as Kemp 1987, 21 on Lomazzo, who shares with Vasari the "message that one who knows his genius and follows it, exactly reaches the peak of excellence in that aspect of painting to which he is inclined, as is seen in Raphael"—on which see Lomazzo 1974, 25.

51 Biow 2015, 57–72.

52 On the structure of the workshop in Renaissance Italy, see Rossi 1980, Thomas 1995 and 2006, and Comanducci 2000, as well as the synthetic discussion in Welch 1997, 83–101 on artistic training and workshop collaborations, and O'Malley 2013, 125–71. For an imaginative description of a typical Italian Renaissance workshop, see Rowland and Charney 2017, 55–60.

53 Pilliod 1998 and 2001 offers one explanation, rooted in Vasari's revenge against such rivals as Tasso, Jacone, Foschi, and Bacchiaccia, who were held in Cosimo I's favor in the 1540s and benefited from ties with the major-domo Pierfrancesco Riccio.

And, of course, hardly any women artists were included, on which see, for instance, Och 2012.

54 Rossi 1994.

55 Gardner 1997.

56 For Vasari, Andrea Verrocchio is a case in point of someone who lacked a natural gift, what he calls here the "benefizio o facilità della natura," but who nevertheless overcame it through long and dedicated study, for, as he puts it, "study will do a great deal [*se ben lo studio ne porta seco la maggior parte*]" (1.549, G3.533).

57 In particular, see Barzman 2000, but also Pevsner 1973, Goldstein 1975, Dempsey 1980, Hughes 1986a/b, and Waźbiński 1987.

58 On the early spaces, see Waźbiński 1987, 267–9.

59 Waźbiński 1987, 275.

60 It is not clear to me where or for whom the *giovani* worked, or indeed if any of this ever took place: were they apprentices, *garzoni* at a more advanced stage in their development as *dipendenti*, working for a *maestro* in a workshop, as Hughes 1986a and Waźbiński 1987, 299 appear to assume? And yet it is somewhat difficult to understand why a *maestro* would allow one of the *visitatori* to critique, as it were, one of his assistant's works of art, especially since the function of the assistant was to adopt and imitate perfectly the style of the *maestro*. Capitolo Ottavo, July 1563, says that if the *giovani* will ask a Console or some reputed member of the Accademia for some help, they [the Console, etc.] will have to go only "nelle case e stanze di questi tali giovani che richiedono d'essere ammaestrati," and not in any other place. From this passage, which implies already a different arrangement of the Accademia from the image emerging from the statutes of six months before, we can assume that the *giovani* can also work at their home—plus in their "working premises [*stanze*]." I am not persuaded by Pilliod 2001, 5, which argues that by the time he wrote the 1568 Giuntina edition of the *Lives*, Vasari aimed to completely replace the independent *bottega* system with a state-sponsored academy of art, although the first version of the statutes puts special emphasis on the idea of transforming the Accademia into a proper Studio, with working premises for the *giovani*, where they can study both theory and practice. At the same time, the emphasis on the teaching and training of the *giovani* seems to become weaker and weaker in one version after another of the statutes. It is indeed very strong in January 1563, but in 1585 it is definitively less present, and very little of it survives in that "redazione" (Waźbiński 1987, 467).

61 Goldstein 1975, 152, 20, Dempsey 1980, 556–7, and Barzman 1989. Not that this ideal fellowship of visual artists did not exist without some real internal friction right from the start, with the very organizing and implementation of the foundational funeral honoring Michelangelo, on which see Wittkower and Wittkower 1964, 20–1 and Barzman 2001.

62 The Accademia's members were not officially released from their obligation to the guilds until Cosimo I ruled favorably on their petition in 1572 (the petition was submitted in 1571). Nonetheless, it is clear that it was conceived from its inception as an organization that would indeed take over guild functions. On its ties to guilds, see Hughes 1986a/b.

63 This seems to have been Vasari's understanding of the purpose of the Accademia, shortly after the first meeting of Compagnia di San Luca, when he convened a gathering to propose the creation of just such an Accademia (G5.507).

3 *PRESTEZZA*/SPEED

1 2.1019, G6.369.

2 Hope 1995, 2005, and 2014.

3 Hope 2014, 14. Nova 2013 argues, as do many, that Vasari was in fact working on the *Lives* earlier than when Hope indicates in his timeline; but see the exhaustive tracking of the timeline, which conforms to Hope's, in Ruffini 2011, 72–103. On the impressive number of works completed by Vasari in that short span of time, along with presumably the *Lives*, see Scoti-Bertinelli 1905, 26–7. The Giuntina edition was written as a direct reworking of the Torrentiniana in three years, from 1564 to 1567, while Vasari was once more engaged in a host of time-consuming commissions.

4 On this, see Hope 1995, 2005, and 2014, Frangenberg 2002, and Ruffini 2011.

5 See, for instance, the definitions of the words under the appropriate entry in the *Vocabolario degli Accademici della Crusca*, 1612.

6 Rubin 1995, 93 suggests that "Raphael's former assistants Giovanfrancesco Penni, Giulio Romano, Polidoro da Caravaggio, and Perino del Vaga … had established a model of efficient bravura, whereby unhesitating design and speed of execution became essential features of their practice, which came to be contrasted with the laborious study of Florentine masters typified by Andrea del Sarto"; according to Rubin, this model of production influenced Vasari's view of the value of speed as he "became a student of Raphael's school." Härb 2015, 9 and 127 sees an even more formative model of *prestezza* for Vasari in Giulio Romano.

7 Important scholarship in this area, to which I am indebted in crafting this chapter, is Clements 1954, Nichols 1996 and 1999, d'Elia 2004, Cerasuolo 2014, esp. 60–9, and Sohm 2015. For how the concept applies to Vasari's work as a draftsman, see Härb 2015, 9, 15, 28, 121, and 136. For interesting thoughts related to "speed" in the visual and verbal arts in modernity, see in particular Schnapp 1999 and 2009. For a lively discussion of the value of speed in literature generally, see Calvino 1988.

8 On the significance of the intensification of the concern for speed in postal delivery in the sixteenth century in Italy, see the synthetic and fascinating observations in Fedele 2012, 67: "l'elemento centrale della rivoluzione comunicazionale del XVI secolo sta nel fatto che le poste permettevano di muoversi alla massima velocità possibile," and *passim*.

9 Barocchi 1984 and Ruffini 2011.

10 See Curtius 1990, 83–5 on the false modesty topos, which Vasari often enough employs in the *Lives*, as in the very epigraph to this chapter.

11 On *facilitas* within the ambit of court culture, where it gets viewed as a sort of courtly virtue, see Warnke 1993, 209–11; on *prestezza* and *facilità* and their relationship to *sprezzatura*, see Clements 1954. On *facilità* and its relationship in Alberti's reasoning about "diligenza congiunta con prestezza," see Baxandall 1972, 123–4. On *facilità* and *prestezza* for Vasari, see the brief but salient comments in Pozzi and Mattioda 2006, 215–18, which highlights some of the more important references in the *Lives*, as well as Cerasuolo 2014, esp. 60–9. For reassessments of Warnke, with thoughts on eccentric artists of the period as "vertical invaders," see Campbell 2004 and Welch 2004.

12 Vasari also has a description of the work in his *Ricordanze*, where he correctly assigns the painting to 1541 rather than the incorrect date of 1542 (indicated in

the *Lives*): "Fecesi dentro il batesimo di Cristo per Santo Giovanni Batista con molti popoli atorno … Eranvi le figure grandi principali braccia sette ('Ricordo' no. 115)." The painting, now lost, was "commissioned by Cosimo I de' Medici for the church of San Giovanni in Florence, as part of the celebrations for the baptism of Francesco de' Medici in 1 August 1541. This was one of Vasari's first major commissions in Florence, and he paid homage to the city's leading painter, Andrea del Sarto, by the similarities with the latter's frescoes in the Chiostro dello Scalzo, the *Preaching of the Baptist* and the *Baptism of the People*." Along with the drawing held in the British Museum, "there is also a pen study for the lower part of the composition in the National Museum in Stockholm, and one related to God the Father in the upper half of the painting was sold at Sotheby's, 1 July 1965, lot 96 (Härb figs. 26–7)." The citations above are taken from the British Museum curator's description accessed online: www.britishmuseum.org/research/collection_online/collection_object_details.aspx?objectId=715210&partId=1&searchText=vasari+drawing&page=2.

13 I have had to rework the syntax of the Italian to adapt it to my prose: "Ben mi penso che ne venissi maravigliata e sodisfattissima" (G6.401).

14 ASF, Segnatura: ASF, Carte Guidi, c. 556, as cited in Palli d'Addario, 1985, 369.

15 On Pitti generally and his relations with Vasari, see Rosen 2003.

16 Frey 1923, 169 (August 22, 1546). See also Giovio's letter to Cardinal Alessandro Farnese, in Giovio 1999, 342–3, where Vasari is once more described as *expedito* (as cited in Sohm 2015, 66 n. 23).

17 Frey 1923, 1.387. Letter dated November 23, 1553.

18 Bottari and Ticozzi 1822–5, 7.510–11 (Federico Zuccaro letter to Antonnio Chigi), as cited in Sohm 2015, 103.

19 Sohm 2015, 83–8, to whom I am indebted, does an excellent job of characterizing this aspect of Vasari as part of his tendency to be hyperbolic about his speed and hyperproductivity and how he is later chastised or ridiculed occasionally for it. See also Parker 2004, *passim*, Barolsky 1991, 12, and Rowland and Charney 2017, 150, 178, 234, and 334. By contrast, on Bronzino's slowness according to Vasari, who complains about it, see Pilliod 2001, 200. For that matter, Vasari's *prestezza* has also been noted by art historians in distinctly negative terms as far back as Lanzi 1809, 189 and 310 ("vi [in Naples] dipinse una quantità considerabile di figure con quella prestezza e mediocrità che fa il carattere della massima parte de' suoi lavori"). In terms of his workshop, Härb 2015, 141 suggests that Vasari's practice of working closely with "humanists who devised *concetti* for individual paintings as well as elaborate programmes for entire fresco decorations"—and Vasari did so, she argues, "perhaps more than any artist of his time"—was "entirely consistent with his constant striving for efficiency and speed of execution." In terms of his drawings, Härb 2015, 27–8 also observes that over time Vasari adopted different drawing techniques in order to increase speed and efficiency: "From the 1550s onwards Vasari seems to have largely abandoned the pen technique, focusing instead on drawings with additional wash to define the shading and volume of the figures. If applied in a bold manner with broad brushstrokes, it is a much faster method than drawing fine hatching with the pen. Though less precise in the definition of individual details, this technique is more suggestive in the rendering of light effects and conveys a more vivid impression. Again, Vasari's preference in his later career for the more rapid pen and wash technique for

compositional drawings surely reflects his striving for improved efficiency and speed in making preparatory drawings."

20 On the grand ceremony and its triumphalism, see Partridge and Starn 1992, 168–212, esp. 183–212, on Vasari's contributions as an "impresario."

21 Sohm 2015, 84 calculates that it took about twice the time. But no matter: this is Vasari mythologizing.

22 The anecdote, which appropriates the classical source of Apelles saying much the same thing, is recorded in Caro 1957–61, 2.62–4 (letter dated May 10, 1548). On the Apelles anecdote and its diffusion in the Renaissance, see Nichols 1999, 73–4.

23 Sohm 2015, 84 observes that Vasari, although he vowed never to make the same mistake again, blundered for the same reason on future occasions, such as the Sala Regia frescoes completed in 1570s.

24 Biow 2015, for instance, discusses aspects of the investment in the emotion of wonder, admiration, "meraviglia" as a response to both visual and verbal art. See also Cast 2009, 1–34, who discusses it in the context of thinking about a language of aesthetic delight in the period.

25 Frey 1930, 565–7 (February 10, 1571, emphasis mine): "Ancora che io abbi passato con silenzio molte settimane, Vostra Altezza saperrà per questa mia come io ho già condotto a fine 56 pezzi di cartoni delle 3 capelle, fra quali sono 12 storie grandi di braccia 5 larghe, alte braccia 7, piene di figure, che in quattro v'è le storie di Tubia con l'angelo Raffaello, 4 di Santo Stefano, 4 di Santo Pietro Martire, il resto sono cartoni delle 3 volte, dove è a San Michele la pioggia degli angeli neri, a Santo Stefano un cielo aperto con gran copia di figure, a San Piero Martire tutte le virtù teologiche e santi e sante de l'ordine di San Domenico: così s'è abozato di colori le 3 tavole, et all'ultimo di questo sarà abozzati 12 quadri grandi per la capella dì San Michele, *cosa che Nostro Signore stupiscie*. E m'ha comandato che io non lassi vederla a nessuno; lui solo con il San Galletto ci viene spesso et ha caro veder lavorare e ragiona meco assai et spesso si tracta dì Vostra Altezza, che nel vero vi ama, et ha dolcezza, quando conto della delettazione ch'ell'ha in ogni sorte di virtù, e vi benediscie a ogni parola, quanto fa del Gran Duca." See also, among other such statements in his letters, the following of January 1, 1571 (Frey 1930, 558, emphasis mine), once more to Francesco I de' Medici: "Gran frutto ho cavato dai suoi documenti, scritti nella sua dolce et amorevole de' XII del passato; che se per gli studi, fatica e sollecitudine s'ha a servire bene e presto Sua Santità, nessuno l'arà servito meglio: e già in questo poco di tempo, che è oggi un mese, oltra che ho fatto tutti e disegni delle 3 capelle, e coperto di colori tutte di mia man sola, non bozze, ma come finite dua tavole, e la terza a Befania sarà come le altre. Cosa, Signor mio, *che ha fatto stupire Nostro Signore*, che mostra averne gran contento."

26 Goldthwaite 1993 and Findlen 1998.

27 Some of this has been traced by Cerasuolo 2014, 60–9.

28 Pliny 1984, 35.109–10, as well as 35.148. Vasari recalls these Plinian examples in G1.196 and 202.

29 O'Malley 2013, *passim* in fact demonstrates that speed became an increasing issue of concern in the fifteenth century in workshops as artists, "painting under pressure" (to use the title of her book), employed different techniques to increase the pace of production.

30 Compare with Armenini as discussed in Cerasuolo 2014, 58–64 and 68.

31 See G4.132, G4.255, G4.428, G4.460, 4.622, G4.625, G5.219, and G5.443.
32 Trachtenberg 2010.
33 As observed by Phillips-Court 2011a, 717–19, Bandello 1990, 264–5, and Cinzio 1968, 222 had also remarked on Leonardo's strange, often slow, meditative habits of painting.
34 See Phillips-Court 2011a for a recent treatment of this in light of Aristotelian and Platonic ideas circulating in the period and in terms of a poetics of ethics.
35 Alberti 1804, and Alberti 1833, 35.
36 Ghiberti 1947, 28.
37 Leonardo 1996, 224 and 226.
38 Gombrich 1966a, 60. I draw on Gombrich's translation of Leonardo here.
39 Pino (in Barocchi 1960–2, 1.119 in particular, as well as 1.114).
40 Dolce, in Barocchi 1960–2, 1.158 (on Apelles) and 1.201. Needless to say, it was typically Tintoretto who was recognized for his speed, and often enough praised for it, later in the century, in contrast to Titian and Veronese, on which see d'Elia 2004 and Nichols 1996 and 1999, 69–99. More broadly, see Cerasuolo 2014, esp. 60–9.
41 Cennini, il Anonimo Magliabechiano, il Anonimo Gaddiano, and Billi have, it is worth noting, nothing to say about "speed." My reading of a variety of treatises on the visual arts, including those written both before and after the *Lives*, indicates that *prestezza* only becomes a matter of significant interest after Vasari elaborates upon it. Antonio Manetti (Saalman, 1970, 47), for instance, congratulates Brunelleschi for his speed once, early on in his late fifteenth-century *Vita*, when it comes to describing how he swiftly completed the panel for the competition for the Baptistry's bronze doors ("Filippo fecie la storia sua in quella forma che la si vede ancora al presente e feciela presto, perche possedeva l'arte gagliardamente"), but then otherwise drops it as an issue of any significant note. To shift beyond the borders of Italy while staying still within the ambit of Italy's influence on others from abroad reflecting on the topic of speed, the Portuguese court artist Francisco de Holanda has some things to say about it in his 1548 treatise on "antique painting," in one instance repeating much of what Leonardo had to observe about the value of sketching things out "rapidly [*depressa*]," as in Holanda 2013, 98; 1918, 1.101, as well as in two other instances mentioned later in this chapter and cited in nn. 55 and 56. But Holanda never aspires to make speed a key feature of a narrative about the historical development of art, as Vasari does only two years later, in 1550.
42 My understanding of printing (and bookselling) of the sixteenth century is indebted to Grendler 1977, Lowry 1979, Quondam 1983, Filippo Bareggi 1988, Richardson 1998, 1999, and 2004, Nuovo 2003, and Fenlon 2007, 233–71.
43 On the *poligrafi* as professional adventurers of the pen, see Grendler 1969, Filippo Bareggi 1988, Bragantini 1996, and Biow 2010, 157–85. On *prestezza* as a shared value of *poligrafi* and visual artists in the sixteenth century, see the observations of Nichols 1996 and 1999, 69–99, d'Elia 2004, and Biow 2010, 157–85.
44 Doni 1972, 80.
45 Doni 1552, c [3]v.
46 "Gli schizzi, de' quali si è favellato di sopra, chiamiamo noi una prima sorte di disegni che si fanno per trovare il modo delle attitudini et il primo componimento dell'opra; e sono fatti in forma di una ma[c]chia e accennati solamente da noi in una sola bozza del tutto. E perché dal furor dello artifice sono in poco tempo con penna o con

altro disegnatoio o carbone espressi solo per tentare l'animo di quel che gli sovviene, perciò si chiamano schizzi." (G1.117). On the fascinating topic of the *schizzo* and its roots in Leonardo's theories of painting, see Grassi 1957, Gombrich 1966a, Longhi 1966, and especially now Cerasuolo 2014, 54–60.

47 Gombrich 1966a, 60.

48 On Pontormo and Vasari's negative appraisal, see Gregory 2009 and Pilliod 1998 and 2001.

49 Armenini 1988, 92; 1977, 146, translation modified for accuracy.

50 As Härb 2015, 127 has observed, not just Raphael but also, and perhaps above all, Giulio Romano served Vasari as the model of workshop efficiency and thus, by extension, the speed of production of visual art.

51 Armenini 1988, 93; 1977, 147.

52 Armenini had conflicting notions of the value of speed. On the one hand, he saw it as a cause of the decline of modern art (Armenini 1977, 85, 142, and 202; 1988, 25, 87–8, and 154), with too many over-eager, over-ambitious, still largely untrained, and/or sometimes greedy artists trying to get things done quickly to turn a profit, although he does indeed recognize that some ceremonial and ephemeral works of art need to be put together quickly for patrons celebrating large-scale public events (see Armenini 1977, 142; 1988, 88). On the other hand, he certainly valued speed when it came to the visual artist rapidly producing sketches as a poet swiftly works out ideas on paper, in keeping with such practices developed by Leonardo (Armenini 1977, 144; 1988, 89–90): "The intellectual part of our soul which gives rise to inventions does so in various ways, and because it is naturally imperfect it cannot create them fully formed. It is necessary, then, to express the subject one part at a time, first one particular or another, or, perhaps, even all, depending on the work's quality and size. This is accomplished by means of the impulse of that first concept which is immediately materialized as a rough outline called a sketch or draft because various postures of figures and other subjects are outlined very quickly [*in un tempo brevissimo*] as they come to mind not fully ordered. This is similar to the extemporaneous versifying of good poets ..." (see also Armenini 1977, 125 and 145; 1988, 71 and 91, on the coupling of *prestezza* with technical mastery: "This method [of drawing] is more like painting and is used by experienced masters since they can very quickly [*con molta prestezza*] and almost effortlessly express in a stroke their entire concept";"it is clear how much this routine [practice of drawing daily] enlivens one's memory, enabling it to recall the things one has seen, and is especially admirable in keeping the hand in practice, making it extremely sure, quick [*spedita*], and ready to meet any contingency, thanks to its having been used habitually in this manner"). On Armenini and *prestezza*, see Cerasuolo 2014, esp. 60–9.

53 On Michelangelo and speed, see the wide-ranging discussion in Clements 1954.

54 Of course, Michelangelo did in fact make use of assistants in painting the Sistine Chapel, on which see Wallace 1987.

55 Holanda 2013, 215; 1918, 241–2, from the end of the third dialogue: "'But now I [Francisco] would like to know this from Signor Michelangelo, to see if he agrees with my opinion; and it is that he tells me which is better, whether to execute a work quickly or slowly [*se fazer depressa qualquer obra, se de vagar*]?' And he responded: 'I will tell you: to execute something with great facility and dexterity is very profitable and good, and it is a gift received from the immortal God that

something which another artist spends many days painting should be done in a few hours; for if this were not so, Pausias of Sicyon would not have labored so to perfect a painting of a child on a panel in a day. Thus he who paints fast [*pintando depressa*] and does not for that reason fail to paint as well as someone who paints slowly deserves far greater praise for this. But if with the facility of his hand he exceeds certain limits which are not allowed to be exceeded in art, he should instead paint more slowly and in a more studied manner; for an excellent and worthy draftsman does not have license to let himself be beguiled by pleasure in his swiftness [*presteza*] of hand if it in anyway distracts him or makes him careless of the great task of perfection, which must always be his aim. Thus working a little slowly or even, if need be, very slowly, or spending a great deal of time and care on works of art, does not amount to a failing if it is for the sake of greater perfection; but only want of knowledge is a defect. And I wish to tell you, Francisco de Holanda, a very great perfection in this science of ours, of which perhaps you are not unaware, a perfection that I believe you will consider supreme; it is that what one must work and sweat over the most in works of painting is this, with a great amount of effort and study, to make the thing so that it looks, after much work, as if it had been executed almost in haste and with almost no effort at all [*que foi feita quasi depressa e quasi sem nenhum trabalho*], and very easily, when that is not the case … Now, Plutarch relates in his book *De liberis educandis* that an inept painter showed Apelles what he was doing, saying "This painting is by my hand, done just now," to which Apelles responded: "Even if you had not told me so, I recognize that it is by your hand and that it was done quickly; and I am surprised that you do not produce many of these every day.""" The anecdote is from Plutarch 9.

56 Holanda 2013, 96; 1918, 98–9.

57 Barocchi 1960–2, 201.

58 Vigenère 1976, 885; translation from Clements 1954, 304.

59 Armenini 1988, 134. On Armenini and *prestezza*, see Cerasuolo 2014, esp. 60–9 and n. 52 above.

60 Barocchi 1960–2, 300, along with the similar observations on Orlando Flacco.

61 Sohm 2015. Rowland and Charney 2017, 25 correctly highlights Vasari's "carefully cultivated modesty."

62 Elam 1998 shows that Tiberio Calcagni recorded annotations directly from Michelangelo, who balked at some of the statements in Condivi's biography; nevertheless, it is clear that Michelangelo had a large hand in the making of it. For a different reading of Condivi's *Life*, see Hirst 1996.

63 See, for instance, also Stimato 2005b, 88–9, and Patrizi 2000, 56.

64 On Tintoretto, Vasari synthetically writes: "Ha costui alcuna volta lasciato le bozze per finite, tanto a fatica sgrossate, che si veggiono i colpi de' pennegli fatti dal caso e dalla fierezza, più tosto che dal disegno e dal giudizio" (2.509, G5.468–9). For the significance of speed in his paintings and the way it is, *pace* Vasari, viewed as a positive feature of his art, see Nichols 1996 and 1999 and d'Elia 2004.

65 Sohm 2015 documents how it took actually longer than a hundred days to complete.

66 Terms all used, of course, in the preface to the third volume.

67 For the rhetorical underpinnings of Renaissance art theory, see Baxandall 1972. For its application to Vasari, see, for instance, Goldstein 1991 and Rubin 1995.

68 For its overarching design, see, for instance, Rubin 1995, but also Barocchi 1984, Pozzi and Mattioda 2006, Cast 2009, and Ruffini 2011. For Vasari as a storyteller, see Introduction, n. 21.

69 On Vasari's home, see, for instance, Cheney 2006 and 2014.

4 *TEMPO*/TIME

1 Translation from Rubin 1995, 114 (T3.284).

2 2.211, G5.185.

3 Biow 2010, 18.

4 Much has been written on the topic of gift-giving in the Renaissance; see in particular Davis 2000. On Vasari receiving such recognition and reward from Cosimo I, see Rubin 1995, esp. 197–215.

5 Warnke 1993, 132–42. Vasari seems to have begun receiving an annual allowance as a court artist in 1554, on which Scoti-Bertinelli 1905, 58 n. 1, citing from the Archivio di Stato di Firenze, filza 394, fol. 6, and Rowland and Charney 2017, 277. As Vasari himself announces at one point in the *Lives*: "Delle quali mie fatiche, ancora che continue, difficili e grandi, ne fui dalla magnanima liberalità di sì gran Duca, oltre alle provisioni, grandemente e largamente rimunerato con donativi, e di case onorate e comode in Fiorenza et in villa, perché io potessi più agiatamente servirlo" (G6.400). Cellini makes similar sorts of pronouncements about how he was favorably treated by the king of France but, conversely, finds Cosimo I to be too mercantile and lacking in the graces of courtly gift-giving, on which see Tylus 1993, 31–53.

6 Ovid 1977–84, *Metamorphoses* 15.234: "Tempus edax rerum." See Cohen 2014 for its appropriation in Renaissance images.

7 By contrast, for the late Italian Renaissance and early modern obsession with training and reinforcing the power of memory, see, for instance, Yates 1974.

8 As Borghini insists in a manner that rehearses the earlier elitist position of Plutarch, no one really cares about the lives of mere craftsmen, none of whom were illustrious and none of whom could have ever possibly done anything worthy of allowing them to rise to the level of being the appropriate subjects of exemplary, humanist-oriented biographies. For Borghini's observation on the matter, see Frey 1930, 102, Letter from Borghini to Vasari, August 14, 1564. Plutarch's remark can be found in Plutarch 1961, 5.

9 Wittkower and Wittkower 1963 and Biow 2010.

10 Woods-Marsden 1987.

11 On epitaphs in the *Lives*, see Gahtan 2011 and 2014, who also places Vasari's gathering together of epitaphs at the end of individual Lives (no fewer than 108 out of the 133 Lives of the Torrentiniana edition) in the broader context of the antiquarian practices of collecting epitaphs in the Italian Renaissance and Vasari's desire to lift up visual artists in stature and canonize others more specifically, even by having epitaphs commissioned for artists. The number of epitaphs in the Giuntina edition is significantly reduced (only a third of the Lives now contain epitaphs, although there are also significantly more Lives), while other strategies come into play, Gahtan reveals, to elevate socially and culturally the status of the visual artists (the inclusion of artist's

portraits, for instance) as Vasari becomes more "curatorial" in his selection of which epitaphs should and should not remain in his (now more museological) book.

12 Gahtan 2014, 57.

13 Dante 1970–5.

14 Boase 1979, 86. The inscription alludes to Aeneid 8.470-1 (Virgil 2000): "Maxime Teucrorum ductor, quo sospite numquam / res equidem Troiae victas aut regna fatebor." Consider as well the similar use of *sospes* on Raphael's epitaph in the Pantheon attributed to Pietro Bembo: "Ille hic est Raffael, timuit quo sospite vinci rerum magna parens et moriente mori."

15 Barkan 1999.

16 Notable in this regard, by contrast, is the work of conservation on the part of Fra Iocondo (Giovanni Giocondo, G4.560, G4.562).

17 Doni 1972, 127. On Doni in general, see Grendler 1969, Filippo Bareggi 1988, Masi 1988, Biow 2010, 157–85, and the updated, thorough bibliography in Masi 2010. On the *Libraria*, see in particular Bramanti 1972 ("Introduzione" to Doni 1972, 10–43), Masi 1988, Bradbury 2009, Biow 2010, 157–85.

18 Marsili-Libelli 1960, 339 and Bongi 1890–5, 1.261.

19 Gregory 2012; see also Lincoln 2000 and Pon 2004.

20 The point is made emblematically in the Life of Andrea del Sarto (G4.380). As Boase 1979, 10–11 observed, Vasari was keenly aware how print conferred fame because "they could easily circulate"; the point is reiterated by Giovio in a letter of April 2, 1547 to Vasari (Frey 1923, 196–7): "La vostra lettera è tutta da filosofo; come spero, che farete in compilare il bel libro delli famosi pictori, qual vi farà al certo immortale, perché in fatto, le cose, che avete fatto a Monte Oliveto in Napoli a quelli tiranni delle frittate grosse e grasse, alla fine fine saranno cacabaldole, colsumate dal sanitro e dalle tarle; ma quello che scriverete, non lo consumerà il ladro tempo, qual suole consumare li visi delle sposate in termine d'uno anno; e voi lo conoscerete per prova, avanti che finisca la prima parte del libro."

21 Related is Vasari's active role as a "restorer," seeking to preserve artifacts, on which see Tiberio 1974, and more recently Nova 2013, Waldman 2014, and Rowland and Charney 2017.

22 Tellingly, Vasari observes that he does not need to describe the *Last Judgment* since there are already so many printed versions of it in circulation (2.691, G6.69). On prints as "aides-mémoires" for Vasari, see Gregory 2012, 133–60.

23 See, for instance, the Life of Andrea Pisano (G2.150). Hence, as well, the importance of the discovery of the grotesques in the Domus Aurea, which gave Italian painters a concrete model for artistic excellence in the art of painting from antiquity.

24 Needless to say, this is true also with regard to Vasari's own paintings, such as fig. 27.

25 For general overviews of the concept of time in the period, see Quinones 1972, Le Goff 1980, Trachtenberg 2010, esp. 25–61, and Cohen 2014.

26 The locus classicus is Petrarch's concern with posterity, best expressed in the final unfinished letter to the *Seniles*, accessible in Petrarch 1992, 672–80.

27 Frey 1923, 196–7 (April 2, 1547).

28 On *goffismo*, see Barolsky 1991, 13–14.

29 Biow 2006, 54.

30 Vasari here draws in a familiar manner in the Renaissance on Aristotle's *Nicomachean Ethics*, here more or less echoing the position of Castiglione: "in tutte le cose si vuole

avere un certo mezzo e star lontano dagl'estremi, che sono comunemente viziosi" (1.803, G4.303).

31 See G3.327–42, G3.559–70, G5.539–52.

32 On Vasari's notion of progress, see Alpers 1960, Gombrich 1960 and 1966b, Rubin 1995, Clifton 1996, and Payne 2001. Vasari's vision of progress within his history certainly includes plenty of artists who contributed little to advance the development of the arts, such as, say, Boccaccino, who died at fifty-eight "senza aver fatto alcun migioramento nell'arte" (G4.312). In this respect, what matters to Vasari are those who manifestly furthered the development of the arts, and the loss of any one masterful work that could have done so represents a substantial loss to the progress he traces and for posterity itself.

33 A point stressed at the end of Boase 1979, 338.

34 On this aspect of Vasari, as something of a braggart, see Sohm 2015.

35 On Baccio's unfinished objects, see, for instance, Waldman 2001.

36 This is also true, to be sure, of Leonardo, whom Vasari identifies as the artist who defines the beginning of the third age of historical development of the visual arts and who likewise stands apart from others in his exceptionality even if he rarely finishes things: "It is clear that Leonardo, through his comprehension of art, began many things and never finished one of them, since it seemed to him that the hand was not able to attain to the perfection of art in carrying out the things which he imagined; for the reason that he conceived in idea difficulties so subtle and so marvelous, that they could never be expressed by the hands, be they ever so excellent" (1.627–8, G4.19).

37 On Michelangelo absorbed in his work, see Biow 2010, 92–129.

38 Lee 1940, 251–2 (my emphasis). Leonardo 1970, 1.61, no. 27. The entire issue of *ut pictura poesis* in the Italian Renaissance has received varied and extensive treatments, some downplaying its importance, others still finding relevance in it.

39 A point emphasized by Andrews 1995 in the context of investigating the ongoing and highly developed Renaissance investment in continuous narrative. There is much written, to be sure, on *ut pictura poesis* and the role of time and narrative in visual art in the Italian Renaissance. For the purposes of this book I have benefited most from: Lavin 1990, Farago 1992, Andrews 1995, Lubbock 2006, Greenstein 2012, Cohen 2014, and Demos 2015.

40 Lavin 1990.

41 There are a plethora of books now on how students were trained to read in the humanist schoolroom, from Grafton and Jardine 1986 to Grendler 1989, or in the university system in Italy in particular and Europe more broadly, not to mention how the clergy was trained to read scripture, on which the *locus classicus* in the period was Augustine's *De doctrina christiana*. More broadly, the entire topic that examines historically how people read and were trained to read in different periods over time is an enormous one in scholarship today.

42 Greenstein 2012, 217 is drawing on the observations of Leonardo, who wrote a good deal about the nature of time in painting and the viewer's experience of temporality, along with Chapman 1975. See also Andrews 1995.

43 Lavin 1990, 2.

44 I borrow these examples from Greenstein 2012.

45 Steinberg 2001; see also Demos 2015. For a far-reaching investigation into the meaning and implications of Leonardo's *sfumato*, see Nagel 1993.

46 For a recent exploration into *ut pictura poesis*, along with *ekphrasis*, see Barkan 2013, 27–74, but in particular Barkan 2011 for ways of connecting word and image in Michelangelo's drawings. See also Phillips-Court 2011b for connections between the verbal (in this instance drama) and the visual in the period.

47 Alpers 1960. On *ekphrasis* in Vasari, see also Rubin 1995, 275–82, and Ruffini 2011, 137–60. For its history, and serious reservations about the way the term has been deployed since the nineteenth century, but above all beginning with Leo Spitzer in critical theory, see Webb 1999 and 2009. For my own explanation of the use of the term in this book, see Chapter 1 n. 6.

48 In and of itself there is nothing unusual in this. Manuals of prayer enjoined viewers, for instance, to meditate on devotional images and respond to them emotively, even committing them to memory as narratives, so that viewers could be drawn even deeper at any given moment into experiencing their faith through a sort of trained, interiorized vision.

49 Interestingly, this sort of emotive metanarrative does not appear in the *Ragionamenti*; there the *ekphrases* are informative and purposely instructional but emotively bland, and they lack, rhetorically, *enargeia*.

50 For a synthetic reading of the painting in Raphael's oeuvre, see Wood 2005, 33–5 and Talvacchia 2007, 38–41. On the relationship of the preparatory drawings to the final paintings, see Nagel 2000, 120–35.

51 See, for instance, Brown 1992 on Perugino losing ground as Raphael absorbs the lessons of Leonardo.

52 Alpers 1960, 195.

53 On spiritual contemplation of images and the interiorizing of them, see, for instance, Andrews 1995, 29–44, and Baxandall 1972, 29–108 on the "period eye."

54 This is, to be sure, a compliment that Vasari reserves for truly great works of art, such as the *Last Judgment* (2.694, G6.73), which appears as if painted in one day.

55 On the centrality of epideictic rhetoric in the Italian Renaissance, see, for instance, O'Malley 1979 and McManamon 1989. Standard overview of the medieval *ars praedicandi* can be found in Murphy 1974. There is a concise discussion of the rhetoric of devotional handbooks as it applies to continuous narratives in visual arts in the Renaissance in Andrews 1995, 29–33.

56 White 1978 and 1987.

57 Payne 2001.

58 Ruffini 2011.

59 On the history of the exegesis of figural readings and their development, see Lubac 1998–2000. Auerbach 1984, 11–78 famously traced the concept of *figura*. For a recent, sensitive reading of the role of typology in the *Lives*, see Blum 2013.

60 It was likewise conventional in the period to refer to Raphael as a *figura Christi*.

61 This large topic is classically addressed in Singleton 1954 and 1958 and Hollander 1969. Reading the *Lives* allegorically, in terms of prefiguration and typology, has been part of Barolsky's influential project, particularly in Barolsky 1990, esp. 44–77. But see also Blum 2013.

62 Ariosto 1982.

63 The issue in a nutshell is this. If the *Lives* offers a teleological view of the development of the visual arts from the fourteenth to the sixteenth century, with Michelangelo as the overriding goal (*telos*) toward which all other artists have progressively, unconsciously, and providentially labored, what are we to make of the period in which Vasari himself produced art, which follows Michelangelo? This is an important question in terms of the temporal structure of the *Lives*. For Vasari is quick to assert in the *Lives* that his own period is *not* one of decline, even if it comes after Michelangelo, who represents the apex of all artistic achievement. How does Vasari get out of this bind? How does the period after Michelangelo not constitute a falling off if Michelangelo really does mark the absolute highpoint? The question is posed, and differently resolved, most recently in Ruffini 2011.

5 *NOTTE*/NIGHT

1 G6.381.
2 2.1049, G6.394.
3 On the crucial concept of *difficultà*, see Summers 1981.
4 I use the gendered "he" advisedly here: Vasari has precious few women artists who are shown to overcome masterfully "difficulties."
5 Baxandall 1988.
6 I am thinking, of course, of the concept of distinction developed in Bourdieu 1984.
7 Barkan 1999 discusses, for instance, how viewers staged such playful competitions amongst themselves regarding who could detect, say, the original antique sculpture from the modern forgery. On the sophistication of some viewers, and how a work of visual art could even be designed for just a single, informed viewer, see Shearman 1992.
8 Milton 2005, 1.63.
9 For Vasari, as for Michelangelo, landscapes were not a key feature of great art and unworthy of the attention of a great talent/genius (2.696, G6.76).
10 Leonardo 1956, 1.117, 2.52.
11 Leonardo 1956, 1.86, 2.66: "*Whether different colors can appear to be of uniform obscurity because of a common shadow.* It is possible for all the different colors with a common shadow to appear to be transmuted into the color of that shadow. This is shown in the shadows on a cloudy night, in which no shape or color of a body is perceived. Since shadow is nothing but the absence of light, either direct or reflected, through which all the shapes and colors of bodies are comprehended, it necessarily follows that when the cause of the light is completely removed, the effect and the perception of the colors and forms of those bodies should be lacking."
12 Edgerton 1975 and 2009 and Kemp 1990.
13 Clark 1976, 103, Hills 1987, 85, and Howard 1992, 217.
14 Leonardo 1956, 1.287, 2.203.
15 Cardinal Farnese's secretary, the humanist Annibale Caro, is the mediator here informing Zuccaro what is required: interestingly, he then goes on to provide a detailed description of what is desired, and it turns out to be not a naturalistic rendering of night but a distinctly allegorical one.

16 Vincenzo Borghini, August 14, 1564 (Frey 1930, 100–3) had this in mind, in line with Pliny's reflections, as he commented warmly on Vasari's renditions of nights: "Vorrei, che questo quadro, dove si mostra la testa, fussi oscuro e paressi notte da dovero: scrive Plinio (eccovi la dottrina in campo), che fu molto celebrato d'un pittore un fanciullo che soffiava nel fuoco, che quello splendore gli ribatteva nella bocca et per certi muri della casa, come la vostra notte di Camaldoli et d'altri, che nel vostro libro raccontate."

17 Admittedly, these translations are not literal, but they capture the spirit of Vasari's thoughts.

18 Weil-Garris Posner 1972 and 1974.

19 It seems to have inspired the Florentine painter Giuliano Bugiardini to render a comical, parodic version of it in a manner that amused Michelangelo himself (G5.283).

20 Buonarroti 1991, poems 101–4, for instance, treating the night.

21 Barbieri 1999, 96, reformulated again in Barbieri 2005, 157 (albeit in the form of a rhetorical question). In any event, as Barbieri amply demonstrates, by the 1520s, overcoming the challenge of painting a nocturne scene had become a matter of keen interest for painters and purchasers of visual art, although it is only with Vasari, I submit, that it becomes a matter of historical concern, here articulated for the first time within a teleological narrative about the development of the visual arts.

22 Moffitt 1989, as well as Weil-Garris Posner 1972. The relevant source about Apelles and the innovative technique of *atramentum* is Pliny 1984 (35.36.97): "His inventions in the art of painting have been useful to all other painters as well, but there was one which nobody was able to imitate: when his works were finished he used to cover them over with a black varnish of such thinness that its very presence, while its reflection threw up the brilliance of all the colors and preserved them from dust and dirt, was only visible to anyone who looked at it close up, but also employing great calculation of lights, so that the brilliance of the colors should not offend the sight when people looked at them as if through a muscovy-glass and so that the same device from a distance might invisibly give somberness to colors that were too brilliant [*coloribus austeritatem occulte daret*]."

23 With the exception of Leonardo's insights already cited, I have not found any sustained discussions before Vasari's *Lives* specifically dedicated to the problem of visualizing the night in pictorial form, other than Pino's rather underdeveloped observation (at least when compared to Vasari's observations) in his *Dialogo di pittura* (Barocchi 1960–2, 1.184). After Vasari, one can consult Dolce in Roskill 1968, 154–5 (once more with underdeveloped observations in this regard), and especially Sorte (in Barocchi 1960–2), 291–2, who thoughtfully addresses the issue as a practitioner: "E perciò dirovvi solo come questo caso, essend'io allora pittore, con li colori imitai, illuminando il paese et i luoghi vicini parte dallo splendore della luna e parte dalli vapori e vampi più vivi dello incendio. Il sereno adunque e stellato cielo della notte con la luna lucente e chiara, come si fa in tutte l'altre cose, rilevai con biaca accompagnata con azzurrino, e nei lumi più vivi e fissi adoperai la biaca senza l'azzurrino, e tutti gli edificii, cioè case, fiume, alberi, e tutte l'altre cose ove non aggiungeva il lume del fuoco da essa luna illuminai, e quelle parti, ove dagli ardenti vapori di esso fuoco erano i splendori della luna occupati, da essi vapori illustrai, ricazzando tutte le cose con l'endego fino e lacca nelle materie più lontane, secondo che meglio mi pareva convenire. Essi vapori più chiari e più

vivi imitai con gialdolino accompagnato con biaca, sfumandoli nelli suoi luoghi con minio e ricazzandoli sempre con cinaprio appresso il minio, et oscurandosi con lacca accompagnata sempre di endego fino. I fumi che non prendevano il lume della luna, per non essere ancora saliti tanto in alto, ma ch'erano d'appresso et avevano i lumi dalli chiarissimi vapori del fuoco, gli macchiai di minio senza gialdolino, ricazzandoli medesimamente col cinaprio e lacca al modo sopradetto, fingendoli alcune chiarette fiamme, scintille e vampi di diverse sorti, secondo che meglio alla somiglianza di quel vivo e naturale mi pareva che convenissero; perciò che questi e così fatti sono soggetti tanto particolari e proprii del giudicio e della mano del pittore, che non si ponno né esprimere, e meno insegnare, se non che in fatto ciò l'operazioni dimostrano. Laonde deve assai bene bastare a sapere le sorti, le qualità e le nature dei colori che s'adoperano, e le tempere et i modi con cui si usano: perciò che colui ch'averà buon disegno e perfetta cognizione del rilevo, farà tutto quello agevolmente con la mano che non si può con la penna insegnare."

24 For a general introduction to Raphael, see Talvacchia 2007 and Hall 1997 and 2005.

25 Rubin 1995, 357–401 in general, 377 in particular.

26 As in, for instance, Pliny 1984, 35.36.65–6.

27 Barbieri 1999, 94 adds appropriately Pietro Lorenzetti's *Betrayal of Judas* and *Last Supper* in the lower church of San Francesco at Assisi, and Pisanello's painting skills in capturing nocturnes (about which Guarino Veronese had written a poem in his praise): "When you paint a nocturnal scene you make the night-birds flit about and not one of the birds of the day is to be seen; you pick out the stars, the moon's sphere, the sunless darkness [*Noctis opus pingens circum volitare volucres/Nocturnas facis et nusquam apparere diurnas:/Astra, globum lunae cernas, sine sole tenebras*]" (from Baxandall 1965, 193). Barbieri also identifies prior northern examples, such as Rogier van der Weyden.

28 Leonardo 1956, 209–92.

29 G1.22, on the *difficultà* of painting in fresco.

30 Giovio 1971, 14.

31 Koslofsky 2011, 2.

32 On artists' tonal use of colors as distinct "modes," see Hall 1992, 92–148, as well as Hall 1987.

33 For an early high regard for Raphael as an exceptional colorist, setting him up over and against Michelangelo, see Shearman 2003, 809. Vasari also famously applauded Raphael's *grazioso* use of color. On the appreciation of Raphael as a colorist, see, for instance, Bell 1997, 85–113 and Hall 1987 and 1992.

34 There are indeed exceptions, such as the *Madonna del Cardellino* (ca. 1506), the *Spasimo di Sicilia* (ca. 1514–16), *St. Michael* (1518), and *The Holy Family of Francis I* (1518).

35 Barbieri 1999, 42.

36 On Sebastiano, see Hirst 1981 (I here cite from p. 48), and for his role as a proxy in Michelangelo's rivalry with Raphael, see Liebert 1984, Goffen 2002, and Barbieri 2005. On the *Pietà of Viterbo* and the nocturnal, see Barbieri 1999 and 2004: she proposes, moreover, that "the iconography of the night setting may also be related to the liturgical context of the offices for Good Friday and Holy Saturday—offices celebrated at night. In this context, the night takes on the symbolic meaning of a vigil, as the faithful await the divine light of the Resurrected Christ" (Barbieri 1999, 47 and 154–60).

37 Barbieri 2005, 157–8.

38 On Giorgione's influence on Sebastiano, see, for instance, Barbieri 1999, 8–19, 53, 97, and 99, and even Vasari himself: "Colorì [Sebastiano] similmente alcune cose a olio, delle quali fu tenuto, per aver egli da Giorgione imparato un modo di colorire assai morbido, in Roma grandissimo conto" (G5.87).

39 Weil-Garris Posner 1972, 366 n. 33.

40 Moffitt 1989. And that had served as an ancient, classical precursor to Leonardo's own innovative art of *sfumato*.

41 In reality smoke-black (also known as "lampblack") is suspended carbon and carbon doesn't get any darker.

42 Hall 1992, 131–6, and Barbieri 2005, 142.

43 On Leonardo's influence on Raphael, see, for instance, Weil-Garris Posner 1974, Brown 1992, and Barbieri 1999 and 2005.

44 On Leonardo's influence on the dark manner of painting, see Weil-Garris Posner 1974.

45 On the salient borrowings on the part of Raphael from Leonardo, and especially the *Adoration*, in the making of the *Transfiguration*, see Weil-Garris Posner 1972, esp. 345–9, and 1974 *passim*. See also Bertini 1961, Mellini 1963, and Cranston 2003 for additional Leonardo underpinnings to the *Transfiguration*.

46 Weil-Garris Posner 1972, 349–50.

47 Weil-Garris Posner 1972, 355 (see also n. 79) nevertheless observes that "Leonardo wrote instructions on the painting of night scenes and that he himself was thought to have painted them." I do not know of any surviving Leonardo paintings devoted strictly to the night, although many were of course dedicated to representing *oscurità* in a manner that was formative for Raphael, as Weil-Garris Posner and others have argued.

48 Weil-Garris Posner 1972, 350–1 also draws out additional nuanced contrasts that come into play with this *paragone* that pits Michelangelo (via Sebastiano) against Leonardo by thinking about the larger *paragone* in the period that pits, more broadly, sculpture against painting: "For Michelangelo … painting was at best only a partial, diminished imitation of sculpture. In practice it meant that painting, like sculpture, was reduced to the representation of finite plastic units (figures), interrelated to some extent by grouping but principally through pose and gesture, and projected into an essentially negative space. Raphael's enthusiastic adoption of a Vincian dark manner in effect bespoke allegiance to an opposed theoretical attitude, which held that painting was the superior art because of its greater ability to achieve *relievo* through the use of light and shade. Painting was also to be preferred to sculpture because of its richer resources for the depiction not only of figures but of all nature, in its visual and poetic totality." Or to put it differently, Raphael and Leonardo can capture "night" better in such paintings as the *Deliverance of St. Peter*, the *Transfiguration*, and the *Raising of Lazarus*, than Michelangelo can in his sculpture of, in fact, *Night*, lodged in the New Sacristy. For additional ways in which the *paragone* between painting and sculpture is inscribed not only into the *Transfiguration* and the *Raising of Lazarus* but also, in important ways, the *Pietà of Viterbo*, see Barbieri 1999, 2004, and 2005.

49 I am referring throughout these concluding paragraphs to Koslofsky 2011.

50 Ekirch 2001 and 2005. "E così in sul primo sonno," Vasari writes of Polidoro da Caravaggio being attacked by his nefarious servant, "assalitolo mentre dormiva" (1.897, G4.469).

51 1.142–4, G2.161–3; Sacchetti novella 161.

52 Boccaccio 1987 has a few stories dedicated to Buffalmacco's exploits at night. For a fine reading of one such episode, see Kirkham 1983–4.

53 G3.102 and G4.468–9.

54 These words are from the instructions Annibale Caro delivers to Taddeo Zuccaro in the painting of Night in the Farnese Villa, as recorded by Vasari in the *Lives*.

55 For visual artists explicitly designated in the *Lives* as having worked through the night, see, for instance, G2.162, G3.49, and G3.72 (in a comical fashion), G3.373, G3.595, G5.177, G5.230, G5.410, G5.493, G5.511, G5.512, and G5.553.

56 Biringuccio 1540, 1959, chapter 10 deals with fireworks, *fuochi arteficiali*.

57 On Giorgione and nocturnes, see Barbieri 1999, 99.

58 Vasari does not seem to recognize the Venetian achievement in this area, although he does seem to think that as inveterate glass-makers they tended to darken their stained glass productions (G1.160). Barbieri 1999, 99–100 and 2005, 157 succinctly documents the Venetian fascination with the nocturnal, a fascination that in turn interested patrons.

59 Howard 1992 and Rzepińska and Malcharek 1986.

CONCLUSION

1 G6.12; 2.649.

BIBLIOGRAPHY

Abbott, Andrew. (1988). *The System of Professions: An Essay on the Division of Expert Labor*. Chicago, IL: University of Chicago Press.

Ackerman, James S. (1997). "Review of Patricia Rubin, Giorgio Vasari: Art and History." *Renaissance Quarterly* 50: 639–40.

Agosti, Barbara. (2013). *Giorgio Vasari: Luoghi e tempi delle vite*. Milan: Officina Libraria.

Ahl, Diane Cole. (2005). "Sia di mano di santo o d'un angelo: Vasari's Life of Fra Angelico." In *Reading Vasari*, ed. Barriault et al., 119–31. London: Philip Wilson in association with the Georgia Museum of Art.

Alberti, Leon Battista. (1804). *Della pittura e della statua di Leonbatista Alberti*. Ed. Girolamo Tiraboschi. Trans. Cosimo Bartoli. Milan: Società Tipografica de' Classici Italiani.

(1833). *Della architettura libri dieci di Leon Battista Alberti; traduzione di Cosimo Bartoli; con note apologetiche di Stefano Ticozzi e trenta tavole in rame disegnate ed incise da Costantino Gianni*. Milan: Spese degli Editori.

(1960–73). *Opere volgari*. 2 vols. Bari: Laterza.

Alford, John A. (1979). "Medicine in the Middle Ages: The Theory of a Profession." *Centennial Review* 23: 377–96.

Alighieri, Dante. *See* Dante Alighieri.

Alpers, Svetlana Leontief. (1960). "Ekphrasis and Aesthetic Attitudes in Vasari's *Lives*." *Journal of the Warburg and Courtauld Institutes* 23: 190–215.

Ames-Lewis, Francis. (2000). *The Intellectual Life of the Early Renaissance Artist*. New Haven, CT: Yale University Press.

Andrews, Lew. (1995). *Story and Space in Renaissance Art: The Rebirth of Continuous Narrative*. Cambridge: Cambridge University Press.

Anonimo Fiorentino. (1969). *Il Codice magliabechiano*. Ed. Carl Frey. Farnborough: Gregg.

Ariosto, Ludovico. (1982). *Orlando furioso*. Ed. Emilio Bigi. 2 vols. Milan: Rusconi.

Armenini, Giovanni Battista. (1977). *On the True Precepts of the Art of Painting*. Edited and translated from the Italian with an introductory study, critical and historical notes, and bibliography by Edward J. Olszewski. New York, NY: B. Franklin.

(1988). *De' veri precetti della pittura*. Ed. Marina Gorreri. Turin: Einaudi.

Ascoli, Albert R. (2008). *Dante and the Making of a Modern Author*. Cambridge: Cambridge University Press.

Auerbach, Erich. (1984). *Scenes from the Drama of European Literature: Six Essays*. Trans. Ralph Manheim. Minneapolis, MN: University of Minnesota Press.

Avesani, Rino. (1960). "Amaseo, Romolo Quirino." In *Dizionario biografico degli Italiani* 2.660–6.

Bacci, M., and P. Stoppelli. (1979). "Cennini, Cennino." In *Dizionario biografico degli Italiani* 23.565–9.

Bakhtin, Mikhail M. (1981). *The Dialogic Imagination: Four Essays*. Trans. Caryl Emerson and Michael Holquist. Austin, TX: University of Texas Press.

Bandello, Matteo. (1990). *Novelle*. Ed. Luigi Russo. Milan: Rizzoli.

Barbieri, Costanza. (1999). "Sebastiano del Piombo and Michelangelo in Rome: Problems of Style and Meaning in the Viterbo Pietà." PhD dissertation, Rutgers University.

(2004). *Notturno sublime: Sebastiano e Michelangelo nella Pietà di Viterbo*. Rome: Viviani Editore.

(2005). "The Competition between Raphael and Michelangelo and Sebastiano's Role in It." In *The Cambridge Companion to Raphael*, ed. Marcia B. Hall, 141–64. Cambridge: Cambridge University Press.

Barkan, Leonard. (1999). *Unearthing the Past: Archaeology and Aesthetics in the Making of Renaissance Culture*. New Haven, CT: Yale University Press.

(2011). *Michelangelo: A Life on Paper*. Princeton, NJ: Princeton University Press.

(2013). *Mute Poetry, Speaking Pictures*. Princeton, NJ: Princeton University Press.

Barocchi, Paola, ed. (1960–2). *Trattati d'arte del Cinquecento, fra manierismo e Controriforma*. 3 vols. Bari: Laterza. Accessible now online through Memofonte.

ed. (1971–7). *Scritti d'arte del Cinquecento*. 3 vols. Milan: Ricciardi.

(1976). "Le postille di Del Migliore alle Vite vasariane." In *Il Vasari, storiografo e artista: Atti del Congresso internazionale nel IV centenario della morte*, 439–47. Florence: Istituto Nazionale di Studi sul Rinascimento.

(1984). *Studi Vasariani*. Turin: Einaudi.

Barolsky, Paul. (1978). *Infinite Jest: Wit and Humor in Italian Renaissance Art*. Columbia, MI: University of Missouri Press.

(1990). *Michelangelo's Nose: A Myth and Its Maker*. University Park, PA: Penn State University Press.

(1991). *Why Mona Lisa Smiles and Other Tales by Vasari*. University Park, PA: Penn State University Press.

(1992). *Giotto's Father and the Family of Vasari's "Lives."* University Park, PA: Penn State University Press.

(1994). *The Faun in the Garden: Michelangelo and the Poetic Origins of Italian Renaissance Art*. University Park, PA: Penn State University Press.

(1999). "Vasari and the Historical Imagination." *Word & Image* 15: 286–91.

(2005). "Fear of Fiction: The Fun of Reading Vasari." In *Reading Vasari*, ed. Barriault et al., 31–5. London: Philip Wilson in association with the Georgia Museum of Art.

(2010). *A Brief History of the Artist from God to Picasso*. University Park, PA: Penn State University Press.

(2014). "Vasari's Literary Artifice and the Triumph of Michelangelo's *David*." In *The Ashgate Research Companion to Giorgio Vasari*, ed. Cast, 121–8. Farnham, Surrey: Ashgate.

Barriault, Anne B. (2005). "Piero di Cosimo the Egg-Eating Elegist." In *Reading Vasari*, ed. Barriault et al., 191–201. London: Philip Wilson in association with the Georgia Museum of Art.

Barriault, Anne B., Andrew Ladis, Norman E. Land, and Jeryldene M. Wood, eds. (2005). *Reading Vasari*. London: Philip Wilson in association with the Georgia Museum of Art.

Bartoli, Lorenzo. (1997). "Rewriting History: Vasari's Life of Lorenzo Ghiberti." *Word & Image* 13: 245–52.

Barzman, Karen-edis. (1989). "The Florentine Accademia del Disegno: Liberal Education and the Renaissance Artist." In *Academies of Art between Renaissance and Romanticism, Leids. Kunsthistorish Jaarbook* 52: 14–32.

(1991). "Perception, Knowledge, and the Theory of *Disegno* in Sixteenth-Century Florence." In *From Studio to Studiolo: Florentine Draftsmanship under the First Medici Grand Dukes*, ed. Larry J. Feinberg, 37–48. Seattle, WA: University of Washington Press.

(2000). *The Florentine Academy and the Early Modern State: The Discipline of Disegno*. Cambridge: Cambridge University Press.

(2001). "The Accademia del Disegno and Fellowships of Discourse at the Court of Cosimo I de' Medici." In *The Cultural Politics of Duke Cosimo I de' Medici*, ed. Konrad Eisenbichler, 177–88. Aldershot, UK: Ashgate.

Bavaj, Riccardo. (2010). "Intellectual History." *Zentrum für Zeithistorische Forschung Potsdam* e.V. Docupedia-Zeitgeschichte, September 13, 2010. http://docupedia.de/zg/Intellectual_History.

Baxandall, Michael. (1965). "Guarino, Pisanello and Manuel Chrysoloras." *Journal of the Warburg and Courtauld Institutes* 28: 183–204.

(1972). *Giotto and the Orators: Humanist Observers of Painting in Italy and the Discovery of Pictorial Composition*. Oxford: Clarendon Press.

(1985). *Patterns of Intention: On the Historical Explanation of Pictures*. New Haven, CT: Yale University Press.

(1988). *Painting and Experience in Fifteenth-Century Italy*. 2nd ed. Oxford: Oxford University Press.

Bec, Christian. (1983). "Lo statuto socio-professionale degli scrittori (Trecento e Cinquecento)." In *Letteratura italiana: Produzione e consumo*, ed. Alberto Asor Rosa, 2.229–67. Turin: Einaudi.

Becchi, Egle, and Monica Ferrari, eds. (2009a). *Formare alle professioni: Sacerdoti, principi, educatori*. Milan: FrancoAngeli.

(2009b). "Professioni, professionisti, professionalizzare: Storie di formazione." In *Formare alle professioni: Sacerdoti, principi, educatori*, ed. E. Becchi and M. Ferrari, 7–27. Milan: FrancoAngeli.

Bell, Janis. (1997). "Color and Chiaroscuro." In *Raphael's "School of Athens,"* ed. Marcia B. Hall, 85–113. Cambridge: Cambridge University Press.

Bellori, Giovanni Pietro. (1751). *Descrizione delle quattro immagini dipinte da Raffaelle d'Urbino nel Palazzo Vaticano*, 29–47. Rome: Eredi del q. Gio. Lorenzo Barbiellini.

(1997). "The Image of the Ancient *Gymnasium of Athens*, or, *Philosophy*." Trans. Alice Sedgwick Wohl. In *Raphael's "School of Athens,"* ed. Marcia B. Hall, 48–56. Cambridge: Cambridge University Press.

Bertini, Aldo. (1961). "La 'Trasfigurazione' e l'ultima evoluzione della pittura di Raffaello." *Critica d'Arte* 8: 1–19.

Bettarini, Rosanna. (1976). "Vasari scrittore: Come la Torrentiniana diventò Giuntina." In *Il Vasari, storiografo e artista: Atti del Congresso internazionale nel IV centenario della morte*, 485–500. Florence: Istituto Nazionale di Studi sul Rinascimento.

Billi, Antonio. (1969). *Il Libro di Antonio Billi; Il Codice dell'anonimo gaddiano*. Farnborough: Gregg.

Biow, Douglas. (2002). *Doctors, Ambassadors, Secretaries: Humanism and Professions in Renaissance Italy*. Chicago, IL: University of Chicago Press.

(2006). *The Culture of Cleanliness in Renaissance Italy*. Ithaca, NY: Cornell University Press.

(2010). *In Your Face: Professional Improprieties and the Art of Being Conspicuous in Sixteenth-Century Italy*. Stanford, CA: Stanford University Press.

(2015). *The Importance of Being an Individual in Renaissance Italy: Men, Their Professions, and Their Beards*. Philadelphia, PA: University of Pennsylvania Press.

Biringuccio, Vannoccio. (1540). *De la pirotechnia. Libri. x. dove ampiamente si tratta non solo di ogni sorte e diversita di miniere, ma anchora quanto si ricerca intorno a la prattica di quelle cose di quel che si appartiene a l'arte de la fusione over gitto de metalli come d'ogni altra cosa simile a questa*. Venice: Rossinello.

(1959). *The Pirotechnia*. Trans. Cyril Stanley Smith and Martha Teach Gnudi. New York, NY: Basic Books.

Black, Robert. (1991). "Italian Renaissance Education: Changing Perspectives and Continuing Controversies." *Journal of the History of Ideas* 52: 315–34.

(2001). *Humanism and Education in Medieval and Renaissance Italy: Tradition and Innovation in Latin Schools*. Cambridge: Cambridge University Press.

Blum, Gerd. (2013). "Vasari on the Jews: Christian Canon, Conversion, and the *Moses* of Michelangelo." *Art Bulletin* 95: 557–77.

Boase, Thomas S. R. (1979). *Giorgio Vasari: The Man and the Book*. Princeton, NJ: Princeton University Press.

Boccaccio, Giovanni. (1987). *Decameron*. Ed. Vittore Branca. Turin: Einaudi.

Bolland, Andrea. (1996). "Art and Humanism in Early Renaissance Padua: Cennini, Vergerio and Petrarch on Imitation." *Renaissance Quarterly* 49: 469–87.

(2006). "From the Workshop to the Academy: The Emergence of the Artist in Renaissance Florence." In *Renaissance Florence: A Social History*, ed. Roger J. Crum and John T. Paoletti, 454–78. Cambridge: Cambridge University Press.

Bongi, Salvatore. (1890–5). *Annali di Gabriel Giolito de' Ferrari da Trino Monferrato, stampatore in Venezia*. 2 vols. Rome: Presso i Principali Librai.

Bottari, Giovanni Gaetano, and Stefano Ticozzi, eds. (1822–5). *Raccolta di lettere sulla pittura, scultura ed architettura*. Milan: G. Silvestri.

Bradbury, Jonathan David. (2009). "Anton Francesco Doni and His *Librarie*: Bibliographical Friend or Fiend?" *Forum for Modern Language Studies* 45: 90–107.

Bragantini, Renzo. (1996). "Poligrafi e umanisti volgari." In *Storia della letteratura italiana*, ed. Enrico Malato, Vol. 4, *Il primo Cinquecento*, 681–754. Rome: Salerno Editrice.

Brann, Noel L. (2002). *The Debate over the Origin of Genius during the Italian Renaissance: The Theories of Supernatural Frenzy and Natural Melancholy in Accord and in Conflict on the Threshold of the Scientific*. Leiden: Brill.

Britton, Piers. (2003). "'Mio malinchonico, o vero … mio pazzo': Michelangelo, Vasari, and the Problem of Artists' Melancholy in Sixteenth-Century Italy." *Sixteenth Century Journal* 34: 653–75.

(2008). "Raphael and the Bad Humours of Painters in Vasari's *Lives of the Artists*." *Renaissance Studies* 22: 174–96.

Brizio, Anna Maria. (1952). "La prima e la seconda edizione delle *Vite*." In *Atti del Convegno internazionale per il IV centenario della prima edizione delle "Vite" del Vasari: Studi Vasariani*, 83–90. Florence: Sansoni.

Brown, David Alan. (1986). "Leonardo and Raphael's *Transfiguration*." In *Raffaello a Roma*, ed. Christoph Luitpold Frommel and Matthias Winner, 237–43. Rome: Edizioni dell'Elefante.

(1992). "Raphael, Leonardo, and Perugino: Fame and Fortune in Florence." In *Leonardo, Michelangelo, and Raphael in Renaissance Florence from 1500 to 1508*, ed. Serafina Hager, 29–53. Washington, D.C.: Georgetown University Press.

Bryce, Judith. (1983). *Cosimo Bartoli (1503–1572): The Career of a Florentine Polymath*. Geneva: Droz.

Bullough, Vern L. (1966). *The Development of Medicine as a Profession: The Contribution of the Medieval University to Modern Medicine*. New York, NY and Basel: Karger.

Buonarroti, Michelangelo. (1991). *The Poetry of Michelangelo: An Annotated Translation*. Trans. and ed. James M. Saslow. New Haven, CT: Yale University Press.

Bourdieu, Pierre. (1984). *Distinction: A Social Critique of the Judgment of Taste*. Trans. Richard Nice. Cambridge, MA: Harvard University Press.

Burioni, Matteo. (2010). "Vasari's *Rinascita*: History, Anthropology or Art Criticism?" In *Renaissance? Perceptions of Continuity and Discontinuity in Europe, c. 1300–c. 1550*, ed. A. Lee, P. Péporté, and H. Schnitker, 115–28. Leiden: Brill.

Bushnell, Rebecca. (1996). *A Culture of Teaching: Early Modern Humanism in Theory and Practice*. Ithaca, NY: Cornell University Press.

Cadogan, Jeanne K. (1993). "Michelangelo in the Workshop of Domenico Ghirlandaio." *Burlington Magazine* 135: 30–1.

(2000). *Domenico Ghirlandaio: Artist and Artisan*. New Haven, CT: Yale University Press.

Calcaterra, Carlo. (1942). "L'incoronazione." In *Nella selva del Petrarca*, 109–18. Bologna: Cappelli.

Calvesi, Maurizio. (1984). "Raffaello: *La Trasfigurazione*." In *Oltre Raffaello*, ed. Luciano Cassanelli and Sergio Rossi, 33–41. Rome: Multigrafica.

Calvino, Italo. (1988). *Six Memos for the Next Millennium*. Cambridge, MA: Harvard University Press.

Campbell, Stephen J. (2004). "Introduction." In *Artists at Court: Image-Making and Identity, 1300–1500*, ed. S. Campbell, 9–18. Boston, MA: Isabella Stewart Gardner Museum.

(2008). "Vasari's Renaissance and Its Renaissance Alternatives." In *The Art Seminar: Renaissance Theory*, ed. James Elkins and Robert Williams, 47–68. New York, NY: Routledge.

(2014). "Artistic Geographies." In *The Cambridge Companion to the Italian Renaissance*, ed. Michael Wyatt, 17–39. Cambridge: Cambridge University Press.

Campbell, Stephen J., and Michael W. Cole. (2011). *Italian Renaissance Art*. New York, NY: Thames & Hudson Inc.

Caro, Annibale. (1957–61). *Lettere familiari*. 3 vols. Ed. Aulo Greco. Florence: Le Monnier.

Carrara, Eliana. (2011). "Fonti vasariane tra la Torrentiniana e la Giuntina." *Atti e Memorie della Accademia Petrarca di Lettere, Arti e Scienze* 72–3: 135–61.

(2015). "Reconsidering the Authorship of the *Lives*: Some Observations and Methodological Questions on Vasari as a Writer." *Studi di Memofonte* 15: 53–90.

Cast, David. (2009). *The Delight of Art: Giorgio Vasari and the Traditions of Humanist Discourse*. University Park, PA: Penn State University Press.

ed. and intro. (2014). *The Ashgate Research Companion to Giorgio Vasari*. Farnham, Surrey: Ashgate.

Castiglione, Baldassar. (1769). *Lettere del Conte Baldessar Castiglione*. Ed. P. Serassi. Padua: Comino.

(1929). *Il cortegiano*. Ed. Vittorio Cian. 3rd ed. Florence: Sansoni.
(1959). *The Book of the Courtier*. Trans. Charles S. Singleton. Garden City, NY: Doubleday.
Cellini, Benvenuto. (1568). *Due trattati uno intorno alle otto principali arti dell'oreficeria. L'altro in materia dell'arte della scultura; dove si veggono infiniti segreti nel lavorar le figure di marmo, e nel gettarle di bronzo*. Florence: Per Valente Panizzij, & Marco Peri.
(1960). *Opere di Baldassare Castiglione, Giovanni della Casa, Benvenuto Cellini*. Ed. Carlo Cordié. Milan: Ricciardi.
Cennini, Cennino. (1933). *The Craftsman's Handbook: The Italian "Il libro dell'arte."* Trans. Daniel V. Thompson, Jr. New York, NY: Dover.
(1971). *Il libro dell'arte*. Ed. Franco Brunello. Intro. Licisco Magagnato. Vicenza: Neri Pozza.
Cerasuolo, Angela. (2014). *Diligenza e prestezza: La tecnica nella pittura e nella letteratura artistica del Cinquecento*. Florence: Edifir.
Chapman, Stanley. (1975). "Towards a Theory of Narrative." *New Literary History* 6: 295–318.
Chastel, André. (1952). "Vasari et la légende médicéenne: L'École du Jardin de San Marc'." In *Atti del convegno internazionale del IV centenario della prima edizione delle "Vite" del Vasari: Studi Vasariani*, 159–67. Florence: Sansoni.
(1961). *Art et humanisme à Florence au temps de Laurent le Magnifique: Études sur la Renaissance et l'humanisme platonicien*, 476–80. Paris: Presses Universitaires de France.
Cheney, Liana de Girolami. (2006). *The Homes of Giorgio Vasari*. New York, NY: Peter Lang.
(2014). "Giorgio Vasari: Artist, Designer, Collector." In *The Ashgate Research Companion to Giorgio Vasari*, ed. Cast, 41–76. Farnham, Surrey: Ashgate.
Cinzio, Giambattista Giraldi. (1968). *Giraldi Cinthio on Romances: Being a Translation of the "Discorso intorno al comporre dei romanzi."* Trans. Henry L. Snuggs. Lexington, KY: University of Kentucky Press.
Cipolla, Carlo. (1973). "The Professions: The Long View." *Journal of European Economic History* 2: 37–51.
(1976). *Public Health and the Medical Profession in the Renaissance*. Cambridge: Cambridge University Press.
Clark, Kenneth. (1976). *Landscape into Art*. New York, NY: Harper & Row.
Clements, Robert J. (1954). "Michelangelo on Effort and Rapidity in Art." *Journal of the Warburg and Courtauld Institutes* 17: 301–10.
Clifton, James. (1996). "Vasari on Competition." *Sixteenth Century Journal* 27: 23–41.
Cochrane, Eric. (1981). *Historians and Historiography in the Italian Renaissance*. Chicago, IL: Chicago University Press.
Cohen, Simona. (2014). *Transformations of Time and Temporality in Medieval and Renaissance Art*. Boston, MA: Brill.
Comanducci, Rita. (1999). "'Buono artista della sua arte': Il concetto di 'artista' e la pratica di lavoro nella bottega quattrocentesca." In *Arti Fiorentine: La grande storia dell'artigianato*. Vol. 2, *Il Quattrocento*, ed. F. Franceschi and G. Fossi, 149–55. Florence: Giunti.
(2000). "Fattori e garzoni al lavoro nelle botteghe d'arte." In *Arti fiorentine: La grande storia dell'artigianato*. Vol. 3, *Il Cinquecento*, ed. F. Franceschi and G. Fossi, 41–55. Florence: Giunti.

(2014). "Vasari's Painters and the Lute." In *Renaissance Then and Now: Danza, musica e teatro per un nuovo Rinascimento, Atti del convegno internazionale di studi ISI Florence, Palazzo Rucellai, 7–9 maggio 2013*, ed. Stefano U. Baldassarri, 65–80. Pisa: Edizioni ETS.

Condivi, Ascanio. (1976). *The Life of Michelangelo*. Ed. Hellmut Wohl. Trans. Alice Sedgwick Wohl. Baton Rouge, LA: Louisiana State University Press.

(1998). *Vita di Michelagnolo Buonarroti*. Ed. Giovanni Nencioni, with essays by Michael Hirst and Caroline Elam. Florence: Studio per Edizioni Scelte.

Cox, Virginia. (1992). *The Renaissance Dialogue: Literary Dialogue in Its Social and Political Contexts, Castiglione to Galileo*. Cambridge: Cambridge University Press.

Cox-Rearick, Janet. (1984). *Dynasty and Destiny in Medici Art: Pontormo, Leo X, and the Two Cosimos*. Princeton, NJ: Princeton University Press.

Cranston, Jodi. (2003). "Tropes of Revelation in Raphael's *Transfiguration*." *Renaissance Quarterly* 56: 1–25.

Curtius, Ernst Robert. (1990). *European Literature and the Latin Middle Ages*. Trans. Willard R. Trask. Princeton, NJ: Princeton University Press.

Dante Alighieri. (1970–5). *The Divine Comedy*. Ed. and Trans. Charles S. Singleton. 6 vols. Princeton, NJ: Princeton University Press.

Davis, Natalie Zemon. (2000). *The Gift in Sixteenth-Century France*. Madison, WI: University of Wisconsin Press.

De Gaetano, Armand L. (1967). "G. B. Gelli and the *Questione della Lingua*." *Italica* 44: 263–81.

(1976). *Giambattista Gelli and the Florentine Academy: The Rebellion against Latin*. Florence: Olschki.

d'Elia, Una Roman. (2004). "Tintoretto, Aretino, and the Speed of Creation." *Word & Image* 20: 206–18.

Demos, Melissa N. (2015). "Time and the Experience of Narrative in Italian Renaissance Art." PhD dissertation, University of Texas at Austin.

Dempsey, Charles. (1980). "Some Observations on the Education of Artists in Florence and Bologna during the Later Sixteenth Century." *Art Bulletin* 62: 552–69.

(1986). "The Carracci Postille to Vasari's *Lives*." *Art Bulletin* 68: 72–6.

Dolce, Lodovico. *See* Roskill.

Doni, Antonfranceso. (1552). *I mondi del Doni libro primo*. Venice: Marcolini

(1972). *La libraria*. Edited with an Introduction by Vanni Bramanti. Milan: Longanesi & C.

Eamon, William. (2010). *The Professor of Secrets: Mystery, Medicine, and Alchemy in Renaissance Italy*. Washington, D.C.: National Geographic Society.

Edgerton, Samuel Y. (1975). *The Renaissance Rediscovery of Linear Perspective*. New York, NY: Basic Books.

(2009). *The Mirror, the Window, and the Telescope: How Renaissance Linear Perspective Changed Our Vision of the Universe*. Ithaca, NY: Cornell University Press.

Ekirch, A. Roger. (2001). "Sleep We Have Lost: Pre-Industrial Slumber in the British Isles." *American Historical Review* 106: 343–86.

(2005). *At Day's Close: Night in Times Past*. New York, NY: W. W. Norton.

Elam, Caroline. (1992). "Lorenzo de' Medici's Sculpture Garden." *Mitteilungen des Kunsthistorischen Institutes in Florenz* 36: 41–83.

(1998). "'Ché ultima mano!': Tiberio Calcagni's Marginal Annotations to Condivi's *Life of Michelangelo*." *Renaissance Quarterly* 51: 475–97.

Emison, Patricia A. (2004). *Creating the "Divine" Artist from Dante to Michelangelo.* Leiden: Brill.

Fanti, Mario. (1979). "Le postille carraccesche alle 'Vite' del Vasari: Il testo originale; spigolature d'archivio per la storia dell'arte a Bologna (II)." *Il Carrobbio* 5:148–64.

Farago, Claire J. (1992). *Leonardo da Vinci's Paragone: A Critical Interpretation with a New Edition of the Text in Codex.* Leiden: Brill.

Fedele, Clemente. (2012). "Quale posta nel XVI secolo? What Postal Service Existed in the Sixteenth Century?" *I Tasso e le poste d'Europa. Atti del 1° Convegno internazionale. Cornello dei Tasso*, ed. Tarcisio Bottani, 65–80. Bergamo: Museo dei Tasso e della Storia Postale.

Fenlon, Iain. (2007). *The Ceremonial City: History, Memory and Myth in Renaissance Venice.* New Haven, CT: Yale University Press.

Ferraresi, Alessandra, and Monica Visioli, eds. (2012). *Formare alle professioni: Architetti, ingegneri, artisti (secoli XV–XIX).* Milan: FrancoAngeli.

Ferrari, Monica, and Filippo Ledda, eds. (2011). *Formare alle professioni: La cultura militare tra passato e presente.* Milan: FrancoAngeli.

Ferrari, Monica, and Paolo Mazzarello, eds. (2010). *Formare alle professioni: Figure di sanità.* Milan: FrancoAngeli.

Filippo Bareggi, Claudia di. (1988). *Il mestiere di scrivere: Lavoro intellettuale e mercato librario a Venezia nel Cinquecento.* Rome: Bulzoni.

Findlen, Paula. (1994). *Possessing Nature: Museums, Collecting, and Scientific Culture in Early Modern Italy.* Berkeley, CA: University of California Press.

(1998). "Possessing the Past: The Material World of the Italian Renaissance." *American Historical Review* 103: 83–114.

Fiorato, Adelin Charles, ed. (1989). *Culture et professions en Italie (fin XVe–début XVIIe siècles).* Paris: Publications de la Sorbonne.

Fragnito, Gigliola. (1998). "Buone maniere e professionalità nelle Corti Romane del Cinque e Seicento." In *Educare il corpo, educare la parola nella trattatisica del Rinascimento*, ed. Giorgio Patrizi and Amedeo Quondam, 77–109. Rome: Bulzoni.

Franceschi, Franco. (1999). "La bottega come spazio di sociabilità." In *Arti fiorentine: La grande storia dell'artigianato.* Vol. 2, *Il Quattrocento*, ed. F. Franceschi and G. Fossi, 65–83. Florence: Giunti.

Frangenberg, Thomas. (2002). "Bartoli, Giambullari, and the Prefaces to Vasari's *Lives* (1550)." *Journal of the Warburg and Courtauld Institutes* 65: 244–58.

Freedberg, Sydney J. (1993). *Painting in Italy: 1500–1600.* 3rd ed. New Haven, CT: Yale University Press.

Freiberg, Jack. (2005). "Vasari's Bramante and the Renaissance of Architecture in Rome." In *Reading Vasari*, ed. Barriault et al., 132–46. London: Philip Wilson in association with the Georgia Museum of Art.

Frey, Karl, ed. (1923). *Il carteggio di Giorgio Vasari.* Munich: G. Müller. Accessible online at: www.memofonte.it/autori/carteggio-vasariano-1532–1574.html.

(1930). *Der literarische Nachlass Giorgio Vasaris.* 3 vols. Munich: G. Müller. Accessible online at: www.memofonte.it/autori/carteggio-vasariano-1532–1574.html.

Gahtan, Maia Wellington. (2011). "Epitaphs in Giorgio Vasari's *Lives.*" *Journal of Art Historiography* 5: 1–24.

ed. (2014). *Giorgio Vasari and the Birth of the Museum.* Burlington, VT: Ashgate.

(2014). "Giorgio Vasari, Collector of Epitaphs." In *Giorgio Vasari and the Birth of the Museum*, 52–63. Burlington, VT: Ashgate.

Gardner, Victoria C. (1997). "*Homines non nascuntur, sed figuntur:* Benvenuto Cellini's *Vita* and Self-Presentation of the Renaissance Artist." *Sixteenth Century Journal* 28: 447–65.

Garin, Eugenio. (1965). *Italian Humanism: Philosophy and Civic Life in the Renaissance.* Trans. Peter Munz. New York, NY: Harper & Row.

(1974). "Giorgio Vasari e il tema della rinascita." In *Il Vasari storiografo e artista: Atti del Congresso internazionale nel IV centenario della morte*, 259–66. Florence: Istituto Nazionale di Studi sul Rinascimento.

Garzoni, Tomaso. (1996). *La piazza universale di tutte le professioni del mondo*. Ed. Paolo Cherchi and Beatrice Collina. 2 vols. Turin: Einaudi.

Gelli, Giovan Battista. (1967). *Dialoghi*. Ed. Roberto Tissoni. Bari: Laterza.

Gensini, Stefano. (1980). "'Poeta et historicus': L'episodio della laurea nella carriera e nella prospettiva culturale di Francesco Petrarca." *La cultura* 18: 166–94.

Ghiberti, Lorenzo. (1947). *I commentarii*. Ed. Ottavio Morisani. Naples: Ricciardi.

Giambullari, Pierfrancesco. (1549). *Origine della lingua fiorentina, altrimenti Il Gello*. Florence: Lorenzo Torrentino.

(1551). *Della lingua che si parla e scrive in Firenze. Et uno dialogo di Giovan Batista Gelli sopra la difficultà dello ordinare detta lingua*. Florence: Lorenzo Torrentino.

Gilbert, Felix. (1965). *Machiavelli and Guicciardini: Politics and History in Sixteenth-Century Florence*. Princeton, NJ: Princeton University Press.

Gilmore, Myron P. (1979). "*Studia Humanitatis* and the Professions in Fifteenth-Century Florence." In *Florence and Venice: Comparisons and Relations*. Vol. I, ed. S. Bertelli, N. Rubinstein, and C. H. Smyth, 27–40. Florence: La Nuova Italia.

Ginzburg, Carlo. (1980). *The Cheese and the Worms: The Cosmos of a Sixteenth-Century Miller*. Baltimore, MD: Johns Hopkins University Press.

Ginzburg, Silvia. (2007). "Filologia e storia dell'arte: Il ruolo di Vincenzio Borghini nella genesi della Torrentiniana." In *Testi, immagini e filologia nel XVI secolo*, ed. Eliana Carrara and Silvia Ginzburg, 147–203. Pisa: Edizioni della Normale.

Giordani, Simone. (2011). "Pittore della cerchia vasariana: Ritratto di Giorgio Vasari, post 1571." In *Vasari, gli Uffizi e il Duca*, ed. Claudia Conforti, exhibition catalog, Uffizi, 104. Florence: Giunti.

Giovio, Paolo. (1971). "Raphaelis Urbinatis vita." In *Scritti d'arte del Cinquecento*. 3 vols, 1.13–18. Milan: Ricciardi.

(1999). *Scritti d'arte: Lessico ed ecfrasi*, ed. Sonia Maffei. Pisa: Scuola Normale Superiore.

Godi, Carlo. (1970). "La 'Collatio laureationis' del Petrarca." *Italia medioevale e umanistica* 13: 13–27.

Goffen, Rona. (2002). *Renaissance Rivals: Michelangelo, Leonardo, Raphael, Titian*. New Haven, CT: Yale University Press.

Goldberg, Edward L. (1988). *After Vasari: History, Art, and Patronage in Late Medici Florence*. Princeton, NJ: Princeton University Press.

Goldstein, Carl. (1975). "Vasari and the Florentine Accademia del Disegno." *Zeitschrift für Kunstgeschichte* 38: 145–52.

(1991). "Rhetoric and Art History in the Italian Renaissance and Baroque." *Art Bulletin* 73: 641–52.

(1996). *Teaching Art: Academies and Schools from Vasari to Albers*. Cambridge: Cambridge University Press.

Goldthwaite, Richard A. (1993). *Wealth and the Demand for Art in Italy, 1300–1600*. Baltimore, MD: Johns Hopkins University Press.

Gombrich, Ernst H. (1960). "Vasari's Lives and Cicero's *Brutus*." *Journal of the Warburg and Courtauld Institutes* 23: 309–11.

(1966a). "Leonardo's Method for Working out Compositions." In *Norm and Form: Studies in the Art of the Renaissance*, 58–63. London: Phaidon.

(1966b). "The Renaissance Conception of Artistic Progress and Its Consequences." In *Norm and Form: Studies in the Art of the Renaissance*, 1–10. London: Phaidon.

Goodchild, Karen Hope. (2014). "Bizarre Painters and Bohemian Poets: Poetic Imitation and Artistic Rivalry in Vasari's Biography of Piero di Cosimo." In *The Ashgate Research Companion to Giorgio Vasari*, ed. Cast, 129–44. Farnham, Surrey: Ashgate.

Gould, Cecil. (1967). *The Raising of Lazarus by Sebastiano del Piombo*. London: National Gallery.

Grafton, Anthony. (1999). "Historia and Istoria: Alberti's Terminology in Context." *I Tatti Studies in the Italian Renaissance* 8: 37–68.

(2006). "The History of Ideas: Precept and Practice, 1950–2000 and Beyond." *Journal of the History of Ideas* 67: 1–32.

Grafton, Anthony, and Lisa Jardine. (1986). *From Humanism to the Humanities: Education and the Liberal Arts in Fifteenth- and Sixteenth-Century Europe*. Cambridge, MA: Cambridge University Press.

Grassi, Luigi. (1957). "I concetti di schizzo, abbozzo, macchia, 'non finite' e la costruzione dell'opera d'arte." In *Studi in onore di Pietro Silva*, 97–106. Florence: Le Monnier.

Greene, Roland. (2013). *Five Words: Critical Semantics in the Age of Shakespeare and Cervantes*. Chicago, IL: University of Chicago Press.

Greenstein, Jack M. (1992). *Mantegna and Painting as Historical Narrative*. Chicago, IL: University of Chicago Press.

(2012). "Mantegna, Leonardo and the Times of Painting." *Word & Image* 15: 217–42.

Gregory, Sharon. (2009). "The Unsympathetic Exemplar in Vasari's Life of Pontormo." *Renaissance Studies* 23: 1–32.

(2012). *Vasari and the Renaissance Print*. Burlington, VT: Ashgate.

Grendler, Paul F. (1969). *Critics of the Italian World, 1530–1560: Anton Francesco Doni, Nicolò Franco, and Ortensio Lando*. Madison, WI: University of Wisconsin Press.

(1977). *The Roman Inquisition and the Venetian Press, 1540–1605*. Princeton, NJ: Princeton University Press.

(1989). *Schooling in Renaissance Italy: Literacy and Learning, 1300–1600*. Baltimore, MD: Johns Hopkins University Press.

Hall, Marcia B. (1987). "From Modeling Techniques to Color Modes." In *Color and Technique in Renaissance Paintings, Italy and the North*, ed. Marcia Hall, 1–29. Locust Valley, NY: Augustin.

(1992). *Color and Meaning: Practice and Theory in Renaissance Painting*. Cambridge: Cambridge University Press.

(1997). "Introduction." In *Raphael's "School of Athens,"* ed. Marcia B. Hall, 1–47. Cambridge: Cambridge University Press.

(1999). *After Raphael: Painting in Central Italy in the Sixteenth Century*. Cambridge: Cambridge University Press.

ed. (2005). *The Cambridge Companion to Raphael*. Cambridge: Cambridge University Press.

Hampton, Timothy. (1990). *Writing from History: The Rhetoric of Exemplarity in Renaissance Literature*. Ithaca, NY: Cornell University Press.

(2009). *Fictions of Embassy: Literature and Diplomacy in Early Modern Europe*. Ithaca, NY: Cornell University Press.

Härb, Florian. (2015). *The Drawings of Giorgio Vasari (1511–1574)*. Rome: Ugo Bozzi, Edizioni per la Storia dell'Arte.

Hibbard, Howard. (1998). *Michelangelo*, 2nd ed. Boulder, CO: Westview Press.

Hills, Paul. (1987). *The Light of Early Italian Painting*. New Haven, CT: Yale University Press.

Hirst, Michael. (1996). "Michelangelo and His First Biographers." *Proceedings of the British Academy* 94: 63–84.

(1981). *Sebastiano del Piombo*. Oxford: Clarendon Press.

Hochman, Michel. (1998). "Les annotations marginales de Federico Zuccaro à un exemplaire des *Vies* de Vasari: La réaction anti-vasarienne à la fin du XVI siècle." *Revue de l'Art* 80: 64–71.

Holanda, Francisco de. (1918). *Da pintura antigua*. Porto: Da Renascença Portuguesa.

(2013). *On Antique Painting*. Translated by Alice Sedgwick Wohl, with introductory essays by Joaquim Oliveira Caetano and Charles Hope, and notes by Hellmut Wohl. University Park, PA: Penn State University Press.

Hollander, Robert. (1969). *Allegory in Dante's "Commedia."* Princeton, NJ: Princeton University Press.

Hope, Charles. (1995). "Can You Trust Vasari?" *New York Review of Books* 5 (Oct.): 10–13.

(2005). "Le 'Vite' Vasariane: Un esempio di autore multiplo." In *L'autore multiplo*, ed. Anna Santoni, 59–74. Pisa: Scuola Normale Superiore.

(2008). "The Audience for Publications of the Visual Arts in Renaissance Italy." In *Officine del nuovo; sodalizi fra letterati, artisti ed editori nella cultura Italiana fra Riforma e Controriforma*, ed. Harald Hendrix and Paolo Procaccioli, 19–29. Rome: Vecchiarelli.

(2014). "Vasari's *Vite* as a Collaborative Project." In *The Ashgate Research Companion to Giorgio Vasari*, ed. Cast, 11–22. Farnham, Surrey: Ashgate.

Howard, Deborah. (1992). "Elsheimer's Flight into Egypt and the Night Sky in the Renaissance." *Zeitschrift für Kunstgeschichte* 55: 212–24.

Hughes, Anthony. (1986a). "'An Academy for Doing' I: The Accademia del Disegno, the Guilds and the Principate in Sixteenth-Century Florence." *Oxford Art Journal* 9: 3–10.

(1986b). "'An Academy for Doing' II: Academies, Status and Power in Early Modern Europe." *Oxford Art Journal* 9: 50–62.

Jack, Mary Ann. (1976). "The Accademia del Disegno in Late Renaissance Florence." *Sixteenth Century Journal* 7: 3–20.

Jacobs, Fredrika H. (2005). "Vasari's Bronzino: The Paradigmatic Academician." In *Reading Vasari*, ed. Barriault et al., 101–15. London: Philip Wilson in association with the Georgia Museum of Art.

James, Sara Nair. (2005). "Vasari on Signorelli: The Origins of the 'Grand Manner of Painting.'" In *Reading Vasari*, ed. Barriault et al., 75–88. London: Philip Wilson in association with the Georgia Museum of Art.

Jamison, Kay Redfield. (1996). *Touched with Fire: Manic-Depressive Illness and the Artistic Temperament*. New York, NY: Free Press.

Jay, Martin. (1998). *Cultural Semantics: Keywords of Our Time*. Amherst, MA: University of Massachusetts Press.

Joost-Gaugier, Christiane L. (2002). *Raphael's "Stanza della Segnatura": Meaning and Invention*. Cambridge: Cambridge University Press.

Kallab, Wolfgang. (1908). *Vasaristudien*. Vienna: K. Graeser and Kie.

Kallendorf, Craig K., ed. and trans. (2002). *Humanist Educational Treatises*. Harvard, MA: Harvard University Press.

Kelley, Donald R. (2002). *The Descent of Ideas: The History of Intellectual History*. Burlington, VT: Ashgate.

Kemp, Martin. (1976). "'Ogni dipintore dipinge se': A Neoplatonic Echo in Leonardo's Art Theory?" In *Cultural Aspects of the Italian Renaissance: Essays in Honour of Paul Oskar Kristeller*, ed. Cecil H. Clough, 311–23. Manchester: Manchester University Press.

(1977). "From 'Mimesis' to 'Fantasia': The Quattrocento Vocabulary of Creation, Inspiration, and Genius in the Visual Arts." *Viator* 8: 347–98.

(1981). *Leonardo da Vinci, the Marvelous Works of Nature and Man*. Cambridge, MA: Harvard University Press.

(1987). "'Equal Excellences': Lomazzo and the Explanation of the Individual Style in the Visual Arts." *Renaissance Studies* 1: 1–26.

(1989). "The 'Super-Artist' as Genius: The Sixteenth-Century View." In *Genius: The History of an Idea*, ed. Penelope Murray, 32–53. Oxford: Blackwell.

(1990). *The Science of Art: Optical Themes in Western Art from Brunelleschi to Seurat*. New Haven, CT: Yale University Press.

(2006). *Leonardo da Vinci: Experience, Experiment and Design*. Princeton, NJ: Princeton University Press.

Kempers, Bram. (1987). *Painting, Power, and Patronage: The Rise of the Professional Artist in Renaissance Italy*. Trans. Beverley Jackson. London: Penguin.

Kennedy, William J. (2016). *Petrarchism at Work: Contextual Economies in the Age of Shakespeare*. Ithaca, NY: Cornell University Press.

Kirkham, Victoria. (1983–4). "Painters at Play on the Judgment Day (Dec. viii, 9)." *Studi sul Boccaccio* 14: 256–77.

Kiséry, András. (2016). *Hamlet's Moment: Drama and Political Knowledge in Early Modern England*. Oxford: Oxford University Press.

Kleinbub, Christian R. (2011). *Vision and the Visionary in Raphael*. University Park, PA: Penn State University Press.

Klibansky, Raymond, Erwin Panofsky, and Fritz Saxl. (1964). *Saturn and Melancholy: Studies in the History of Natural Philosophy, Religion, and Art*. New York, NY: Basic Books.

Koslofsky, Craig. (2011). *Evening's Empire: A History of Night in Early Modern Europe*. Cambridge: Cambridge University Press.

Ladis, Andrew. (2008). *Victims and Villains in Vasari's Lives*. Chapel Hill, NC: University of North Carolina Press.

Land, Norman E. (2005). "Vasari's Buffalmacco and the Transubstantiation of Paint." *Renaissance Quarterly* 58: 881–95.

Lanzi, Luigi. (1809). *Storia pittorica della Italia dal risorgimento delle belle arti fin presso al fine del XVIII secolo*. Vol. 1. Pisa: N. Capurro.

Larson, Magali Sarfatti. (1977). *The Rise of Professionalism: A Sociological Analysis*. Berkeley, CA: University of California Press.

Lavin, Marilyn Aronberg. (1990). *The Place of Narrative: Mural Decoration in Italian Churches, 431–1600*. Chicago, IL: University of Chicago Press.

Le Goff, Jacques. (1980). *Time, Work, and Culture in the Middle Ages*. Trans. Arthur Goldhammer. Chicago, IL: University of Chicago Press.

Le Mollé, Roland. (1985). "Le invention sémantique chez Vasari." *Revue des études italiennes* 31: 36–57.

(1988). *Georges Vasari et le vocabulaire de la critique d'art dans les "Vite."* Grenoble: Ellug.

Lee, Rensselaer W. (1940). "*Ut Pictura Poesis*: The Humanist Theory of Painting." *Art Bulletin* 22: 197–269.

Lenzoni, Carlo. (1556). *In difesa della lingua fiorentina, et di Dante. Con le regole da far bella et numerosa la prosa*. Florence: Lorenzo Torrentino.

Leonardo da Vinci. (1956). *Treatise on Painting [Codex Urbinas Latinus 1270]*. 2 vols. (vol. 1 Translation, vol. 2 Facsimile). Translated and annotated by A. Philip McMahon. Princeton, NJ: Princeton University Press.

(1970). *The Notebooks of Leonardo da Vinci, Compiled and Edited from the Original Manuscripts*. 2 vols. Ed. Jean Paul Richter. New York, NY: Dover Publications.

(1996). *Scritti scelti*. Ed. Anna Maria Brizio. Turin: Unione Tipografico Editrice Torinese.

Lewis, C. S. (1960). *Studies in Words*. 2nd ed. Cambridge: Cambridge University Press.

Liebert, Robert S. (1984). "Raphael, Michelangelo, Sebastiano: High Renaissance Rivalry." *Source: Notes in the History of Art* 3: 60–8.

Lincoln, Evelyn. (2000). *The Invention of the Renaissance Printmaker*. New Haven, CT: Yale University Press.

Lomazzo, Giovanni Paolo. (1974). *Scritti sulle arti*. 2 vols. Ed. Roberto Paolo Ciardi. Florence: Marchi & Bertolli.

Long, Pamela O. (2001). *Openness, Secrecy, Authorship: Technical Arts and the Culture of Knowledge from Antiquity to the Renaissance*. Baltimore, MD: Johns Hopkins University Press.

(2011). *Artisan/Practitioners and the Rise of the New Sciences, 1400–1600*. Corvallis, OR: Oregon State University Press.

Longhi, Roberto. (1966). L'inizio dell'abbozzo autonomo." *Paragone* 195: 25–9.

Looney, Dennis. (2009). "The Beginnings of Humanistic Oratory: Petrarch's *Coronation Oration*." In *Petrarch: A Critical Guide to the Complete Works*, ed. Victoria Kirkham and Armando Maggi, 131–40. Chicago, IL: University of Chicago Press.

Lowry, Martin. (1979). *The World of Aldus Manutius: Business and Scholarship in Renaissance Venice*. Ithaca, NY: Cornell University Press.

Lubac, Henri de. (1998–2000). *Medieval Exegesis: The Four Senses of the Scripture*. Trans. Mark Sebanc. Grand Rapids, MI: W. B. Eerdmans; Edinburgh: T&T Clark.

Lubbock, Jules. (2006). *Storytelling in Christian Art from Giotto to Donatello*. New Haven, CT: Yale University Press.

Mac Carthy, Ita. (2009). "Grace and the Reach of Art in Castiglione and Raphael." *Word & Image* 25: 33–45.

ed. (2013a). *Renaissance Keywords*. London: Legenda.

(2013b). "Grace." In *Renaissance Keywords*, ed. Ita Mac Carthy, 63–80. London: Legenda.

(2014). "Ariosto's Grace: The View from Lodovico Dolce." *Modern Language Notes* 129: SS 45–59.

Maginnis, Hayden B. J. (1993). "Giotto's World through Vasari's Eyes." *Zeitschrift für Kunstgeschichte* 56: 385–408.

(2004). "In Search of an Artist." In *The Cambridge Companion to Giotto*, ed. Anne Derbes and Mark Sandona, 10–31. Cambridge: Cambridge University Press.

Malatesta, Maria. (1995). "Introduction: The Italian Professions from a Comparative Perspective." In *Society and the Professions in Italy, 1860–1914*, ed. M. Malatesta, trans. Adrian Belton, 1–23. Cambridge: Cambridge University Press.

ed. (1996). *I professionisti*. Annali 10 of *Storia d'Italia*. Turin: Einaudi.

Mammana, Simona. (2005). "Lenzoni, Carlo." *Dizionario biografico degli italiani* 64: 395–97.

Marrou, Henri Irénée. (1938). *Saint Augustin et la fin de la culture antique*. Paris: E. de Boccard.

(1956). *A History of Education in Antiquity*. Trans. George Lamb. New York, NY: The New American Library.

Marsh, David. (1980). *The Quattrocento Dialogue: Classical Tradition and Humanist Innovation*. Cambridge, MA: Harvard University Press.

Marsili-Libelli, Cecilia Ricottini. (1960). *Anton Francesco Doni scrittore e stampatore*. Florence: Sansoni Antiquariato.

Masi, Giorgio. (1988). "'Quelle discordanze sì perfette': Anton Francesco Doni 1551–1553." *Atti e memorie dell'Accademia toscana di scienze e lettere La Colombaria* 53: 11–112.

(2010). "Bibliografia: Anton Francesco Doni." www.nuovorinascimento.org/cinquecento/doni.pdf (accessed 2015).

McClure, George. (2004). *The Culture of Profession in Late Renaissance Italy*. Toronto: University of Toronto Press.

McHam, Sarah Blake. (2011). "Pliny's Influence on Vasari's First Edition of the *Lives*." *Artibus et Historiae* 32: 9–23.

(2013). *Pliny and the Artistic Culture of the Italian Renaissance: The Legacy of "The Natural History."* New Haven, CT: Yale University Press.

McIver, Katherine. (2005). "Vasari's Women." In *Reading Vasari*, ed. Barriault et al., 179–88. London: Philip Wilson in association with the Georgia Museum of Art.

McMahon, Darrin M. (2013). *Divine Fury: A History of Genius*. New York, NY: Basic Books.

(2014). "Return of the History of Ideas?" In *Rethinking Modern European Intellectual History*, ed. Darrin M. McMahon and Samuel Moyn, 13–31. Oxford: Oxford University Press.

McManamon, John M. (1989). *Funeral Oratory and the Ideals of Italian Humanism*. Chapel Hill, NC: University of North Carolina Press.

Mellini, G. L. (1963). "In margine alla 'Trasfigurazione' di Raffaello." *Critica d'Arte* 10: 39–55.

Merrill, Elizabeth. (2017). "The *Professione di Architetto* in Renaissance Italy." *Journal of the Society of Architectural Historians* 76: 13–35.

Milton, John. (2005). *Paradise Lost*. Oxford: Oxford University Press.

Moffitt, John. (1989). "Leonardo's 'sfumato' and Apelles's 'atramentum'." *Paragone* 40: 88–94.

Morandi, Matteo, ed. (2013). *Formare alle professioni: Commercianti e contabili dalle scuole d'abaco ad oggi*. Milan: FrancoAngeli.

Moretti, Franco. (2013). *Distant Reading*. London: Verso.

Moyer, Ann. (2006). "Distinguishing Florentines, Defining Italians: The Language Question and Cultural Identities in Sixteenth-Century Florence." In *Nation, Ethnicity, and Identity in Medieval and Renaissance Europe*, ed. Philip M. Soergel, 131–58. New York, NY: AMS Press.

Murphy, James Jerome. (1974). *Rhetoric in the Middle Ages: A History of Rhetorical Theory from St. Augustine to the Renaissance*. Berkeley, CA: University of California Press.

Murray, Penelope. (1989). "Introduction" and "Poetic Genius and Its Classical Origins." In *Genius: The History of an Idea*, ed. Penelope Murray, 1–8 and 9–31. Oxford: Blackwell.

Mutini, Claudio. (1977). "Caro, Annibale." In *Dizionario biografico degli italiani* 20: 497–508.

Nagel, Alexander. (1993). "Leonardo and sfumato." *RES: Anthropology and Aesthetics* 24: 7–20.

(2000). *Michelangelo and the Reform of Art*. Cambridge: Cambridge University Press.

Nencioni, Giovanni. (1952). "Sullo stile del Vasari scrittore." In *Atti del Convegno internazionale per il IV centenario della prima edizione delle "Vite" del Vasari: Studi Vasariani*, 111–15. Florence: Sansoni.

(1965). "Il Vasari scrittore manierista?" *Atti e memorie dell'Accademia Petrarca di lettere, arti e scienze*, n.s. 37: 260–83.

Nichols, Tom. (1996). "Tintoretto, *Prestezza* and the *Poligrafi*: A Study in the Literary and Visual Culture of Cinquecento Venice." *Renaissance Studies* 10: 72–100.

(1999). *Tintoretto: Tradition and Identity*. London: Reaktion Books.

Nigro, Salvatore. (1983). "*Scriptor necans*." In *Introduction to Torquato Accetto, Della dissimulazione onesta*, ed. S. Nigro, 19–26. Genoa: Costa & Nolan.

(1984). "Le livre masqué d'un secrétaire du xviie siècle." *Le Temps de la réflexion* Fall: 183–211.

(1987). "Lezione sull'ombra." In *Introduction to Torquato Accetto, Rime amorose*, v–xxi. Turin: Einaudi.

(1991). *Il segretario di lettere*. Palermo: Sellerio.

Nochlin, Linda. (1971). "Why Are There No Great Women Artists." In *Women in Sexist Society: Studies in Power and Powerlessness*, ed. Vivian Gornick and Barbara K. Moran, 480–510. New York, NY: Basic Books.

Nova, Alessandro. (2013). "'Vasari' versus Vasari: La duplice attualità delle *Vite*." *Mitteilungen Des Kunsthistorischen Institutes in Florenz* 55: 55–71.

Nuovo, Angela. (2003). *Il commercio librario nell'Italia del Rinascimento*. 3rd ed. Milan: FrancoAngeli.

Och, Marjorie. (2012). "Vittoria Colonna in Giorgio Vasari's Life of Properzia de Rossi." In *Wives, Widows, Mistresses, and Nuns in Early Modern Italy: Making the Invisible Visible through Art and Patronage*, ed. Katherine McIver, 119–37. Farnham, Surrey: Ashgate.

Oettinger, April. (2005). "Michelangelo's Snowman and the Art of Snow in Vasari's *Lives*." In *Reading Vasari*, ed. Barriault et al., 203–11. London: Philip Wilson in association with the Georgia Museum of Art.

O'Malley, John W. (1979). *Praise and Blame in Renaissance Rome: Rhetoric, Doctrine and Reform in the Sacred Orators of the Papal Court, c. 1450–1521*. Durham, NC: Duke University Press.

O'Malley, Michelle. (2013). *Painting under Pressure: Fame, Reputation and Demand in Renaissance Florence*. New Haven, CT: Yale University Press.

Ovid. (1977–84). *Metamorphoses*. Ed. Frank Justus Miller. 3rd ed., rev. G. P. Goold. Cambridge, MA: Harvard University Press.

Palli d'Addario, M. V. (1985). "Documenti vasariani nell'Archivio Guidi." In *Giorgio Vasari: Tra decorazione ambientale e storiografia artistica: Convegno di studi, Arezzo, 8–10 October, 1981*, ed. Gian Carlo Garfagnini, 363–89. Florence: Olschki.

Panofsky, Erwin. (1962). "Artist, Scientist, Genius: Notes on the 'Renaissance-*Dämmerung*'." In *The Renaissance: Six Essays*, ed. Wallace K. Ferguson, 121–82. New York, NY: Harper Torchbooks.

(1968). *Idea: A Concept in Art Theory*. Columbia, SC: University of South Carolina Press.

Paoletti, John T., and Gary M. Radke. (2012). *Art in Renaissance Italy*. 4th ed. Upper Saddle River, NJ: Pearson Prentice Hall.

Park, Katharine. (1987). "Medical Profession and Medical Practice in the Italian Renaissance." In *The Rational Arts of Living*, ed. A. C. Crombie and N. Siraisi, 137–57. Vol. 50. Northampton, MA: Smith College Studies in History.

Parker, Deborah. (2004). "Bronzino and the Diligence of Art." *Artibus et Historiae* 49: 161–74.

Partridge, Loren, and Randolph Starn. (1992). *Arts of Power: Three Halls of State in Italy, 1300–1600*. Berkeley, CA: University of California Press.

Patrizi, Giorgio. (2000). *Narrare l'immagine: La tradizione degli scrittori d'arte*. Rome: Donzelli.

Payne, Alina. (2001). "Vasari, Architecture, and the Origins of Historicizing Art." *RES: Anthropology and Aesthetics* 40: 51–76.

Petrarch, Francesco. (1975). *Opere latine*. Ed. Antonietta Bufano. Vol. 2. Turin: Unione Tipografico Editrice Torinese.

(1992). *Letters of Old Age*. Trans. Aldo S. Bernardo, Saul Levin, and Reta A. Bernardo. 2 vols. Baltimore, MD: Johns Hopkins University Press.

Pevsner, Nikolaus. (1973). *Academies of Art, Past and Present*. New York, NY: Da Capo Press.

Phillips-Court, Kristin. (2011a). "Vasari, Leonardo, and il vero ritratto del tradimento et inumanità." *Sixteenth Century Journal* 42: 709–35.

(2011b). *The Perfect Genre: Drama and Painting in Renaissance Italy*. Burlington, VT: Ashgate.

Pignatti, Franco. (2000). "Giambullari, Pierfrancesco." *Dizionario biografico degli italiani* 54: 308–12.

(2011). "Molza, Francesco Maria." *Dizionario biografico degli italiani* 75: 451–61.

Pilliod, Elizabeth. (1998). "Representation, Misrepresentation, and Non-Representation: Vasari and His Competitors." In *Vasari's Florence: Artists and Literati at the Medicean Court*, ed. Philip Jacks, 30–52. New Haven, CT: Yale University Press.

(2001). *Pontormo, Bronzino, Allori: A Genealogy of Florentine Art*. New Haven, CT: Yale University Press.

Plaisance, Michel. (2004). *L'Accademia e il suo principe: Cultura e politica a Firenze al tempo di Cosimo I e di Francesco de' Medici*. Manziana: Vecchiarelli.

Pliny, the Elder. (1984). *Natural History*. Trans. H. Rackham. Vol. 9. Cambridge, MA: Harvard University Press.

Plutarch. (1961). *Plutarch's Lives*. Trans. Bernadotte Perrin. Vol. 3. Cambridge, MA: Harvard University Press.

Pon, Lisa. (1996). "Michelangelo's *Lives*: Sixteenth-Century Books by Vasari, Condivi, and Others." *Sixteenth Century Journal* 27: 1015–37.

(2004). *Raphael, Dürer, and Marcantonio Raimondi: Copying and the Italian Renaissance Print*. New Haven, CT: Yale University Press.

Pozzi, Mario, ed. (1996). *Discussioni linguistiche del Cinquecento*. Turin: Unione Tipografico Editrice Torinese.

Pozzi, Mario, and Enrico Mattioda. (2006). *Giorgio Vasari: Storico e critico*. Florence: Olschki.

Preimesberger, Rudolf. (2011). *Paragons and Paragone: Van Eyck, Raphael, Michelangelo, Caravaggio, and Bernini*. Los Angeles, CA: Getty Research Institute.

Quinones, Ricardo J. (1972). *The Renaissance Discovery of Time*. Cambridge, MA: Harvard University Press.

Quintilian. (2001). *Institutiones oratoriae*. Trans. Donald. Russell. Cambridge, MA: Harvard University Press.

Quondam, Amedeo. (1983). "La letteratura in tipografia." In *Letteratura italiana*, ed. Alberto Asor Rosa. Vol. 2, *Produzione e consumo*, 555–686. Turin: Einaudi.

(2007). *La conversazione: Un modello italiano*. Rome: Donzelli.

Ragghianti Collobi, Licia. (1974). *Il Libro de' disegni del Vasari*. 2 vols. Florence: Vallecchi.

Rebhorn, Wayne A. (1976). "Thomas More's Enclosed Garden: Utopia and the Humanist Tradition." *English Literary Renaissance* 6: 140–55.

Reilly, Patricia L. (2014). "Artists' Workshops." In *The Cambridge Companion to the Italian Renaissance*, ed. Michael Wyatt, 84–99. Cambridge: Cambridge University Press.

Richardson, Brian. (1998). "The Debates on Printing in Renaissance Italy." *La bibliofilìa* 100: 135–55.

(1999). *Printing, Writers, and Readers in Renaissance Italy*. Cambridge: Cambridge University Press.

(2004). "Print or Pen? Modes of Written Publication in Sixteenth-Century Italy." *Italian Studies* 59: 39–64.

Robinson, Andrew. (2011). *Genius: A Very Short Introduction*. Oxford: Oxford University Press.

Rosand, David. (2000). "Raphael's *School of Athens* and the Artist of the Modern Manner." In *The World of Savonarola: Italian Elites and the Perceptions of Crisis*, ed. Stella Fletcher and Christine Shaw, 212–32. Aldershot, UK: Ashgate.

Rosen, Mark. (2003). "Don Miniato Pitti and the Second Life of a Scientist's Tools in Cinquecento Florence." *Nuncius: Annali di Storia della Scienza* 18: 3–24.

Roskill, Mark W. (1968). *Dolce's Aretino and Venetian Art Theory of the Cinquecento*. New York, NY: Published for the College Art Association of America by New York University.

Rossi, Paolo L. (1994). "The Writer and the Man: Real Crimes and Mitigating Circumstances—il caso Cellini." In *Crime, Society, and the Law in Renaissance Italy*, ed. K. Lowe and T. Dean, 157–83. Cambridge: Cambridge University Press.

Rossi, Sergio. (1980). *Dalle botteghe alle accademie: Realtà sociale e teorie artistiche a Firenze dal XIV al XVI secolo*. Milan: Feltrinelli.

Rota, Arianna Arisi, ed. (2009). *Formare alle professioni: Diplomatici e politici*. Milan: FrancoAngeli.

Rowland, Ingrid D. (1997). "The Intellectual Background of the *School of Athens*: Tracking Divine Wisdom in the Rome of Julius II." In *Raphael's "School of Athens,"* ed. Marcia B. Hall, 131–70. Cambridge: Cambridge University Press.

(1998). *The Culture of the High Renaissance: Ancients and Moderns in Sixteenth-Century Rome*. Cambridge: Cambridge University Press.

(2005). "The Vatican Stanze." In *The Cambridge Companion to Raphael*, ed. Marcia B. Hall, 95–119. Cambridge: Cambridge University Press.

Rowland, Ingrid D., and Noah Charney. (2017). *The Collector of Lives: Giorgio Vasari and the Invention of Art*. New York, NY: W. W. Norton.

Rubin, Patricia Lee. (1995). *Giorgio Vasari: Art and History*. New Haven, CT: Yale University Press.

Ruffini, Marco. (2009). "Sixteenth-Century Paduan Annotations to the First Edition of Vasari's *Vite* (1550)." *Renaissance Quarterly* 62: 748–808.

(2010). "La prima ricezione de *Le vite*: Postille venete alla Torrentiniana." In *Le Vite del Vasari: Genesi, topoi, ricezione*, ed. K. Burzer, C. Davis, S. Feser, and A. Nova, 183–90. Venice: Marsilio.

(2011). *Art without an Author: Vasari's "Lives" and Michelangelo's Death*. New York, NY: Fordham University Press.

Ruggiero, Guido. (2015). *The Renaissance in Italy: A Social and Cultural History of the Rinascimento*. Cambridge: Cambridge University Press.

Rzepińska, Maria, and Krystyna Malcharek. (1986). "Tenebrism in Baroque Painting and Its Ideological Background." *Artibus et Historiae* 7: 91–112.

Saalman, Howard, ed. (1970). *The Life of Brunelleschi by Antonio di Tuccio Manetti*. Trans. Catharine Enggass. University Park, PA: Penn State University Press.

Saccone, Eduardo. (1978). "Trattato e ritratto: L'introduzione del *Cortegiano*." *Modern Language Notes* 93: 1–21.

(1983). "Grazia, Sprezzatura, and Affettazione in the *Courtier*." In *Castiglione: The Ideal and the Real in Renaissance Culture*, ed. Robert W. Hanning and David Rosand, 45–67. New Haven, CT: Yale University Press.

(1987). "The Portrait of the Courtier in Castiglione." *Italica* 64: 1–18.

Sacchetti, Franco. (2004). *Trecentonovelle*. Turin: Unione Tipografico Editrice Torinese.

Scapecchi, Piero. (2011). "Chi scrisse *Le vite* del Vasari: Riflessioni sulla *editio princeps* del 1550." *Letteratura e arte* 9: 153–9.

Schlosser, Julius Ritter von. (1977). *La letteratura artistica: Manuale delle fonti della storia dell'arte moderna*. Trans. Filippo Rossi. 3rd ed. Florence: La Nuova Italia.

Schnapp, Jeffrey T. (1999). "Crash (Speed as Engine of Individuation)." *Modernism/Modernity* 6: 1–49.

ed. (2009). *Speed Limits*. Milan: Skira.

Scholar, Richard. (2013). "The New Philologists." In *Renaissance Keywords*, ed. Ita Mac Carthy, 1–10. Oxford: Legenda.

Scoti-Bertinelli, Ugo. (1905). *Giorgio Vasari, scrittore*. Pisa: Nistri.

Shearman, John K. G. (1967). *Mannerism*. Harmondsworth: Penguin.

(1992). *Only Connect …: Art and the Spectator in the Italian Renaissance*. Princeton, NJ: Princeton University Press.

(2003). *Raphael in Early Modern Sources (1483–1602)*. New Haven, CT: Yale University Press.

Sherberg, Michael. (2003). "The Accademia Fiorentina and the Question of the Language: The Politics of Theory in Ducal Florence." *Renaissance Quarterly* 56: 26–55.

Simonetti, Carlo Maria. (2005). *La vita delle "Vite" vasariane: Profilo storico di due edizioni*. Florence: Olschki.

Singleton, Charles S. (1954). *Dante's "Commedia": Elements of Structure*. Baltimore, MD: Johns Hopkins University Press.

(1958). *Journey to Beatrice*. Baltimore, MD: Johns Hopkins University Press.

Siraisi, Nancy G. (1990). *Medieval and Early Renaissance Medicine: An Introduction to Knowledge and Practice*. Chicago, IL: University of Chicago Press.

Snyder, Jon. (1989). *Writing the Scene of Speaking: Theories of Dialogue in the Late Italian Renaissance*. Stanford, CA: Stanford University Press.

Sohm, Philip. (2000). "Ordering History with Style: Giorgio Vasari on the Art of History." In *Antiquity and Its Interpreters*, ed. Alina Payne, Ann Kuttner, and Rebekah Smick, 40–54. Cambridge: Cambridge University Press.

(2015). "Giving Vasari the Giorgio Treatment." *I Tatti Studies in the Italian Renaissance* 18: 61–111.

Sontag, Susan. (1989). *Illness as Metaphor; and Aids and Its Metaphors*. New York, NY: Picador/Farrar, Straus and Giroux.

Spagnolo, Maddalena. (2007). "Considerazioni in margine: Le postille alle *Vite* di Vasari." In *Arezzo e Vasari: Vite e postille*, ed. Antonino Caleca, 251–72. Foligno: Cartei & Bianchi.

Stack, Joan. (2000). "Artists into Heroes: The Commemoration of Artists in the Art of Vasari." In *Fashioning Identities in Renaissance Art*, ed. Mary Rogers, 163–76. Aldershot, UK: Ashgate.

Steinberg, Leo. (2001). *Leonardo's Incessant "Last Supper."* New York, NY: Zone Books.

Steptoe, Andrew. (1998). "Artistic Temperament and the Italian Renaissance: A Study of Giorgio Vasari's *Lives*." In *Genius and the Mind: Studies of Creativity and Temperament*, ed. Andrew Steptoe, 253–70. Oxford: Oxford University Press.

Stimato, Gerarda. (2005a). "Dai *Ricordi* alla *Vita*: Giorgio Vasari biografo di se stesso." *Letteratura e arte* 3: 83–105.

(2005b). "La formazione dell'artista rinascimentale nelle *Vite* di Giorgio Vasari: Tra apprendistato tecnico e modelli socio-culturali." *Schifanoia: Notizie dell'Istituto di Studi Rinascimentali di Ferrara* 28–9: 87–94.

Struever, Nancy S. (1970). *The Language of History in the Renaissance: Rhetoric and Historical Consciousness in Florentine Humanism*. Princeton, NJ: Princeton University Press.

Summers, David. (1981). *Michelangelo and the Language of Art*. Princeton, NJ: Princeton University Press.

(1987). *The Judgment of Sense: Renaissance Naturalism and the Rise of Aesthetics*. Cambridge: Cambridge University Press.

Talvacchia, Bette. (2007). *Raphael*. London: Phaidon.

Tanturli, Giuliano. (1976). "Le biografie d'artisti prima del Vasari." In *Il Vasari, storiografo e artista: Atti del Congresso internazionale nel IV centenario della morte*, 275–98. Florence: Istituto Nazionale di Studi sul Rinascimento.

Tempesti, Anna Forlani. (2014). "Giorgio Vasari and the Libro de' disegni: A Paper Museum or Portable Gallery." In *Giorgio Vasari and the Birth of the Museum*, 31–52. Burlington, VT: Ashgate.

Thomas, Anabel. (1995). *The Painter's Practice in Renaissance Tuscany*. Cambridge: Cambridge University Press.

(2006). "The Workshop as the Space of Collaborative Artistic Production." In *Renaissance Florence: A Social History*, ed. Roger J. Crum and John T. Paoletti, 415–30. Cambridge: Cambridge University Press.

Thomas, Ben. (2013). "Disegno: Superficial Line or Universal Design?" In *Renaissance Keywords*, ed. Ita Mac Carthy, 31–44. London: Legenda.

Tiberio, Claudio. (1974). "Vasari restauratore." In *Il Vasari, storiografo e artista: Atti del Congresso internazionale nel IV centenario della morte*, 533–65. Florence: Istituto Nazionale di Studi sul Rinascimento.

Trachtenberg, Marvin. (2010). *Building-in-Time: From Giotto to Alberti and Modern Oblivion*. New Haven, CT: Yale University Press.

Trapp, J. B. (1982). "*The Poet Laureate*: Rome, *Renovatio* and *Translatio Imperii*." In *Rome in the Renaissance: The City and the Myth*, ed. P. A. Ramsey, 93–130. Binghamton, NY: Center for Medieval and Early Renaissance Studies.

Trexler, Richard. (1980). *Public Life in Renaissance Florence*. New York, NY: Academic Press.

Tribby, Jay. (1991). "Cooking (with) Clio and Cleo: Eloquence and Experiment in Seventeenth-Century Florence." *Journal of the History of Ideas* 52: 417–39.

(1992a). Body/Building: Living the Museum Life in Early Modern Europe." *Rhetorica* 10: 139–63.

(1992b). "Of Conversational Dispositions and the Saggi's Proem." In *Documentary Culture: Florence and Rome from Grand-Duke Ferdinand I to Pope Alexander VII*, ed. Elizabeth Cropper, Giovanna Perini, and Francesco Solinas, 379–90. Bologna: Nuova Alfa Editoriale.

Tylus, Jane. (1993). *Writing and Vulnerability in the Late Renaissance*. Stanford, CA: Stanford University Press.

Vasari, Giorgio. (1823). *Ragionamenti del Signor Giorgio Vasari sopra le invenzioni da lui dipinte in Firenze nel Palazzo Vecchio con Francesco Medici allora Principe di Firenze*. Pisa: N. Capurro.

(1938). *Il libro delle Ricordanze di Giorgio Vasari*. Ed. Alessandro del Vita. Arezzo: Reale Istituto di Archeologia e Storia dell'Arte.

(1966–87). *Le vite de' più eccellenti pittori, scultori, e architettori nelle redazioni del 1550 e 1568*. 6 vols. Ed. Rosanna Bettarini and Paola Barocchi. Florence: Sansoni.

(1967). *Le vite de' più eccellenti pittori, scultori, e architettori*. 9 vols. Ed. Paola della Pergola, Luigi Grassi, and Giovanni Previtali. Revisions by Aldo Rossi; notes and bibliography by Giovanni Previtali and Paola Ceschi. Novara: Istituto Geografico De Agostini.

(1996). *Lives of the Painters, Sculptors and Architects*. Trans. Gaston du C. de Vere. Intro. David Ekserdjian. New York, NY: Knopf.

(2009). *Le vite dei più eccellenti pittori, scultori e architetti*. Rome: Newton Compton Editori.

Vigenère, Blaise de, trans. (1976). *Les images*. Reprint of 1614 ed. New York, NY: Garland Publishing.

Virgil. (2000). *Aeneid*. Trans. H. Rushton Fairclough. Rev. G. P. Goold. Cambridge, MA: Harvard University Press.

Vitale, Maurizio. (1978). *La questione della lingua*. Palermo: Palumbo.

Vocabolario degli Accademici della Crusca. Accessed online. http://vocabolario.sns.it/html/index.html.

Waldman, Louis A. (2001). "Bandinelli and the Opera di Santa Maria del Fiore: Privilege, Patronage and Pedagogy." In *Santa Maria del Fiore: The Cathedral and Its Sculpture*, ed. Margaret Haines, 217–52. Fiesole: Cadmo.

(2014). "*Vadunt ad habitandum hebrei*: The Otto di Balia, Vasari, and the Hiding of Murals in Sixteenth-Century Florence." *Mitteilungen des Kunsthistorischen Institutes in Florenz* 56: 351–4.

Wallace, William E. (1987). "Michelangelo's Assistants in the Sistine Chapel." *Gazette des Beaux-Arts* 110: 203–16.

(2010). *Michelangelo: The Artist, the Man, and His Times*. Cambridge: Cambridge University Press.

Warnke, Martin. (1993). *The Court Artist: On the Ancestry of the Modern Artist.* Trans. David McLintock. Cambridge: Cambridge University Press.

Watkins, John, ed. and intro. (2008). "Toward a New Diplomatic History of Medieval and Early Modern Europe." *Journal of Medieval and Early Modern Studies* 38: 1–14.

Watts, Barbara J. (1995). "Giorgio Vasari's *Vita di Michelangelo Buonarroti* and the Shade of Donatello." In *The Rhetorics of Life-Writing in Early Modern Europe: Forms of Biography from Cassandra Fedele to Louis XIV*, ed. Thomas F. Mayer and D. R. Woolf, 63–96. Ann Arbor, MI: University of Michigan Press.

Waźbiński, Zygmunt. (1987). *L'Accademia Medicea del Disegno a Firenze nel Cinquecento: Idea e istituzione.* Florence: Olschki.

Webb, Ruth. (1999). "Ekphrasis Ancient and Modern: The Invention of a Genre." *Word & Image* 15: 7–18.

(2009). *Ekphrasis: Imagination and Persuasion in Ancient Rhetorical Theory and Practice.* Farnham, UK: Ashgate.

Weil-Garris Posner, Kathleen. (1972). "Raphael's *Transfiguration* and the Legacy of Leonardo." *Art Quarterly* 35: 342–74.

(1974). *Leonardo and Central Italian Art, 1515–1550.* New York, NY: New York University Press.

Welch, Evelyn. (1997). *Art and Society in Italy, 1350–1500.* Oxford: Oxford University Press.

(2004). "Painting as Performance in the Italian Renaissance Court." In *Artists at Court: Image-Making and Identity, 1300–1500*, ed. S. Campbell, 19–32. Boston: Isabella Stewart Gardner Museum.

White, Hayden V. (1978). *Tropics of Discourse: Essays in Cultural Criticism.* Baltimore, MD: John Hopkins University Press.

(1987). *The Content of the Form: Narrative Discourse and Historical Representation.* Baltimore, MD: John Hopkins University Press.

Wierzbicka, Anna. (1997). *Understanding Cultures through Their Key Words: English, Russian, Polish, German, and Japanese.* New York, NY: Oxford University Press.

Wilkins, Ernest Hatch. (1951). "The Coronation of Petrarch." In *The Making of the "Canzoniere" and Other Petrarchan Studies*, 9–69. Rome: Edizioni di Storia e Letteratura.

Williams, Raymond. (2015). *Keywords: A Vocabulary of Culture and Society.* 2nd ed. New York, NY: Oxford University Press.

Williams, Robert. (1988). "Vincenzo Borghini and Vasari's 'Lives.'" PhD dissertation, Princeton University.

(1997). *Art, Theory, and Culture in Sixteenth-Century Italy: From Techne to Metatechne.* Cambridge: Cambridge University Press.

(2007). "The Artist as Worker in Sixteenth-Century Italy." In *Taddeo and Federico Zuccaro: Artist-Brothers in Renaissance Rome*, exh. cat., ed. Julian Brooks, 95–103. Los Angeles: J. Paul Getty Museum.

(2014). "Vasari and Vincenzo Borghini." In *The Ashgate Research Companion to Giorgio Vasari*, ed. Cast, 23–40. Farnham, Surrey: Ashgate.

Witt, Ronald G. (2000). *"In The Footsteps of the Ancients": The Origins of Humanism from Lovato to Bruni.* Leiden: Brill.

Wittkower, Rudolf. (1971). *Architectural Principles in the Age of Humanism.* New York, NY: W. W. Norton.

Wittkower, Rudolf, and Margaret Wittkower. (1963). *Born under Saturn: The Character and Conduct of Artists: A Documented History from Antiquity to the French Revolution.* New York, NY: Random House.

(1964). *The Divine Michelangelo: The Florentine Academy's Homage on His Death in 1564.* Introduced, translated, and annotated by Rudolf and Margot Wittkower. London: Phaidon.

Wood, Jeryldene M. (2005). "Young Raphael and the Practice of Painting in Renaissance Italy." In *The Cambridge Companion to Raphael*, ed. Marcia B. Hall, 15–35. Cambridge: Cambridge University Press.

Woodhouse, J. R. (1967). "Vincenzo Borghini and the Continuity of the Tuscan Linguistic Tradition." *Italian Studies* 22: 26–42.

(1971). "Borghini's Theory of the Decay of Tuscan." *Studi secenteschi* 12: 101–15.

Woods-Marsden, Joanna. (1987). "'Ritratto al Naturale': Questions of Realism and Idealism in Early Renaissance Portraits." *Art Journal* 46: 209–16.

Woodward, William Harrison. (1963). *Vittorino da Feltre and Other Humanist Educators.* New York, NY: Bureau of Publications, Teachers College, Columbia University.

Yates, Frances A. (1974). *The Art of Memory.* Chicago, IL: University of Chicago Press.

Zimmermann, T. C. Price. (1976). "Paolo Giovio and the Evolution of Renaissance Art Criticism." In *Cultural Aspects of the Italian Renaissance: Essays in Honour of Paul Oskar Kristeller*, ed. C. H. Clough, 406–24. Manchester: Manchester University Press.

(1978). "Renaissance Symposia." In *Essays Presented to Myron P. Gilmore*, ed. Sergio Bertelli and Gloria Ramakus, vol. 1, 363–74. Florence: La Nuova Italia.

(1995). *Paolo Giovio: The Historian and the Crisis of Sixteenth-Century Italy.* Princeton, NJ: Princeton University Press.

Zuccaro, Federico. (1961). *Scritti d'arte di Federico Zuccaro.* Ed. Detlef Heikamp. Florence: Olschki.

Zuccolin, Gabriella. (2010). "I chirurghi del Trecento: Formazione dottrinale e professionale." In *Formare alle professioni: Figure di sanità*, ed. Monica Ferrari and Paolo Mazzarello, 58–77. Milan: FrancoAngeli.

INDEX